James Maidment, William Hugh Logan, John Wilson

The Dramatic Works of John Wilson

James Maidment, William Hugh Logan, John Wilson

The Dramatic Works of John Wilson

ISBN/EAN: 9783337340902

Printed in Europe, USA, Canada, Australia, Japan

Cover: Foto ©Thomas Meinert / pixelio.de

More available books at **www.hansebooks.com**

DRAMATISTS OF THE RESTORATION.

WILSON.

Printed for Subscribers only.

450	copies	Small Paper.
150	,,	Large Paper.
30	,,	Whatman's Paper.
3	,,	Vellum.

THE DRAMATIC

WORKS OF JOHN WILSON.

WITH PREFATORY MEMOIR, INTRODUCTIONS,

AND NOTES.

MDCCCLXXIV.

EDINBURGH: WILLIAM PATERSON.

LONDON: H. SOTHERAN & CO.

MURRAY AND GIBB, EDINBURGH,
PRINTERS TO HER MAJESTY'S STATIONERY OFFICE.

TO

WILLIAM JOHN THOMS, Esq., F.S.A.,

ETC. ETC. ETC.,

THE ORIGINATOR, AND, FOR

A QUARTER OF A CENTURY, EDITOR OF

NOTES AND QUERIES,

THESE, THE DRAMATIC WORKS

OF

JOHN WILSON, of Lincoln's Inn,

NOW FOR THE FIRST TIME COLLECTED,

ARE, WITH MOST SINCERE REGARDS, INSCRIBED BY

THE EDITORS.

CONTENTS.

THE information hitherto afforded us respecting John Wilson, the author of the plays contained in this volume, through the medium of Langbaine and other contemporaneous authorities, and reiterated by the editors of the *Biographia Britannica*, the *Biographia Dramatica*, and the rest of the more modern writers, is of a very scanty kind, resolving itself into the mere fact, that towards the end of the seventeenth century he was Recorder of Londonderry. That a man of such great ability as Wilson, and who in his time had rendered himself in some degree prominent in Ireland as an adherent and supporter of the cause of James II., should have been thrust into the shade, or, as it were, almost totally extinguished, may perhaps be accounted for by reason of his political principles, the tone of the times on the sudden accession of the House of Orange being coloured by the prevailing influence of the popular power, which could recognise only its own supporters. The continuation of Langbaine—London, 1699, 12mo—contains this brief notice of John Wilson:

"An author, of the place of whose birth I am ignorant. He was once Recorder of Londonderry, and some time resided in Dublin, where he wrote 'Belphegor,' which was afterwards acted in London. He died about three years since, near Leicester Fields, but where buried I know not. He is author of four plays, viz.:—

"Andronicus Comnenius: a Tragedy. 4to, 1663. Plot from Heylin's Cosmography in the Description of Greece, Cantacusenus, Leunclavius, etc.

"Belphegor; or, the Marriage of the Devil: a Comedy. 4to, 1690. Acted at the Queen's Theatre in Dorset Garden. Plot taken from a novel of Machiavel and Quevedo's novels.*

"The Cheats: a Comedy. 4to. Printed two editions, the

* In Machiavel certainly, but not in Quevedo.

last 1671.* This play met with applause when first acted, and is a diverting comedy.

"The Projectors: a Comedy. 4to, 1665. This play met with no great success."

John Wilson was the son of the Rev. Aron Wilson of Plymouth, from whom he derived a competent patrimony. He became a student of Lincoln's Inn, and was called to the bar on 31st October 1646; 22 Car. I. It is believed that he became secretary in Ireland to the Duke of York, through whose influence he was appointed, shortly before the death of King Charles II., to the office of Recorder of Londonderry; but this he seems to have vacated about the time of the siege, which began 18th April and continued till 1st August 1689, during which, as there were neither mayor nor sheriff, the vocation of recorder would be a dead letter. It is evident that Wilson shortly afterwards went to Dublin, no doubt to join King James there, and that, hoping in the ultimate ascendency of the Jacobite cause, he remained a resident for some years afterwards. He appears to have died in London in 1696.

That he was not quite so unknown to fame, as hitherto the writers respecting him have indicated, these contemporaneous lines will evince:

. . . . . .

"Ellis in great discontent went away,
  Whilst D'Avenant against Apollo did rage;
Because he declared *The Secrets* a play
  Fitting for none but a mountebank stage.

John Wilson stood up, and wildly did stare,
  When on a sudden stept in a bold Scot;
And offer'd Apollo he freely would swear
  The said Maister Wilson might pass for a sot.

But all was in vain; for Apollo, 'tis said,
  Would in nowise allow of any Scotch wit;
Then Wilson in spite made his plays to be read,
  Swearing he'd answer for all he had writ."

These lines are from "The Sessions of the Poets, to the tune of Cock Laurel," in the 1st vol. of "Poems of

* This is an error. "The Cheats" ran through four editions.

Affairs of State from the time of Oliver Cromwell to the abdication of K. James Second. Written by the greatest wits of the age." Lond. 8vo, 6th ed., 1716. Vol. i. ;—a continuation of "A Tryal for the Bays, in imitation of a satyre in Boileau, by the Duke of Buckingham, and the Earl of Rochester."—See the Works of his Grace, George Villiers, late Duke of Buckingham, vol. i. p. 155, 8vo, 3d ed. 1715.

Besides the four plays enumerated, which are in themselves works of immense merit, he wrote the following books :—

1. Moriæ Encomium : or, the Praise of Folly. Written originally in Latin by Des. Erasmus of Rotterdam, and translated into English by John Wilson. Licensed, Roger L'Estrange. London, printed for William Leak, and are to be sold at the Crown in Fleet Street, between the two Temple gates. 1668, 12mo.

2. Jus Regium Coronæ : or, the King's Supreme Power in dispensing with Penal Statutes ; more particularly as it relates to the two Test Acts of the twenty-fifth and thirtieth of his late Majesty, King Charles II. *Argued by Reason*, and confirmed by the Common and Statute Laws of this Kingdom. In two parts. Auctore, Jo. Wilsonio, J.C.

Sir Edw. Coke, 1 *Inst.* 64. *Imperii Majestas, Tutelæ Salus.* London, printed by Henry Hills, printer to the King's most excellent Majesty, for his household and chapel ; and are sold at his printing house, on the Ditch side, in Blackfriars. 1688. 4to, pp. 79.

The dedication runs thus :—

"TO THE HONOURABLE SOCIETY OF LINCOLN'S INN.

"It is my honour, gentlemen, that I served a double apprenticeship within your walls; and however I have for many years discontinued, it is not possible that any man, bred in a society of so much learning and air, should have altogether forgotten what he once imbibed.

"The loyalty of your house, excepting some single person here and there, was in the worst of times exemplary; nor were y' last in bringing the King back again to his. And because the dispensing power best secures him in it, and the kingdom under it, unto whom more justly could I make a proof of it, than to that honourable body, from whom I received it?

"Such, gentlemen, is the discourse I herewith present ye; and in that being now no longer mine, but yours, as none are more able, be also as pleased to defend it; or so kind, at least, to say this of your old acquaintance: That he spoke his thoughts;

that he believed them true; and on that account would not willingly quit them, till he be better informed.—Gentlemen, your most humble servant, JOHN WILSON."

The postscript is this:

"What has been the common want to the reader suits better with this matter to give it here, and that is, the occasion of what I have written, which lies thus:—

"His Majesty, through the greatest of difficulties, and the repeated but fruitless attempts of an exclusion, had, by the death of his late royal brother King Charles II., come at last to the crown; nor was it scarce on his head when a double rebellion did more than threaten it. Upon this, the King (sole judge of the danger of the kingdom, and in what manner to avoid it), being little other than necessitated either to trust those few he had tried, or those many others that had been for excluding him, grants commissions to certain persons, not qualified according to the said statute 25th Car. II., with a *non obstante* to that statute. This begat some popular disputes touching the King's dispensing power, and those a desire in me of satisfying my own judgment; and, being confirmed myself, I thought it my duty to strengthen others.

"In short, it was written about Easter 1686, and has but lately come to my hands again; by which means I wanted the advantage of rivetting it with that solemn judgment in point (in B.R.) in the case of Godwin *versus* Sir Edward Hales upon this statute, which was not till the Trinity term following. However, finding that so great a foundation for a further superstructure, I went on with the argument upon that other Test Act, 30th Car. II., as it severally respects a Peer of the realm and a member of the House of Commons; and finished it with this: that the King might lawfully dispense with that statute also. But this being out of my hands, and having little to recover it by but some imperfect notes, I thought fit to publish this first part for the present, with assurance, nevertheless, of that second part to follow it; though neither of them had been further thought on, but that, the same dust being raised anew, it was but charity to keep it from blinding the people."

He also wrote:

3. A Discourse of Monarchy, more particularly of the Imperial Crowns of England, Scotland, and Ireland, according to the Ancient, Common, and Statute Laws of the same; with a close for the whole as it relates to the succession of his Royal Highness, James, Duke of York. *Deut.* iv. 32—'Interroga de diebus antiquis qui fuerunt ante te, ex die quo creavit Dominus hominem super terram,' etc. London: printed by M. C. for Jos. Hindmarsh, bookseller to his Royal Highness, at the Black Bull in Cornhill, 1684. 8vo.

The table of contents gives for Section 10th the following heads, which will show the nature and tendency of Mr. Wilson's book :—

"A close from the whole, by way of inquiry whether an exclusion of his Royal Highness the Duke of York may be of more advantage or disadvantage. The advantage proposed; and whether an Act for security of religion may not be as safe as a Bill of Exclusion. The moral impossibility of introducing the Romish religion, though the Prince were of that persuasion. The reason why the kingdom followed the Reformation under Edward VI., Queen Mary, Queen Elizabeth. That the case cannot be the same at this day. The crown of England an ancient entail, with the danger of innovations. Objection that such things have been done; so has a King been murdered. More particularly answered in Edward IV., Queen Mary, and Queen Elizabeth; all three excluded by Parliament, yet came to the crown. No man changes but in hopes of better. The advantages of continuing as we are. It is a bar to pretenders; the same as to competitors. Disorders avoided. No new family to be provided for. The indignity of a repulse avoided. Suppose Scotland and Ireland be of another opinion, the former of which has by Parliament asserted the right of succession of that crown, notwithstanding any religion, etc. Lastly, all occasions of jealousy taken away. Objection answered. Disadvantages that have attended the laying by the right heir. Examples from old Rome, and usurpations at home. The revolt from Rehoboam; our loss of France. With a conclusion from the whole, more particularly as it relates to his Royal Highness."

The dedication runs thus :—

"TO THE MOST HONOURABLE JAMES, DUKE OF ORMOND, ETC.,
LORD-LIEUTENANT OF IRELAND.

"*May it please your Grace,*

"It was a saying of the late Earl of Ossory (Lord-Deputy of Ireland, your son, at what time he delivered up the sword of that kingdom to the Lord-Lieutenant Berkeley), '*Action is the life of Government.*' Common experience tells us, usefulness is the end of action, and without which (like a glass-eye to a body), a man rather takes up a room than becomes any way serviceable. The sense of this put me on those thoughts I herewith present your grace; and unto whom more fitly, than to a person in the defence of which few men sate longer at helm, or suffered more; you, that hung not up your shield of faith in the temple of despair, and never seemed more worthy of the great place you now fill than when farthest from it. Nor am I in the so doing without some prospect of advantage to myself; inasmuch as, if censuring, the age shall handle me roughly on this account, under your great patronage I shall fight in the shade.

"And now, my lord, I was just breaking off when it came into my head that I had, in some of our late pieces, found Sir Edward Coke often quoted, especially to the defence of those notions which had better slept in their forgotten embers; and therefore I thought it not altogether foreign to the matter that I used the words of St. Peter (2 *Peter* iii. 16), touching St. Paul's Epistles, '*in which*' (saith he) '*are some things hard to be understood, which they that are unlearned and unstable wrest, as they do also the other scriptures, unto their own destruction.*' I have purposely made use of him in many places as an high assertion of monarchy and prerogative; those that find him otherwise,

'Habeant secum, serventque;'

or let him lie indifferent, my argument depends not singly on him; while I humbly took leave to advert, and am, may it please your grace, your most obedient, obliged, humble servant,

"JOHN WILSON."

In addition to a poetical epistle "to His Grace James, Duke of Ormond," Lord-Lieutenant of Ireland, printed at London in 1677, Wilson addressed the following verses to the duke's son:—

"To his Excellence Richard, Earl of Arran, etc., Lord-Deputy of Ireland. A Poem. '*Nec deficit alter aureus, et simili frondescit virga metallo.*' Dublin. Printed at His Majesty's printing house for Joseph Wild, bookseller in Castle Street. 1682. Folio."

"To his Excellence Richard, Earl of Arran, Lord-Deputy of Ireland, on the occasion of his Grace James, Duke of Ormond, etc., Lord-Lieutenant of the same (his father's), going to England and leaving the Government to him.*

"Hence the nice wits that are so squeamish grown,
Nothing will down with them but what's their own!
It has been said (yet tax'd) I *freeze* and *burn*,
And the same instant both *rejoice* and *mourn*.
And why, I pray, mayn't different notes agree?
Take away discords, where's the harmony?

Both are met here: We mourn one sun gone east,
And joy: another rising in the west;
Such—such as had the ancient Persian
View'd the Parelia, this double sun
Had made him stagger at the smart surprise,
Nor yet resolv'd, divide his sacrifice.

'Tis now past twenty times since th' Ormond stem
First branch'd itself in such a princely brain;
And may it yet increase, and multiply
Its scatter'd rays into a galaxy!

---

* James, Duke of Ormond, returned Lord-Lieutenant in 1684.

Spread-eagles join in body; Lucifer
And Vesper are the same alternate star;
The elements, Castor and Pollux, too,
Relieve each other, and in that still new.

Nature had never made a second day
Without a night's repose: that short allay
Stamp'd us another, and that timely care
Stepp'd in, and sav'd the infant world's despair.

And now 'tis but a day from sun to sun;
The one takes up, the other holds it on:
Seasons to seasons give a fresh supply;
The year absolv'd, comes the Epiphany.

Such your most noble father, sir's, with you;
He closes one, and you begin the new:
And be his motions yours, I'll boldly say,
The sun withdrew, and yet we lost no day.

J. WILSON."

This will be found in a folio volume in the British Museum,—Sig. $\frac{807.\ 9.\ 5}{28}$,—immediately following which this ill-humoured rejoinder occurs in MS.

"On Mr. Wilson's admirable copy of verses dedicated to his Excellency the Earl of Arran:—

"Hence the nice wits who are so squeamish grown,
Nothing will down with them but what's their own!"

"'Twas wholesome council, and 'twas fairly done,
To tell them their dull fare before they come;
Their puny stomachs never would digest
This nauseous stuff of thine, this porters' feast.
But yet, methinks, 'twas prodigal to rhyme
Out of that slender shallow stock of thine;
Thy name in preface might have done as well:
'Here, little Wilson, here doth dulness dwell.'
For who the devil with appetite would look
On such a dish, and dress'd by such a cook?
Who can endure, dost think, to see thee run
For an old threadbare simile to the sun?
A thing the very Phillis-fools despise,
And far more bright than the fair Celia's eyes.
But thus from thy parelia to fall
To Lucifer and Hespers; worst of all
To treat thy prince with scraps pick'd here and there
From sacred Lilly and the famous Hare.
Tell me, for sure thou did'st it out of sport,
To show thy worst; or was't compos'd in court,
Where thou that Latin cub of thine brought forth,
To boast thy haughty ignorance in both?

By heaven, were I in 's Excellency's case,
I'd hang the wretch that did me this disgrace.
'Tis time, indeed, the style may serve to show
When sun's in Cancer, when in Scorpio,
To help a wretched almanac's dull sale,
And martyrdom of Christmas pies bewail.
But never, sure, did flattering poet kiss
The hands of prince in such a style as this—
A style whose panegyric is abuse,
Which nothing but his madness can excuse;
For mad he is,—at least he is possess'd,
The fiend Belphegor heaves within his breast,—
Else why should he poetic strains essay
Since the sad fate of that unhappy play? *
'Tis true his 'Cheats,' tho' stol'n, had great applause,
And thence, alas! sprang the unlucky cause
Of his succeeding trifles. Swell'd with praise,
The fiend Belphegor he from hell must raise;
Thence these lewd lines (which surely were not stol'n—
They're dull enough, I'm sure, to be his own).
Thus a vile fawning dog, if heretofore
He chance to please you once, will ne'er give o'er;
Impertinent about your feet he 'll play,
Till you are forc'd to spurn the cur away."

Prior to the appearance of Wilson's play, *Andronicus Comnenius*, an anonymous author had written one on the same subject. It is titled, "Andronicus: A Tragedy. Impiety's long Success, or Heaven's late Revenge. *Discite justitiam moniti, et ne temnite Divos.* London, printed for Richard Hall, and are to be sold at the stationers in London, 1661. 12mo."

Mr. Geneste has overlooked this play, of which the author gives this account in his Address to the Reader:—

"Let me acquaint thee with the pedigree and progress (not to say pilgrimage) of this tragedy. It was born some eighteen years since in Oxford, thence carried by a casualty to York. The author thereof, conceiving this (the only copy) utterly lost, found it, beyond his expectation, in London some months since.

"Thus, weary with long wandering, it hopeth at last to find

* As the play of Belphegor was not printed until 1690, and Geneste notes that it was "licensed October 13, 1690," it may be inferred from what this writer says, that an earlier edition had been acted prior to 1682 without success. We may therefore assume that Wilson improved the piece before printing it.

quiet repose and candid reception, reader, with thee. It hath in it some *negative goodness*, namely, nothing therein which in the least degree trespasseth on piety, charity, or modesty. Besides, it presumeth on something *positive*, viz. variety and verity—the one to please, the other to profit. And if the poet brought the varnish, the historian, I am sure, gave the groundwork.

"What moved the author to make it may invite thee to read it,—diversion of his mind from the troubles of the times. I have done, when I have remembered thee of what I have read in Mr. Herbert: '*A verse may find him out who shuns a sermon.*' And such is the genius of our times, that those who dislike more serious matters may benefit by these lighter treatments of their time. If the author hereof hath intrench'd on his fancy, upon him who wrote the life of Andronicus in the *Holy State*, he doubts not but to obtain his pardon, as also hopes to have thine for his failings herein.—PHILANAX."

There is a formidable list of *dramatis personæ*, which is as follows:—

1. *Maria Cesarissa*, daughter to Manuel, late Emperor of Constantinople.
2. *Zena*, the Empress, mother to Alexius.
3. *Eudoxa*, } ladies of honour to Zena.
4. *Irene*, }
5. *Artemia*, a court lady, wife to Menander.
6. *Anna*, Empress to Alexius, afterwards to Andronicus.
7. *Juletta*, maid of honour to Anna.
8. *Alexius*, son of Manuel, and Emperor.
9. *Andronicus*, kinsman, murderer, and successor to Alexius.
10. *Isachius*, next of the imperial line, at last Emperor.
11. *Ducas*, a prince of the blood.
12. *Basilius*, patriarch of Constantinople.
13. *Monobius*, a hermit newly quitting his cell.
14. *Cleobulus*, an aged privy councillor.
15. *Paleologus*, a young courtier.
16. *Lapardus*, an instrument to promote Andronicus.
17. *Menander*, a courtier, and husband to Artemia.
18. *Crato*, a statesman.
19. *Assotus*, a dissolute man, and debaucher of Alexius.
20. *Panergus*, engineer-general to Andronicus in all his villainies.
21. *Philobiblus*, tutor to Alexius.
22. *Spiculator*, an executioner.
23. *Nurse*, *Servants*, *Surgeons*, *Messengers*, and *Citizens*.

The Scene: CONSTANTINOPLE.

A contemporaneous reader of the copy of this play in the British Museum has issued summary judgment upon its merits, by writing "verry badd" at the beginning of the first scene, and repeating his expressive phrase after the word "Finis." Without adopting this early reader's opinion, we content ourselves by saying that it is an eccentric production, and the poetry is in most instances truly original. In the first scene between Maria Cesarissa and her nurse, Alexius is thus spoken of:—

"*Nur.* Have patience, madam; matters may amend:
The Emperor's yet a child.
Mar. And child in judgment he will ever be.
No monster doth more hate a looking-glass
Than he a book; his wit's too short to measure
A noble sport or honourable pleasure.
Only he sits, and sots, and drinks, and sleeps:
The stews are brought him, or he to th' stews.
Nur. Andronicus will shortly here arrive,
And by him all things will be rectified.
Mar. Well, I could tell you something if I durst.
Nur. Madam, do!
If I reveal it, let me be accurst.
Sooner the very stones themselves shall speak.
Mar. That's not impossible;
In churches oft I have seen *speaking stone.*
Nur. Midnight shall turn a clack sooner than I.
Mar. 'Tis this: I do not think Andronicus
Will help us any whit.
Nur. Know you the man?
Mar. Were all faults lost, in him they might be found."

There are other passages equally, if not more grandiloquent than this, and some of the situations are bordering closely on the ludicrous; but to pursue the subject farther would be only to bestow our tediousness too long upon our patient readers, who, if they wish to peruse the play itself, will find the only copy, it is believed, extant, in the King's Library, British Museum.

JAMES MAIDMENT.
W. H. LOGAN.

EDINBURGH, 1*st November* 1873.

THE CHEATS.

A

The Cheats: A Comedy. Written in the year 1662. Hor. Serm. 1.—'*Ridentem dicere verum, Quis vetat?*' Imprimatur, Nov. 5, 1663. *Roger L'Estrange. London, Printed for G. Bedell and T. Collins, at the Middle-Temple-Gate; and Cha. Adams, at the Talbott, over against St. Dunstan's Church in Fleet Street.* 1664. *4to.*

The Cheats. The Second Edition, 1671.

The Cheats. The Third Edition. Printed by James Rawlins for John Wright, Moses Pitt, Thomas Sawbridge, and Gabriel Collins. 1684.

The Cheats. The Fourth Edition, corrected, with the addition of a new Song. By J. Wilson of Lincoln's Inn, Gent. Printed for J. Walthoe in Vine-Court, Middle-Temple. 1693.

THE comedy which follows is cleverly written, and in style resembles that of Ben Jonson more than of any other writer. On its earliest production on the stage it was received with applause, which was not diminished on every fresh revival. Langbaine, in speaking of the author, says: "His play called *The Cheats* having the general approbation of being an excellent comedy," while the editors of the *Biographia Dramatica* are equally laudatory. They remark: "This play met with general approbation, and very deservedly; notwithstanding which, the author's modesty induced him to make an apology for its faults, in a preface to the earlier editions." Geneste, although he affirms that "some parts of it are very dull," corroborates the general opinion that "on the whole it is a good play." The "preface" alluded to, however, as will be seen, is more a disavowal of any intention of personality than an apology for faults.

The popularity of *The Cheats* caused the issue of several editions. The text presently adopted is that of the fourth, it being the last published during the author's lifetime, and "with the addition of a new song." Prior to the introduction of this song, and the short relative dialogue preceding it, which now appears in the concluding scene, Whitebroth immediately followed up the dance with the words: "Why so? We're all friends," etc., the play ending as now.

Although this comedy was acted frequently before the fourth edition appeared in 1693, none of the actors' names are earlier given; but it is evident that the cast is that originally made, several of them being at that date dead or retired from the stage.

William Wintershall or Wintersell died in July 1679. He is spoken of in Buckingham's *Rehearsal*, and in the prefixed Key is characterized as a most judicious actor, and the best instructor of others. Downes says he was a good performer in tragedy and comedy, and that, as "Cokes" in *Bartholomew Fair*, Nokes fell short of him. Downes commends him highly as Master Slender. Pepys, on 28th April 1668, has this entry: "In the King's house, and there did see *Love in a Maze*, wherein very good mirth of Lacy, the clown, and Wintershall, the country knight, his master."

William Cartwright was one of Killigrew's company at the original establishment of Drury Lane. By his will, dated 1686, he left his books, pictures, and furniture to Dulwich College, where also his portrait still remains.

Oldys in his notes says, in reference to the library in Dulwich College, "to which Mr. Cartwright, a player, who was bred a bookseller, and had a shop at the end of Turnstile Alley, gave a collection of plays, and also many excellent pictures."

"Here comes in the Queen's purchase of plays [formerly Mrs. Oldfield's], and those by Mr. Weever, the dancing master, Sir Charles Cotterell, Mr. Coxeter, Lady Pomfret, and Lady Mary Wortley Montague."

Pepys mentions Cartwright thus: "2d Nov. 1667.—To the King's playhouse, and there saw *Henry the Fourth;* and, contrary to expectation, was pleased in nothing more than in Cartwright's speaking of Falstaffe's speech about 'What is Honour?'"

Cartwright and Wintershall belonged to the private house in Salisbury Court.

Nicholas Burt, as a boy, was first under Shanke at Blackfriars, and then under Beeston at the Cockpit, where he used to play the principal female parts, particularly "Clariana" in *Love's Cruelty.*—WRIGHT'S *Historia Histrionica.*

On the 11th October 1660, Pepys says: "Here, in the Park, we met with Mr. Salisbury, who took Mr. Creed and me to the Cockpit to see *The Moor of Venice*, which was well done. Burt acted the 'Moor;' by the same token, a very pretty lady that sat by me called out to see Desdemona smothered. With Mr. Creed to Hercules Pillar, where we drank." Davies, in his *Miscellanies*, observes that Burt ranked in the list of good actors after the Restoration, though he resigned the part of "Othello" to Hart. Pepys, on the other hand, contradicts this in some degree. There is this entry in his diary, of 6th February 1668-9: "To the King's playhouse, and there, in an upper box,—where come in Colonel Poynton and Doll Stacey, who is very fine, and by her wedding ring I suppose he hath married her at last,—did see *The Moor of Venice*, but ill acted in most parts. Mohun, which did a little surprise me, not acting 'Iago's' part by much so well as Clun used to do; nor another Hart's, which was 'Cassio's;' nor, indeed, Burt doing the 'Moor's' so well as I once thought he did."

Pepys does not appear latterly to have thought much of Burt. He had recorded his feeling respecting him on a previous occasion thus: "11th Dec. 1667.—Attended the Duke of York, as we are wont, who is now grown pretty well, and goes up and down Whitehall, and this night will be at the Council. Here I met Rolt and Sir John Chichly; and I met Harris, the player, and talked of *Catiline*, which is to be suddenly acted at the King's house; and there all agree that it cannot be well done at that house, there not being good actors enough; and Burt acts 'Cicero,' which they all conclude he will not be able to do well. The King gives them £500 for robes, there being, as they say, to be sixteen scarlet robes."

Charles Hart was great-nephew, as is believed, to William Shakespeare, and one of the most celebrated tragedians of his time. Some have said that he was Nell Gwyn's first lover. Others, again, assert that Nell's first admirer was Robert Duncan or Dungan, for whom she obtained a commission in the Guards. —CUNNINGHAM'S *Story of Nell Gwyn*, p. 27. See also *Notes and Queries*, 3d series, i. 286. It is very questionable whether either were in that position, or whether she herself was aware of who was her first lover, her earliest life having been passed in no very reputable company. However, it is not a matter of consequence, as she had a pretty accurate idea of who was the father of the ancestors of the Dukes of St. Albans, her surviving issue. Sir George Etherege, in a satirical poem printed in the *Lives of the Most Celebrated Beauties*, etc., 1715, says she was "protected" by Lacy, and afterwards by Hart. At all events it is certain that, previous to her elevation to Royal favour, Nell received instructions in the Thespian art from both these gentlemen.

Malone says: "Charles Hart, the actor, was born about the year 1630, and died in August 1683. If he was a grandson of Shakespeare's sister, he was probably the son of Michael Hart, her youngest son."

Hart, who used to play "Cassio," while Burt played "Othello," became soon so superior to Burt that he took the lead of him in almost all the plays acted at Drury Lane. Othello was one of his master parts.—DAVIES. He also became great in Wycherly's *Plain Dealer*.

Hart and Clun, as boys at Blackfriars, played female parts. Hart was Robinson's boy or apprentice; he acted the "Duchess" in the tragedy of *The Cardinal*, which was the first part that brought him into notice. The principal actors, such as Robinson, formerly performed on the sharing system. Usually the sharers were not more than twelve. The inferior actors were retained, by the name of hirelings, at a weekly salary defrayed by the sharers, each of whom was entitled to have a boy for youthful or female parts. For the services of these boys their masters received a stipulated sum.

Hart and Killigrew, soon after the theatre in Drury Lane was burnt down, 1671–2, sent Jo. Haynes to Paris to examine the machinery displayed in the French opera, with a view to the adoption of its best features in this country. The King's company, after being burnt out, took refuge in the theatre in Lincoln's-Inn-Fields, which had been vacant since the November previous. They opened on 26th February 1671–2, with the play of *Wit without Money*.

Richard Robinson, above mentioned, circa 1616, usually performed female characters himself. (See *The Devil is an Ass*, act ii., scene 3.) In 1647 his name occurs, with several others, prefixed to the dedication of the first folio edition of Fletcher's plays. He served in the King's army in the civil wars, and was killed in an engagement by Harrison, who refused him quarter, and who was afterwards hanged at Charing Cross.

The patent of the Theatre Royal, Drury Lane, of which Mr. Hart and Major Mohun formed part of the company, having descended from Thomas to Charles Killigrew, "in 1682 he joined it to Dr. Davenant's patent, whose company acted then in Dorset Garden, which, upon the union, were created the King's company; after which Mr. Hart acted no more, having a pension to the day of his death from the united company. I must not omit to mention the parts in several plays of some of the actors, wherein they excelled in the performance of them. First, Mr. Hart in the part of 'Arbaces' in *King and no King*, 'Amintor' in *The Maid's Tragedy*, 'Othello,' 'Rollo,' 'Brutus' in *Julius Cæsar*, 'Alexander.' Towards the latter end of his acting, if he acted in any one of these but once in a fortnight, the house was filled as at a new play, especially 'Alexander'—he acting that with such grandeur and agreeable majesty, that one of the court was pleased to honour him with this commendation, that Hart might teach any king on earth how to comport himself."—DOWNES' *Roscius Anglicanus*, edit. 1789.

In Rymer's *Dissertation on Tragedy* he is thus noticed:—"The eyes of the audience are prepossessed and charmed by his action before aught of the poet can approach their ears; and to the most wretched of characters Hart gives a lustre which dazzles the sight, that the deformities of the poet cannot be perceived."

Again, Downes: "He was no less inferior in comedy, as 'Mosca' in *The Fox;* 'Don John' in *The Chances;* 'Wildblood' in *The Mock Astrologer*, with sundry other parts. In all the comedies and tragedies he was concerned, he perform'd with that exactness and perfection that not any of his successors have equall'd him."

It would seem that, through Hart's "excellent action" alone, Ben Jonson's *Catiline* (his own favourite play), which had been condemned on its first representation, was kept on the stage during the reign of Charles II. With Hart this play died.

The cause of Hart retiring from the stage was by reason of his being dreadfully afflicted with the stone and gravel, "of which he died some time after, having a salary of forty shillings a week to the day of his death."

Clun was barbarously murdered on the night of the 4th of August 1664, on his way out of town to his country house, after having performed the character of the "Alchymist," which was one of his best parts. Pepys says he was "set upon and murdered; one of the rogues taken, an Irish fellow. It seems most cruelly butchered and bound," naively adding, "the house will have a great miss of him."

Five years afterwards, Clun still dwells in Pepys' remembrance. "17th April 1669.—At noon, home to dinner, and there find Mr. Pierce, the surgeon, and he dined with us; and there hearing that *The Alchymist* was acted, we did go, and took him with us to the King's house, and it is still a good play, having not been acted for two or three years before; but I do miss Clun for the 'Doctor.'"

"Ben Jonson had one eie lower than t'other, and bigger, like Clun, the player. Perhaps he begott Clun."—AUBREY'S *Lives*, 8vo, 1813.—Art. BEN JONSON.

John Lacy was originally a dancing master. He subsequently procured a lieutenant's commission in the army, which ere long he quitted for the stage. Pepys characterizes him as an admirable actor, and Langbaine says he "performed all parts that he undertook to a miracle, insomuch that I am apt to believe, that as *this* age never had, so the *next* never will have, his *equal*, at least not his superior." He was notable in eccentric parts, such as Frenchmen, low Irishmen, Scotchmen, etc. He died in 1667.

The King would appear, from the following entry of Pepys, 8th May 1663, to have preferred Lacy to Clun: "Took my wife and Ashwell to the [new] Theatre Royall, being the second day of its being opened. The house is made with extraordinary good convenience, and yet hath some faults, as the narrowness of the passages in and out of the pit, and the distance from the stage to the boxes, which I am confident cannot hear; but for all other things is well; only, above all, the musique being below, and most of it sounding under the very stage, there is no hearing of the bases at all, nor very well of the trebles, which sure must be mended. The play was *The Humorous Lieutenant*, a play that hath little good in it, nor much in the very part which, by the King's command, Lacy now acts instead of Clun. In the dance, the tall devil's actions were very pretty."

Langbaine speaks of Lacy as the most perfect actor of his time; he was one of the recruits which they engaged in the King's Company, for there is no trace of his having ever acted before the Restoration. He wrote three plays, and died about the year 1684.—DAVIES. See an account of Lacy in the *Biographia Dramatica*; also, in his own collected works, in this edition of the *Dramatists*.

Lacy played "Falstaff" during the life of Cartwright. On account, I suppose, of his superior excellence, Langbaine speaks of his admirable representation of "Falstaff."—DAVIES.

Downes, in detailing the new plays acted, among others mentions *The Rehearsal*, in which last Mr. Lacy,

"For his just acting, all gave him due praise,
His part in *The Cheats*, *Jony Thump*,
Teg, and *Bayes!*
In these four excelling, the Court gave him the bays!"

Michael Mohun, better known as Major Mohun, he having held a commission during the civil wars, was brought up as an actor under Robinson, as Hart and others were. In his youth he acted "Bellamente" in *Love's Cruelty*, "which part," according to Wright, "he retained after the Restoration." Mohun and Shatterel were, according to the same authority, boys along with Burt under Beeston, afterwards at the Cockpit. Major Mohun remained in the "United Company" after Hart's retirement. "He was eminent for 'Volpone;' 'Face' in *The Alchymist;* 'Melanthius' in *The Maid's Tragedy;* 'Mardonius' in *King and no King;* 'Cassius' in *Julius Cæsar;* 'Clytus' in *Alexander;* 'Mithridates,' etc. An eminent poet [thought by Thomas Davies to have been Lee] seeing him act this last, ventured suddenly this saying: 'Oh, Mohun, Mohun! thou little man of mettle; if I should write 100 plays, I'd write a part for thy mouth.' In short, in all his parts he was most accurate and correct."—DOWNES' *Roscius Anglicanus.*

Davies further observes, that Lee "was himself so good a reader of his own tragedies, that Mohun frequently threw down his part, in despair of approaching to his excellence of expression."

Pepys has this entry of Mohun's first appearance after the Restoration: "20th November 1660.—Mr. Shepley and I to the new playhouse, near Lincoln's-Inn-Fields (which was formerly Gibbon's Tennis Court), where the play of *Beggar's Bush* was newly begun; and so we went in, and saw it well acted. And here I saw for the first time one Moone, who is said to be the best actor in the world, lately come over with the King: and, indeed, it is the finest playhouse, I believe, that ever was in England."

Mohun appears to have had the ear of his majesty, for on the occasion of the Honble. Edward Howard's play, called *The Change of Crowns,* having given offence to Charles—15th April 1667—and performances at the theatre having in consequence been forbidden, he interceded, and "got leave for them to act again, but not this play." Pepys calls it "a great play, and serious; only Lacy did act the country gentleman come up to court, who so abuses the court with all the imaginable wit and plainness about selling of places, and doing everything for money. The play took very well." "Knipp tells me the King was so angry at the liberty taken by Lacy's part, to abuse him to his face."

Davies records that "King Charles II., being asked how he liked Mohun's acting in a certain play, said that Mohun, or Moon, as usually pronounced, shone like the sun, and Hart like the moon." Waldron, commenting on this anecdote, says: "Charles II. is somewhere characterized as having never said a foolish thing, nor ever done a wise one. This play upon the words sun and moon might pass for wit in a king, but would not be so reputed in a subject."

Rymer, in *The Tragedies of the Last Age Considered*, thus criticizes these two actors: "We may remember (however we find this scene of 'Melanthius' and 'Amintor' written in the book) that at the theatre we have a good scene acted; there is a work cut out, and both our Æsopus and Roscius are on the stage together. Whatever defect may be in 'Amintor' and 'Melanthius,' Mr. Hart and Mr. Mohun are wanting in nothing. To these we owe what is pleasing in the scene, and to this scene we may impute the success of *The Maid's Tragedy*."

In *A Comparison between the Two Stages*, this anecdote is given: "The late Duke of Monmouth * was a good judge of dancing, and a good dancer himself. When he returned from France, he brought with him St. André, then the best master in France. The Duke presented him to the stage; the stage, to gratifie the Duke, admitted him, and the Duke himself thought he might prove a mighty advantage to 'em, tho' he had nobody else of his opinion. A day was published in the bills for him to dance, but not one more besides the Duke and his friends came to see him. The reason was, the plays were then so good, and Hart and Mohun acted 'em so well, that the audience would not be interrupted for so short a time, tho' 'twas to see the best master in Europe."

Mohun acted, in 1682, in *The Persian Prince*, by Southern; and "Burleigh," in *The Unhappy Favourite*, by Banks, in 1685.

Geneste observes: "Robert Shatterel was a performer of repute. William Shatterel seems to have been an actor of the lowest rank." William Shotterel or Shatterel, as his name is frequently printed, is the actor who was associated with the others just enumerated. He performed such characters as "Voltore," in *The Fox;* "Sir John Daw," in *The Silent Woman;* "Poyns," in *King Henry IV.*, etc.

The actress who played "Mrs. Whitebroth" in the present comedy, whose name is printed "Covey," must have been Mrs. Corey. Her name appears in the list of those who had acted under Killigrew's patent, and who remained on the union of the two companies in 1682. Downes gives the list as follows:—Major Mohun, Mr. Cartwright, Mr. Kynaston, Mr. Griffin, Mr. Goodman, Mr. Duke Watson, Mr. Powel, sen., Mr. Wiltshire, Mrs. Corey, Mrs. Bowtell, Mrs. Cook, Mrs. Montfort, etc.

On 26th November 1720, *The Cheats* was played at Lincoln's-Inn-Fields—"not acted twenty years"—"Whitebroth," Mr. C. Bullock. On the 20th May following it was again performed. The cast then was "Scruple," Griffin; "Mopus," Harper; "Afterwit," Leigh; "Jolly," Diggs; "Runter," Boheme; "Double Diligence," Bullock; "Tyro," Pack; "Bilboe," Egleton; "Titere Tu," H. Bullock; "Mrs. Whitebroth," Mrs.

* See notes appended to the *Masque of Calisto*, in Crowne's Works, vol. i. of this series.

Gifford; "Mrs. Mopus," Mrs. Elsam; "Mrs. Double Diligence," Mrs. Gulick; "Beatrice," Mrs. Knapp; "Cis," Miss Stone. Geneste has this remark: "Alderman Whitebroth is omitted —C. Bullock was no doubt ill. The bill for January 23, 1720, gives us reason to suppose that Egleton played 'Apish' [in *The Quaker's Wedding*], May 10, 1721, in consequence of C. Bullock's illness."

In all the editions of *The Cheats* prior to the fourth, the second prologue is thus headed: "Another. Intended, upon the revival of the play, but not spoken."

The licence granted by Sir Roger L'Estrange for this play was simply a licence for printing, in terms of an existing act which terminated in 1679. Sir Roger had no connection with the stage.

Further reference as to the actors of the time may be made to the introductory memoir of Sir William Davenant, in the first volume of his Dramatic Works in the present series.

THE AUTHOR TO THE READER.

—Non omnibus unum est
Quod placet, hic, Spinas colligit, ille, Rosas.
—PETRON. ARBITER.

I HAVE ever had so little faith for apologies, that I rather believ'd they did more hurt than good, and, for the most part, left things in a worse condition than they found them. The sense of this made me pass some late censures in silence, and perhaps might have oblig'd me to the same still, had I not found a dust rais'd, and believ'd it my concern to blow it off, —at least, endeavour it. To come to the matter: this comedy was lately acted, and, as it fares with things of this nature, variously receiv'd; nor could I well have expected other. It were too much fondness, not to say worse, to tax that freedom in another which I should think hard to be denied myself. No, this is nothing of the point. All that I take notice of is this, how justly it may have deserv'd all that has been said upon 't; unless people would have it dealt with like Don Quixote's library,—some burnt for the curate's sake, others for the barber's, and not the least for the good woman's. Not to detain you longer in the porch, I have at present but this short request, that it may speak for itself. And first, to take the parts as they lie, I shall begin with Bilboe and Titere Tu, the one usurping the name of a Major, the other of a Captain; whereas, in truth, and as may be gather'd from their discourse, they never were either, or scarcely anything like it,—a humour that can be no wise strange to any man that knew this town between the years '46 and '50, and, being so understood, will be as unlikely to prove an occasion of scandal to any person of honour; for if I have shown the odd practices of two vain persons pretending to what they were not, I think I have sufficiently justified the brave man even by this reason, that the exception proves the rule. And further, if there be anything in their language that may seem loose, be pleased to consider who they are that speak it; and then I hope you'll thus far absolve me as to say, I had as ill brought 'um in with a pair of beads at their girdle, as my Puritan constable with a feather in his cap. But secondly, for the second scene; I am confident I may pass it and come to the third, where, and in other parts of the play, if you meet with a small pretender to astrology, physic, the Rosicrucian humour, fortunetelling, and I know not what,—or in the fifth act, *qualiacunque voles vendentem somnia,* I shall, instead of plea to it, only enlarge my request, That you would but run over the late adventures of that kind, the sad effects of which may be well fear'd to live among the people when the persons that writ 'um may be either dead or forgotten. Nor do I think I ought to ask pardon that I have taken a Levite to this teraphim, since whoever shall give himself the trouble of inquiry will, without the least force, easily find that both alike have spoken vanity. But fourthly, for what concerns Runter, though I think I might have let that pass too, yet, because I would not be misunderstood, give me leave to believe that no wise man can conceive either profession, viz. common or civil law, could be intended in it. For as to the first, those that know my way of education will be ready to excuse me thus far, that had I design'd that I must necessarily have laid it another way, and perhaps, too, might have been able to have done 't; or, if I had struck at the latter, that I was not so altogether a stranger to it as not to have run it higher. Let this suffice to both, that I made use of no more than what serv'd to my purpose. And so I leave it to a favourable interpretation, and come to the fifth scene, viz. Mr. Scruple; where, if any man shall say I have trod too near upon religion, I hope, upon his second thoughts, I may trust my cause with him, when, if he shall rightly understand it, he will easily perceive that I have only shown how that venerable name has been abus'd, and that best thing made bawd to the worst actions. Lastly, to any man that shall say such or such humours have either been in the town before, or formerly writ upon, give me leave to offer this to the first, that Comedy either is or should be the true picture of virtue or vice, yet so drawn as to show a man how to follow the one and avoid the other; in doing which, if I had fram'd anything that was not, I had not only belied the town, but wrong'd myself. Doth not Martial say of his epigrams, '*Dictavit auditor?*' And was not *Quicquid agant homines*, Juvenal's farrago? As to the second, if it has been said so long since that there is nothing which has not been before, I hope, if I may have border'd upon anyone that has gone before, I am thus far excusable that I have purposely declin'd both his matter and his way. To which, if the contrary shall chance to be objected, I think it enough at present to say, I am in possession; and a bare 'they say,' without showing it, will not be sufficient to evict me out of it. To be short, were there nothing more, even this were enough, that there is hardly anything left to write upon but what either the ancients or moderns have some way or other touch'd on. Did not Apuleius take the rise of his *Golden Ass* from Lucian's *Lucius?* And Erasmus his *Alcumistica* from Chaucer's *Canon's Yeoman's Tale?* And Ben Johnson his more happy *Alchymist* from both? The argument were everlasting, *Sed Cynthius aurem vellit, et admonuit;* and therefore, upon the whole matter, whoever may have seen the play, or shall happen to read this, I have but two things more to beg of him,—the one, that by a new comment he pick not out any ill meaning which I never intended—*Improbe facit, qui in alieno libro ingeniosus est;* the other, that he remember that of the tragedian—*Si judicas, cognosce.* And then, perhaps, I may have deserv'd his thanks, that I thus hung out the buoy to discover the rock, and drew the curtain from an old cheat, to no other end but to prevent a new. Farewell!

LINCOLN'S INN, *Nov.* 16, 1663.

THE PROLOGUE.

CUSTOM prevails, and somewhat must be said
To tie your hands, and save the author's head.
'Tis a new play! you'll cry. What then? 'Twere too,
Too much to find you meat and stomachs too.
But since it must, expect no bill of fare.
No! I shall only tell ye—what's not here!
  We've no sententious sir, no grave Sir Poll,
No little pug nor devil,—bless us all!
No tedious sieges to the music room,
Nor frisks abroad! No,—our scene's all at home!
But if you ask me, how? 'Troth, I've forgot.
And, now I think on 't, it may spoil the plot
To give 't you beforehand. Whate'er it be,
Have but a little patience and you'll see.

ANOTHER.

Upon the revival of the Play, after it had been suppressed by a faction.

SAD news, my masters! and too true, I fear,
For us! Scruple's a silenc'd minister.
Would ye the cause? The brethren snivel and say,
'Tis scandalous that any cheat but they.
Well,—to be short; h'as been before the triers,
And, by good fortune, is got out o' th' briers.
Where, if he lost a limb to save the rest,
No hurt; here's yet enough to know the beast!
Nor let the sisters pule! I'll tell y' a thing,—
He may be libb'd, and yet have left a string!

THE EPILOGUE.

SPOKEN BY MOPUS.

I HAD almost forgot! Let's see—what weather?
Nor fair—nor foul,—indifferent,—both together;
Clear, if no clouds nor miz'ling. If there should,
It shall proceed from former causes. Good!
So much for doctrine! To apply it, now!
Ye've had a play, but whether good or no,
'Tis past my globe; yet guess, the weather will
Prove fair enough unless you make it ill.
'Tis you must make the play or stand or fall;
Therefore, by me, to you, and you, and all,
The author bows. And perhaps reason for 't—
Some men the judge, others the jury court;
The one more just if unconcerned; the other
More pitiful; if he claps both together
He means no hurt, for in a common hall
Noise carries it. He fain would please you all.
You've had for pit, for box, for gallery too;
Keep your own posts and he is well enou'.
But, if you must lash out, and think you can't
Be wits yourselves unless you pique and rant,
At your own peril be 't; and further know,
Who gives a character, in one, gives two.
He hopes the best,—nor will we be perplext;
Laugh hearty now, and he shall fix you next!

THE PERSONS.

With some of the first Actors' names.

WHITEBROTH, *An Alderman,*	MR. CARTWRIGHT.
RUNTER, *A Civilian,* . .	MR. WINTERSAL.
AFTERWIT, *A Gentleman, Suitor to Beatrice,* . . .	MR. BIRT.
JOLLY, *His Friend,* . .	MR. HART.
TYRO, *A young Squire, Pretender to Beatrice,*	——
SCRUPLE, *A Nonconformist,* .	MR. LACY.
MOPUS, *An Astrological Physician,*	MR. MOHUN.
BILBOE, TITERE TU, *Two Hectors; the one usurping the name of a Major, the other of a Captain,* .	MR. CLUN and MR. SHATTEREL.
DOUBLE DILIGENCE, *A Puritan Constable,*	——
TIMOTHY, *The Alderman's Servant,*	——
MRS. WHITEBROTH, *The Alderman's Wife,*	MRS. COVEY.
MRS. MOPUS, *The Astrologer's Wife,*	——
MRS. DOUBLE DILIGENCE, *The Constable's Wife,* . .	——
BEATRICE, *The Alderman's Daughter,*	——
CIS, *The Alderman's Maid,* .	——

The Scene—

LONDON.

THE CHEATS.

ACT I.—SCENE I.

Enter BILBOE *and* TITERE TU, *as meeting.*

T. T. HOH! Major! *Quibus Hector*, etcetera?

Bil. Why, faith, the old trade still—here, and there, and everywhere. But how now, captain?—Latin! Latin!—Send us fair weather! From small beer and ends of Latin, deliver me.

T. T. Troth, I rise with as little of 't this morning as the rest of my neighbours; and yet once to-day, 'twas a measuring cast whether I had English enough to carry me to bed.

Bil. For why, my Man o' Memphis? New adventures?

T. T. Small game. However, 'tis better than idleness. A man would pick straws rather than not keep his hand in use. Anything, good Major, in an honest way.

Bil. Thou'rt in the right, boy. But, hark ye! did ye bite?

T. T. Yes; and I've struck him.

Bil. A squire? Another squire?

T. T. He may be one in time; but for present he is only a small bachelor of the law, new come to town to learn breeding.

Bil. I'll say this—and a fig for thee—he has as hopeful a tutor as man need have rak'd hell for.

T. T. Mean you me, sir, or Runter the civilian, to whose care his father by his last will committed him?

Bil. Runter? Hah! hah!

T. T. Why, he thinks himself a learned man; and 'tis some sign that others are of the same opinion. I can assure you, he missed the Chancellorship of Dunstable as narrowly as ever any man that went without it.

Bil. Nay, nay, nay! the gentleman will be well bred, there's no doubt of 't. But what's the business?

T. T. Compositions, Major, compositions; a small collation to save the effusion of Christian blood. That thou hadst seen him while the Prudential and my Second were discoursing the business! He looked so like a sick horse, he would neither eat nor drink before he knew whether he should live or die; but as soon as the sum was agreed, and we had shaken hands upon 't—Whip, says Jethro!—he was got drunk ere I could wet my whistle.

Bil. But are the pence numbered? Do they cry chink in thy pocket? How many yellow boys, rogue? how many yellow boys?

T. T. Why, faith, Major, none; but we are to take a £100 together, which will be all one.

Bil. But who must lay it down, Captain? who must lay it down?

T. T. I have a small broker that for £40 or £50 has undertaken to procure it.

Bil. That may do well; but hark you! where does your horse stand? I hear of a purchase, and must out to-night.

T. T. No more, good Major; no more of that doleful tune; the very remembrance of 't puts me into a cold sweat.

Bil. 'Twas a pretty nag—thou hast not sold him?

T. T. Would 'twere no worse.

Bil. He is not stol'n? No rogues among ourselves, I hope?

T. T. Neither.

Bil. Or is he dead?

T. T. In law, I think he be. I was t'other night upon the randan, and who should I meet with but our old gang, some of St. Nicholas' clerks? Pad was the word, the booty set by the Chamberlain; we took it, and shar'd it, but, coming home, were all snap'd by a hue and cry for another business, wherein I was not concerned; which Mr. Constable perceiving, and imagining me as very a rogue as the rest, and that I would be glad to escape upon any terms, he takes me aside and tells me, that though I was not in this, yet there were others wherein I had been; and therefore (because I looked like a civil gentleman, merely drawn in by ill company) if I would give him my horse he would let me escape. You may easily believe he did not speak to a deaf man, or one that had no mind to understand him. I closed with him, got me to my company, made them dead drunk, and when they were fast asleep fairly march'd off.

Bil. That is to say, ran away.

T. T. And a good shift too. You are put to none of these hazards, Major. You lie as safe in the constable's house as a thief in a mill, or (to use a more familiar expression) some of our friends in Newgate.

Bil. Yes, I could have better accommodations abroad; but he is my loving friend.

T. T. His wife, you mean.

Bil. Why,—she's a good girl. And now you talk of these trumperies, what's become of your small cockatrice, the astrologer Mopus his wife?

T. T. I ha'n't seen her since my last mischance; I must ev'n to her for new riggings. I hope her husband has had a good term of 't. I'd live like a prince if I could perform the tenth part of what his bills promise. But see, Major! yonder's your pinnace sailing by—

Enter DOUBLE DILIGENCE *and his wife.*

Ah! how she booms! Prithee, hail her, man. Would I had the furling of her mainsail!

Bil. Landlord, well met! How now, landlady? This is better than wish. I must give you a barrel of oysters and a bottle or two of wine ere we part, honest landlord. [BILBOE *hugs him.*

D. D. Oh,—good Major,—another time; we are going to exercise now.

Bil. But, dear landlord—— Captain, advance, and know this gentleman, my friend and landlord; he is the honestest fellow, and the best natured thing——

D. D. Thank you, good Major, I have always your good word.

Mrs. D. Ay, indeed, husband, that you have; and more behind your back than ever I told you of.

[T. T. *comes up and salutes* D. D.

T. T. Worthy sir, your servant's humble servant.

D. D. Alas, good Captain!—Indeed and truly,—sweet sir,—the Major and I are old friends.

T. T. And may you long continue so.

D. D. I thank you, sir. Come, my joy, shall us walk? I should be loth to have Mr. Alderman there before us.

Mrs. D. Ay, my dear, I stay for thee.

[*Exit* D. D.

Bil. But hark you, hussy—

[*He whispers her back.*

Where shall you and I exercise? Can't you drop him, or give him the slip for an hour or two?

Mrs. D. Oh, no. We are to be at the Repetition at Mr. Alderman's—'tis Friday night. But I shall see you anon. Farewell, good Major. Your servant, sir.

[*Exit.*

T. T. Your servant, lady.

Bil. Captain, prithee let's meet to-morrow, in the afternoon, at Mother Formal's, the midwife's, and bring your small harlotry with you. We'll be merry.

T. T. A match—a match! [*Exeunt.*

SCENE II.

Enter JOLLY *and* AFTERWIT.

Aft. You are so wise! I have observ'd, this world
Dwells most abroad; seldom or ne'er at home.
Most men can counsel others; few themselves.

Jol. Hah! sentences. There's somewhat troubles you!
What is 't? And can you call me friend, and yet
Not let me bear my part? Friends should be one;
Breath, hope, fear, will, and nill the same, in common.
Aft. Why, what were you the better if you knew?
You cannot give me ease.
Jol. However, try!
A handsome fellow, and a fair estate,
And wit at will!—thou mayest command the town.
Leave off this fooling.
Aft. I'm beholden to you.
Can you, with all your wisdom, tell me now
Where this shoe wrings me?
Jol. No.
Aft. Then pray believe
I know; and if you are my friend, forbear
A further scrutiny.
Jol. My life, in love!
Not past that boy's disease—that troublesome itch?
Come; we'll be jovial, and divert the humour.
Aft. Suppose I were, is not the world the same?
Love is the bond of nature; and without it
The universe were but a besom unbound—
Sand without lime.
Jol. I need no further symptoms
To make the crisis. Hah! And you believe
This dainty philosophical poultice
Will work the cure? If I have any skill,
There were a better remedy.
Aft. For shame,
Thou infidel to all that's good or lovely!
May'st thou die in thy heresy, and ne'er know
What a good woman means, unless, perhaps,
For thy conversion.
Jol. This was intended
For a small curse. But I must thank my friend.
And if he were not turn'd bigot, I think
Might satisfy him. You're in love, forsooth!
All in good time. But have you not yet consider'd

What 'tis? How much more misery beyond it
Than on this side of 't? You may fancy castles,
And forty I know not what's; but they're of snow;
Come one good show'r, and farewell my fine gewgaw.
Aft. Thou art a strange fellow. What dost think of those
Have gone before us, and commend it too?
Jol. One woodcock makes no winter. But, I pray,
What are the persons? Are they not concern'd?
These married men are like boys in the water.
Ask 'um how 't goes: Oh! wonderous hot, they cry,
When yet their teeth chatter for very cold.
If you must love, love on; but go no further.
Women enjoy'd, like rivers in the sea,
Lose both their taste and name. Suppose 'um Junoes
In the pursuit, they're clouds in the enjoyment.
Aft. Thou'rt like the fox, that, having lost his tail,
Would fain persuade the rest to mak 't a fashion.
Prithee give over.
Jol. Troth I've scarce begun.
Suppose her handsome, she's a honey-pot
I' th' sun; if otherwise, you'll ne'er endure her:
If honest, insolent, though ne'er so ugly:
She thinks you are beholden to her for't;
And yet, who knows how long she may be so.
Is she the map of modesty? perhaps
'Tis but your own opinion; love is blind.
There's many pass for such, whose husbands yet
Could, if they durst, tell you another tale.
Is she a housewife? can she make a band?
Order a dairy? cure a broken shin?
Examine your accounts, and at year's end
Pray tell me what you've saved. Is she highborn?
Twenty to one she's proud, and quickly scorns you.
What are you better for those doughty acts
My lord her great-great-grandfather perform'd
The Lord knows where? or t'ave her portion paid you
In genealogies, gilt spurs, and cantons?*
Aft. Come—I can hold no longer. Have you done?

* A term in heraldry.

Jol. With your good patience, a word. Consider,
'Tis like a battle, to be fought but once;
And therefore, it must be so, be sure
She be your equal, and if possible virtuous—
At least not tainted with her mother's vices.
And now, if after this thou dar'st be wiving,
Th'art a bold fellow; and that's all I'll say.
Heav'n keep thee yet within the power of hellebore.
Aft. Prithee be n't so severe. Thou art my friend,
And I'll deal plainly with thee. That estate
Which you believe so fair (and wer't not for
My father's debts, and some small slips of mine,
Might have look't somewhat like it) is at present
At that low ebb, that if I don't look to 't
In time, it will be past recovery.
Come; the red petticoat must piece up all.
Jol. 'T 'as a half face of reason. As you say,
Desperate causes must have desperate cures.
But what is he has got this hank upon 't?
Aft. Did you ne'er hear of Alderman Whitebroth?
Jol. Ay, there's a Jew indeed! I'll tell thee what—
He has a daughter; thou shalt have her too,
Tho' it be but to be reveng'd of him.
Aft. There spake my friend. Oh! but her father——
Jol. What?
Aft. Will never give consent.
Jol. To chuse—she'll make
The better wife, to justify her folly.
Aft. Prithee be serious.
Jol. Good faith, I am;
And if thou hast her not, one way or other,
I'll be thy bondman. We'll about it straight.
[*Exeunt.*

SCENE III.

Enter MOPUS, *solus, with a book, etc.*

Mop. Saturn and Jupiter come to a trine in Taurus and Capricorn. Huh! We shall have strangers come to town, and their wives ne'er miss 'em in the country. Next month they all meet in the house of Mercury, he being lord thereof and significator of speech: it may intend advocates, cryers of courts, splitters of causes, oyster wives, and broom-men——Hold!—Saturn—(nothing but this malevolent planet) in the sign Virgo, in conjunction with Venus in her detriment. Beware, women, of green gowns; great men, of stone and cholic; and costermongers, of rotten pippins. Again, *pars torturæ*, coupled with the *Catabibason*—that is to say, the Dragon's Tail—huh, huh—children shall be subject to convulsion fits, young wenches to the falling evil, and old women to cough out their teeth.—[*He makes a pause.*]—But all this is no money. Many an honest man has but one house, and maintains his family very well; but, such an unlucky rogue, the whole twelve will hardly pay my rent. Now, a pox take these citizens, and then a man might get some money by 'um. They are so hidebound, there's no living by 'um; so clunch-fisted, a man would swear the gout were got out of their feet into their hands; 'tis death to 'um to pluck 'um out of their pockets. I am sure my bills bid as high as the proudest—they cure all diseases, and resolve all astrological questions, and they'll hardly quit cost for pasting 'um up. Here dwells an astrological physician, reads one; And there let him till I trouble him, answers another. His Majesty's most excellent operator, says one; Yes, upon post, quoth another. And thus you see how an artist is valued. O ignorance! ignorance! well may'st thou be mother of devotion; but I am sure thou art the stepdame of art. If it were not for the good women, with their groats and their vinegar bottles, and now and then a young wench to enquire of her sweetheart, I might e'en hang myself; nay (which were worse), my wife would cry her trade were the better o' th' two. But husht! I hear somebody coming. Ten to one but 'tis my young Squire, with his mercer's wife to have her fortune read—I could with less trouble and more certainty have told her husband's. I hear 'um—husht!—my wife understood their meaning, and might have put 'um together without troubling of me.

Enter MRS. MOPUS.

Oh! is it you? How goes all causes?

Mrs. Mop. But ill enough, I'm sure. I wonder what I'm the better for a husband in you. Here you sit moping and moping all day upon a book, and at night you are as sleepy as a gib'd cat.

Mop. Oh ho! I'm in thy debt, but thou shalt be paid it altogether. Is it not better to receive £100 at one payment than to dribble 't shilling and shilling?

Mrs. Mop. But you'd be loth, though, if your wife had an occasion, that she should borrow, though 'twere but sixpence.

Mop. Thou sayest right; but I dare trust thee further. Prithee go in and look after the house; we shall have some or other come popping in presently.

Mrs. Mop. To mighty purpose! 'Tis well you get so much. Methinks trading is grown extreme dead. Time was when your honest citizens' wives, and no ordinary madams, and their gallants would come and be merry here; but now——

Mop. A little patience, good wife; 't 'as been a long vexation the gentry are not come to town yet. And yet we have some doings, too.

Mrs. Mop. Yes; a company of fribbles, enough to discredit any honest house in the world. No; I'd have you know, I am for none of your skip-jacks. No. Give me your persons of quality; there's somewhat got by them. Besides, a woman need not be ashamed to sit jig by joul with the best of the parish; and who dare say black is her eye?

Mop. Prithee be quiet. I expected a young squire and his mistress; but I believe she could not get out, her husband is so jealous of her.

Mrs. Mop. Now, out upon her; could she not have took another woman with her? He has been a good one himself, I warrant you, that shall offer to suspect two women together. Marry hang these jealous-headed coxcombs, these ass-cuckolds, that believe their ears to be horns ; and such have you been in your time too—that you have.

Mop. Well, well ! go in — all shall be mended. Prithee, in !

Mrs. Mop. No, indeed, I don't intend it ; I must have some money first. Do you think I can go always in one gown ? Pray don't mistake yourself. Besides, I must buy the child a new coat ; and Mr. Scruple expects I should carry him something for his pains amongst us. Indeed, husband, he is a precious able man.

Mop. Yes, he is able—able to speak more with ease than another man can hear with patience. Away, you fool !

Mrs. Mop. Nay, good husband ; how do you think a woman can love you, if you will not let her do as the rest of her neighbours ? I warrant you for them, not one of them mist the meeting to-day ; and I hope you have found that they are not the worst customers we have. Marry come up here—

[*She strikes the book out of his hand.*

'Tis a fine thing that a woman can have no money but what she must ask her husband for ; and then, too, to have all this clutter about it. Give me some money, or I'll make my complaint to Mr. Scruple.

Mop. Be quiet, and thou shalt have anything. I must e'en stop her mouth to be rid of her.

[*This and the next aside.*

If once she set up her clack, the cataracts of Nile are but still music to 't. Come, we'll in, and see what may be done. [*Exeunt.*

Scene IV.

Enter Runter *and* Tyro.

Ru. Indeed, your father was my old acquaintance and very good friend. Ah ! how it tickles my lungs to think how many mad frolics we have had at robbing of orchards and stealing pudding-pies. I hope I may take it for granted that you visited the University? Pray, which of 'um, and what College?

Ty. Gotam College, sir; the University of Rumford.

Ru. My fellow-collegiate! You and I must be acquainted. A graduate, I hope, sir?

Ty. Yes, sir, a small one; I went out bachelor last horse fair.

Ru. And I doctor, in the throng. We must be better acquainted. You're come up to study?

Ty. My mother would have it so.

Ru. Then let me advise you. Study both laws, but chiefly the civil: you would not think what advantage 'tis to be a general man.

Ty. I shall follow your directions, sir.

Ru. Then, when you come to practice, you must get you a good brass towel and a steel countenance, and ever carry so much patience as not to be discouraged at anything; for I am to tell you a great truth, that our profession rots at the wrong end—the young ones die, and the old ones live. But how, I pray? Even like bawds and medlars, never ripe till rotten; that is to say, seldom or never get money till they are past the use of 't. And then, perhaps, what with a little favour and a great deal of money, they may chance to arrive at last to the height of sleeping out a cause.

Ty. I thank you, sir; and I think I shall be able to remember it.

Ru. Then you must ever be obsequious to great men; not that you expect any good from 'um, but, as the Chineses worship the devil, that they do you no hurt. Then be sure to keep your chamber; it will keep you. I kept mine many a long year, and nothing came; but at last, thanks to my stars and these good times, it came to the purpose.

Ty. I know this to be true; for my mother would be continually preaching it to my father.

Ru. Then you must never examine your cause,

whether it be good or bad. If it be good, and of no great concernment, it will carry itself; if bad, there's your master-piece to help it out. Every fool can manage a good cause; but he's your man can set the nose to which side he pleases, and make something out of nothing.

Ty. I hope I shall have the grace to put it in practice; and wish my father were alive, to thank you.

Ru. Then, if at any time you find you have the worst end of the staff, leave off your cause and fall upon the person of your adversary; put it boldly and enough of 't, and somewhat must stick; no matter how true or false, it begets a prejudice to a person, and many times forejudges the cause. For example, now, to give you an instance in a gentleman, a friend of mine, a great master of this way of pleading: A gentleman, with a long comely beard, demurs to his client's bill; my friend takes him up at first hop, and demurs to his beard; calls it a vow-beard, and that he had made an oath not to cut it till the King came in; and hark you, had he had twenty arguments, he might have better spared the other nineteen than that one. I could tell you of as good a one of my own, and upon as great a person as any this day in Europe—ah! how I firk't him up, with—a chip of the old block, and twenty as good—but enough of this now. The thing is sufficiently known, and it ill becomes a man to set out his own virtues. But try this, and do it boldly, and never doubt of clients. A modest lawyer!—A silent woman!—A paradox in nature.

Ty. I can but thank you still, sir.

Ru. I had almost forgot one thing, and no way inferior to any of the rest. If you find any commotion in the state, be sure to strike in with the first. If you get nothing—*cantabit vacuus*—you'll pass in the crowd; if you do, you'll have money enough to purchase your pardon, and perhaps, too, get in to be some great man's advocate. Chew the cud upon this for the present, and as I find you growing up to 't, I shall instruct you further. [*Exeunt.*

SCENE V.

Enter WHITEBROTH (*coughing*), MRS. WHITEBROTH, BEATRICE, CIS, *and* TIMOTHY, *laden with books.*

Wh. I do profess, this Mr. Scruple is a singular man.

Mrs. Wh. Ay, indeed is he; I never edified under any man like him. But how d'you, my lamb? how d'you?

Tim. A vengeance over-grown one. I have seen many a ram in my time has not been so big by the head and the horns. [*Aside.*

[WHITEBROTH *coughs all the while.*

Bea. How d'you, sir? You don't look well.

Wh. Nothing but a cold, my child—nothing but a cold! I hope 'twill away again. [*He coughs again.*

Mrs. Wh. Cis, Cis! a stick of licoras, Cis.

Enter DOUBLE DILIGENCE *and his Wife.*

Cis. I have some candied ginger, forsooth.

Mrs. Wh. Here, chick, prithee bite a bit of 't; 'tis the most sovereign thing, next a pepper-posset, as can be.

D. D. Save your good worship! It fell in an ill time. I am afraid it may beget an obstruction of justice, by hind'ring your worship's sitting on the bench.

Wh. How d'you, neighbours both? How d'you? You're welcome—[*coughs*]—I am afraid I sat a little too long in the cold—[*again*]. Come, neighbour Diligence! you and I'll walk in, and leave the women to entertain Mr. Scruple.

D. D. I wait upon your worship.

[*Exeunt* WHITEBROTH *and* DOUBLE DILIGENCE.

Mrs. Wh. Timothy!

Tim. Madam?

Mrs. Wh. Quickly, good Timothy, quickly—run in and get the towels. After, good Cis, after him; and see they be through warm.

[*Exeunt* TIMOTHY *and* CIS.

Enter SCRUPLE.

Oh, Mr. Scruple, Mr. Scruple! Alas, good man, how he sweats! Tim! Tim! Tim! A towel, Tim, a towel—quick, quick, quick!

Enter TIM.

Tim. Here, forsooth.

Mrs. D. Now, blessing o' your heart, good Mr. Scruple; you have taken a great deal of pains to-day.

Tim. Or his lungs have, which is all one. [*Aside.*

Mrs. Wh. Truly, and indeed, a great pains-taker. Come, Mr. Scruple, you have stood long to-day; pray sit down—[*they pull him down into a low chair and rub him*]—we must rule you here. Will you have a candle, sir? Alas, poor man! how wet the collar of his shirt is! Feel, Diligence; I prithee feel.

Mrs. D. Now, beshrew me, but 't 'as work'd quite through his doublet, coat, cloak, and all.

Sc. Hum, I am refreshed; yea, in good sooth, I am.

Mrs. Wh. Will you have a lemon-posset, sir?

Sc. I fear me it is too cold.

Mrs. Wh. Will you go to bed, sir? or have a fresh shirt? How do you, sir?

Tim. Troth, very ill upon a text.

Sc. I am well enough; only a qualm—a qualm.

Mrs. Wh. What say you to your collar of S'S, then?

Sc. That would not be amiss—there's no false Latin in 't.

Mrs. Wh. Quickly, Tim, quickly!—a pint of sack, a quart of cider, and a handful or two of sugar; and put 'um into the great bowl. Run, Timothy, run! Dear child, do thou help him.

Tim. Call you me this his collar of S'S?—[*aside*]—You shall have it presently.

[*Exeunt* TIMOTHY and BEATRICE.

Mrs. D. I am afraid you are not well, sir.

Sc. Yes; I am so so. You would not think how 't

has recover'd me. One would hardly believe what a rejoicing to my spirit it is to see you thus eager and, as it were, hungry for your food. Ah! be the same still. You cannot lay out yourselves, nor I myself, forth enough, in these ways. Pray mark it. We cannot lay out ourselves forth enough, one to another. These often duties put us into a spiritual posture of war. Ah! it is best fighting together. Ah! what a precious thing it is when we are concern'd together, and—ah!—ah! as a man may say, wrap't up in one common cause and interest. Ah! good sisterly women, consider it, and lay it upon your hearts. But how does Mr. Alderman? Methought I heard him cough ere while. How does he?

[*The women answer him in a long-drawn sigh*]. Hui!

Mrs. Wh. Now, indeed, I think he sat too long in the cold. He has gotten a heavy cough of 't.

Sc. To see the frailty of man's nature! How weary of every thing that is good!—how irksome it is unto us! I dare undertake he should have sat at a lewd stage-play a whole afternoon—nay, with his hat off too—and—ah, been ne'er the worse.

Mrs. Wh. But are these stage-plays such lewd things as you make them?

Sc. Why, truly, you are my bosom-sisters, and I may speak truth to you. Nay, they are not; for you may find good moral things in them—vice deprest, virtue encourag'd, and the like. However, we have thought fit to rail at 'um, for fear the people should set their hearts upon 'um, and consequently undo us. I have often lectured at 'um in a morning, and in the afternoon stol'n behind a pillar to hear 'um.

Enter TIM.

But see, here comes Timothy.—[*He starts.*]—Avaunt! This bowl is scandalous—it looketh like a wassail.—[TIM *offers to go out.*]—Nay, hold, Timothy! Though the bowl be scandalous, 'tis pity the good creature should be spoil'd. Pray, next time, let me have the great tankard; I am of opinion, too, it holds more.—[*He drinks.*]—The

Casuists speak comfortably in this point. A man may eat and drink abundantly without any necessity, but merely for his pleasure. Nay, he may *usque ad vomitum ingurgitare,* provided always he do not prejudice his health thereby; because it is allowable in the natural appetite to be taken up with those actions that are proper thereunto. We must deny ourselves; we may not deny the creature. Pray observe it. I say, we may not deny the creature; it being given us not for our sustentation only, but contentation also. Timothy! Prithee once more, good Timothy.

Tim. Here, sir. [SCRUPLE *drinks again.*

Mrs. Wh. Now, much good may it do your heart, good Mr. Scruple.

Mrs. D. Indeed he deserves a good thing, he makes so much of it when he has it.

Sc. This is napping gear, and well encourag'd. But, pray, no more of this bowl; pray no more of 't. For this time it may pass. Now, trust me, it has such a pleasant farewell, it invites a man to drink often of it. Timothy!

Tim. Here, sir! [SCRUPLE *drinks again.*

Sc. I do assure you, special stuff, and too good for the wicked; it may strengthen them in their enormities. But come; let's go visit Mr. Alderman. Timothy, is all out?

Tim. Yes, sir—not a drop left.

Sc. Then pray speak to Ruth to dress up the great tankard, and bring it in to Mr. Alderman's chamber.

Tim. It shall be done, sir. [*Exeunt.*

ACT II.—SCENE I.

Enter TIMOTHY, *solus.*

Tim. Huh! he grows worse and worse. I have been with the doctor, and he'll be here presently. Precious Mr. Scruple is departed, but so like a dog outlaw'd, that unless the devil owes me a spite, I may be troubled with a mourning cloak. I am sure I have deserved it. I am the general officer of this house, like my mistress's silver sack-posset-bason—screw a handle to 't, and 'tis her bed-pan; put a cover to that, her warming-pan; take off both, it serves to wash her hands in the morning, and for a sack-posset at supper. In the stable I am groom; in the garden gard'ner; at the market, caterer; in the cellar, butler; upon all visits, her gentleman usher; and above stairs, his *valet de chambre.*

Enter MOPUS.

My noble doctor! you're a man of your word.

Mop. How does your master?

Tim. Alack, sir! I thought you could have told that by the stars. I have heard say, learned men know everything.

Mop. Yes! I could have erected a Scheme, but I thought it unnecessary. How does he take his rest?

Tim. But ill; and complains of heats and gripings.

Mop. I'll set him right again—unless the stars——

Tim. What, good sir?

Mop. Have pre-decreed the contrary; and if so, we must submit. Will you let your mistress know I am here?

Tim. I shall, sir. [*Exit* TIMOTHY.

Mop. So—there's half the disease; I shall easily pick the rest out of the good woman. If all things hit right, this alderman may prove a good milch-cow.

Enter MRS. WHITEBROTH.

Madam! your humble servant.

Mrs. Wh. You're welcome, sir. Nay, what d'you mean? Pray, sir! Indeed there's nobody expects it. Pray be pleas'd, I can assure you, no—in truth I do not—pray, sir!

[*She does this to make* MOPUS *put on his hat.*

Mop. O—your servant. Have you sav'd the Alderman's water, as I ordered?

Enter CIS *and* TIMOTHY.

Mrs. Wh. Yes, sir! Cis, Cis! thy master's state.

Cis. O! Tim, Tim! 'twas in the silver tankard, and the cat overthrew it.

[*This and the next to be spoke aside.*

Tim. There stands some dead ale upon the table, put that i' the urinal; he'll tell as much by one as t'other. [*Exeunt* TIMOTHY *and* CIS.

Mop. A most fortunate face—I never met with more lucky lines. You'll live to bury the Alderman —and—shall marry—let me see—a lord.

Mrs. Wh. Indeed, sir? I believe you can tell.

Mop. Nay, I am certain of it. Hereafter I may chance to tell you his name; but for the present, be sure he is a viscount at least.

Mrs. Wh. This—[*she gives him money*]—and my thanks. A viscountess! I'll promise you, I'll take it no longer as I have done.

Enter CIS *with an urinal.*

Mop. Oh! let me see 't. High-colour'd—his blood's inflam'd. Feverish—feverish.

[*At every stop he shakes the urinal.*

Mrs. Wh. Indeed, sir, he burns like fire.

Mop. Sick—sick—sick! He cannot rest.

Mrs. Wh. Ay, indeed! You are as right.

Mop. Sometimes up, and sometimes down.

Mrs. Wh. Truly, he has not been out of his bed since he first took his cold till just now.

Mop. Huh—a cold!—[*Aside.*]—Pains in his limbs, coughing, and now and then wind. This froth and feather in the water is a certain token.

Mrs. Wh. Now, bless me, sir! how is 't possible you should hit things so right?

Mop. How do you hit your mouth in the dark? One's as easy as t'other—that is to say, to a man of art. I could tell you a thousand things; but time is precious. May I not see the Alderman?

Mrs. Wh. O, by all means. I hear him coming.

Enter WHITEBROTH.

O, my dear, here's a gentleman has told me all your distemper, as right. [WHITEBROTH *coughs.*

Wh. And what does he think of it?

Mop. Pray, bend your wrist, sir.—[*He feels his pulse.*]—All will do well again. A purge and a vomit—a purge and a vomit. Gi' me a pen and ink. [*He writes.*

Mrs. Wh. Would not some *Parma Citty* do him good? Truly, I would be loth he should want anything.

Mop. You do well. Let me see—what says the College? *Sperma cœti, confectio quædam*—pox on't, I have forgot the rest. *Sperma cœti!—sperma cox comb.* They're a company of quacking fools. 'Tis *Parmacitty*, and takes its name from the city of Parma. Hang this foisting—I'll trust ne'er a doctor of them all.—[*He tears the paper.*]—Have a little patience, madam, and I'll send you a preparation of my own. In the mean time, your servant. I am staid for at present. [*Exit.*

Mrs. Wh. Farewell, good doctor. Come, my heart! rest thyself within. [*Exeunt,* WHITEBROTH *coughing.*

SCENE II.

Enter JOLLY *and* AFTERWIT.

Jol. And how d'you like her now?

Aft. Could I like heav'n?
Prithee, forbear these questions.

Jol. And much good may she do thee. Thou sha't have her. I've laid the plot, and I am sure 'twill take.

Aft. As how, my Jolly?

Jol. Not so hasty. I have an odd humour in my pocket will strike fair to it. [*He pulls out a printed bill;*

Aft. What's here? A printed bill! Prithee let's hear 't.

Jol. 'In the name of God, through the light of the Son, by the revelation of the Spirit, I cure these diseases, perfectly and speedily, without any annoyance to the body, which commonly happens through college bills and apothecaries' medicines, with which the devil has deceived the world these many hundred of years.

'The new disease (otherwise called the Great Pox) with all its appendices, in few days, with herbs that I gather in the woods, and gums of trees—agues of all sorts, in three fits—gout, whether knotted or running, in four or five dressings—dropsy—timpany—rickets—spleen—convulsion—yellow and black jaundies, stone, strangury, and collick, in six hours. All kinds of fluxes, most distempers of the head, shortness of breath, and ptisick, at first sight. And have ever by me a most approved remedy against green sickness, barrenness, and fits of the mother.'

Aft. 'Twas fairly vied. Who bids more?'

Jol. He comes again: 'As also (to let the world see how wide of their mark they are like to run that as boldly as ignorantly dare adventure on physic without the knowledge of astrology), I resolve these ensuing astrological questions:

'The sick, whether they shall recover or not; the party absent, whether living or dead. How many husbands or children a woman shall have; whether one shall marry the party desir'd, or whom else. Whether a woman hath her maidenhead or not, or shall be honest after marriage, or her portion well paid. If a man be wise or a fool. Whether it be good to put on new clothes. If dreams be for good or evil. Whether a child be the reputed father's; or shall be fortunate, or not. Ships at sea, whether safe or not. Of law-suits, which side shall have the better. And generally, all astrological questions whatever.

'*Iatros Iatrophilus Mopus*,

'A Servant of God, and Secretary of Nature.'

Aft. Hah, boys! if this wo'n't take 'um, the devil take 'um. But what are those hard words?

Jol. Oh! a physician, a friend to physicians—The only true thing in all his bill. These quacks are the best friends physicians have; they make work for 'um. What dost think is come into my head?

Aft. How is it possible I should know? I am no Œdipus.

Jol. Why, this fellow must be a cheat; and, I am confident, with a little help, would be able to do our business. Prithee let's to him. But see, your mistress! To her!

Enter BEATRICE *and* CIS.

Aft. This is such fortune, I forgive my stars
All their unkindness.

Bea. Is this natural? Or do you carry set forms about you, to be used as occasion shall serve?

Aft. Faith, neither. So much excellence must needs inform a statue, and make a post rhetorical.

Bea. Demonstrations! Why, how now, Mr. Afterwit?

Aft. Just as you see. How d'you like him?

Jol. Well said! To her again. If I can make no sport, I'll mar none. How now, Cis?

Cis. The better for your asking, I thank you, sir.

Jol. Hark you—a word.

[JOLLY *and* CIS *walk aside.*

Aft. So fair, and so unkind! Sure Nature dotes,
She twists such contradictions; or, what's worse,
Has lost her wits, and would have all like her.

Bea. Whence this new fury?

Aft. Can you read your self
And ask that question? Were you made thus lovely,
To make me miserable? Would you had less
Divinity or more humanity.

Bea. Then you're in love, it seems! or at least would
Make me believe it. Don't I know, you men
Speak anything? Women are fools, and can't
For shame but credit it.

Aft. You wrong my truth,
By all that's good!
Bea. No more. Admitting yet
What I can scarce believe, why must you crop
That flower, which, as it grows, may peradventure
Look fair and lovely; but once gather'd, withers?
Give me love refined—a love that flames
Upon itself, not fed with grosser fuel;
A love that loves the virtue, not the sex.
Aft. And such is mine. But fancy not this new
Philosophy of immaterial flames.
Hearts may meet hearts, and souls piquere * with souls;
But if they come no nearer than the eyes,
For want of matter to maintain 'um, die.
Bea. Be judge yourself. Who but the needy pray?
Once fill your belly, you've no more to say.
Aft. Yes. To give thanks, and ruminate upon
Those blessings which grow faster than we reap 'um.
Come, come, be wise, and trifle not away
That youth would make an emperor too happy.
All seek their like, and like the needle, tremble,
And never settle till it reach that North.
I'd rather be an owl than phœnix,
If I must live alone.
Bea. These morals, sir,
Might have been better. But since you'll needs
Make me believe you love me, court my father;
For notwithstanding the respect I bear you,
I must declare, I've neither eyes nor ears
To anything but what he shall direct.

Jol. You need say no more. Mind what I told you, and leave the rest to me.—[*He speaks this to* CIS.]—What! have you done yet? A good soldier, now,

* Or 'pickeer'—coquette. Literally, to skirmish before a battle begins.

Y^e^ garrison, wth some commons and the Scotch horse *picquoring* awhile close by the walls on the east, drew off, after they had failed in snapping Col. Graye's small regement of hors at Stanwick, with much ado gott into the towne without losse.—TULLIE'S *Narrative of the Siege of Carlisle*, p. 6.

would have carry'd the town with half this do. Ha' done your grace for shame; and fall to your meat.

Aft. Sure my father went to heaven, I'm so unfortunate. Well, be it as 't will, I love you; and were I to speak seven years, I could but say the same thing. Come! I'll wait on you. [*Exeunt.*

SCENE III.

Enter SCRUPLE *and* MRS. WHITEBROTH.

Sc. I can't away with it; unfeignedly, I cannot. A man may profess it is lawful—yea, assuredly it is; and therefore, I profess if any of my flock shall so much as straggle into his pastures, I shall not only turn them out of my fold for rotten sheep, but they shall for ever be to me as publicans; that is to say, as the learned have most ingeniously observ'd, *Publicanus, quasi publicus canis.*

Mrs. Wh. Why, good Mr. Scruple, a member should not be cut off for one failing.

Sc. Good, me no goods, good Mrs. Whitebroth; I tell thee here, sister of mine, it is a wilful failing—a very wilful failing.

Mrs. Wh. For why, I pray? The man is learned—I am sure he told me all my husband's distemper before he so much as saw him.

Sc. Told ye! Ay, there's the point. And I must tell you too, he must needs use some unlawful means.

Mrs. Wh. Alas! It cannot be. His wife, good woman, is one of us; and do you think, if he were such, she would ever suffer it?

Sc. Why, there's the blind. The woman is a sisterly woman, and an often frequenter; which he allows of only to deceive the world, as if he were! Well, well, mark what I say!—if he has not made some secret express contract with Satan, I'll be your teacher no longer. If you had ever read Doctor Faustus, this would not be so strange to you.

Mrs. Wh. Now, goodness defend it!

Sc. Come, come, 'tis great pity it is not look't into. I dare undertake, had this fellow set up in Spain, he had been in the Inquisition long ere this. But we, the more light we have, the less we see. We are wilfully, stiff-neckedly blind; indeed we are.

Mrs. Wh. Be not too rash. Many a good body's wrong'd, or many of our brethren and sisters are not what they should be.

Sc. Yes! that was always the malice of the devil and his instruments. But this fellow is a profest reprobate. I have read his bills, and spoken with several that have been with him, and they tell me he has a globe ever standing upon his table, and never answers any question propos'd without first turning that. And why may not the devil be in that globe, as well in the pummel of Paracelsus's sword, and Doctor Dee's cristall? D'you mark me that, gentlewoman? Answer me that!

Mrs. Wh. Nay, pray, Mr. Scruple, I must go to him; all that he told me was without his globe. I mean no hurt.

Sc. That may be something in the case. Let me see, what say the Casuists? If anything help you, it must be the intention; and that we are forc'd to make use of in many cases, especially such as we cannot hinder, and correct the viciousness of the means by the purity of the end. For example: if a woman, great with child, long for another man besides her husband, and this husband will not give consent, in this case we say, and so we generally agree, that she may follow her natural inclination; provided always she have no intention of sin, but only to satisfy her longing; for, *Actus non facit reum, nisi mens sit rea.*

Mrs. Wh. Now, blessing on you, good sir; I always thought so.

Sc. In like manner: if a woman of a godly parentage do fall into a holy fornication, not out of lust but love, and thereupon prove with child, in such a case we say that it may be lawful to procure abortion; provided always it be not with intention of murder, but only to save life or reputation. Nay, further, lest the profession should be scandal'd by it, we hold it better to trust Providence, by foreswearing the fact, than to fall into the hands of men by confessing the infirmity of the flesh. And in this, as many other things, we agree with some gentlemen abroad; and truly, where we do differ, the difference between us is so fine and nice, we can hardly perceive it ourselves. There is, as the schoolmen term it, an identificadunity of principles common to us both. They have their private shrifts; so we. They call it a venial sin with a sister, and in case of necessity can forgive a neighbour's wife; so we. They allow regulating by tumults; so we. And lastly, they deny all this in plain words, but grant it in effects; so we.*

Mrs. Wh. What's this to me? May not I go, good Mr. Scruple?

Sc. If your intention be right, you may. However, for fear of the worst, I will go with you; I should be loth to lose one of the best sheep in my flock for want of a little care. Come, Mrs. Whitebroth, I did not think to have done so much; but you have such a winning way with you, such a power upon me, I can deny you nothing—indeed I cannot. Come! we must now and then comply with one another's weakness.

[*He leads her off.*

Mrs. Wh. 'Tis a good hearing, sir. I thank you.

[*Exeunt.*

* Who shall decide when doctors disagree,
And soundest *casuists* doubt like you and me?—POPE.

What arguments they have to beguile poor, simple, unstable souls with, I know not; but, surely, the practical, casuistical, that is the principal, vital part of their religion, savours very little of spirituality.—SOUTH.

Morality, by her false guardian drawn,
Chicane in furs, and casuistry in lawn.—POPE.

Scene IV.

Enter Bilboe, *leading* Mrs. Double Diligence; *and* Titere Tu, *leading* Mrs. Mopus.

Bil. Come, gipsy! how came you to light on this house? 'Tis a rare convenience.

Mrs. D. Oh! she's our midwife.

T. T. And, faith, they are good necessary things, and generally tractable before they grow rich.

Mrs. Mop. How do you know? I never met you here before.

T. T. Time enough now.

Mrs. D. But pray, Major, is this gentleman married?

Bil. Hang him, rogue—every man's boots serve his turn.

T. T. And better so than going barefoot. I am not married, sweet lady, but a lover still.

Mrs. D. A pretty gentleman!

Mrs. Mop. He was, you would have said, had you known him when I knew him first; but now——

T. T. As good as ever, my girl! Dear Mopus!

[*He hugs her.*

Mrs. Mop. Away, Captain! You do so mousle one!

Bil. Nay, have a care of him. I say no more.

Mrs. Mop. Marry! I hope you are not in earnest.

T. T. And thou hast no more wit than to believe him. As sound as a bell, wench; as sound as a bell.

[*He capers.*

Mrs. Mop. Indeed, Captain, I hope the best. But sure there's somewhat in 't—he does not fine up himself, as he was wont.

T. T. I seldom regard fashions; anything serves me. *Drape de berry* in the summer keeps out the heat, and stuff in the winter lets it in. I must confess, I have three or four as rich suits for Flanders lace, gimp, and embroidery, as any in the town.

Mrs. Mop. But where are they, good Captain, where are they?

T. T. Why, faith, I have had 'um all in my head this twelvemonth, but could never yet get one of them upon my back.

Mrs. Mop. Troth, Captain, 'twould not be amiss at this time if you open'd your head and took one of 'um out.

T. T. The jade's too hard for me. Hark you!

[*He picks her pocket.*

Mrs. Mop. O, good Captain! It must buy the child a new coat.

T. T. Hang him, brat! one of thy old petticoats will serve. Bestow money upon puppy-dogs!

Mrs. Mop. You always serve me thus. Pray, Captain! Give me some of 't again.

[*He leads her aside, and whispers.*

T. T. Not a cross, by this good light. D'you hear me?

Bil. And must thy Major have no hatchments? Prithee, disburse, disburse! Dear landlady!

[*He hugs her.*

Mrs. D. Indeed I have no money. One would think your meat, drink, lodging, washing, and wringing were worth somewhat.

Bil. Irish beef, by this good Tilbury—nothing but sheep's heads and Irish beef.

Mrs. D. 'Tis but too good for you, unless you were more thankful. Many an honest gentleman would be glad of your orts.*

Bil. Prithee, my best landlady, let the small gem or the superfluous petticoat march.

Mrs. D. I will not always endure this! For once—— But shall we be merry then?

[*She plucks out a piece wrapt up.*

Bil. As merry as thou wilt, my joe. Hang pinching! we'll never pine ourselves, though our heirs smart for 't.

Mrs. D. Here, Major, here's an old Elizabeth has not seen light these seven years.

Bil. And ev'n let her go. She has been prisoner

* Leavings.

long enough, of all conscience. Come, Captain, let's be merry!

T. T. By this hand, 'tis true.—[*Speaking to* MRS. MOPUS]—I love thee above all flesh alive. Fear nothing! All's well, and as right as my leg.

Bil. And that's crooked, to my knowledge.

Mrs. Mop. Nay, good sir; you do but jest!

T. T. Hang him—hang him! I have said enough. And now I'm for you. *Be true, cuckolds; be true, be true*, etc. [*He sings.*

Mrs. Mop. Hoop holyday! That's old.

T. T. You are for new faces too! Pray, Major, will you oblige this lady?

Bil. Who, I? With all my heart. But I've got so strange a cold, and drunk so much French wine of late, that, by this old companion of my side, 'twill be but once remov'd from howling.

Mrs. D. However; pray venture! I never knew a good voice without an excuse. Pray, try!

Bil. My landlady might command me anything. But I'm so out of tune. *Ta,—la, la, la, la.* Hang 't!

T. T. Let him alone, and you won't be rid of him. He's like the blind beggars of Bolonia; a man must give 'um a halfpenny to sing, and twopence to hold their tongues.

BILBOE SINGS.

I.

COME, give the wench that is mellow,
And a pox take all fools that are yellow;
'Tis the horn, the horn,
The advancing of the horn,
Dubs a cuckold an alderman's fellow.

II.

Let no man disorder his rest
By believing bull's feathers in 's crest;
When you've said what you can,
A cuckold is a man,
Or most of our fathers were beasts.

III.

Then let us sing, At it, and at it;
And let ev'ry one catch that can catch it;
All opinions agree
In one of these three—
The horn, the pot, or the placket.

Bil. La, you now! Did not I tell you as much? I'll have my pipes clear'd against we meet next.

Mrs. D. But when shall that be?

Bil. When you will; provide it be for all night, and out of town.

Mrs. D. That's impossible!

Bil. Not at all. You may leave word, you are gone to a woman's labour.

Mrs. D. Hah! hah! But her husband——

Bil. What?

Mrs. D. Will discover the contrary.

Mrs. Mop. Puh! puh! Never let that trouble you. His knowledge does not lie that way. You know, Captain, I have slipt a man into his tables ere now, and he not a farthing the wiser.

T. T. Ay, that thou hast, I'll be sworn.

Bil. Come, come! let's in, and discourse it further. A bottle and a fiddle, and then good-night.

T. T. A match, a match! Lead up before, Major!
[*Exeunt.*

SCENE V.

Enter RUNTER *and* TYRO.

Ru. What think you of it? She is a handsome gentlewoman, and her father's heir.

Ty. Think, do you say? I'll promise you, my stomach wambles* at her already.

* This word has long been in use in Scotland as well as in England. The celebrated Henry Erskine, Dean of the Faculty of Advocates, when pleading before a venerable Senator of the

Ru. Leave it to me. I will not do with you as I do with my clerk, snip half profits. But you know, sir, somewhat ought to be done. *Danda est ossa.*

Ty. Whatever you please, sir. If this take, I will down into the country, get me an able clerk, and turn Justice of peace.

Ru. And so you may. The Alderman is gone to take the air, and ten to one but he makes this way homeward. I did once, at distance, propose such a thing; and, now I perceive you relish it, I'll present you to him. But to pass the time till he comes—you say you are a bachelor of law? I'll try your wit. I have a case here referr'd to me; pray observe it, and give me your opinion in 't. I take it, it runs through the whole twenty-four letters. These common lawyers are our younger brothers, but they have given us the start; they never let anything come to us but what they can make nothing of themselves.

Ty. Pray, sir, let me hear 't.

Ru. You shall. 'Tis thus:—[*he reads*]—'Abigail, a *femme sole*, seised in tail of the manor of Black-acre, makes a feoffment in fee to Cutbeard, upon condition that if Daniel shall release Emanuel of and from all actions relating to Ferdinand, that then Gregory shall satisfy Humphry of and for all marriage-portions intended by Jeremy to be given Knipperdoling, with his wife's daughter Lettice; which, Maximilian perceiving, and believing that Nicholas had a more than ordinary influence upon Oliver, procures Peter to discharge Quintilian, and engage Rowland to estate his wife Susan in the capital messuage of Tonguewell (with a certain salt-marsh and under-woods thereunto belonging), and stop his daughter Ursela's mouth with

College of Justice somewhat slow of comprehension, advanced, and most pertinaciously urged, a plea of which his Lordship did not perceive the force, although he gave his full attention to the learned lawyer's subtle arguments. When concluded, his Lordship did not venture to deliver judgment, but calmly said: 'Weel, Hairry, there may be a great dale in what ye say, but I'll just let it wimble-wamble in my wame, an' I'll let ye ken what I think o't the morn.' This mode of dealing with a case is now termed 'taking it to avizandum.'

a wind-mill and a water-mill left her by her mother. Whereupon, Winifred, having lately recovered, in a pre-contract against Xenophon, makes a lease to Younker, who re-leases to Zachary, who enters upon Abigail, who re-enters upon him, and, ejecting him out of the premises, burns his principal evidences.' And now, sir, what think you? Where has this man his remedy?

Ty. I should think, sir, he were gone at common law.

Ru. You are always hankering after the common law. How shall we hedge in the jurisdiction of 't?

Ty. Indeed I cannot tell. But, they say, here is a learned astrologer, that undertakes to tell such things by the stars. Perhaps it might not be amiss to consult him.

Ru. Hark you! I dare trust you. He knows no more of law than you or I do. Now, by my troth, but it is a difficult case, and I have given my opinion in 't both ways—the devil's in 't if one of 'um ben't right. But, as I told you, the Alderman—his constable and he are a little private; they'll have done presently.

Enter WHITEBROTH *and* DOUBLE DILIGENCE.

Wh. How do you say it was?

D. D. Why thus, an't please you: I had, according to the duty of my office, just walk'd my round, when lo! about the first of the morning, we perceived a kind of glimmering, as of Guido Faux's lanthorn; and we said unto it—'Stand! And what art thou? and what meaneth that light at this unseasonable hour of the night?' when presently a voice answered—'Nay, but what are ye?' and we said—'The watch.' And to our seeming, it said again—'Harm watch, harm catch;' and there fell a shower, as it had been of chamber-pots; and we were most lewdly bepist, and some pates broken.

Wh. A plain case. The King's majesty's authority affronted, in the representative person of my neighbour

Double Diligence, the constable. Bring 'um before me; I 'll make 'um know what's what.

D. D. Will it please your worship to grant me your warrant? I had one from mistress's worship, during your sickness, but could make nobody obey it.

Wh. How? not obey her warrant? I'd have 'um to know she is, in my absence, as good a justice of peace as myself. Are not man and wife one person in law? Not obey her warrant! Let me see who dares deny 't! Come, neighbour, come, I smell a rat; what would you say now, if this should prove to be a Bull from the Pope. I say no more.

[RUNTER *and* TYRO *come up.*

Ru. Save you, Mr. Alderman! I am glad to see you so well abroad again.

Wh. Doctor Runter! my loving friend and neighbour, well met.

Ru. This is the gentleman, sir, I told you of. He is a thriving young man, and you may do what you will with him.

Wh. I shall be glad to be acquainted with you, sir.

Ty. I hope the doctor will oblige me in 't.

Wh. Methinks the air is somewhat sharp. Come, Doctor, take your friend with you. [*Exeunt.*

ACT III.—SCENE I.

Enter JOLLY, AFTERWIT, *and* BOY.

Boy. Be pleas'd, gentlemen, to take a turn or two in this room. My father is a little private with a person of honour, but will be with you presently.

[*Exit.*

Jol. Where are we now? Nor better, nor worse, but a downright astrological bawdyhouse. The devil of anything could I see in t'other room but two or three chairs broke in the back, half-a-dozen empty gally-pots and a death's-head between two syringes.

Aft. You may guess forty times, and not hit so right again. I believe him a better artist at bawdry than conjuring.

Jol. Not a jot the worse instrument. Do but hear him, and you'll quickly judge. And if you love me, pray let me manage the conference. He's somewhat long. Where is this man of learning?

Enter MOPUS.

Mop. Here, sir! A poor old man; one or other will never let him be quiet till he is in his grave. Your commands, gentlemen?

Jol. Why faith, this gentleman and myself have receiv'd so large a character of you, that we are come to wait on you in the behalf of a friend of ours.

Mop. I have done somewhat in my time, and hope I shall never be too old to do good.

Jol. You say well. There is a friend of ours, that for the present shall be nameless, has got a small mischance. You may guess what I mean.

Mop. Well, sir, I apprehend you, and will set him right again.

Jol. Then you take it for granted it must be a man. Suppose it be a woman, does that alter the case?

Mop. Sir, I'll deal plainly with you. If your friend be a man, I'll cure him for five pieces; but if a woman, I shall not take her in hand under twenty.

Jol. Why this great difference?

Mop. O sir, not without reason. The sooner you cure a man, the sooner you have him again. He's a constant Termor. But a woman—ah! sir, she brings grist to mill—cure her once and she grows cunning; you'll hardly hear of her more. I shall not bate anything of twenty pieces to cure her. But this I'll do with you—I'll patch her up against Term for forty shillings.

Jol. Hah! hah! Let this satisfy you; 'tis a man. [*He gives him money.*]—I'll send him t'you.

Mop. Pray do; and leave him to me. And if there

be any virtue in sassa, guaiacum, or turpentine, you need not fear him.

Aft. A rare rogue! [*Aside.*

Jol. Well, sir, I shall. But this is not all our business. We are well satisfied that you are a person of occult learning. Pray, sir, oblige us.

Mop. You look like gentlemen, and I am confident are so. I'll be free with you. I could discover a secret of nature to you, and for the expence of a brace of hundred pounds put you in possession of 't. It will give you the knowledge of all things—past, present, and to come; and long life, health, youth, blessedness, wisdom, and virtue shall be added to it.

Aft. As paper and pack-thread. [*Aside.*

Mop. But, if you should not make a right use of it, by living soberly, temperately, and enjoying it, as if you had it not; but shall mis-employ it, in swaggering, gluttony, worldly pride, and sensuality, you shall not only lose it for the present, but be out of all hopes of finding it again for the future. And this is that which we call our Magisterium Elixer, or Rosycrucian Pantarva. The father of it is the sun, the mother of it the moon, its brothers and sisters the rest of the planets; the wind carries it in its belly, and the nurse thereof is the earth.

Jol. Pray, sir, proceed; and disclose this son of gold.

Mop. Hermetically, I shall. It is situated in the centre of the earth, and yet falls neither within centre nor circumference; small, and yet great; earthy, and yet watery; airy, and yet very fire; invisible, yet easily found; soft as down, yet hard above measure; far off, and yet near at hand. That that is inferior, is as that which is superior; and that which is superior is as that which is inferior. Separate the combustible from the incombustible, the earth from the fire, the fluid from the viscous, the hot from the cold, the moist from the dry, the hard from the soft, the subtile from the thick—sweetly, and with a great deal of judgment, *per minima,* in the caverns of the earth—and thou shalt see it ascend to heaven, and descend to earth, and receive the powers of superiors and inferiors. Comprehend this, and be happy! Thou hast discover'd the balsam of sulphur, the *humidum radicale* of metals, the sanctuary of nature; and there is little or nothing between thee and the mountain of diamonds, and all the spirits of astromancy, geomancy, and coschinomancy are at your command.

Jol. Pray, sir, how call you that? That last again!

Mop. Coschinomancy, sir; that is to say, the most mysterious art of sieve and sheers. I must confess, I was once of the mind to have oblig'd the world with a discourse upon this subject; but since that, the world and I have been better acquainted, and I find it base and unworthy.

Jol. Troth, sir, 'tis pity but you went on; such a Quixotism in philosophy must needs please every man. For my own part, I dare promise you, you shall want neither money nor coals as long as this gentleman's purse and mine can supply you.

Mop. Why, truly, sir, encouragement may do much. I am neither Mede nor Persian; upon good demonstrative reasons I may be persuaded.—[*A bell rings within.*]—What pity it is, that beast of mankind, that Goth to all good literature,—for he deserves no better from me,—Dioclesian, burnt all the books of this art, and for no other reason but that he fear'd, forsooth, they would make gold too common. A wise fellow,—another Lycurgus,—to avoid drunkenness, cut down the vines. You see by this he confest it feasible.

Enter BOY.

Boy. Sir, I must speak a word with you in haste.

Mop. Gentlemen, I'll wait on you again instantly.

Jol. By no means. We shall have further business to you, and will see you again. We follow you.

[*Exit* MOPUS.

What say you, now? Is not this a special rogue?

Aft. As ever breathed. But to my business—I am afraid I shall want present money; I could never find any wheels move merrily without greasing.

Jol. Nor I neither. And therefore, to prevent the worst, try to get t'other £1000 of the Alderman, and crossbite him with his own money.

Aft. And that I can. He has offer'd it me!

Jol. And do it. If a man must break, a £1000 will signify little in the sum. Come, mind your business, and you cannot miscarry if you would!

[*Exeunt.*

SCENE II.

Enter WHITEBROTH *and* TIMOTHY.

Tim. I am glad to see your worship tread so lusty and strong again. I hope you'll be better for 't.

Wh. Ay, Tim. 'Twould have vex't a man, to have just got an estate, and strait pipt o'er the pearch he had ere he had time to look upon 't. Mr. Scruple put divers things very home to me, and 'twas ten to one but all had come out, but that I thought with myself there was no such need yet. Come, Tim, leave that, and let's see how affairs stand at present. How have you done with your rotten raisins? Did they yield well?

Tim. Troth, sir, the wine-coopers have done their part; they have made you at least sixty pipes of wine out of 'um. But they advise your worship to get your money for 'um before they stir out of your cellar; for however they may be palatable enough as long as they lie there, yet, as soon as you stir 'um, they'll kick up their heels.

Wh. Good enough to be pist against a wall an' they were worse. And now I think on't, you remember the country vintner, that bought the pipe of Canary on shipboard, and gave it to Rascal-Mark, to cheat the Customhouse? See it be cran'd off into another pipe, and fill'd up again with your new what d' you call it? 'Tis good enough for sinners. If he discover it, you may tell him 'tis his own mark.

Tim. It shall be done. But, sir, Mr. Spendal was to have waited on you yesterday touching a bond of his of £500, which he says is paid, and you promis'd to deliver up.

Wh. O ho! let me see. Here 'tis—[*he reads*]—'If the said Spendal shall content, satisfy, and pay,' etc. Why, see—the condition of the obligation, which is made for his benefit, and not mine, says, *if he shall content.* Pray tell him, notwithstanding the payment of the money, his bond is forfeited; for I am not contented. Does he think I can be content with six per cent.? I have no more to say to him; I'll take my course. Pray mind your own business. Have you receiv'd the Jew's money, and sent him the pack of left-handed gloves I order'd you?

Tim. Yes, sir; 'tis done.

Wh. Put tricks upon me! Make me buy a round parcel of gloves; and now you know I have 'um by me, if I will not bate a third part of the money, you have occasion but for half of 'um, and be hang'd. I'll Jew you, with a horse pox. I have receiv'd half your money, and you shall have half the gloves—that is to say, all the left-handed ones. You may truck them off with maim'd soldiers; if not, I'll make you pay sauce for t'other. Reach me that book—and while I remember it, go into my chamber, and upon the table you'll find a £1000 in half-crowns; pray weigh 'um one by one, and lay by such as are over weight, and see 'um melted down. 'Tis a hard world, and fit every man make the most of his own.—[*The bell rings.*]—See, who's at door! [*Exit* TIMOTHY.

[WHITEBROTH *reads.*]—'Taken up on Bottomry, upon the good ship call'd the *Mary*, to be paid with interest, after the rate of £30 per cent., within ten days after her coming to anchor in the River of Thames, £1700'—So, so, that's paid: All got. She's sunk at New-found-Land. Besides, I have insur'd a £1000 upon her myself. How wealth trowls upon an honest man! The master deserves a £100 extraordinary for this, and shall have it. This is the fifth ship he has sunk for me. '*Item*, Paid the Irish army, in Peru dollars.' Ay, there's a sweet business.

Enter TIMOTHY.

Who's that?

Tim. Sir, Mr. Afterwit desires to see you.

Wh. Stay him a while without; I'll be for him presently.—[*Exit* TIM.]—Here's a squire, too, will be worth me somewhat. Let me see his account. 'Lent his father, upon judgment, £4000. *Item*, More upon a statute, £3000. *Item*, Upon mortgage, £2500. *Item*, Upon his own account, upon bond, £500. *Item*, More, £300. *Item*, Bound to me, for other men, £1000.' Pox o' these bonds! I must persuade him to take another £1000, and hedge all into one good mortgage. To see how this world goes round! My great-grandfather was a wealthy citizen, and left my grandfather a gentleman, forsooth! But what between my my father and him, they so order'd the business that they left me nev'r a groat. This fellow's grandfather was a law-driver, and swallow'd my father up; his father set the estate a moving, and this will set it quite away. His first ancestor cheated mine, and I hope I shall be able to requite his love upon his posterity. Thus, you see, the wheel comes round to the same point again. This city is like the sea—few estates but ran out of 't at first, and will run into 't at last. Timothy!

Enter TIMOTHY.

Desire my friend to walk in!

Enter AFTERWIT.

Mr. Afterwit! the welcomest man alive! You were wont to come and sit with me; but now, you're grown such a courtier you forget your old friends. On my conscience you want money, or I had not seen you now. Away with 't! 'tis all but dirt! You shall not want a £1000 as long as I can help you; nay, an' 'twere £10,000, to do you good. The son of my old friend!

Aft. I thank you, sir, and shall make use of you! But I'll promise you, this was purely visit.

Wh. I am the more beholding to you.—[*The waytes play within.*]—Hark, Tim! Beat out those rogues. What would they have?

Tim. They are the waytes, sir. They bid you good morrow every morning; and they are now come to congratulate your worship's recovery.

Wh. I'll give 'um nothing; they are the cause of more beggars and bastards. When a man would sleep quietly, they wake him, and be hang'd; and then the good woman plucks him by the sleeve, and cries: 'Heark, husband, heark! the waytes! heark!' Come, Mr. Afterwit, we'll out of the noise. 'Tis as dreadful to me as the last trump. [*Exeunt.*

SCENE III.

Enter SCRUPLE *and* MRS. WHITEBROTH, *conducted by a* BOY.

Sc. 'Tis a fine child! I'll try his wit. How far have you learnt, youth?

Boy. Sententia puerilis, sir.

Sc. A good boy! You may in time come to your *genus* and *species.*

Boy. I am past that already—

> 'Quæ genus, aut flexum variant quæcunque novato
> Ritu deficiunt superantve, heteroclita sunto.'

Sc. A most emphatical description of us, sister Whitebroth. We are a kind of heteroclites; and oftentimes sav'd even contrary to rules. A witty child! Let's see! *Byssus, abissus;* how render you that?

Boy. Byssus, a bottomless pit; *abissus,* a more bottomless pit.

Sc. Child, thou art in the right. There is a great —great—great bottomless bottom. Indeed there is!

Boy. Please you to give me leave to ask you one word?

Sc. With all my heart, child. What is 't?

Boy. What's the English of *adolescentior?*

Sc. Adolescentior!—Hum! *Adolescentior!*—Haw! *Adolescentior*—Ay——that is as much as to say—*adolescentior*——Now, fie child! Ask questions with that dirty face? Go wash it, child—go wash it! Fie, child, fie!

Boy. It signifies a ladder. *Adolescens*, a lad; *adolescentior*, a lad-der.

Sc. I profess I did not observe it. I see a man may live and learn every day. Go, child, wash your face, and let your father know I am here.

Boy. Yes, sir; I shall. [*Exit* BOY.

Sc. Now, indeed, Mrs. Whitebroth, this is your fault. I am present in body, but absent in mind. I could chide you now. But I hear him coming.

Enter MOPUS, *as from his study.*

Did not I tell you of that globe? 'Tis well I did not venture you by yourself. I'll sift him.

Mop. Worthy sir, and you, good madam, most welcome! Be pleas'd to let me know your commands, and you shall see I am so great a reverencer of your coat that my whole art shall lie at your feet.

Sc. He speaks like other men.—[*Aside.*]—You call it right; it is a coat indeed—no cassock, but a good, plain, honest, distinguishing jump.* But to our business. I have heard, sir, you are a man of art; and therefore I would fain know what you conceive of this notable conjunction of Satan and Jupiter in October next, which the learned believe to be the forerunner of doomsday, if not the thing itself.

Mop. Saturn and Jupiter, you mean, in Sagitary?

Sc. The same. What may it portend? Good or evil?

Mop. Much good, no doubt! Wherein, though I

* The weeping cassock scar'd into a jump,
A sign the presbyter's worn to the stump.—CLEAVELAND.

dare not be positive, yet, as far as Trismegistus, Albobazen, Haly; Messahala, Zael, Rabbi Abraham; Albubater, Avenezra, Albumacer; Guido, Bonetus, Hispalensis, Firmius; Alchindus, Proclus, Monteregius; Albertus Teutonicus, Averrois; and the most ancient Chaldeans, Egyptians, Moors, Jews, or Arabians have discourst, either this or the like, I shall give you my opinion.

Sc. I profess, a great-read man!

Mop. And here we are to observe, which of the two planets, Saturn and Jupiter,—this the very best, that the very worst,—is strongest at the time of his conjunction; for according to his nature will the effects follow.

Sc. In truth, learnedly. Pray, sir, on!

Mop. The last conjunction of these two planets happened——

Sc. Pray, sir, no chance or happening. Was, I pray!

Mop. Then, was in February 1643, in 25 degrees of Pisces—a sign of the wat'ry triplicite, not known in nature before, which produced those monstrous actions not heard of in the world before. And now, forasmuch as their conjunction is in Sagitary, the day-house and triplicite of Jupiter, we may conclude it is the more considerable, in regard they have wholly left the aquatic trigon, and will for many years make their conjunction in the fiery tranquillity; for when any alteration from one trigon to his contrary happens——

Sc. Good sir, no happening, let me beseech you; for look you, d'you see, as this—good sir, things come not by hap or chance.

Mop. Well, what you please. It is impossible but that some admirable effects, quite opposite to the former, must needs follow. And of this opinion is the learned Haly, and, generally, all the ancients and moderns.

Sc. But suppose it should be otherwise?

Mop. Then we're mistaken; and that's very unlikely, amongst so many learned men. As we ordinarily converse in the world, we may be mistaken; but *in cathedra* (that is to say, our studies), 'tis impossible.

Sc. A pretty word for a study. *Cathedra, quasi cathedra.* But pray, sir, what effect do you conceive this conjunction may have upon the whore of Babylon?

Mop. Why, truly, that is somewhat uncertain; in regard it will depend so much upon that great eclipse of Sol in Cancer in the house of the moon, the 22d day of June 1666, and will appear almost total at Rome. For my part, I expect some or other should marry her up, and make an honest woman of her, or otherwise (as Mr. Brightman, upon his pair-royal of sixes, has most excellently observ'd) she is likely to get such a clap she'll hardly claw it off again in haste.

Sc. I do profess, you have handled the point notably. I am convinc'd—there is no devil in this globe.

Mrs. Wh. La! you know, Mr. Scruple, you'll trust me another time; won't you?

Sc. Reproach not my good meaning. Certainly, sir, you must needs have added a rare collection to your own observation.

Mop. Yes, I have some toys, for so the world esteems 'um. However, to me they are jewels.

Sc. As what, good sir?

Mop. Many, many. In particular, a treatise of the philosopher's stone, written by Janbosher, Adam's tutor, whom you find recorded in the Indian books written by Isagarith about a hundred years before his time.

Sc. I thought letters had not been so ancient.

Mop. Alas! there are diverse very good authors, writ before the Flood. I have some half a dozen of 'um within, if I could tell where to find 'um. Men of my profession cannot well be without 'um. When I see you next, I'll show you the very *autographum* by which Seth drew his pillars.

Sc. Yes; that were worth the seeing. And, now I find you so near the Flood, give me the exact time and the language of that time, and I'll say you're a scholar.

Mop. For the time, it was, according to our computation, the 5th day of June, in the 1656th year of the world, one month and seventeen days, nor more nor less; and by all good tokens, upon a Friday—*Sol in Gemini.* The Dominical letter that year D—fifteen minutes precisely after sun-setting.

Sc. I see you're very exact.

Mop. Alas! we must be so; half a minute's loss so many years ago had been the Lord knows what by this time. Then for the language, notwithstanding anything that has been said to prove it high Dutch, I am clearly of opinion it was Hebrew, or some other jargon.

Sc. Nay, there you must bate me an ace;* for, though I look upon it as obscure as the head of Nile, yet, as far as it may be lawful to pry into unreveal'd mysteries, I dare boldly pronounce it to have been Welsh.

Mop. Welsh! *Afedrwch chwi Gymeraege?*

Sc. Why, truly, no; but I have a little look'd into the learning of the tongue, and that for two reasons. The one, for the honour of my nurse; for I am to tell you I suck'd a Welsh nurse, and so, by a *synecdoche*—[*he pronounces it long*]—may be called a Welshman. The other, that I have observ'd it makes an excellent sound in a country church, and consequently is tantamount to all the Eastern languages, and, I'll promise you, as guttural (that is to say, throteral)—*Y Cradog, Crugog, Crogwch, Y Gwan wr hull fu gan (r) hwch.*

Mop. O' my word, there's no more than *Kawse Pobi* in this. Pray, sir, how do you English it?

Sc. It matters not; or if it did, 'tis not the custom. But I had almost lost the argument. I say 'twas Welsh, and thus I prove it. 'Tis confest of all hands, that before the confusion of tongues there was but one language; which being so, 'tis more than probable that Gomer, the first grandchild of Noah, and first ancestor of the Welshmen, spake the same lan-

* 'Excuse me there.'—NARES. See Davenant's Works, vol. i. p. 158.

guage that his grandfather did; and that from him, by continu'd succession, it has been deriv'd to them. For example: Ask a Welshman at this day what countryman? He will answer, *Cimro glan*, a true Welshman; that is to say, *Gomera glan*. In like manner, for his language, *Gymeræge quasi Gomeræge;* both from Gomer. And, truly, I take the Cimbrians to be much the same—*Cimbri quasi Cambrit, quasi Cymbri, quasi Gomeri.* And again, *Mumgumri, quasi Mount Gomery*—the very seat of Gomer himself.

Mop. This is draper, diaper; napkin, nipkin; pipkin, King Pepin.

Sc. Most excellent! I see you have studied etymology. I might yet further, and, I think, without much difficulty, make it out that the mountains of Ararat were Penmenmaure in Wales; and the most ancient Egyptians originally Welsh, as may be more than suspected from their deification of leeks. But I had rather come nearer home. What, pray, were the Galli Senones that sack'd Rome? Welshmen, no doubt; the very name speaks it—*Gallus, Guallus,* or *Wallus*, a Welshman. In like manner, the *Gallo-Græcians*, under *Brennus*, the same—*Brennus, Brenn,* or *Brenning*, a king, in Welsh. But what do I go about to prove that which nobody dares deny? I'll give you but one smart parting blow. The red-streak't apple which makes such excellent cyder, what was it originally but the Welsh crab?

Mop. Sir, you have shown yourself a person of no ordinary learning; and because I see you are a *virtuoso*, be pleased to walk in with me, and I may chance to show you some rarities not unworthy your perusal. And you, madam, if you have any commands for me, I'll receive 'um there.

Sc. We'll follow you, sir. [*Exeunt.*

SCENE IV.

Enter WHITEBROTH, TYRO, *and* TIMOTHY.

Wh. You're welcome, sir! and I have heard so well of you from the doctor, your friend, that I'll show you fair play. Catch her, and take her. Timothy!

Tim. Your pleasure, sir.

Wh. Go, bid my daughter come hither.

[*Exit* TIMOTHY.

'Tis a good girl, and will make a good wife; and I hope, whoever marries her will be a good husband to her. She will deserve it, though I say it.

Ty. Never fear it, sir. If ever I kill her, 'twill be with kindness. My mother would always say——

Enter BEATRICE.

I was the best natur'd thing!

Wh. Come hither, Beatrice. I am going abroad, and will leave you to entertain this gentleman till I come again.

Bea. I shall obey you, sir.

[TYRO *goes backward, scraping.*

Wh. Nay, to her, man. Never fall into the rear when you should charge.

Ty. I warrant you, sir, for one.

[*Exit* WHITEBROTH; TYRO *struts.*

Bea. What, in the name of goodness, have we here? By my father's last words it should be a sweetheart, forsooth! How it struts, like a crow in a gutter! I have a great mind to hear it speak! [*All this aside.*

Ty. Methinks, madam, this is a very fine room.

Bea. It cannot be otherwise, sir, while you are in it.

Ty. Alas! good madam, 'tis your goodness! Truly, pray, what a clock do you count it?

Bea. He has a mind to show his watch; but I'll prevent him.—[*Aside.*]—'Tis much about four, sir.

Ty. I have a thing in my pocket corrects the sun.

[*He pulls out a large brass watch.*

Bea. How do you call it, good sir?

Ty. The vulgar call it a watch; but according to the learned, 'tis a *trochleal horadeixe.*

Bea. He that made it was as little sparing of his stuff, as t' other of his breath, that new-christen'd it by so stubborn a name.

Ty. Will your ladyship be pleas'd to accept it? I assure you 'tis at your service. It shall be part of your *parafernalia.*

Bea. By no means, sir. You speak in phrase!

Ty. Alas! madam, 'tis the way of the learned. Term is three-quarters of the art. Here's this, now—[*he points to a wooden standish*]—I warrant you, you would have called it an ink-box, or at best a standish.

Bea. It appears no other to me at present.

Ty. Nor yet to me. But the word's too common; a butcher would have said as much. Oh, no! 'Tis a ligneous pixid, accommodated with two plumbeous receptacles or stanneous repositories for ink and sand. Or, more laconically, an *escritoire.*

Bea. You're learned, sir!

Ty. Thanks to a good tutor, some small foundation. I must present you something.—[*He takes out a flageolet.*]—What say you to this? Your better sort of gentlemen seldom go without one of them in their pockets. [*As* TYRO *plays,*

Enter AFTERWIT *speaking to* TIMOTHY.

Aft. A suitor, say'st thou? 'Tis a puppet!

Tim. You may be too confident, sir.

Aft. There!—[*He gives* TIMOTHY *money.*]—And if your master comes to hear of it, tell him I was drunk.

Tim. I shall, sir. [*Exit* TIMOTHY; AFTERWIT *reels.*

Aft. How now! Where's the Alderman? What have we got here? A glister-pipe?

[*He strikes off* TYRO'S *hat, and kicks him.*

Bea. Forbear, sir! Know where you are!

Ty. The hat cost more money than to be made a football.

Aft. Ha! reply? Madam, your fan!

Ty. Murder! murder! murder!

[*Exit* TYRO, *and runs against a post.*

Bea. Was there ever such rudeness?

[*She offers to go out.*

Aft. Nay; you shall only stay to see I am not drunk. I thought this the best disguise I could use to keep your father from believing I made any pretences to you. Well, madam, I love you, and you know it. You may be proud. Farewell! [*Exit.*

Bea. A mad wooer! However, would my father lik'd him! [*Exit.*

SCENE V.

Enter WHITEBROTH, RUNTER, TIMOTHY, DOUBLE DILIGENCE, *all the women, and* SCRUPLE *leading two of them.*

Ru. Good Mr. Scruple, satisfy my conscience. An oath adds no legality to the action. If I swear to kill a man, must I do it?

Sc. Why, thus—hum!—haw!—[*He grows pettish.*] —Conscience! me no conscience. I came not hither to resolve any man's conscience; it is not my way. Truly, I hope, neighbours—[*he alters his voice*]—I may not only hope, but dare say, that you are all so well satisfied of what I have deliver'd to you, that you are really convinc'd that they are truths not to be question'd. You know I meddle not with conscience; I came to teach ye.—[*He raises his voice.*]— Did I for this preach up the holy covenant? told you you must deny learning and reason, and give the good cause a lift? Was it for this that that zealous son of thunder, Mas' Andrew, told you that he came to you with a commission to bid you subscribe? that it was a spiritual contract in letters of flesh? and that he came a wooing to you for him that had commissionated him, and therefore call'd upon you to come and be handfasted by subscribing the contract? Did I for this convince you of the lawfulness of the thing, and, as it were, compel you to the wedding? And will you call that holy violence a Spanish inquisition? Have I done all this, and will you now fall back? Shall our old lease run out, and the land be sow'd with cockels again? Ah! ha!

[*The women answer him with a long-drawn* Hui!

Ru. This is not the point. I cannot deny but that I took it myself; but then, was then; and now, is now.

Sc. Ah! be stedfast, and do not believe I speak this out of particular egotism, or fondlishness to myself. Ah! no. This thing of selfishness is a very nothingness; a mere—mere—— Ah! do but consider it.—[*He is out, and turns it off.*]—(And pray, neighbours there, leave your whispering, and mind the matter in hand.)—Hum!—I say—hum! do but consider what acting, wonder-working, advancing, and Christian-comforting times, these were. How the rebuke of the poor, belied, slander'd people was taken away, and their reputation clear'd! Ah—ah! what great things were wrought upon the spirits of men, even through the bowels of difficulty! Aa! Antichrist was dying in his limbs; nay, dying upwards. And this kingdom, that was once so given to it that it was call'd the Pope's Ass—ah! how was it become (as the Assembly most happily found it out) the chief of the ten horns that were to gore the whore! Ah—aa! good people, do not fear. There are more Assemblies coming, and more purses opening to carry on the work. Ah! comfort yourselves, that though these land-destroying sins of superstition, innovation, and idolatry were sins in the kingdom, they were not sins of the kingdom; and a nation was never destroy'd without national sins. Mark that, beloved; pray mark that!—[*The women again*—hui.]—Aa! rouze up yourselves, and let this beget in you, as it were—hum! haw!—new spiritual mouth-waterings. Let it not be said of you that you began well, but gave it over when there was most need of you. Aa!—no—If we must perish, 'tis better to perish in hope than fear. Aa!—we must be a doing people as well as a saying people.—[*The women again*—hui.]—It is not enough that you have done well already, but you must press forward; and like the Grecian, that when his hands were cut off clap'd hold with his teeth.—Ah—aa!—do you but stand in the gap, and there is a block in the way; it cannot be got over. The nation cannot be destroyed as long as you are in 't. Ah! then, do not despond in this day of trial, this day of treading down and not building up. Aa!—give not up this good old cause, which you have so long contended for with so much precious blood and so much precious treasure. Aa!—forsake it not, lest the malignants rejoice; lest the malignant and disaffected say, 'You've fought to much purpose.'—Aa!—bear it yet but a little, and you will see Dagon totter; and when he is once running down hill, he will not stop till he come to th' bottom.—[*Here he sinks his voice.*]—In the meantime,—ah!—what remains? but that (forasmuch as the sword is yet out of our hands)—ah!—but that we, as it were, descend from ourselves in petitioning for toleration and preservation of our mortal bodies against the rude enemy; and that we promise to be their servants in everything that we shall judge to be righteous. [*Here, all*—hui.

Ru. There I hold with you, good Mr. Scruple; and the Codes are of the same opinion. *Tempori, aptare decet.* Come, let 's in, and consult the Form.

Sc. I am for no Form. Yea, I hate the name; I abominate it. *Forma, bonum fragile est.* [*Exeunt.*

ACT IV.—SCENE I.

Enter BILBOE *and* TITERE TU, *fighting.* BILBOE *drives* TITERE TU *round the stage.*

Bil. I'll make a rogue of you, sirrah!

T. T. Why, Major! Nay, good Major! Have a care!

Bil. Thou son of a woman! do'st think men are bulls, and get their money by roaring? Cheat me of my share, you dog?—[*T. T. has one leg over.*]—Are you earthing, you rogue? I'll unkennel you!

T. T. Nay, Major—Major, what d'you mean? Nay, nay, nay; flesh and blood is not able to endure this. —[*He takes his sword in both hands, winks, and runs again at t'other;* BILBOE *runs off.*]—Nay; I am bound to follow no man. Do you think I am obliged to fight you by the mile? [BILBOE *peeps in.*

Bil. The rogue's afraid, or he had mischieft me.—[*He comes on again.*]—Sa, sa, sa, sa!

T. T. Hold, Major, hold! 'Fore George, you might have spoiled a man so.

Bil. Why, sirrah? You stinking, lousy totterdemallion! you raggamuffin, tarrarag rogue! who made you a captain? Was it not I? Speak!

T. T. No, troth, was it not. 'Twas even the box-keeper of the *Three Kings,* and the *Fleece* link-boys made us both—you a Major, and me a Captain.

Bil. Why, you Rotterdam villain, deny it if thou canst! Did not I pick thee up at a threepenny ordinary, brought you into gentlemen's company, dub'd you a knight of the blade, taught you the method of making new plots and borrowing half-a-crown of your landlady upon the hopes of 'um, and after all this sign'd your certificate to make you capable of those arrears you never fought for? And do you now forget your patroon, sirrah? do you forget your patroon?

T. T. And, good Major, recollect yourself too, if you please. Don't you know that I know that you were never above a corporal in all your life, and that, too, not till fighting was quite out of fashion? Bow the stick on t'other side, and 'twill be straight.

Bil. I must kill the rogue!—[*They fight again, as before.*]—'Twas bravely fought! Thou hast acquitted thyself like a man of mettle. Let's breathe!

T. T. Did not I, if you are yet cool enough to hear truth, teach you your top, your palm, and your slur?

Shew'd you the mystery of jack-in-a-box,* and the frail die? Taught you the use of up-hills, down-hills, and petars? the wax'd, the grav'd, the slipt, the goad, the fullam, the flat, the bristle, the bar;† and, generally, instructed you from prick-penny to long-lawrence? And is the question now, Who is beholden?

Bil. That ever friends should fall out about trifles!—[*They drop their swords and embrace.*]—Prithee, let's discourse the business quietly; and since 'tis gone so far as to be taken notice of in the town, cross and pile‡ between us who shall wear his arm in a scarf.

T. T. Agreed! But hold! the devil a cross have I!

Bil. Or I. Then knots and flats! Our swords shall serve. This, knots; that, flats. I cry knots!

T. T. And I flats! Twirl up!—[BILBOE *twirls up his sword.*]—'Tis flats! 'Tis yours, Major; all thine own, boy!

Bil. Well, it can't be help'd. A man's ne'er the worse man for a mischance. But hark you, Captain! upon honour, no talking!

T. T. No, no, no! First blood! first blood! And now, Major, you think I cheated you? By this good Morglay! the rogue was resolved to fight, and I had no reason but to suffer it to be taken up. I'll be sworn, I got not so much as a reconciliation supper by 't!

Bil. This is it, when men must manage their business by themselves. All covet, and all lose. You think you are well enough if you can but say your gamut by rote, though you are not able to prove a note of 't. Come, come! I must tell you there's more

* Substituting empty boxes for others of like appearance full of money.

† These terms are applicable to false or loaded dice, or to the knavish mode of handling them.

‡ Cross and pile—a chance play with money, such as that now called pitch and toss.

> Whackum had neither cross nor pile,
> His plunder was not worth the while.—HUDIBRAS.

This I humbly conceive to be perfect boys' play; *cross*, I win, and *pile*, you lose; or, what is yours is mine, and what's mine is my own.—SWIFT.

required to be a rogue than to say I will be a rogue! A man would have thought one of your years and education might have easily guessed who would fight and who not.

T. T. Pox on 't! 'tis past!

Enter TYRO.

Prithee, no more of 't! See! here comes my squire I told you of! Noble squire! Your servant! Pray, Major, be pleas'd to know my friend!

[BILBOE *and* TYRO *salute.*

Ty. Oh, Captain, I have been all about to look for you! Not fighting, I hope?

T. T. No! The Major and I have been only measuring blades. Here's the pretty'st thing you ever handled. Hey, dash!—[*He foins at* TYRO.]—Toledo to an inch; right Thomas de Ayala! Upon my credit, but two of 'um came over in three ships. Do but see how finely 'tis mounted! Sa, sa! Observe—how true it bends! Ah! for a pass in *flanconade!*—[*At* TYRO *again.*]—'Tis a trusty steel, and has been the death of——

Bil. A thousand frogs! [*Aside.*

T. T. More than I'll speak of; or, to tell you truth, dare. But hark you, squire! hast thou any noble achievements for thy man of Mars? Must the great Turk die? Speak! His breath hangs on thy lips!

Ty. Why, truly, Captain, I came to ask your advice. I have been most lamentably abus'd; nay, in the presence of my mistress, too!

T. T. Send him a cartel, boy! send him a cartel, and I'll carry it! Is he of mortal race?

Ty. Why, truly, Captain, I cannot tell what he is. But this I am sure, he had a good material hand and hoof.

Bil. How, Captain? This gentleman is your friend?

T. T. He is; and I'm engaged in honour to see him righted!

Bil. 'Twas bravely spoke. And pray, think of no second but myself. Good sir!—[*to* TYRO]—set forth the truth, the whole truth, and nothing but the truth; it may be matter of life.

Ty. Then, so 't please you, thus:—I was entertaining my mistress with this little bauble——

[*He shows the flageolet.*

Bil. 'Tis somewhat beneath the standard, I must confess. But pray, on!

Ty. When, of a sudden, a rude, roaring roisterer—

Bil. His name, good sir?

Ty. Truly, I could not learn that. It being in the city, 'tis probable it was some merchant or other got drunk.

Bil. Not unlikely. Proceed!

Ty. I say, then, this rude fellow, without scarce saying a word, gives me a good sound box.

Bil. Not to interrupt you, sir, was it the bucketoon or the bucketado? Logically or rhetorically? That is to say, with the clunch fist or open palm?

Ty. Why, truly, neither. But, as near as I can remember, it was with the back of the hand on the cheek; for, with the same motion, he strook off my hat. Thus, Major! [*He strikes off* BILBOE'S *hat;* BILBOE *stoops, takes it up, and rubs it.*

Bil. O, ho! the *De rere main!* Why, then, the question will be singly this—whether a blow with the back of the hand upon the cheek may be call'd a box on the ear. For my part, I am clearly of opinion not.

T. T. To take it literally, I grant it you. But then answer me whether it were not a probable box o' the ear? I take it 'twas.

Bil. So far I agree with you, Captain. But pray, sir, the rest?

Ty. Then, as if his foot had kept time with his hand, he gave me such a kick *in ano,* that, to avoid him, I had almost beaten out my brains against a post!

Bil. This last of the post was your own act, and may by no means be call'd his. However, upon the whole matter, you are wrong'd, and we'll see you righted!

Ty. Thank you, good Major! I am beholden to you!

T. T. D'you hear me, Squire? You see what pains the Major has taken in your business—you must present him!

Ty. 'Tis my intention. Pray, let's meet here about an hour hence, and we'll further consider of 't!

T. T. We'll attend you. Your servant!

[*Exeunt severally*

Scene II.

Enter Mopus, *solus.*

Mop. So, so! the trade goes merrily on! Let it hold but one seven years, and I shall go near to fine for Alderman.

Enter Mrs. Mopus.

Mrs. Mop. O Mopus! Mopus! Here's the constable's wife to have her fortune read! She had a bastard before she was married! has had two husbands, and one daughter by this! One Major Bilboe is her sweetheart; and I more than believe our Alderman has a finger in the pie too! [*Exit* Mrs. Mopus.

Mop. The devil's in 't if I miss her fortune! I shall be conjuror whether I will or no.

Enter Mrs. Double Diligence.

Save you, gentlewoman! Your business with me?

Mrs. D. Indeed, sir, I have heard you are a cunning man, and can tell a woman anything!

Mop. Such things have been done, and may again. Let me see your hand!—[*She gives him her hand; he pores on it.*]—Three husbands! The first dead; the second living—a man of authority!

Mrs. D. Now, indeed, sir, he is a constable! Bless me!

Mop. Your third shall be very rich—a common-councilman at least! and you shall have children by him!

Mrs. D. How many have I had already?

Mop. Let me see? One daughter, and no more—that is, since you were married!

Mrs. D. To see what learning can do!

Mop. Ah, mistress, I travell'd hard for 't! I have been where never any man was before me or since! I'll speak a bold word—I have been so far that I might have put my finger in the very hole where the wind came out; and all this for a little knowledge!

Mrs. D. Methinks 'tis a great deal! Pray, a little more!

Mop. You should have three diseases; and if you 'scape the first and second you may arrive to the third. You shall bury all three husbands, and be very fortunate toward your latter end! You were born—[*he turns his globe*]—under Cancer; and have receiv'd a hurt by fire, hot water, or some other way!

Mrs. D. Now truly, but I burnt my hand with a smoothing iron! and all to be scal'd my foot, with taking down the pot one day, when my maid was gone abroad with her sweetheart!

Mop. You have a natural mark, before or behind, or somewhere about you, between your head and your heel!

Mrs. D. That's more than I know; but I'll have my husband look to-morrow morning!

Mop. You are pretty neat in your house; somewhat nimble, witty, subtile, and a good bed-fellow!

Mrs. D. Indeed, sir, I know not why; but I've been told so!

Mop. Double-minded; often changing your resolution; prone to be angry, but quickly gone; and now and then love a bit in a corner!

Mrs. D. 'Tis best eating when one's a-hungry.

Mop. Your good days are Monday, Wednesday, Friday. Your evil, Tuesday and Thursday. Saturday, indifferent. Your good fortune lies south and by north; and therefore direct your affairs that way, and place your chamber door and bed to that side!

Mrs. D. Now, beshrew me, sir, but I'll observe your directions!

Mop. Once more your hand! Your *Mons Veneris* is exalted. You love! Ay, marry, that you do!

Mrs. D. Nay, now, sir! what d'you mean? I love nothing but what all women do,—their husbands!

Mop. Two strange thwarting lines across the *cingulum.* You have a sweetheart or two besides your husband!

Mrs. D. Who? I, sir? I'd have you know I'm no such! I am as honest a woman as any in the parish! I scorn your words!

Mop. No doubt of it. Let me see how your hand agrees with my globe. He is——[*he turns his globe, and describes* BILBOE]—Suppose I should name him to you? B-I-L—Bilboe! He belongs to the sword.

Mrs. D. Oh, sir, have a care! If my husband should hear you, he would run horn-mad, and knock both our brains out with his staff of authority!

Mop. To show you more of my art—You had a bastard before you were married; and there is an old fellow that haunts you.—[*He describes the Alderman.*]—What say you?

Mrs. D. Oh, good sir! If you discover me I am undone!

Enter BOY.

Boy. Sir, there are two gentlemen below desire to speak with you.

Mop. I will wait on 'um presently.—[*Exit* BOY.]—Never fear me! We are oblig'd, by our order of the Rosie Cross, to keep all confessions secret. 'Tis our Alderman; that's more!

Mrs. D. If you should betray me, now?

Mop. I will not—I will not! But hark you—upon condition still you give me a bit too!

[*He colls* her.*

* Clasps. This stage direction is in the first ed. only.

Mrs. D. Oh, sir! 'tis impossible! Your wife's in t'other room! The gentlemen stay for you below! Somebody's coming up! Mrs. Mopus! Mrs. Mopus!

[*She speaks as if she would not be heard.*

Mop. Hang her, jade!

[*As* MOPUS *kisses and pulls her,*

Enter JOLLY *and* AFTERWIT *behind them.*

Aft. See! see! see! I' faith, Mr. Doctor, is this your living soberly, temperately, and enjoying it as if you had it not? [Mrs. D. *scuttles away.*

Jol. Is this your magisterium, elixar, or Rosycrucian pantarva? No, sirrah! The father of this is the devil; the mother, his dam; its brothers and sisters, the tribe of whore-hoppers; the wind carries it from bawdy-house to bawdy-house, and the nurse thereof is a suburb-tantrum!

Mop. A plague o' this boy! Undone for ever!

[*Aside.*

Jol. Are you so hot? I'll cool you! D'ye hear me? Give the next porter half a crown, and let him fetch Double Diligence, the constable! I am mistaken, or the woman we found here was his wife!

Aft. Keep him in the mean time.

Jol. I warrant you, he stirs not!

[AFTERWIT *offers to go out.*

Mop. Gentlemen! Good gentlemen! As you are men, you undo me for ever! Study wherein I may serve you!

Jol. Stay a little!—[*to* AFTERWIT.]—Confess, and you shall see what we'll say to you! Art not thou a damn'd cheating rogue? How hast thou the impudence to believe that anything but fools should come near thee?

Mop. Nor would I, by my good will, deal with other. Do you take the wise men, and give me the fools; and then see who'll have the most practice! There are but two sorts of people in the world—*aut qui captant, aut qui captantur; aut corvi qui lacerant, aut cadavera quæ lacerantur.* Which the great Albumazer has most significantly rendered by cheaters and cheatees. If it were not for fools, sir, how should knaves live?

Jol. An ingenious beginning! If it hold, much may be said!

Mop. You are gentlemen, and, I see, understand. I'll be plain with you. Examine the world, and you'll find three-quarters of 't downright fools; and for the rest, six parts in seven little besides band and beard; and yet they make a great bustle in the world, and pass for shrewd men! And can you blame me, then? Did you ever hear a fishwife cry stinking mackarel? or a citizen, gumm'd velvet? No! The best in the town, though the worst in his shop! Here we have a learned consultation, whether my lady may eat butter with her eggs, or have her posset turn'd with lemon or ale. Yonder another keeps a sputter, with his new, new, new! the walley'd * mare, and the cropt flea-bitten; a book with a hard title; a new-found language in Ireland; Turk and Pope; the flesh-office; my lady's dog; the safest way of cutting of corns; a bag of writings; a house of the Bank-side; the christening of another Turk; a Franciscan proselyte, gentlemen-ushers and maid-servants; dentifrices and lozenges. Another daubs you whole volumes with the difference between sufficient and efficacious. Another, whether the lining of Aaron's ephod were sky-colour'd or sea-green; and hack and hew so desperately about their goats' wool, a man would bless himself to see such piles of elaborate nonsense! And now, gentlemen, am I the only man in fault? The worst you can say is, the people have so little wit as to give me money; and I am so mad as to pocket the injury! Does this satisfy?

Aft. Rogue enough! But is 't not possible to make thee honest?

Mop. Try me. I have a wife and three children—

* Having eyes with an undue proportion of white.

Wall-eyed slave! whither wouldst thou convey
This growing image of thy fiend-like face?—SHAKESPEARE.

the devil take my wife and two of them, if ever I fail you!

Aft. A safe wish. But suppose I should order it so that a young lady come to you, could you so read her fortune as to make her marry me? You know how to play your part if you please!

Mop. And if I don't to your advantage, cut my throat!

Aft. Ye must know 't at last. I had as good tell him the person. [*To* JOLLY.

Jol. So you may; and do!

Aft. Hold up thy hand! To make thee honest, here's twenty pieces for thee; and if thou dost thy business, I'll give thee two hundred more. What sayest thou?

Mop. If I betray you, or do not my best, be seven years in killing me!

Aft. You know Alderman Whitebroth?

Mop. Know him! Why, I am his doctor!

Aft. 'Tis his daughter. You know your work?

Mop. And if you don't do 't, I'll run my country! And now, gentlemen, you shall say I am honest. You observ'd the woman that was here when you came in?

Aft. Yes; what of her?

Mop. Why, she is the Constable's wife, whom, to be short, the Alderman cuckolds.

Jol. Hah! Are you sure of it?

Mop. By the help of this globe, I made her confess that the Alderman and one Bilboe play *level de coile* with her. But (I may tell it you now) my wife gave me the first hint of 't.

Jol. Hah! hah! Thou art honest! Bilboe? A Hector! He lies in the Constable's house?

Mop. The same! Make what use of it you will; I'll promise you to follow your directions.

Aft. This was better than wish! Come, we 'll lay our heads together, and you shall hear of us suddenly!

Scene III.

Enter Whitebroth, Runter, Timothy, Beatrice, *and* Scruple, *leading* Mrs. Whitebroth.

Wh. Was he so drunk, d'you say?

Tim. As ten thousand beggars!

Wh. So, so! his money's jogging already! Alas, Mr. Runter, you hear what he says? He was drunk!

Tim. Indeed, sir, I was never but half so bad in all my life, and then I was maudlin for a whole month after.

Sc. And well it became you! Compunction is good, Timothy.

Ru. What say you, sir? Mr. Tyro is a civil, hopeful gentleman, and, I am sure, loves your daughter!

Wh. Nay, speak to her. There she is!

Bea. Love me! 'Tis more than ever he told me yet!

Sc. He is a little modest. *Ingenui vultus puer, ingenuique pudoris.* Truly, I think you could not have chosen better.

Bea. I chosen, sir? You will not persuade me, I hope, that I am in love? If I am, I can assure you 'tis not with him!

Mrs. Wh. How, child! Not be rul'd by your father? Indeed, husband, it would be worth your while to have an eye upon her!

Wh. And your own too, good wife!

Sc. It should be both your care. You must provide a husband for her in time, or she will provide one herself.

Wh. Come, leave this discourse to another time. You know we have business!

[*Exeunt.* *Manet* Timothy.

Tim. What pity 'tis that this Monsieur le Coxcomb, Tyro, should have my young mistress! A fool, that knows not the use of money, but to play at bob-farthing and span-counter. Afterwit has most right to her, for his estate's sake. Come, come, he is a gentleman; and if things hit right, thou shalt have her, boy! [*Exit.*

SCENE IV.

Enter BILBOE (*his arm in a scarf*) *and* TITERE TU *at one door*, TYRO *at another.*

Ty. Alas, Major! Your arm in a scarf?

Bil. Why, faith, a small badge of honour! And I was drest up in haste, that I might not fail you.

Ty. How was it, good Major?

Bil. Nothing, nothing, but a small brush about the wall, and I know not why; but I fancied he might be the person that affronted you. To be short, he made me this pass in second, and I turn'd it so nimbly in tierce, that I made the sun shine clean through him!

T. T. Lightning! by this hand, lightning! Well!
[*He claps* BILBOE *on the back.*

Bil. Uh! Have a care, Captain! [BILBOE *shrinks.*

T. T. Go thy ways; and if thou takest a swing in quart* for 't, there hangs as brave a fellow as has hung there these forty years!

Ty. No murder, I hope, good Major?

Bil. Let him look to that! I neither know nor care. Don't be troubled, boy. I have an arm yet left to fight thy battles!

Ty. I thank you, sir. Be pleased——
[*He gives* BILBOE *money.*

Bil. O sir! Your love——

T. T. Ne'er doubt him, Squire. I'd as leif have him upon his stumps as twenty others upon no legs.

Ty. Well, gentlemen, courage! For my own part, I fear no flesh alive. No, upon my life and soul, don't

* Continuing the fencing terms used by Bilboe, Titere Tu purposes this for a pun—'quart,' or 'quarter,' also signifying an upright beam, meant here to express the gallows.

I! And I believe the same of you. You may fight—you are men of the sword! But for me, a man o' th' law! How say you, Captain?

T. T. By no means, Squire!

Bil. Say no more—He's dead!

Ty. Nay, good Major, have a care! No more murder!

Bil. What you please. I'll use him the better for your sake.

Enter AFTERWIT.

Ty. See, Captain! this is he!

T. T. Pray, sir, withdraw; and hazard not yourself! It may prove dangerous. [*Exit* TYRO.

Aft. I have out-stay'd my time—[*to himself.*]—With your favour, sir, what's o'clock?

T. T. Look upon the dial.—[TITERE TU *turns up his breech to him.* AFTERWIT *kicks him on the face thereof, takes away his sword, and sets one foot on him.*

Aft. It wants a gnomon. [BILBOE *steps in.*

Bil. Hold thy death-threatening hand! He is a captain! Let him die fairly! You do well to presume upon this scarf! I ha'n't been wont to see such things and carry my hands in my pocket.

Enter JOLLY.

But——

Jol. Thou art not mad, man? Hold!

Aft. The rogue has affronted me for speaking kindly to him. Be quick, and let me know the cause, or I'll nail thee to the ground for an example to others!

Bil. You have injur'd a worthy friend of ours,—Squire Tyro!

Aft. If that be all, rise! There's your sword!

Bil. By no means, sir!—[BILBOE *claps between 'um.*]—'Tis against the law of arms to hold a sword against any man has had our life at his mercy.

Jol. Major Bilboe, I think?

Bil. The same, sir. I should know that face too.

Certain, sir, I have had the honour to be drunk in your company ere now!

Jol. And not unlikely! We must not part with dry lips now. Afterwit—our friend—dost not remember we were merry together, at——

Aft. Oh! Your servant, sir! [*They salute.*

Jol. Come—all friends! Well, Major, to renew our acquaintance, I have the best humour for you. 'Twill get you the pence, and all of us mirth!

Bil. And what may it be?

Jol. Dismiss your friend to the next tavern, and I'll tell you! [BILBOE *whispers* TITERE TU.

T. T. Methinks I find a dislocation in my crupper. Your servant, gentlemen!

[TITERE TU *goes limping off.*

Bil. Your servant, you rogue, your servant! Now, sir, your commands?

Jol. To the point, then! If you are honest to us, it may be worth you £500. If not, we are two to one, persons unstain'd in our reputation; and if we deny, your affirmation will signify little! Will you be trusty?

Bil. As steel, my boy! What is 't?

Jol. You lie at Double Diligence, the Constable's house?

Bil. I do. What then?

Jol. And now and then, for diversion, with your landlady?

Bil. No wounding of reputation, good gentlemen! She's a pretty fly-boat; two men won't sink her!

Aft. Nor three, I warrant you!

Bil. It may be not. Have you a mind, gentlemen?

Jol. Oh, no, sir! I hope Alderman Whitebroth visits you pretty often?

Bil. For his rent, or so.

Jol. Then we know more than you. He has a lick at her too. Will you assist us in a design?

Bil. By the faith of a soldate and a man of arms, I will!

Aft. To engage you, then, here's twenty pieces for

you. You must trepan him with the Constable's wife. If you find her shy, you may bring in her husband for a share. My neck on 't, you square him out of a £1000 at least! He'll do anything rather than to have it known!

Bil. Do 't? and thank you too! The bed-pad is the safest pad. Here's my hand; I'll be honest to you!

Jol. Well, see you are; and let's hear from you again as soon as you can. In the mean time, do you two go to the Captain. You know whither I am going. Farewell! [*Exeunt severally.*

SCENE V.

Enter CIS, *sola.*

Cis. That I could meet with Mr. Afterwit now! He'll never get such another opportunity! And at home 'tis vain to think it.

Enter JOLLY.

Jol. O! Cis! Well met! 'Tis my good girl!

[*He calls and kisses her.*

Cis. Nay, pish! stand away! Come, do what you will, but don't you rumple my handkercher!

Jol. Alas, poor thing! I warrant, you much minded what I spake to you of last! Have you said anything to your mistress about it?

Cis. Yes, that I have! And she likes him well enough; but she will never marry without her father's consent. She loves him well, but her father's estate better!

Jol. A good crafty wench! Let us but secure her, I'll warrant the estate! And if thou dost it, Cis, I'll promise thee a good portion, and a better husband!

Cis. What would you have me do?

Jol. Lose no opportunity of commending Mr. Afterwit to her,—a gentleman—a fine man—a handsome man — a proper man — and, you dare warrant, a good woman's man. And, hark you, you may tell her how Tyro had hir'd a couple of fellows to hector him, and that he came off bravely—and all this for her!

Cis. Indeed, sir, I will not fail you in a tittle!

Jol. But were 't not possible to get her to Mopus's, to have her fortune read?

Cis. Suppose I should? What then?

Jol. The work were done!

Cis. Then trouble not yourself. She made me steal out before, and is just following me to that purpose. But, hang him, he knows as much as my horse! I had almost told her how Tim and I cheated him with some dead ale in a urinal instead of my master's water, but that Mr. Scruple and my old mistress have so cried him up.

Jol. Have a care of stories; they may spoil all. The fellow is ignorant enough, there's no doubt of 't. But yet, as long as they believe him knowing, will be easily able to do my friend's business. Prithee, desire her to make him show her her husband's face in a glass. Doubt nothing, but follow your instructions. I must to Afterwit, and let him know whither his mistress is going.

Cis. Well, trust to me! Begone! I hear her coming! [*Exit* JOLLY *at one door*,

Enter BEATRICE *at another.*

Bea. O! Cis! I am stol'n out with much ado! Shall we go? What dost think of him?

Cis. Truly, I take him for a huge cunning man. He has told all the maids of the parish the strangest things; and, they say, can show one one's sweetheart's face in a glass!

Bea. If he can do that I'll believe him! I am so strangely troubled with dreams, it passes——

Cis. And so have I been too; and thought several times to tell you of a strange thing in our house, but that I was afraid you would laugh at me.

Bea. But tell me! What was 't?

Cis. Why, last New-Year's Eve, when all the house were in bed, I swept up the hearth, and smooth'd the ashes, and next morning found the print of a wedding ring and a grave upon them. I am confident we shall have a wedding and a burial out of our house this year—my old master die, and my young mistress married!

Bea. Away, fool! If I marry, I promise you it shall not be Tyro! 'Tis such a piece of ginger bread!

Cis. Marry hang him! 'Tis all the news that he hir'd a couple of fellows to murder Mr. Afterwit; but he has paid 'um to the purpose. And they say the quarrel was about you!

Bea. Then in short time I shall be town talk, and work for knights adventurers. I should be sorry he were hurt—I would. But come! I long to hear what this fellow will tell me! [*Exeunt.*

ACT V.—SCENE I.

Enter MOPUS, JOLLY, *and* AFTERWIT.

Jol. Make haste! I left 'um coming.—[*The bell rings.*]—Here they are!

Mop. Then do you step into the next room—[*to* AFTERWIT]—and when you hear me cry 'Jubeo,' take the small stool in your hand, and come in; stand upon it behind her chair, and look upon the glass; and be sure, when you have done, to take the stool along with you!

Jol. I must be gone; I have appointed Runter. Have you prepared the Alderman's dose?

Mop. 'Tis here!—[*He shows a small vial.*]—And as soon as I have despatch'd you, I am resolv'd to visit him, and give him half a score drops of it in somewhat or other; but so qualifi'd, it shall not only distemper him, but do him no further hurt. A glass of stomach water will fetch him again while you say——What's this?

Enter Boy.

Boy. Sir, there is a gentlewoman or two at door desire to speak with you.

Mop. Desire them to walk in! Here, here! this way! and you there!

[*Exeunt* Jolly, Afterwit, *and* Boy *severally.*

So; if this take, I shall save my credit, and get good money to boot!

Enter Beatrice *and* Cis.

Madam! your servant! What service have you for me?

Bea. I have heard my mother so talk of you, I could not be quiet till I came to you too.

Mop. I am not wont to make my art common. But do you propose what you will, and I'll do my best to resolve you.

Bea. Then, truly, sir, I have been extremely troubled with dreams, and would fain know what they mean.

Mop. And shall, madam, if art can do 't. Dreams are certain motions or fictions of the soul, signifying some good or evil to come; wherein, notwithstanding, we chiefly regard how the moon stands affected. What were yours?

Bea. Methought my father was chosen Lord Mayor, and that Cis and I were pounding spices, to make an entertainment, and at last, methought, we fell together by the ears in our smock-sleeves.

Mop. For the first, 'twas an ill sign—a sign of your father's death. For death is like the Mayor of the town within his own corporation—subject to none, and has no companions. Then, as to your pounding of spices, that betokens matrimony; for the pestle represents the man, and the mortar the woman. Lastly, as to your fighting, infallibly the same; and that the rather the persons being stript, as you say they were. Have you more?

Bea. Yes, sir. Methought I was married to a man with a great jolt-head.

Mop. A sign of dignity. If there had been a brazen face to 't, the better, for 'tis the first step to 't.

Bea. There were divers others, but I have forgot 'em. Pray be pleas'd to give me some general hints, that I may the better observe 'um for the future!

Mop. Anything, good madam, to serve you. To dream of loss of eyes betokens help, for most men help the blind. If but one eye, but half what was expected. For a married woman to dream of beheading, loss of her husband; to a maid, loss of her maidenhead. Of leeks and cheese, that she shall marry a Welshman. Of hanging, matrimony; for they both go by one destiny.

Bea. Pretty, indeed. Pray, sir, some more!

Mop. To dream of loss of fingers betokens want of employment, to a lawyer. Of broken pates, good luck, to chirurgeons. Of cutting high capers, hanging, to a thief. Of a midwife, revealing of secrets. Of grasshoppers and crickets, more words than performance. Of a post and pillars, a Mayor and Alderman. Of a calf's head and pertinents, a foreman and his fellows. Of being abed with a handsome lady, ill luck, because 'tis not true. Of having a true friend——

Bea. Ay! what sign's that?

Mop. A sign he's mistaken. But enough of this! Good madam, your hand!

Bea. Here! And pray, tell me my fortune.

Mop. I cannot make it better or worse; but such as it is, you shall know presently.—[*He pores on her hand.*]—A fair table—the line of riches well extended—very large wheels of fortune. You will be a good housekeeper, rich, and fortunate. These lines betoken husbands. You will have, let me see, if your first husband dies before the mark's out of your mouth, a second; and then, perhaps, a third. These interferings, children;—you will have—some half a dozen, more or less. Yet once again—pray, let me see how your hand agrees with my globe!

[*He steps to the table and turns his book and globe.*

Bea. What think'st thou of him, Cis?

Cis. No doubt but it is all true. They say he can show one's sweetheart's face in a glass. Good madam, remember to try him!

Mop. You shall have a husband in a very short time. As to his person, he is, *etc.*—[*He describes* AFTERWIT.]—He has some incumbrances upon his estate at present, but shall recover them all, and be very happy, fortunate, and honourable.

Bea. But does he love me?

Mop. I am sure he does. And without him, you'll be very unhappy. He is a most excellent person. He receives his knowledge from Mercury in Virgo. His completeness of body from Caput Draconis in Gemini. Saturn and Venus, in Libra, direct him to the light of nature. Fortuna major and Populus, figures of geomancy, give him health, and Puella befriends him. Mars, in Cancer, is his enemy; Jupiter, in Capricorn, somewhat uncertain; and two ideas of geomancy conspire against him. But he shall receive treasures from the sun and jewels from the moon; and his guardian angel shall defend him, and make the spiteful dragon bite his tail in Sagitarius, because he cannot be reveng'd of him.

Bea. But is 't not possible to see this excellent person?

Mop. 'Tis a thing I rarely do—I seldom practise beyond the stars; but if you'll promise me to sit quiet, and not talk it abroad, I will, for once, show you the height of art.

Bea. Well, sir, I promise. But pray, no noise!

Mop. No; he shall rise with music. Boy!

Enter BOY.

My glass, and the enchanted chair!

[*Exit* BOY. MOPUS *draws a circle.*

Bea. Oh, good sir, have a care!

Mop. Be still! The spirit knows my meaning, and I dare not baulk him. Fear not; you are as safe as if you were in your father's house.

Enter BOY, *with a glass and a groaning chair.*

Here, madam, sit down; and you, sweetheart, at your mistress's feet. Sirrah!—[*He speaks aside to the* BOY.]—Take your lute, and when you see the gentleman preparing to come in, play a lesson or two.—[*Exit* BOY.]—Now, madam, sit still, and fear nothing!

[*He takes his book, waves his rod, and reads.*

"MAZOL TOB.

"Bombomachides Cluninstaridysarchides, qui præpositus es Utopiæ, et terram incognitam solus delineasti—Conjuro, et confirmo te, et super te, O nihilum potens! per nomen stellæ, quæ est sine nomine—per solstitium solis, et lunæ dodecatimarion; per Tiberii spintrium, et Claudii apocolocyntheosin; per cingulum Veneris, et garragantue ταῦρον; per alpha, beta, gamma, delta, coph, resch, schin, tau—per omnia predicta, et alia ubicunque quæ nunquam fuerunt, nec usquam futura sunt. Conjuro super te Bombomachides (occulta qualitas, et tamen magne) quod relictis agris Gurgustidoniis, et Gogmagogorum antiquissima sede, in instanti venias, pro me labores, et perimpleas omnem petitionem hujus dominæ, juxta velle, et votum suum. Veni! Veni! Veni! Per omnia predicta—jubeo—veni!"

[*The lute plays. Enter* AFTERWIT; *looks over her chair, as directed, and after a little time exit.* BEATRICE *and* CIS *rise, and look behind the chair.*

Now, madam, you have seen the *ne plus ultra* of art! And if I might advise you, I would have you comply with your destiny; without it, you will be miserable.

Bea. And perhaps with it. Do you know the gentleman?

Mop. I never saw him in my life till now; but as I beheld him in the glass, methought he had a promising aspect, and agreed in everything with what I have told you. Do you know the face?

Bea. Yes. And if my father were consenting to 't, it should be the first thing I would.

Mop. I can but wish you well. Yet one thing I'll do—'tis yet in my power. If you have no mind to him, avoid seeing him before you have slept; and let me know it before sunrising to-morrow, and I may prevent it. If otherwise, 'tis past the art of man.

Bea. I thank you, sir!—[*She gives him money.*]—O! Cis, what shall I do? Is there no back way? If I can but miss him now, I'm well enough!

Cis. Have a good heart, madam! What must be will be.

Mop. You had best let my boy conduct you. Boy!

Enter BOY.

You know the back way to the Alderman's? Show it this lady, and wait on her as far as she pleases to command you. [*Exeunt* BEATRICE, CIS, *and* BOY. Your servant! So, so! things go as they should! Where are you, sir?

Enter AFTERWIT.

Your work's as good as done. She's gone the back way; you will easily get before her upon the turn of the street. Now's your opportunity! Make haste and meet her, and she can't refuse you.

Aft. 'Twas well contrived! Your servant!

[*Exeunt.*

SCENE II.

Enter BILBOE *and* MRS. DOUBLE DILIGENCE.

Bil. I thought what you were! Is this your going to Repetition? I'll tell my landlord!

Mrs. D. Indeed I could not help it—I could never be rid of him! But I am sure I always loved you best. I hope you will not undo a woman!

Bil. Nay, nay! that's nothing to me. I am resolv'd, unless you engage to do one thing.

Mrs. D. Anything, good Mr. Bilboe, that I can. What is 't?

Bil. When will the Alderman be here?

Mrs. D. At night, after the watch is set. What then?

Bil. Why, you must join with me to trepan him. It may be worth us £1000!

Mrs. D. 'Tis impossible! No one will believe him to be such a man.

Bil. They'll never know it. He'll be hang'd ere he'll let the business come upon the stage.

Mrs. D. I'll never yield to it! You shall have what money you will!

Bil. Hang money!—fly brass!—the devil's a tinker!

Enter DOUBLE DILIGENCE.

Honest landlord! I see you are for the watch. Twenty to one but I beat up your quarters. I'll make you run, i'faith!

D. D. Yes—after you, Major; I have done it forty times!

Bil. Why, how now, man? melancholy? Thou lookest as if thy head were full of accounts!

D. D. And, truly, you are right. I was just considering how to patch up my account with Mr. Alderman. Indeed he ties me to hard meat. I cannot take a rat but he makes me account to him for half profits; and yet I allow him as good as £40 a year for the keeping of one poor gate. Would I were once overseer of the poor, or churchwarden—there were somewhat to be got by that! I'm sure this will hardly keep life and soul together.

Bil. Hang care! I'll tell thee what—thou hast the honestest woman to thy wife this day in the parish. Poor soul, how she's been plagued by this Alderman!

Mrs. D. Nay, Major! what d'you mean?—[*She pulls him by the elbow.*]—You won't, I hope, Major!

Bil. She was ashamed to tell you herself, and would not be quiet till I had promised to do it. This old goat is perpetually soliciting her—would one think it? Troth, I should have guest him fuller of Mercury than Venus; but a man may be deceived.

D. D. How! The Alderman? See what 'tis to have an honest woman to one's wife. I warrant you, had she been right, as they say, she had never discover'd it. Now, my dear chick, how I love thee!

Bil. Leave your slobbering, and consider what to do. My advice is, that we trepan him; the thief is rich, and will bleed well.

D. D. That would be somewhat! But how is 't to be done?

Bil. He will be here by that time the watch is set. The Captain and I will do 't.

D. D. If we could get a good round sum between us, 'twould do no hurt. You may compound with the Captain for a small matter.

Bil. Let me alone with him! He's hard at hand! I'll fetch him! Don't you be out of the way!

[*Exit* BILBOE.

D. D. Indeed, wife, this is a providence, and may do us good! Grant we may make a right use of 't.

Enter WHITEBROTH.

Wh. Not gone yet! I must rattle* him.

[*Aside to himself.*

D. D. Save your good worship, sir!

Wh. Alas, Mr. Double Diligence, that you should be thus negligent of the peace of the kingdom! Don't you know there are a number of dangerous people abroad, and your watch not set yet? Now, truly, but you are to blame; and I could find in my heart to have you complain'd of.

D. D. I was just going—your worship sees I am ready!

Wh. Pray keep your watch together, and walk your round in person—you cannot be too secure. Here!

* Thrash.

Here's somewhat for your watch to drink. I have given 'em nothing a great while.

D. D. 'Tis a fourpence-halfpenny, sir. Will your worship be pleased to have the odd halfpenny again?

Wh. No, no! No matter!—let it go for a crust.

D. D. We thank your worship.

[*Exit* DOUBLE DILIGENCE.

Wh. I just met my doctor, and he has given me the rarest cordial—methinks I am so flippant! Now, my little mouse! How do you? Shall we walk in?

Mrs. D. Indeed, sir, I am somewhat ill.

[*He calls her.*

Wh. Prithee leave these excuses! Thou knowest I love thee. [BILBOE *and* TITERE TU *peep in.*

Bil. See, Captain! see!

T. T. Ah! the old rogue!

Wh. Come, come!—you must! I've had no rent a good while!

Mrs. D. Indeed, sir, we've a hard bargain of 't. I hope your worship will consider us against next quarter.

Wh. Why—you pay me no money! You know I take it out, as they say.

Mrs. D. Ay, but Mr. Scruple's very hard upon my husband, and won't believe but he has a double lease.

Wh. I'll order that hereafter. Prithee come!—the cuckold is secure. Good faith, you shall!

Mrs. D. I cannot—nor will I! Pray unhand me!

[*They struggle.*

Enter BILBOE *and* TITERE TU, *with their swords drawn.*

Bil. How's this? My landlady! Cuckold my honest landlord! Kill him! kill him!

[*They both lay at him with the flat of their swords.*

Wh. Good gentlemen! spare my life! Oh—oh!

T. T. Hold! hold!—better geld him!

Bil. Agreed! agreed!

[MRS. DOUBLE DILIGENCE *runs in.*

Wh. Oh! good gentlemen, 'twill break my wife's heart! Good gentlemen, I am an Alderman!

Bil. Thou an Alderman? I'll undertake he stole this chain! Gi' me 't!—[BILBOE *takes it off and pockets it.*]—I'll find out the truth.

T. T. Come, brother!—Uncase! uncase!

[*They strip him to his canvas doublet and satin skirts.*

Enter DOUBLE DILIGENCE.

D. D. I had forgot my night-cap! How now? what's here? Stand! I require you, in their majesties' name, to keep the peace! Stand! What are you? Thieves! thieves! Down with 'em, Mr. Alderman! Alas, good sir, what makes your worship in this condition?

Bil. Landlord, I am confident this is no Alderman. The rogue has serv'd my landlady!—A man would not serve a dog so!

D. D. How? Stick a bull's feather in my cap!—make me a knight o' the forked order! Is this true, Mr. Alderman? is this true?

Wh. Failings, brother Diligence, failings! Pray, let the business be ended between ourselves, and I will patiently submit to a church rebuke.

D. D. One good action is worth two rebukes and three chastisements. Pray, gentlemen, keep him here till I fetch the watch. I will have it recorded, to my own honour, the example of all succeeding Constables, and terror of Justices—that a Constable once in his time laid a Justice of peace by the heels. I'll be with you instantly.

[*He offers to go out,* WHITEBROTH *stops him.*

Wh. Good neighbour, this will be as great a scandal to our fellowship as that abomination of the elder's maid in Bell Yard.

Bil. Hold, landlord! Is he an Alderman in earnest?

D. D. Yes—yes! But I'll Alderman him!

[BILBOE *holds him.*

Bil. By no means!—Stay! The old gentleman may take cold—pray, sir, put on your clothes! 'Twas well I asked the question—I would not have it go further for five thousand pounds. An Alderman!

Wh. Thank you, good sir! Pray take up the business.

Bil. Come, landlord! Hang 't—'tis done, and can't be help'd. He shall give you a thousand pounds.

D. D. A thousand pounds?—Out upon 't!

Wh. A thousand pounds, sir! Alas, I thought ten pounds or so!

Bil. How?—ten pounds! Send we make him accept a thousand pounds! 'Tis a foul business—the more you stir, the worse 'twill be. Will you refer 't me? I hope to deserve a hundred pounds of you myself.

Wh. What you will; but pray beat it as low as you can.

Bil. Come, landlord! what say you? The gentleman's willing to give you a thousand pounds.

Wh. Oh! undone!—I'm a poor man!

D. D. Tell me of a thousand pounds?

T. T. Nay, now, Mr. Constable, you're unreasonable.

D. D. Well, then, let him throw in the lease of my house too, and for your sake, Major, I'll do 't.

Bil. He shall—he shall! Burn it, 'tis but an old house—giv't him. Troth, I was afraid we should not have got him so low. You heard what he said—'twas for my sake, too. I hope you'll consider it.

Wh. Well, if it must be so, no more words of 't. I'll send you a thousand pounds to-morrow, and convey over the house when you please. Oh—oh!—an undone man!

Bil. In the meantime, a bond, as you use to say, for mortality's sake, would do no hurt.

Wh. What you will—I must obey.

Bil. Be not troubled. The flesh was good flesh, and worth the money.

Wh. But the sauce, though, was devilish dear.

Bil. Hark you, landlord! Run to your neighbour Squeeze, the scrivener, for a couple of blank bonds. Make haste! And when the work's done we'll drink abundantly, and remember the founder.

D. D. Truly, I like it well—exceedingly well. It

is good to be thankful. Pray, take the Alderman in, and I'll be with you instantly. [*Exeunt severally.*

SCENE III.

Enter AFTERWIT, BEATRICE, *and* CIS.

Aft. Now, you see, madam, to how little purpose we cross our stars.

Bea. Had you but miss'd me now,
I should have ventur'd that, and perhaps stav'd
That misery which always follows rashness.

Aft. Trust me! I warrant you, things will go right.
Now for a small hedge-priest to make the knot;
We'll tie it faster as we've better leisure.

Enter RUNTER *and* JOLLY.

Keep back a little—I would not have them see us yet. [*Exeunt* AFTERWIT *and* BEATRICE.

Ru. Indeed I won't! You have been large to me already. [JOLLY *would press money upon him.* You must excuse me.

Jol. Upon one condition I may.

Ru. What's that, good sir?

Jol. That you will give me leave to put it in the diurnal.

Ru. I must confess, I should be loth to be the author of so ill a precedent. But if I should take it, how shall I be able to serve your friend?

Jol. I have told you.

Ru. Hah! But such an opportunity will never happen.

Jol. I am certainly inform'd he is now upon 't. For being taken very ill of a sudden, he has resolved to publish that draught which you made for him, and has lain in your hands ever since his last sickness. Now, instead of that, let him seal and deliver this settlement upon my friend, in consideration of marriage with his daughter, and the work's done.

Besides, if he should discover it, I have him so sure upon other accounts he dares not mutter.

[RUNTER *peruses the deed.*

Ru. You are a notable gentleman. You have done extreme prudently in leaving a blank for the first words, "This indenture," etc., and that the parchment is plain at top. I will fill it up with "*In nomine domini*," for fear some one should look over my shoulder while it is doing; when once 'tis over 'tis easy indenting it, and scraping out "*In nomine domini*," and instead thereof puting in, "This indenture made," etc. Trust me with it.

Jol. Shall my friend depend upon you?

Ru. D'you think me a knave? A word's enough. Yet, if you would be rul'd by me, I would advise you to engage Mr. Scruple in the business; he will be able to do much in 't.

Jol. Will a parsonage of £300 a year do 't? If it will, my friend has such a one newly fall'n, and giv'n me order, as I see occasion, to present it him. But do you think he will conform?

Ru. I warrant you he does both. Leave it to me to make him. I must confess he has been somewhat violent heretofore; but of late I can assure you very instrumental.

Enter SCRUPLE.

Here he comes. Pray, leave us not; there will be little said but what you may be privy to. Save you, Mr. Scruple.

Sc. And your worship too. I have been looking you everywhere. Mr. Alderman presents you with that health he wants himself, and desires you to come to him, and bring with you that draught of his will which was engross'd when he was last sick. I left that learned artist Dr. Mopus with him, who shakes his head, and wonders at this sudden alteration. He says they drank a glass of ale together but few hours before; but, truly, now he doubts him.

Ru. Why! what's the matter?

Sc. The doctor had a hard word for 't, but I have quite forgot it. He is taken with a strange scouring and vomiting—the doctor knows not what to make of him—death's in's face.

Ru. Alas, poor gentleman! I'll wait on him immediately. That things should fall so cross! His daughter is just married.

Sc. How! married? I am sure he knows nothing of it, for his intention of sending for you was, that he might so dispose his estate that the Court of Aldermen might not have the fingering of it.

Ru. It can't be helpt—'tis done. But hark you! 'tis to a worthy gentleman, and one that has so great an esteem for you, that having a parsonage of £300 a year in his gift, and now void, he is resolved to dispose it to no one till you have refused it.

Jol. This is true, I can assure you, sir; and by me has made the offer to this gentleman in your behalf, who, I think, knows me too well to doubt the truth of 't.

Ru. Indeed I do. I'll take care your presentation shall be dispatched out of hand. But—you must conform, and sign with the cross.

Sc. Well—well! The sign of the Cross or the sign of the Blue Boar shall break no squares. £300 a year! I do assure you, a worthy gentleman!

Enter AFTERWIT, BEATRICE, *and* CIS.

Jol. He comes himself, and his fair bride. Madam! All joy!

Bea. Of what? Will you persuade me into 't?

Sc. Indeed, Mrs. Beatrice, give you much joy. In truth, a very worthy gentleman. I am sorry it was not my good fortune to have yok'd you together.

Aft. Perhaps it may not be too late yet. You know wise men always marry their daughters both ways. It is not impossible but that Mr. Alderman and myself may be made friends—his daughter is still alive. How says my dear?

Bea. Nay, pish! You're such a man!

Aft. I shall be glad, sir, to be better known to you, and hope my friend has made you a small present from me. Had it been better, your worth deserves it.

Sc. Alas! sweet sir! I thank your love—I have accepted that already. You are an obliging person.

Ru. Come, madam! you're melancholy! Be cheery! All will do well. Mr. Scruple, a word—I think it were not amiss if you went before, and let him know I am coming.

Sc. With all my heart. Have you anything further wherein I may serve this worthy person and his lady?

Ru. Why, truly, yes. You will do well to keep him in the same mind of making his will. Since the young couple are together, and 'tis too late now to part them, we must do something to secure them an estate.

Sc. You say well; and I will join with you in anything, provided always you carry it prudently, for fear of scandal. A blot is no blot till it be hit.*

Ru. You must have a care that no one be in the room but ourselves—not so much as his wife.

Sc. By no means. If they should, I will cause 'em to withdraw, upon pretence of giving him some ghostly counsel, or the like. Farewell! You'll find me there.

Ru. Not a word! Make haste, and be sure to break the marriage to the good woman before the Alderman comes to know it. Watch your time!

Sc. I warrant you! [*Exit* SCRUPLE.

Ru. Madam, your father has sent for me, and I must leave you for the present; but you shall be sure to hear from me suddenly. In the meantime, if you please to repose yourselves at my house, you shall be welcome. You cannot be safer nor nearer if any occasion should be.

Omnes. With all our hearts! [*Exeunt.*

* Referring to a movement in the game of backgammon.

Scene IV.

Enter Scruple, *discoursing to himself.*

Sc. Three hundred pounds a year, and conform! A fair opportunity; and if I slip it, may I never have another! But hark you, Mr. Scruple, you must subscribe! Well, and I will do 't! But what will the brethren say? How will the sisters take it, when it shall be told 'um, *Vir gregis ipse caper de erraverat?* Why, 'twas an act of my hand, not an act of my heart! But stay!—what needs this? Has not the direction of the intention a faculty to null promises? I take it it has. What say the Casuists? If a man promises, and had no intention to perform when he made it, he is not oblig'd, unless there be an oath or contract in the case; for, when a man says simply I will do thus or thus, it shall be conceived he meant if his mind did not alter, for otherwise were to deprive him of his natural liberty. But there is an oath in the case, friend Scruple, there is an oath! How will you do, now? Well, suppose there be two! I take it the case has been determin'd long since. I may take it *pro forma*, by a previous protestation, nevertheless that it shall not be prejudicial to me in anything that I shall act to the contrary hereafter. If not, our brethren are clear in the point. Equivocation, in cases of necessity, may be lawful. 'Tis a *pia fraus!* I'm sure, at worst, it is a probable opinion; and all probable opinions are equally safe in themselves. But hold ye, brother! Are not oaths to be taken according to the meaning of the exactor of the oath? Perhaps they are. What then? Suppose I bring a probable opinion for the meaning of the taker. The extremes are wide; but I have found an expedient,—and yet not mine, but our brethren's still. The swearer is not bound to the meaning of the prescriber of the oath, or his own meaning. How, then? Sweetly!—to the reality of the thing sworn.

I think the hair is split! But who shall be judge of that? Of that hereafter. In the mean time, here is £300 a year, and a goodly house upon 't! I will conform, reform, transform, perform, deform, inform, any form! Form—form—'tis but one syllable, and may be swallowed!

Enter MRS. WHITEBROTH *and* MRS. MOPUS.

Mrs. Wh. Now, bless the good man! what's that he says? Form—form! Marry, I hope you don't intend to conform?

Sc. Form is a good word—a very good word! *Forma dat esse rei!* And without it, sister of mine, you could be neither seen, felt, heard, nor understood!

Mrs. Mop. Now, goodness defend him!—In the highway to Egypt again!

Sc. Mistake me not; I am neither for highways nor high places! But——

Mrs. Wh. But what? I hope you are not in earnest. Will you forsake the good old cause?

Mrs. Mop. Mr. Scruple spew up the Holy Covenant?

Sc. It forsook me, not I it.

Mrs. Wh. What will the vile cavalier say?

Mrs. Mop. How will the despisers of the brethren bristle?

Mrs. Wh. How will the old enemy erect himself?

Mrs. Mop. And the holy sisters be humbled?

Mrs. Wh. Who shall carry on the great work?

Mrs. Mop. Or perfect that which you have begun?

Mrs. Wh. Mr. Scruple transmogrify?

Mrs. Mop. Ah, no! [*Both of them*—Hui!

Sc. You say right; you are my workmanship! I have been working you these twenty years, and you are wrought! But alas!—I speak not this to you—there are a number of dissenting brethren, and I have tried 'em this way and that way and t'other way, and, to say truth, every way, but never the nearer; and therefore I'm ev'n resolv'd to try what the old way will do.

Mrs. Wh. Ah, Mr. Scruple, do you know what you say? The old way!

Mrs. Mop. The old whore! [*Both*—Hui!

Sc. Yes; the old way, though no old whore! Wherein, notwithstanding, I do no more than whatever was, is now, and ever will be. Mark what I say, and observe it. Our brother Fox, that had so little wit as to write his *Book of Martyrs*, had yet enough to keep himself from being one of the number!

Mrs. Wh. Ah! what will become of the flock?

Mrs. Mop. And the little lambs—how shall they play?

Mrs. Wh. Who shall destroy the chickens of the wolf?

Mrs. Mop. And break the leviathan's eggs i' the shell?

Sc. Come, sisters of mine, you live on the blind side of the world! I find the cause and its interest deserted by most people, unless it be some few that, having found how sweet a thing it is to head a faction, make use of us, as the monkey did of the cat's paw, to scrape the nuts out of the fire! I need say no more, unless it be that I have a fair opportunity of £300 a year offer'd me.

Mrs. Wh. Ay, do—do! and see who'll repent it first. Never expect more Friday night suppers!

Mrs. Mop. Nor the sweet society of brethren and sisters!

Mrs. Wh. What fellowship is there in stockfish and oil?

Mrs. Mop. Or, instead of jellies, to be swill'd with frummetry?*

Mrs. Wh. To exchange your venison for red herrings and mustard?

Mrs. Mop. And virgin pullets for ling and haberdine?† [SCRUPLE *shakes his head, and sighs*—Huh!

Mrs. Wh. Who will be gainers now?

* Hulled wheat boiled in milk, and seasoned with cinnamon and sugar.

† Salted cod.

Mrs. Mop. Or whose the loss when this happens?

Mrs. Wh. When the benevolence shall dwindle to an Easter penny?

Mrs. Mop. And purifying dinners into crack'd groats?

Mrs. Wh. When you're at charge of a gown for Sundays and holidays?

Mrs. Mop. And the cassock comes out of your own pocket?

Mrs. Wh. When the boys cry after you it grows too fast?

Mrs. Mop. And the knot of your surcingle sits in the wrong place? [*Again, but louder*—Huh—hu!

Mrs. Wh. And will you, then, leave us? Let not £300 a year be anything in the case; we will allow you four! Pray consider! Did we ever forsake you? What did you lose by your last imprisonment?*

Sc. Now cannot I forbear, but I must accept your £400 a year. Let a man strive never so much against it, natural affection will return upon him. Comfort yourselves—that is to say, be comforted; I will not forsake you! *Conclusum est contra*, etc. I will not conform; nay, verily, I will not!

Mrs. Wh. Ah, Mr. Scruple!

[*They both hang on him. Cough within.*

Sc. Hark! I hear the Alderman! Run in—run in! I'll follow you instantly!

[*Exeunt* MRS. WHITEBROTH *and* MRS. MOPUS.

So, now 'tis £400 a year, and not conform! The women are good comfortable women, and I ought not in conscience to leave 'em. But hear me, brother! what will you do with your new parsonage? Why, I will get some or other instituted and inducted into 't, to save a lapse, and take a bond of £500 of him to resign at six months; which he will forfeit, of course, as not doubting but to be reliev'd against it as

* Instead of this last inquiry, the first, second, and third editions have: 'What have you lost by throwing yourself on your friends? If the worst come to the worst, we will forsake our carnal husbands and carnal children, and march off to New England together.'

simoniacal. So, there's £500 got too! He's gone every way—at common law, 'tis his own bond; in equity, he might have resign'd. But why so fast, friend Scruple? Had not you as good sell it outright to avoid dispute? I cannot tell. But now, I remember me, the Casuists take a notable difference—that is to say, between money given (*pro valore beneficii*) as the full price, and (*tanquam motivum ad resignandum*) for your good will or so. The first, they generally agree to be simony; but for the latter, they leave it as a controverted point, positively denied by very few but such as have money to give.

Enter WHITEBROTH *led by* MOPUS *and* TIMOTHY. WHITEBROTH *coughs.*

Alas, good sir, how does your worship? Pray, sir, how do you like him?

Mop. Troth, but ill; I'm half afraid of him!

Wh. Who's that? Mr. Scruple?

Sc. Yes, sir. How do you?

Wh. Uh—uh—very ill! Is the Doctor coming?

Sc. He'll be here immediately. Poor man! he was half distracted when I brought him the news.

Enter RUNTER.

He's come! How he sweats with haste!

Ru. My dear friend, how do you?

Wh. Oh, oh!—ill, ill!—uh, uh, uh! Have you brought my old will with you? Let me see 't! Uh—uh—uh!

Ru. Yes, sir; here 'tis!

[RUNTER *gives it* WHITEBROTH; *he peruses it.*

Sc. Indeed, sir, 'tis piously and discreetly done to settle affairs, so that there may be no wrangling in case you should do otherwise than well.

Mop. I wonder my boy comes not. I have sent him for a rosicrucian preparation has fetcht a man again after he has been dead a day and half! I hope it may do good. However, for fear of the worst, you do well to settle your estate; it may ease your head.

Wh. Uh—uh—uh! Here, Doctor, put some wax to 't! Set the table nearer, and give me my seal!

[RUNTER, *in putting on the wax, puts the change upon him; he signs and seals the false deed, and coughs all the while.*

Ru. Sir, you are weak! Do you deliver this as your act and deed?

Wh. Yes, I do! Pray, gentlemen, be witnesses to it!

Enter BOY. *They witness it.*

Mop. Oh, are you come at last? Here, sir—here's the most sovereign cordial in all the world! I was seven years in making one poor pint and a half of 't!

Wh. I thank you, sir.—[*He drinks.*]—Uh—uh! It warms me strangely! Uh!—uh!

Mop. Pray, forbear coughing; you are weak! How do you feel yourself now?

Wh. I cannot tell; but methinks it does me good.

Mop. I see by this sudden operation 'twill do the work! You were best to walk in, and rest yourself on your couch awhile before the fire!

Ru. I must run home a little upon some urgent occasions, but will see you again presently.

[*Exeunt severally.*

SCENE V.

Enter DOUBLE DILIGENCE, *and his wife*, BILBOE, TITERE TU—*the men drunk.*

Bil. Why, Captain!—What! all a mort?

T. T. Faith I was contemplating upon the pence.

Bil. And thou shalt have 'em, boy. See here, my bully!—[*He pulls out* WHITEBROTH'S *chain.*]—Here's that will fetch 'em.

Mrs. D. Dear Major, give it me!

Bil. Thou shalt have anything, my jo! Captain,

courage! we'll be merry to-night, and have a wedding, though 't be but a Westminster one.

T. T. What you will.

D. D. Well said, Major. Ah, for a fiddle now! Odds nigs!

Bil. I hate those Puritan oaths. If thou must swear, swear like a man of office!

D. D. The old boy still. Now could I caper through the moon! Hey, toss! Hang one fiddle, we'll have a whole kennel! Come, you jade, dance!

Mrs. D. Alas, Major! How pitifully my husband is cut! He'll be so sick to-morrow morning.

Bil. Yes, faith; he has got a rattle as big as a drum.

D. D. Major! a word! Do you think my wife's a whore?

Bil. Such another word, and, by all the bones of my back——

D. D. Nay, good Major! I was once a little jealous, till she told you of the Alderman; but now, I dare trust her to Lecture by herself.

Mrs. D. What's that you say to me?

Enter AFTERWIT, BEATRICE, JOLLY, RUNTER, *and* CIS.

D. D. Stand! Who comes there? Knock 'em down! What are you? I am the Constable!

Aft. The fellow's mad.

Mrs. D. No, sir! He's a little overtaken, as they say.

D. D. Stand off! down with 'em! Stand! Treason! I command you to apprehend one another.

Jol. Many a good time has this fellow's head been broken to keep the peace whole. Prithee take him away.

Bil. Landlord, they're friends.

D. D. Which?—where! Here I could have 'em, and there I could have 'em.—[*He fences with his staff.*] —Mr. Runter? I profess I knew you not!

Ru. Then ha' done now! Come, gentlemen, what say you? The business must be discovered, first or last, and as good now and perhaps better than another time.

Aft. I like it well, but think it were not amiss to lessen the company. We will not appear all at once.

Ru. However, let 'em be within call.

Jol. Pray, gentlemen, keep together; we shall have occasion to use you presently.

Bil. You see my arm's in a scarf—much cannot be expected from me. But, for a dead lift, we'll make a shift to change hands. Gi' the word of command there—faces about, etc.

Jol. And hear me, Major! Lend me your chain, and let it be your care to provide some abominable music. We'll bring him to our bow, or run him to death with fiddlers.

Bil. I warrant you. Here!—[*He gives him the chain.*

Exeunt all but JOLLY, AFTERWIT, *and* BEATRICE. *To them enter* SCRUPLE, *and* MRS. WHITEBROTH.

Mrs. Wh. How?—married? Oh, my child! my child!

Sc. You might have believed me sooner. How often have I told you she was in her teens? and, you know, *teen quasi teeming.* I may be a little free with you. Young girls are like nuts—you must gather them when they begin to be brown at bottom, or they'll fall of themselves.

Mrs. Wh. But, truly, I hope it is not so plain as you make it.

Sc. How think you?

[AFTERWIT *and* BEATRICE *come up and kneel.*

Mrs. Wh. Oh, my child! my child! Thy father is pretty hoddy again, but this will break his heart quite. Oh, my child! Has he not hurt thee?

Enter WHITEBROTH, MOPUS, *and* TIMOTHY; *after them* MRS. MOPUS.

Aft. No great sign of death, mother.

Wh. What's all this clutter? Here's a noise for a sick man, with all my heart!—[AFTERWIT *and* BEATRICE *kneel to him.*]—How's this?

Sc. Nothing but matrimony, sir, and conjugal love.

Wh. And were you pimp to 't? I hope you have made sure of her portion. I can assure you her grandfather left her not so much as a grey groat.

Aft. I have enough in her.

Wh. Much good may 't do you!

Bea. Good sir, forgive me!

Wh. Out of my doors! The wench is pretty handsome, and will be able to get her own living if the parish will but keep the children.

Aft. I must not hear this language. Know you this? A good honest settlement upon myself—[*he shows the deed*]—and your daughter, in consideration of marriage.

Wh. Ha!—settlement!—and in consideration of marriage? I was not drunk, sure! When was this done?

Aft. Only a little crop sick—very lately.

Sc. Indeed, sir, you desired this gentleman and myself to be witnesses to it. I know my hand again.

Mop. I saw you sign, seal, and deliver it.

Wh. I published only my will.

Mop. I know not what your meaning was, but you delivered it as your act and deed.

Wh. Timothy! fetch me the Constable

Jol. Sir, he'll save you that trouble; I met him just coming to you about a suspicious person, whom he apprehended with this chain in his pocket.—[*He shows the chain.*]—You cannot imagine whose it should be?—[WHITEBROTH *makes no answer, but holds up his hands, and walks.*

Enter full butt upon him BILBOE, DOUBLE DILIGENCE, TITERE TU, *and* MRS. DOUBLE DILIGENCE.

Wh. Cheated! cheated!—as I'm an Alderman, purely cheated!

Aft. How can that be? You have the reputation of as shrewd a man as any upon the bench.

Wh. Ah! rogues all! rogues all! [*He walks again.*

Jol. What say you, sir? Here's the Constable now.

Come, come; be wise! Your daughter has married a gentleman. Is not this better than a Smithfield bargain—give me so much money, and my horse shall leap your mare?

Wh. Don't worry me with words! I'll consider of 't.

Sc. Good sir, marriages are made in heaven.

Wh. Then I'll be sworn I had ne'er a friend there.

Cis. Truly, nor I neither; for indeed, methinks, they are very long in coming down. [*Aside.*

Sc. Now, verily, sir, but this a just judgment upon you for hoarding up your moneys, and suffering the good old cause to starve.

Wh. Screech-owl! But where's my doctor?

Jol. Why, troth, sir, you cannot blame him; he is somewhat loth to appear till he see how things are like to go. Come, pray, sir.

Wh. Well, sir, I see by this chain the Major and you understand one another. Let's have no more words; all parties shall be satisfied. Give me 't!

Jol. There—and may you long live to wear 't. You may come down—all's well.

[*To* RUNTER, *peeping above.*

Wh. Come, son and daughter; the business is done, and I forgive you both. And if that settlement be not large enough, I'll make you a new one upon demand. You shall have your own estate back in present, and, as you love your wife, the rest after our deaths. And so you have my blessing.

Aft. and Bea.—[*kneel*]—We thank you, sir.

Wh. Come, let's be merry! and, as late as 'tis, send for the music—we must have a dance at least.

Jol. See what 'tis to forecast a man's business right. They are gone for, and will be here instantly.

Wh. But we forget the main thing—the posset. Quickly, Cis, and get one ready. [*Exit* CIS.

Mrs. Wh. How's this? music!—dancing! posset! Are they lawful, good Mr. Scruple?

Mrs. Mop. Are they not the rags of the whore?

Sc. Thereafter as they may be used. I will consider it a little, and give you my opinion. [*He walks.*

Enter RUNTER.

Wh. O my doctor! you're a fine gentleman! Good faith, you are!

Ru. Who—I? I care not if all my faults were writ in my forehead.

Enter TYRO.

Wh. It must be in shorthand then, or there will want room.

Jol. Here's Tyro too. You're even come time enough to dance at your mistress's wedding!

Ty. How! My mistress's wedding?

T. T. Even so. Alas, that I had known of this before!

Ru. Women will have their wills. Let her go—I have another guess-thing in chase for you.

Ty. And shall I have her?

Ru. Thou shalt. And hark you!

[RUNTER *having whispered him, he shrugs, and scratches his elbow.*

Sc. Hum—I am full, and shall discourse 'em gradually. And first, of the first—music. Yes, certainly, it is lawful. But what music; that's the question. We'll examine it a little. Cymbals—they are Jewish; the harp—malignant and Irish; organs—antichristian; the flute—a mere hornpipe; the fiddle—out upon 't! most abominable; it ushers in revels and May-poles. What then? Why, truly, I agree with the Assembly—bagpipes; a harmless, innocent music, and most agreeable to the discipline and practice of our brethren of the kirk. Besides, it has (as the learned observe) a specific quality, to mollify and soften the most brutal natures—witness the bears.

"Emollit mores nec sinit esse feros."

But, secondly, for dancing:—why, truly, that may be lawful too. But here, too, the point will be the same—what dancing? Country dances—they are pagan; French dances—fie, fie! antic; our ordinary dancing—villanous; 'tis mixed and promiscuous—a very

Nicolaitanism. The benchers' measures, I must confess, they come somewhat near were they not superstitious. What then? Why, the men may dance in one room, and the women in t'other. Lastly, for the posset:—and, truly, here I'm in a great wood. But not to dwell upon the letter whether posset, or p-osset, I shall take it as it lies before me—posset—and, truly, that may be lawful too. Lemon-posset is cooling; carduus-posset, *benedictus;* and sack-posset comfortable; but wedding-sack-posset—there's the point! Truly, I half doubt it, and that for fifteen reasons—hum——

Jol. A plague o' these fiddlers! We shall be murdered ere they come.

Sc. I say, for fifteen reasons. First, from the name of the things,—*posset*, from *posse*, to be able, and from that fond supposition first brought into weddings—an invention merely carnal. But secondly, for that it ministreth abundance of unsavoury discourse. Thirdly, for that the grace before it is none at all, and the grace after it lewd. Fourthly, that it is eaten by the parties chiefly concerned, only in spite. Fifthly, hum—haw—I say, fifthly——

Enter Fiddles.

Jol. Servavit Apollo! Strike up! strike up! One noise best drowns another.

Sc. A wholesome observation lost.

Jol. 'Twill keep cold for another time.

Wh. Come, gentlemen, one dance, and then for the posset! [*They dance.* TYRO *pipes.*

Jol. Yet, with your favour, Mr. Alderman, a song would do no hurt.

Wh. I think so too.

Sc. But ye don't consider 'tis Saturday night, and past sunset.

Jol. Or you, that the room's next the street, and most of the neighbours will take it for a psalm.

Wh. Well said, Mr. Jolly! and we will have it. Begin!

A Song.

Do it, do 't! Ay, but what, my good fellow?
Canst thou tell me what 'tis makes a glad man?
Shall I flatter to thrive,
Or be honest and live
The same beast I was born, and die mad—man?

Shall I bow to the calves of the season?
Or cry up the Sir Pol of the nation?
Or the college of fools,
Or those moulds of the schools
That spoil forty for one that they fashion?

Shall I speak to the world, I've the meagrim,
By adorning the furrs and the custard?*
By the conjugal itch,
Or the plague of being rich,
And be damned for another man's bastard?

Shall I bluff like the man of great business?
Or set a starch'd face upon folly?
Shall I pet and repine,
Turn love-sick and whine,
Or kick the world round, and be jolly?

That! O that! And while Gotam Hall statists
Buzz their heads with this fop and that clatter,
Who'll be the next mayor
Shall be least of my care,
Or who Pope on this side the water.

Then away with 't! And thy foot to mine, boy!
Here's a glass! and again! 'twill ne'er hurt you.
Drunk, drunk, and dead drunk,
And perpetually drunk,
Oh, 'tis the reward of virtue!

[*He drinks it off.*

* Qy. Costard—the head?

Wh. Why, so—we are all friends! And now, you that are for the posset, follow me!

Jol. Well moved! well moved!—the bride begins to be sleepy.

Bil. Lead on before, there; I'll bring up the rear. Come, landlord, bear up for the bar of Chester; and since we have had so good fortune to-day, we'll henceforth boil our beef in sack, and make the beggars drunk with the porridge. [*Exeunt.*

THE END.

ANDRONICUS COMNENIUS.

Andronicus Comnenius: A Tragedy. By John Wilson. Juvenal, Sat. 13.—'*Fatebere tandem, nec surdum, nec Tiresiam, quenquam esse deorum*'—'*At last you'll find, that heaven is neither deaf nor blind.*' *London, Printed for John Starkey, at the Mitre, between the Middle-Temple Gate and Temple-Bar, in Fleet Street.* 1664. *4to.*

Andronicus Comnenus, or, according to Wilson, Comnenius, was, as Gibbon truly observes, a remarkable instance of the truth of the old proverb, that "bloodthirsty is the man who returns from banishment to power"—an adage of which Marius and Tiberius were striking instances, and of which Andronicus is a still more striking illustration.* He was the youngest son of Isaac, who had the title of Sebastocrator, "which approached the dignity, without sharing the power, of the Emperor,"† and grandson of the Emperor Alexius Comnenus I.

He was "one of the most conspicuous characters of the age, and his genuine adventures might form the subject of a very singular romance. To justify the choice of three ladies of royal birth, it is incumbent on me to observe, that their fortunate lover was cast in the best proportions of strength and beauty; and that the want of the softer graces was supplied by a manly countenance, a lofty stature, athletic muscles, and the air and deportment of a soldier. The preservation in his old age of health and vigour was the reward of temperance and exercise." "Dexterous in arms, he was ignorant of fear: his persuasive eloquence could bend to every situation and character of life; his style, though not his practice, was fashioned by the example of St. Paul; and in every deed of mischief he had a heart to resolve, a head to contrive, and a hand to execute."

In selecting a portion of the life of Andronicus as a fitting subject for his drama, Wilson has taken the latter part of his sanguinary career, when, by his intrigues, his hypocrisy, and the aid of those he subsequently betrayed, he succeeded in placing on his brows the Byzantine diadem; and it cannot be denied that our Author has been successful in the manner in which the true history has been epitomized, and in the language used for that purpose, which is throughout poetical and appropriate. The scenes where Andronicus declines the purple, and especially the one where, after murdering Alexius, his youthful associate, he courts his widow, Alice,‡ is not much inferior to the well-known passage of words between Richard III. and the Lady Anne, the widow of the only son of Henry VI. There is a singular resemblance between the Andronicus of Constantinople and Richard of England: both were murderers, and both mar-

* *History of the Decline and Fall of the Roman Empire*, chap. xlviii. London, 1791. Vol. ix. p. 104.

† Ibid. p. 86.

‡ A daughter of Louis VII., King of France. In the *Dramatis Personæ* she is called Anna.

ried the widows of the parties they had murdered. But the Eastern Potentate exceeded in acts of atrocity the King of England, whose deeds of murder sink into insignificance when compared with the wholesale slaughters perpetrated by the last male representative of the illustrious race of the Comneni.

Gibbon has devoted several pages* of his valuable work to this *unchristian* Christian, who avenged the fancied wrongs he had suffered from his cousin, the Emperor Manuel, upon his widow, the Empress Maria, and their son Alexius. "In the first months of his administration, his designs were veiled by a fair semblance of hypocrisy, which could delude only the eyes of the multitude. The coronation of Alexius was performed with due solemnity; and his perfidious guardian, holding in his hands the body and blood of Christ, most fervently declared that he lived and was ready to die for the service of his beloved pupil."

Thus, in his protestations, Andronicus went far beyond Richard, who never profaned the religion he professed by falsehoods of this description. After thus declaring the boy Emperor, the credulous citizens of Byzantium were easily induced to assume that the associating of Andronicus as joint-ruler with the boy-emperor was the only way of saving the empire from ruin.

Amongst his earliest acts of vindictive revenge, was that perpetrated by him upon the Empress Maria, whom he accused of treasonably corresponding with the King of Hungary. He caused her to be apprehended and tried before a "tribune, which, without requiring any proof, or hearing any defence, condemned the widow of Manuel; and her unfortunate son subscribed the sentence of her death. Maria was strangled, her corpse was buried in the sea, and her memory was wounded by the insult most offensive to female vanity—a false and ugly representation of her beauteous form."

The fall of Alexius was not long deferred. He was strangled with a bow-string; and the veteran tyrant, after surveying the body of his innocent victim, kicked it with his foot, exclaiming, "Thy father was a knave, thy mother a whore, and thyself a fool." As a suitable conclusion to this bloody episode, Andronicus married the widow of his murdered colleague. To complete this fearful tragedy, he put to death all those friends by whose zeal and activity he was enabled to assume the purple.

After a sanguinary reign of three years, in the course of which Andronicus, from time to time, destroyed every member he could find of the imperial family, including his own half-sister, the Princess Mary, it came to his knowledge that there still existed a descendant of Alexius the Great,† named Isaac

* Chap. xlviii.

† Alexius I. was father of the Princess Anna Comnena, who wrote his life, a work which "betrays in every page the vanity of a female author." He assumed the purple in 1081, 1st April. The Princess Anna is introduced by Scott in *Count Robert of Paris*.

Angelus, who, although by a female descent, might at some future period occasion him trouble. He resolved upon his death; and, having given orders for his execution, retired with his Empress and a favourite mistress to one of the delicious islands of the Propontis, to enjoy the pleasures of their fascinating society free from interruption of every kind.

The proscribed Isaac did not tamely submit to the bow-string; he bravely defended himself, slew the executioner, and fled to the church of St. Sophia for sanctuary, where he was surrounded by a crowd of the citizens, who, becoming apprehensive what might be the consequence of their daring to obstruct the tyrant's order, took courage, and exclaimed: "What should we fear? Why do we obey? We are many and he is one: our patience is the only bond of our slavery."

At dawn, the populace were beyond control. The prisons were forced open, and the liberated inmates swelled the crowd of malcontents. Isaac was proclaimed Emperor.* Andronicus, after a futile attempt to recover his position, attempted to escape by sea, but was captured and dragged in chains to the presence of his successor, who abandoned him to the tender mercies of his captors. The description of the tortures inflicted on this monster need not be here detailed, as our author has sufficiently enumerated them in his drama.

Geneste remarks that this tragedy has, "on the whole, considerable merit, particularly in the character of Andronicus," an opinion, we venture to think, in which our readers will concur. It is well put together, and the interest never flags from the commencement to the end. The tyrant's son Manuel is admirably drawn, and his virtuous character affords a strong contrast to the vicious one of his parent. Manuel is represented as one worthy of the Grecian diadem, and in the drama shines as a brilliant star amongst the lesser lights by whom he is surrounded. After the dethronement of Andronicus, it is erroneously said by Gibbon that he became King of Trebizond, a country of which much has been said, but of which little is known.

Had Wilson been aware of the fate of Manuel, he would not have put the commonplace morsels of morality with which the tragedy terminates in the mouth of Isaacus Angelus, who, so far from feeling commiseration for the Prince, made him a captive, deprived him of his eyesight after the Oriental fashion, and afterwards, it is believed, put him to death.

The two infant sons of the Prince, Alexis and David, fled with their aunt Tamar to Colchis, where they grew up to man's estate. In 1206 Alexis made himself master of Trebizond, where he ruled until his death in 1222.

The most original character of the piece is that of Philo, the "zany" of Andronicus, who adheres to his master in all his

* 1185, Sept. 1.

fortunes, and dies for him. It may be conjectured, as nothing is recorded of him in Gibbon, that he was a myth, the creation of Wilson's fancy. The dialogue between Manuel and Philo, in which the Prince endeavours to convert him to virtue, is, we fear, more poetical than real.

Wilson has produced a noble tragedy, written in excellent blank verse, at a period when the ear of the public was corrupted by the wretched jingle of rhyme, made fashionable as a French importation, and patronized by the king and his courtiers. Perhaps on that account it was never acted on the stage.

TO MY FRIEND A. B.

If ever you give yourself the divertisement of reading the preface to my comedy of *The Cheats*, you may remember I did as good as protest against apologies; and yet the case happens to be such at present, that I find myself, how unwilling soever, engaged to tread that path yet once again. To tell you how long since this tragedy was first written, or why it has not been since acted, were but in effect to suspect your memory. 'Tis enough to me that you know both, and I doubt not will be ready to do me right as you see occasion. I pass it, and, according to our wonted freedom, shall only speak a few words to the thing: A story of the Eastern Empire, between the years 1179 and 1183, and such, perhaps, as might not be thought altogether unparallel to what ourselves have seen, were not the one but too fresh in our memories, and the other too far removed from our knowledge. And now, methinks I hear you charging me with a *non bene conveniunt*. The story of three or four years cramped into fewer hours! And why not? My design was a history, and if I have kept the connection, I may reasonably presume I have observed enough; nay, further, if I have dealt with it as Procrustes with his guests,—lopped some, or stretched others,—be pleased to consider, 'twas for the same reason, that I might the better fit them to my own model. To be short, if I have once again made my thoughts legible, and myself the subject of every man's opinion, how weak soever, be pleased, to such cavils as you may chance to meet with, to oppose this:—That notwithstanding I may have written some few plays, yet the stage is the last thing I shall pretend to; and therefore, though possibly I could wish *ut placerent quas fecissem fabulas,* yet I was never so much in love with a full cry, as to believe that all opened alike, or that the approbation of one wise man was not more worth than the noise of a multitude. Let me not seem immodest if I close all with that of Plautus—

> "Virtute ambire oportet, non favitoribus ;
> Sat habet favitorum semper qui recte facit."

Farewell !—Yours, etc.,

J. WILSON.

Jan. 15, 1663.

THE PERSONS.

ALEXIUS COMNENIUS, *A Youth, the Son and Successor of Manuel Comnenius, Emperor of Constantinople.*

ANNA, *His Wife, a Daughter of France, afterwards married by Andronicus.*

MARIA CÆSARISSA, *Half-sister to Alexius, and Wife to Cæsar, an Italian lord, only mentioned, but appears not.*

SEBASTUS, *The Husband of Xene, the Widow of Manuel, who, by debauching the Emperor's youth, had got the management of affairs.*

ANDRONICUS COMNENIUS, *A Prince of the blood, banished by Manuel; but, being called home to counterpoise Sebastus, usurps upon Alexius, murders him, and marries Anna.*

MANUEL, *His Son.*

<table>
<tr><td>CONTO,</td><td>Admiral of the Gallies.</td><td rowspan="4">All of them, together with Maria and Basilius, a bishop, often mentioned, but appears not, of the conspiracy to bring in Andronicus.</td></tr>
<tr><td>CONSTANTINUS,
DUCAS,
LAPARDAS,</td><td>Lords of the best extraction.</td></tr>
<tr><td>STEPHANUS,</td><td>Captain of the Guard to Alexius, and afterwards to Andronicus.</td></tr>
<tr><td>BASILIUS,</td><td>President of the City; both confidants to Andronicus.</td></tr>
</table>

MAMALUS, *Secretary of State during the time of Manuel, laid by by Sebastus.*

PHILO, *Andronicus's Zany.*

ISAACUS * ANGELUS, *A Gentleman of the blood, afar off, but living obscurely in a monastery, not taken notice of by Andronicus; but, the rest of the blood being destroyed, he is in a tumult set up against Andronicus, and carries the Empire.*

CITIZENS. SERVANTS.

GUARDS. FIDDLERS.

The Scene—

CONSTANTINOPLE.

* Throughout the play, as originally printed, this character is styled "Isacius."

ANDRONICUS COMNENIUS:

A TRAGEDY.

Act I.—Scene I.

Enter Lapardas *and* Ducas.

Du. 'Tis strange! and were 't not for that ready faith
I owe your lordship, I had sooner taken
Another article to my creed. A woman!
And yet so large a soul! Your lordship's merry!
La. Troth, no; she fixt me, Ducas! When I saw
How she first took the question, stated it,
Ran the whole matter, and, where danger offer'd,
Past it with such a careless scorn. Believe me
It made me wonder into what narrow cranny
My soul had crept!
Du. You've such a knack at speeching,
You either find them good, or make them so.
Rack me no longer, dearest sir; let's have it!
La. And willingly. We met—you know the place;
Nor was th' appearance small. And as in councils
There never was a fool,—at least that would
Be thought so,—ev'ry man let fly his bolt!
One offer'd this, another that. The point
Was common danger. All agreed the thing,
But few the way of helping it—that plague
And mischief of great actions, "Let's do better,"
Had so unhing'd their souls, until Maria
Summ'd up their little all, told them th' 'ad lost
The question, and 'twas not their wellbeing

But being was the point—not what Greece should be,
But whose it was! And when they threw in doubts,
That thou hadst seen her how she blew them off!
Snufft at their scruples! "And is this," quoth she,
"The lion in the way? Can danger baulk
Men once resolv'd? Be that bugbear mine!
I dare encounter it, and act, whate'er
You all dare think!"

Du. 'Twas a brave virago!
A wonder of her sex! A phœnix, sure!

La. Ay, you'd have sworn it, had you heard that world
Of which this is but an imperfect globe—
A wrong side of the hangings!

Du. But, my lord,
How was it relish'd? Did not their seats grow warm?

La. No; but they all lookt wistly one on t'other,
As who would say, 'twas true enough, but yet
Some passages might have been well forborne.

Du. What was the issue?

La. Why, they all shook hands,
And by a general vote center'd in this:
That men and monies must be rais'd, to break
The present faction, and themselves would do 't!
Next, that Andronicus be invited home
To head the forces, which Maria pray'd
Might be her part o' th' work. Which once agreed,
Sooner than thought they fell into their gears;
Each man subscrib'd his task, gave order straight
For her instructions, and have since despatcht her.

Du. But no account as yet?

La. Not possible!
'Tis scarce two months since she departed hence,
And we forbade all packets. But this night
She is expected. Good my lord, be there!
Your proxy'll serve no longer. I have told them
Your gout is over!

Du. I shall, my lord! My fate
Runs hand in hand with yours!

Enter MAMALUS.

But see! Who's coming yonder? I'm mistaken,
Or 'tis Mamalus! He was an honest courtier
And our true friend; why should not he make one?
La. He is best able. All the affairs of Greece
Have pass'd his hand, and with no ill success.
Du. Let's try! My honour for his secrecy!
La. With all my heart! See, he comes up to you!
Du. Mamalus, save you! 'Tis an age, or better,
Since we last met.
Ma. The loss, my lords, was mine!
La. But whence, our friend?—turn'd courtier again?
How goes all there?
Ma. Troth, I've scarce seen the place
Since my great lord and master, Manuel, died.
I can nor fawn nor truckle.
La. Pettish, I warrant! I'm asham'd, Mamalus!
Is it a courtier's part to show his teeth
Before he bite?—to breathe a pitiful revenge
Ere he have power to act? No! Great men's injuries
Are best remedied by not understanding them,
Or seeming t' 'ave forgot them; whereas, otherwise,
Y' are sure to be prevented with a greater.
Have a good heart! I not forbid thee strike;
But do it sure.
Ma. Your lordship's wide o' the mark.
Yet since you name the Court, when were you there?
Du. Troth, we come there, and that is all. We're grown
Barely spectators—idle lookers on.
Sometimes, perhaps, out of a compliment,
To countenance a business, or concur,
We're call'd to council too.
La. And what of that?
Matters of consequence we must not know.
Nor is it out of love to us, but fear
Of what may follow, that we've kept our heads.
Ma. And can you blame me, then, that have no stake,

If I sit out, when you that have the greatest
Have such ill carding?

Du. Break his neck that packt them!
Come, join with us—shuffle and cut again!

Ma. I am no conjuror; your lordship must
Speak plainer ere I understand you right.

La. Give us thy hand and word for secrecy!

Ma. You have them both.

La. Then, to be short, we're lost,
And so's the empire! Now, to recover it,
Most of the lords and officers of state
Are join'd; nor want we men, or arms, or money!
Andronicus the head—at least we hope so.

Ma. But why, my lords, such haste? Must a man lop
A limb 'cause out of joint?—knock out his brains
To cure the headache? What's to be done but once
Should be considered twice! Mutations
Are ever dangerous, even where the thing
Might have been good and profitable at first;
It being impossible to provide against
Those inconveniences we can't foresee.

La. But there's no other way! Has not Sebastus
Turn'd us quite topsy-turvy, disoblig'd
The nobles, trampl'd under foot the commons?

Ma. 'Tis granted! But why this last remedy?
Bear it a little—time may work it off!
Come, come! close with him! Blow the bladder stiff,
And it must crack! By pulling others down
He has o'erbuilt himself!

Du. We've often thought so,
But find it otherwise.

Ma. Admitting yet
You must be changing, how are you secure
He that comes next shall not be worse? Who, pray,
Shall keep the keepers?

Du. We have order'd that.

Ma. But why Andronicus, of all the world?

Du. Why? He's a soldier, and a Prince o' th' blood,
And valiant enough!

Ma. So much the worse!
What were a virtue in another, in him
May prove a crime! He is too near the crown
Already, and this gives him th' occasion
Of grasping that he has so long design'd!
I dare not—nay, I must not join! The wolf
Shall never have my voice to make him shepherd!
But yet, to show your lordships I'll be secret,
I'll trust you with as much. You may remember
My master banisht him; but why, I'll tell you.
He is a Prince of the most daring soul
E'er dropt from Heaven—industrious, vigilant,
Kind, affable, magnificent.
Yet all this good—nay, all his lusts and passions
Are slaves to his ambition! Take him there,
Nothing can hold him. Laws, religion, all,
Sacred or civil, are no more than—this!

Du. But we'll provide for that. We'll tie him up
Fast under hand and seal, well backt with oaths!

Ma. Tie him with oaths! Hah! You may sooner hold
An angry lion with a clew of thread,
Giants with rotten tow! Th' old emperor found it,
When, having forgiv'n him so oft, he still
Broke out anew—swore and forswore again;
Until necessity made him resolve
To kill or banish him—which last took place.
Pray Heaven 't 'as altered him! Howe'er, let me
Remain your lordships' servant!

Both. Friend, you mean! Farewell!

[*Exit* MAMALUS.

La. 'Tis time that we went too.

Du. I wait your motion. [*Exeunt.*

SCENE II.

Enter SEBASTUS *and* CONSTANTINUS.

Con. Now, good my lord! h' 'as been an ancient servant

Unto our family! 'Tis the least I can!
Pray let him have it!

Seb. How was your lordship saying?
I did not mind you well, my head's so full! [*Scratches.*

Con. O' th' simples!—[*Aside.*]—Come, I beg but seldom.
Shall I send him to kiss your hands?

Seb. Matters of State
Beat all things out!

Con. No; 'tis your oval crown [*Aside.*
Lets nothing in!

Seb. But, good my lord, what is 't?
It must be somewhat more than in my power
When you're denied.

Con. Troth, 'tis a very nothing!

Seb. Why, then, you have it! Is your lordship pleas'd?

Con. Hah! yours is pleasant; 'tis a little odd thing—
The majordomo to his majesty's bears.

Seb. Certain, my lord, it is too mean a place;
And he might find much better. What is 't worth?

Con. Not much above a hundred crowns a year,
Besides the blessing that attends an office.

Seb. Stay! Majordomo?—Let me see! I doubt
Somewhat was done in 't lately.—[*Scratches.*]—Oh! I have 't!
Alas! my lord, 'tis gone—dispos'd, in troth.
Now I'm so sorry!

Con. But to whom? or how?

Seb. Why, I'm mistaken, or the Emperor gave it
To—[*scratches*]—an old servant of his father's.

Con. Strange!
Eagles do seldom stoop so low.

Seb. Then 'twas
My wife—and like enough it might be so!
But there are other things as good, or better,
And might be found if men were diligent.
Trust me, I am so vext; I'll tell my wife
What a displeasure she hath done your lordship.
[*Exit.*

Con. Your lordship's! Gone!—dispos'd! My life, this fellow
Would sell his soul, were any man so mad
To bid him money for 't! Was this a thing
To be believ'd? The devil of such a servant
Or office I yet ever heard or dreamt;
But now I see 'tis good to try one's friends
Ere a man needs 'em. And the same have I
The nature of this beast. Now is he gone
To hunt a chapman; but the scent, beloved,
Will be cold ere you light on one! Dull Greece!
Where is thy soul? What magic or what fate
Has dampt thy spirits? Canst thou live, yet be
Bull'd by this urchin? Canst thou breathe, yet suffer
Such a slave ride thee?—such a tinsel bauble?
No! Know, fond man, though Greece be fast asleep,
Her genius wakes; nor shall thy formal nothing
Brave it much longer! Dirt thou art, and dirt
Shall be thy last, and sudden too! 'Tis done
The better half, what is once well begun! [*Exit.*

SCENE III.

Enter PHILO, *solus, with a letter in his hand.*

Ph. Hah! hah! hah! hah! hah! hah! To see this world!
Luck's all! 'Tis better to be fortunate
Than be a rich man's son! Here are boys scrambling:
One gets an apple, t'other a broken pate!
There's good luck and bad luck!
Yonder a knot of rogues rebel: the poor ones
Hang for example, and the great ones are [*Scratches.*
Ev'n what they please—good luck and bad luck too!
'Tis now two years since first my master sent me
To manage his design within this city,
And what have I done there? Only deserv'd
For to be hanged! Many an honester man
Than both has marcht that way! But the luck's all!

See!—[*Shows his letter.*]—I've receiv'd intelligence from him
That what we have been hammering so long
Is just dropt into 's mouth! 'Tis offer'd him!
Here is a kennel of such precious curs
They cannot rule themselves; and now they court
The devil to part stakes! I hope he will
Remember them in time! Troth, they deserve it.
Well, I must to them; but, to bring me there,
Find out Maria! Now, the wit of woman!
I see they may be trusted with more secrets
Besides their husbands'; though, in troth, I judge
'Twas the best place to lodge one safe—wise men
Ne'er look for 't there!

Enter MANUEL *in a disguise.*

But what have we got here?
A piece of poetry in prose? Hah! hah!
A small philosopher, but that he wears
A brawling-iron! He walks as if he were
Measuring feet with the Antipodes,
Or treading out the Saxon ordeal!
Sure it would speak! I'll step aside and see.

Man. Vain state of wretched man, that only knows
What yet he found too soon—his misery!
Where is that happiness philosophers
So much contend for? I have often met
The name, but ne'er the thing!—sure 'tis their stone,
In other words; or, having trod that path
So long, I must have reach'd my journey's end.
One would have thought my birth, to say no more,
Had been enough t'ave given me title to 't.
But now, I am convinc'd 'tis but a dream,
An airy fancy; or if yet there be
More in 't, 'tis negative, and to be happy
Is only not to be miserable!

But what do I thus fondly to complain
In such a common case? Trace far and near,
And all alike—no satisfaction!
Now I see nature took a fall when young,

She has so limpt e'er since. What's all this world
But several purlieus of wild beasts that walk
On their hin' legs, wherein not always strength,
But such as have the cleanliest conveyance,
Drive the dull staring herd before them?
What's all that noise and cry of public good
But a conspiracy of the richer sort
To grind the poor, and fence themselves with laws
To keep that safely they've unjustly got?
What makes a traitor but a ruin'd cause?
Or heretics, but being less in number?
Nay, what are even our greater ties become
But bawds to interest, and specious names
To cover great men's wrongs? Who, then, would live
That had but soul enough to die? or be
A pris'ner when the keys of his own prison
Hung by his side, and might discharge himself?
And so will I—[*draws*]—'tis worthy of my blood!
Here—[*sets the hilt to ground*]—take your virtue back again who gave it!
And by your leave——

[Philo *comes from behind the hangings and trips his sword away.*

Ph. And mine too, if you please!

Man. Still more misfortune! What art thou? 'Twas rude
To take that from me which thou darest not give!

[Manuel *riseth and runs upon the other's point.*

Ph. Stand off! Nay, since you must pursue your folly,
Hold! there's your sword again—[*draws*].

[*They fight and close; in the close* Philo *knows him, throws away his sword, and kneels.*

My honour'd lord!
Now, shall I bless or curse my hand?

Man. Begone!
And tempt thy fate no longer!

Ph. My best lord!
Yet hear me speak——

Man. Rise, and be sudden then!

Ph. I shall.—[*Riseth.*]—And, since this combat of your passions
May've checkt each other, give your reason time
To breathe a while! Consider what you're doing!
It is an injury to yourself and nature.
Nature preserves itself, and taught not this,
Nor promis'd any by privation bliss.
Man. Injurious to myself it cannot be!
I'm willing; injury supposes force,
Nor yet 'gainst nature; for then surely they,
Whom no religion aw'd, as having 't not,
Had never us'd, at least affected, it.
Then take your argument, or tell me why
Nature yet left it in our power to die?
Ph. She could not help it. To have made a man,
And yet denied him liberty of will,
Had been t'ave given him wings and clipt them too.
Yet, take 't with its restriction, she ne'er meant
Because you might you should destroy yourself.
If all should do the same, where were the world?
Man. What's that to me? would the whole world lay here! [*Claps his hand upon his heart.*
And I'd soon solve the question.
Ph. Yet show me
Some late example of this kind; this humour
Has worm'd itself quite out of date.
Man. Disuse
Is a poor argument. Let children fear
To sit alone because their candle's out:
It is enough to me there is yet left
This remedy and triumph over fortune.
Begone!
Ph. I must not. 'Tis now worth yourself
To dare to live! Who ever sunk his ship
Because he fear'd a storm might do it for him?
Or kill'd himself to save his enemy pains?
Life is a warfare, and who quits the field
Without a lawful passport runs away.
Man. And so do thou, and quickly, or, by this
[MANUEL *shakes his sword at him.*

I shall too soon confute your argument!
Ph. What will your noble father say?
Man. Ha! Father!
There's magic in the word; 't 'as chill'd my blood
Into a palsy. Hence! I dare not trust
My resolution, nor thy tattle, longer.
Ph. How will he bear 't, I say, when he shall hear
His son thus sacrific'd to his return?
Man. Return! There's witchcraft in thy breath!
Begone!
And stagger me no longer with false hopes.
Ph. Credit me once! By all that's great or good,
He's now in Greece—nay, near this city too.
Man. Shall I believe thee? No! it must not be!
Somewhat within me whispers 'tis not so.
Yet say he were! He has believ'd me lost
These many years; and why should I now add
New sorrows to myself or him—to see him,
And yet want power to help him?
Ph. Fear not that
You have! I'll chalk you out the way; and if
You see him not ere many hours shall pass,
As glorious as the sun broke through a cloud,
Then let that mischief you design'd yourself
Fall headlong upon me!
Man. Well, for a while
I'll give thee hearing! [*Sheathes his sword.*
Take up that, and help me
To put it on again. So—so! 'Tis well!
[PHILO *takes up his grey periwig, and helps him on with it again.* [*Exeunt.*

SCENE IV.

Enter CONSTANTINUS, STEPHANUS, *and* BASILIUS.

Bas. 'Twas a good humour!
Const. Good! I'll undertake
You shall not think that thing he shall not swallow.

Bas. 'Tis such a starcht intelligible ass!
Ste. And may become a fair a twelvemonth hence.
Const. A dainty fine new-nothing!—an odd scheme
Of knave and fool, where yet the fool's ascendant,
And lords the horoscope—too much the fool
To conceal handsomely the knave, and yet
Not knave enough to act the cunning fool!
I shall forbear a farther lecture on him;
I'm sure he'll stink ere I get half way through him!
Ste. I would he knew how well his friends thought of him!
[*To them* CONTO, LAPARDAS, *and* DUCAS.
Bas. See! here are more of them!
Const. My lords, all health!
[*They salute each other.*
What say you?
Shall we fall to our business?
Cont. When you please!
[*They take their seats.*
Const. You know, my lords, what we resolv'd on last.
Have you received any account as yet?
Is our Maria safe, or the work done?
Cont. She is returned this night, and sent me word
She would be here. But what is done I know not.
Ste. 'Tis a brave lady! Troth, I half despair'd
T' have heard of her so soon!
Cont. Pray heaven it ben't
Too soon to all our costs!
Your lordships know he is ambitious.
Const. And who is not, pray?
It is the spur of every generous fool!
And were not you the same, what make you here?
Du. But 't had been prudence t'ave secur'd ourselves.
Const. I hope there's no such need. Here comes a lady

Enter MARIA, *led by* PHILO.

Will quickly end the difference. Let's go meet her!
[*They all rise and go to meet her.* *Exit* PHILO.

Madam! you're well return'd! And yet not I,
But Greece, must speak it!
Omnes. Royal Maria, welcome!
[*They all kiss her hand.*
Mar. My lords and gentlemen, I thank you!
And am sufficiently repaid my pains
In your acceptance. Please you keep your seats,
And I'll acquaint you what I've done.
Const. Blest madam!
Our life and death hang on your lips! And yet,
Methinks that face speaks a good augury.
Mar. Then know, my lords,
I have despatcht your message, and here bring you
All you could ask or think. The sea proved calm,
The willing winds smil'd on the enterprize,
And left me not till I had reach'd Onæum,*
Where I soon found Andronicus—his fame
Needed no guides—but, in that blest retirement,
That all those things which we call happiness
Might have took copy from 't, but still come short.
Not to amuse you longer, I presented
Your letters, and he read them o'er; but when
He saw the business, troth, he wept, and wisht
It had been in his power to have complied;
But he was old, and had given o'er the world
To younger men, and his ambition now
Was for a better. Yet he sigh'd and wept,
And wept and sigh'd, and sigh'd and wept again.
And thus he kept me many days. Yet still
I press'd him forward—told him Greece was sunk
Unless he buoy'd it up—that the court had
More factions than lords—the commons prest—
The empire shatter'd—nothing could restore 't
But his lost hand; beseecht him to forget
His banishment and him that laid it on.
At length he paus'd, and, pausing, askt me how
It could be done? He was but one; and arms,
Not lazy wishes, must accomplish it!
On which I show'd him all the whole design—

* Onium—a place of the Peloponnesus, near Corinth.

The persons' names, what force we had already,
And what expected to be hir'd from thence.
Well, to be short, I did at last prevail,
And with his help procur'd five thousand foot;
Yet left him not till I had seen all shipt,
And safe amidst our fleet, where he now rides,
Before the city, and resolves to land
This very night, and sack her round ere morn.
'Tis more than time, my lords, that you were gone—
There's one came with me has your orders ready.

Cont. But what conditions has he sign'd?

Mar. Much more

[*She throws them a blank.*

Than you desir'd; he bids you write your own,
And he hath sworn religiously to observe them.

Cont. What's here?—a blank! 'Tis what I thought—h'as sworn
To nothing, and nothing he'll perform. Would I were fairly rid on 't!

Lap. So would I!

Du. And I!

Lap. We're fool'd so prettily!

Cont. Or we may, in time!

[CONTO, LAPARDAS, *and* DUCAS *rise, walk, and whisper.*

Bas. Did ever men confound a business so?
My soul! we're lost!—we shall all be discover'd!

Ste. I know not what their fear may do. 'Twere best
To knock them i' th' head, and give it out
The soldiers did it. If our business thrive,
We're well enough; if not, we save ourselves.
The dead can tell no tales.

Bas. 'Twere not amiss!
What says my lord?

Const. Let's hear him once again!
And, Royal madam, see what you can do.

Mar. Well, my good lords, what would you now be at?
Are you resolv'd as yet?

Cont. Why—we'll consider 't,
[*They offer to go out,* MARIA *stops them.*
And send you back our answer.
Mar. How's this? Consider! Is 't your fear, or fate?
Blisters of greatness, whom the stupid age—
Dull as yourselves—calls lords! What prompts you this
Irresolution? You all confess
The Empire flames, and yourselves must burn with it;
And yet, forsooth, you first strain courtesy
Who shall begin, or which the way, to quench it.
Nor is that block sooner remov'd, but that
You stumble on another; and then, too,
When one would think you had been all resolv'd.
You must be now secure! Call you this lording?
I shame to hear 't, and, but my sex forbids,
I should suspect your mothers! Was 't for this
My glorious father* made all Asia bow,
Confess his empire, and, had nature pleas'd,
Shak't all the world—at least brought t'other eagle
Back to her nest again? Was it for this—
For this, I say, your famous ansires spread
Their flying banners far as earth had shore,
Only to leave the empty fame to you?
Away! Agree! Occasion calls you forth!
Show whose you are, and justify your mothers!
Const. 'Tis a brave mettled Amazon!
[CONTO, LAPARDAS, *and* DUCAS *walk up and down, biting their lips.*
Ste. Y' faith,
She nettles them!
Mar. For shame, my lords! Resolve—
Time runs away! 'Tis execution
Makes counsel's walk invisible, and, like arrows,
Outrun the eye, and hit the mark ere seen.
What is 't you fear? If 't be Andronicus?
You have his honour, and his oath engaged.
Or if Sebastus? Fancy not to meet

* The Emperor Manuel.

Augustus' arts, nor yet Tiberius' cunning.
No, no! he's nothing but a thick-skull'd stallion—
A very sot—and such a snivelling coward,
'Tis favour to call him so. Then, courage, lords!
Challenge your birthright! Be no more tame fools,
Dull heavy beasts, so jaded from your spirits
That honour cannot spur you up. Come, come!
Mind what you should—'tis now too late t' advise,
For Greece at present wants more hands than eyes.
Cont. Why, I still meant it.
Lap. We'd as good be lost
In going through as lose our heads for nothing.
Du. Nay, I'll do what you will—what you resolve
To do, do quickly.
Mar. Now you speak like men!
Come, my lords! all 's well again. And for aught
That yet remains, we'll better order it within. [*Exeunt.*

SCENE V.

Enter ANDRONICUS, *solus.*

THUS far 'tis well, and I return'd again!
To thank thee, Greece; nor have thy wrongs been sown
On barren ground, but such as shall repay
The principal, with its forbearance too.
I am a Prince—who dares deny 't? He breathes
His last that answers no! He damns his soul
In that one negative! There's but a step
'Twixt me and the Imperial crown! Nor should
That coward wear 't that dares not venture for 't.
Was this the reason, my blind mistress, that
You stroock at me? That thus you deal with all,
Fortune, like butchers, makes the fairest fall:
But stay! I'm still upon my feet, and will
Keep up my chin in spite of her! If she
Will not assist, the world shall know I can
Do it without her help; nor shall she share

A doit i' th' praise, when I, arrived at top,
Thus grasp my wish! Yet say I were as flat
As she could lay me—at the lowest ebb—
I would not yet give out; 'twere poor to fear:
Who is past hope he should be past despair!
I'll run the hazard, then; and if I fall,
What in me lies I'll pluck all after me,
Nor leave behind me such a one that shall
So much as mutter 't. No! my very name
Shall fright the world, and make future times
Fondly attempt my history, but not reach it.
Who follow, tread where men have trod before;
Who is example, must be something more! [*Exit.*

ACT II.—SCENE I.

Alarums, as at the sack of a town; shouts within.
Enter SEBASTUS, *as in a fright.*

Seb. Undone! undone! That ever man should be
Lost ere he dreamt it! Whither shall I run
To hide myself?—[*Shout.*]—Hark! they 've won the city.

Enter ALEXIUS *and* ANNA.

Alex. What sudden noise is this?
Seb. I cannot tell.
Anna. Who should tell, then?
Seb. They say Andronicus
Has landed thirty thousand horse and foot,
And is now storming of the city.
Anna. One would have thought you should have looked to this.
Seb. Who would imagine banishment a place
To raise an army? Or suspect the fleet?
Alex. No doubt but he's well back'd by some at home.
Anna. Too true, I fear me!

Seb. Will 't please your Majesty to get away
Ere 't be too late?

Alex. No! I have done no wrong,
Unless to wear a crown may be call'd such.

Seb. You will do well enough, whoever suffer.
[*To* ANNA.
Pray think on me!

Anna. Yes, I'll remember you!
And if my word will do 't——

Seb. Do 't, without doubt!

Anna. I'll have thee hanged, thou coward! Take thy sword,
And if thou canst not find a man that loves thee
So well as to die by thy side, yet go!
And thrust thyself amidst thy thickest foes:
It may deceive the world. Thy life's not worth
His pains that takes it from thee. [*Alarum—shouts.*

Seb. Hark! again!
The palace is beset! I've but one shift,
And if that fail me, then good night to all.

Enter ANDRONICUS, *as giving orders to some within.*

And. See that the soldiers make no outrages
Upon the palace; there are Franks enough
Within the city, and good pillage too.
Set your guards round; be sure no great ones 'scape.
And if you take Sebastus, bore his eyes out!
But see!—the Emperor!—I must to him. Heaven
[*Goes up to him, and kneels and kisseth his feet.*
Preserve your majesty, and confound your foes.

Alex. Cousin, you're well returned, and might have been
As welcome with fewer followers. However, rise!
Give me thy hand, and unto Heaven thy knee.

And. Next that, unto my prince. And do not think,
[*He riseth.*
Dread sovereign, that I intend you hurt
Although I knock'd thus rudely. All my aim
Was to remove your wardship, and I've done 't.
And now you 're free—free as the air you breathe!

Make the experiment! and, if you doubt my faith,
Bid me return to banishment,—I'm gone.

Anna. I know not why, but I don't like his looks. [*Aside.*

Alex. Cousin, I thank you, and believe you too.
The helm requires your help; I cannot trust it
Into a better hand. But pray, forget
Those injuries my father put upon you.
I am no otherwise entitled to them
Than as I am his son.

And. Had they been more,
I could have past them all, yet never cancel'd
That double tie of loyalty and blood!
'Twas not his fault, but my unlucky fate,
To have my love misconstrued; not the burthen
That grieved me, but the hand; not banishment,
But that 'twas caused by him! However, let
Revenge sleep with his ashes! I will pay
All mine in service to your majesty;
And to that end have I embark'd at present.

Alex. Pray, let me see you often! Farewell!
[*Exeunt* ALEXIUS *and* ANNA.

And. All happiness attend your Majesties!
Yes! you shall see me—ay, and feel me too,
Ere you're much elder. Th' 'ast a double crime—
First, that th' art Emperor; next, that Manuel gat thee.
Curs'd Manuel! would thou liv'dst, I'd make thee feel
The weight of my revenge. I scorn to raze
Thy monument, or to ungrave thy dust;
I rather wish the rest of all my foes
Entomb'd as fairly. But thy son, thy wife,
Thy friends, or whatsoever may prop either,
I will destroy; and make this boy to know,
They're fools who trust a reconciled foe.

Enter PHILO.

How now! what news? Have you dispos'd the army
Into good quarters? Are the lords well pleased?

Phil. Yes! as success can make them. And the people

Call you the public father—scarce a house
Without its bonfire!

And. Then the groundwork's laid!
But, prithee, tell me—for I must acknowledge
Thy management—how gat you this odd rabble?
Their tempers are more different than their faces—
'Twould puzzle the devil to suit them into pairs.

Phil. O, sir! I've ta'en more shapes than Proteus knew—
Been everything to every man—divided
And subdivided them again! Most men
Have their blind sides, but these are blind on both.

And. But how didst pick them out?

Phil. He that will make
Aught of the husband must begin with th' wife.
I've dealt 'twixt bark and tree, turn'd Confessor,
And now and then held forth; talked of ingoings
And of outgoings, so thin and bodyless,
That I was forced t' assign six or seven marks
To know it by,—twelve consequent effects,
Nineteen persuasions, besides ways to get it—
Innumerable.

And. You are merry, Philo!
I fain would give myself the loose. Proceed!

Phil. And since your highness gives me leave, I shall
Set out my cattle.
I've one—but he's a scabbed sheep—a tailor,
And he's been studying these twenty years
A querpo * cut of government. I told him
'Twas special good, and must be well received!
Another, a philosopher by fire;
And he has broke his brains to find the powder
To cleanse houses of office without stinking;
And him I have possess'd 'tis the first step
To the philosopher's stone—too great a thing
For any private man. However, he

* Close. Literally, a dress close to the body.
"I would fain see him walk in querpo, like a cased rabbit, without his holy fur upon his back."—Dryden.

Should, as the first inventor, have the patent!
T' other a one-eyed cobbler,—him I humoured
As a fit instrument to stitch a hole
I' th' commonwealth, when in a trice he threw
His wax to th' devil, and his awl to 's dam!
T' other a meal-man; and he was for sifting
The flour of pure doctrine from the bran
Of superstition, which his neighbour baker
Liked well, and cried he 'd leave the leaven out!
There's scarce a trade of which I have not one.
And, to keep all together, I've a small Levite.
He does so tew * the Pope, that man of sin,
The whore of Babylon; and when he takes a run
'Gainst sense and Antichrist, the clock can't stop him!
And. 'Tis such a rope of sand! Howe'er, they have
Done their work well enough.
Phil. And are apt matter,
Ready disposed for what you 'd have them next.
And. But what was he that skuttled by my side
As I came in? He went as if his head
Would run away with 's shoulders!
Phil. Can you blame
A bowl to wabble that hath lost its bias?
He's been an old State-martyr.
And. I remember him:
He was a scribbler in the old Emperor's days.
Phil. And has done special service for your highness—
Not that he loves you more than him, but hates
Whatever's uppermost.
And. Then 'twere best hang him
To please the people.
Phil. You may do what you will;
'Tis but a halter lost.
And. But what was he?
Don't you remember him that led the van,
And stormed the citadel? I saw it all!
Thrice he came on, and thrice beat back again;
But, as a happy omen to my cause,

* Annoy. This word is still in use in the north of England.

Brought off th' Imperial eagle in his hand;
Rallied his men upon the spot again,
Mounted the walls afresh, and leapt among 'em;
And, as you've seen a flock of sheep, when one
Breaks through the hedge the rest straight follow him,
So here his soldiers, as ashamed to see
One single man give battle to the Empire,
Leapt after him, and while you'd say What's this?
Carried the place! Canst tell me what he was?

Phil. Yes; he's a gentleman of noble blood.
And if your highness please to ratify
What I have done, the regiment is his.

And. With all my heart, and thank him too! Where is he?

Phil. Here, in the palace, sir.

And. Go, fetch him to me!

Phil. I shall! [*Exit* PHILO.

And. This single soul is worth two Empires!
Just such another had my Manuel been,
But that he fell too soon. For all the rest,
How I could hate them! What's the best of men
That he must be beholden to such slaves?
But it must be! I have a greater work
For them to do—over their shoulders I
Must climb th' Imperial throne, no matter how!
He that attempts a wickedness must lay
Thorough a greater wickedness his way!
Sin sin must hide. Thus architects do roll
Stone upon stone, and so cement the whole.
I have my agents that shall buzz the people *
How fit it is Alexius' youth should have
One that may help and share in government.
And whom more fit than I, whom every mouth
Terms the preserver of their liberty?
Nor shall they want rewards! Tush, 'tis but lent;
I can as easy pluck it back as squeeze
A sponge that's full. One need not far to find
A staff to beat a dog, nor circumstance
To make him guilty that's before foredoom'd!

* Spread secretly among the people.

Thus, when they've done, I'll throw the rod i' th' fire,
And break the ladder when 't 'as raised me higher!

Enter PHILO, *conducting* MANUEL.

Now thou hast brought me something! How he looks,
As he would shake the world! You're welcome, sir!
I have sent for you, first to acknowledge, next
To thank, your valour.

Man. 'Twas my duty, sir.

And. Call't what you will, I do assure you thus [*Hugs him.*
I cherish it. And now, to let you know
How I can value virtue where I find it,
I ratify whatever Philo promised!
I've a strange curdling in my blood—what ails me? [*Aside.*

Man. I thank your highness.

Phil. So do I; you never
Could have bestow'd it better.
[PHILO *plucks off* MANUEL'S *disguise.*

And. Ha! what's this?
Some devil has assumed my Manuel's shape
To vex my soul; but I shall conjure him, [*Draws.*
And blow this thicken'd cloud to air again.
[MANUEL *kneels.*

Man. Your blessing, Royal sir! Forbear, a while!
I am your son, your Manuel, not slain
As was supposed.

And. Stand up, and let me feel thee!
[ANDRONICUS *feels him.*
'Tis flesh, and warm; and now I own thee too!
Welcome, my Manuel, to thy father, welcome!
Let me embrace my son! Methinks I'm young,
And have snatch'd forty years from time; my blood
Beats high and strong again. But, prithee, tell me!
Twenty at least have sworn they saw thee fall,
But, like thyself, opprest, not overcome.

Man. How 'twas I fell, I know not; but next day
A countryman, searching to find his son
Among the dead, found me almost one wound,

But yet not breathless, and in charity
Convey'd me to his house, and used me so
As he had known whom 'twas he entertain'd.
And that I am, next Heaven, I owe 't to him!
And. Philo, take care two thousand crowns be sent him,
And my faith, too, to his next wish—
He was an honest man!
Phil. It shall be done, my lord.
And. Come, Manuel!
I'm but too happy now! Some little mischief
To turn this tide, lest, swelling up, it tear
Its banks, and drown what it but thought to cheer.
[*Exeunt.*

SCENE II.

Enter MAMALUS, *solus.*

Mam. Unhappy Greece, or more unhappy me,
That live to see this day! How is thy sword
Turn'd on thyself, and thine old foe invited
Unto the funeral of thy liberty?
Pray Heaven, my augury prove false! But yet
Methinks I see a cloud hang o'er thy head,
And, I'm afraid, will break too soon! That State
Is past its zenith that ne'er learns to do
But by undoing, and that ne'er sees order
But where disorder shows it! Some curst star
Has fired the people, and our seditious peers
Bring fuel to 't! If one should ask them now
What they would have, not one of them can tell,
But praise those times of old they only heard of,
And damn the present, though they neither know
What 's the disease nor yet the remedy.
And now Andronicus is the great idol,
The father of his country, and what not!
A man may safer speak 'gainst Heaven than him,—
Him, whom last year they cursed, and, ten to one,
Will do 't again before the next be past.

Nor will he lose his time: he knows they 're clay,
And may be moulded to what shape he pleases.
The people is a skittish beast, and must
Be smooth'd and stroked till he get into the saddle.
He's at it now; but if he once get there,
Which Heaven forbid, they'll find both switch and
spur.
His age has more of fire than Phaeton's youth—
He knows no mean; but, as his soul is large,
So is his courage! Think and act to him
Are the same things, only remov'd in time.
He 's not like others; he was born to rule
Within an empty sphere,—for such he'll make it,
And christen that solitude with the name of peace!
Others, they're like t'ave none.

Enter CONTO *leading* MARIA, CONSTANTINUS, DUCAS, *and* LAPARDUS.

But see! my friends
That brought him in! My life, they rue it first!

Omnes. Mamalus! well met!

Mam. Your lordships' servant!
[*They salute.*

Mar. And now, my lords, will you believe me next?
Is not Andronicus the same I promis'd?

Const. Yes, troth he is! and praise can add as little
Unto him as detraction take from him.

Cont. But yet it does no hurt to talk a little—
One may observe more than another does.
It did me good to see how he receiv'd us,
Manag'd the storm, and, when that brush was over,
How he embrac'd us with the same even temper,
As though he had not been concern'd at all.
Certain he must be wise!

Mar. His long experience
Must do 't, if yet it had not found him so.

Du. And for his valour, ask the meanest soldier,
And he will swear it was his great example
Put courage in them all; and, like the soul,
Did actuate the whole and every part.

Cont. Most strangely liberal! Has giv'n the fleet
Ten thousand crowns, besides what other presents
Has made to th' officers! What pity 'tis
The Empire lost so brave a man so long;
Or, since it has him now, age creeps upon him.
Mar. The greater is his glory! Had he been young,
It had not been so much, though yet he has
Outstript whatever I or heard or read.
I'll vie his autumn with the pride of spring.
Const. But hark you, gentlemen! you don't consider
How much work's yet to do. The Council waits us!
Will 't please your highness walk?
Mar. Lead on, my lord!
The Duke and I will follow.
[*Exeunt* CONSTANTINUS, CONTO, *and* MARIA.
Manent LAPARDUS, DUCAS, *and* MAMALUS.
Lap. Now, my good friend,
That are so costive of your faith, how think you?
Is not Andronicus a gallant person?
Mam. You know I told it you, and only doubted
How long 'twas possible to keep him so.
Then are you safe, and only then, when 'tis not
Within his power to hurt you if he would!
I hope you've tied him up by hand and seal,
Though you have done no more.
Lap. It needed not.
We have his honour and his oath engag'd.
Mam. To what?
Du. We'll tell you that another time.
Mam. How willingly these lords would cheat themselves! [*Aside.*
Lap. Methought you said he was ambitious;
But I'll be sworn he is the humblest man
I ever met with.
Mam. And that may be pride,
For aught we know. Who was the prouder, pray—
Diogenes, that spurn'd at everything,
Or Alexander, that sate out at nothing?*
'Tis dangerous. There is a rule in ethics,

* Was never satiated with conquest. (?)

That pride which riseth from humility
Is hardest cured; because the vice is grounded
Upon the virtue, and the sin built on
That that should be the cure.
Lap. What should one talk
To make an infidel a proselyte?
Farewell!
Du. Farewell!
Mam. My noble lords, your servant!
[*Exeunt by several ways.*

SCENE III.

Enter ANDRONICUS *and* PHILO.

And. But did they relish it?
Phil. 'Twas not dislik'd,
Nor much approv'd; but yet they drank your health,
And swore you were the best and bravest Prince
That Greece e'er bred! I only threw it out
As 'twere by chance, then catch'd it back again,
To make them follow it. What in the lump
Would fright, by piecemeal giv'n goes easy down.
And. It was discreetly manag'd! You must ply them
For fear it cool!
Phil. I warrant you 'tis done!
The women are all agog—they would fain see
Another show; besides, I've promist them
One's husband shall be this, and t'other's that!
Let it ferment a while—'twill do itself.
And. I like it well! Leave me, and tell Basilius
And Stephanus that I expect them here.
[*Exit* PHILO.
And. What's the best workman without tools? I think
I am fitted pretty well: the fleet mine own,
In spite of Conto, and the fool dreams it not;
The city sure, upon Basilius' score;
The guards, on Stephanus' account; the army,

Upon my own! He that can lose this game,
By my consent should never play another!
And why should I suspect my fortune, then?
Who courts her, loses her. She is a whore,
And must be ruffled! So will I! She never
Coy'd it to him that boldly offer'd at her!
I'll forward then! But, as men get up-stairs,
Step after step, 'tis somewhat long, but sure.
He that will get through a crowd, he must
First wedge an elbow, then a shoulder in,
And press on still till the whole body follow.
I must court everything, submit to all,
Tie up myself! Yet what of that? A lion
Is still a lion though his claws be par'd:
They'll grow again. He that doth otherwise
Falls foul of that odd solecism of power,
To will the end, yet not the means endure!

Enter to him, BASILIUS *and* STEPHANUS.

Welcome, my friends! for that and nothing else
Must be the name hereafter. 'Tis we three
Must make a new triumvirate, and share
Greece and her glory, and throw in the world
As overweight. What is 't you may not have
As cheap as ask? But give yourselves the trouble
To wish, and 'tis your own. Is it estate?
The Empire and her wealth lie at your feet.
Is it command? The provinces are yours.
Is it revenge? Mark out your head, and have it.
Would you a beauty? 'Twill be offer'd you.
Wives by their husbands, daughters by their mothers.
And to complete all this, would you have honour?
I am your servant, only mind yourselves!
What say my noble friends?

Ste. 'Tis seal'd and done!
Nor shall the fate or fortune of the Empire
Stave it off longer.

Bas. I have giv'n my hand,
Nor would I pluck it back to save my head;
Nay, though the universe depended on 't.

And. Spoke like yourselves, my friends!—[*Hugs them.*]—Thus men resolve!
Nothing remains but that we deal like friends;
That's free and plainly. Have you discours'd the thing
Unto your cousin, Basilius? What says he?
Bas. Yes, and 'twill do! But here's a gentleman
Will scarce believe 't.
And. And why, my Stephanus?
Ste. Pox o' these holy cheats! He humm'd and haw'd,
Told me a sleeveless story, could not tell
What God might suffer, and, I know not what,
Of dispensations and of providence.
Pleaded his holy function; but at last
Promis'd neutrality and secrecy.
And. Oh! then he's sure enough.
Bas. My life for yours!
Do you but make it law, he'll make it gospel!
Ste. Nay, there's no doubt he can.
Bas. Trust me for him,
The thing is now abrewing! But great designs
Are like great wheels—if once they move too fast,
'Tis odds they fire themselves. Besides, the people
Must not be rid too hard; they travel best
When they play with the bit i' their mouths—if once they get it
Between their teeth, 'twill try your horsemanship!
A man must deal with them as we break horses,
Show them the saddle first, then let them smell 't;
Lay it i' the manger; set it on their backs,
Your foot i' the stirrup; let them feel your weight
Once and again, and, as you find them coming,
Fall gently into the saddle; off again!
And use them thus but half a dozen times,
They'll take the rest themselves.
And. He's in the right!
And I had former thoughts, whether were best
For my design the people or the nobles;
But have resolv'd upon the first. They're won

With half the do, and easier kept; engage them,
Though never so implicitly, they drive
Furiously on! They're like a conjuror's devil—
Find them but work enough, you need not fear them:
Without it, 'ware yourself. Our first work, then,
Is to divide them, and to keep them so
Till we be safe ourselves. We must have parties
And antiparties, factions and antifactions,
Until they break to nothing; then you'll have them
Be glad of anything! Distune a viol,
And you may set it to what tone you please.
Ste. But is 't not requisite your highness were
Of every of them—at least underhand?
One would not think what an endearment 'tis
When they believe that he that has the power
Is theirs, and singly theirs—it girds them to you.
And. And what says Basilius?
Bas. Extremely good,
Nay, necessary! If the people are mad,
He's madder far that will not be mad with them!
What should a sober man in drunken company
But have his brains knockt out?
Ste. Besides, by this
You'll raise a dust before the grand design!
'Tis hard to see the bait in troubled waters.
And. Now, you're my friends I'm sure! I see you love me, [*Hugs them.*
You've advis'd so true and honestly.
Bas. On, my lord, and trust me for the city!
Ste. And for the guards, myself! I'm sure I can
Form them to anything. Nor are they mine
But to your highness' service.
And. My best friends! [*Again.*
Let's keep this knot inviolable; and, however
Our present actions may seem flat and dull,
They'll credit us when they are seen at full.

Scene IV.

Enter Philo, *and four Citizens drunk.*

Phil. Troth, we were merry! Is not this better than
Small beer and homilies?
1 *Cit.* Yes; but methinks
I cannot find my feet!
2 *Cit.* Nor I my head,
But by the noise in 't! Now, were I scholar,
Would I confute philosophy, and prove
The world went round.
3 *Cit.* Faith, neighbour, at this time
I could say somewhat to that point.
4 *Cit.* If so,
It had been roasted to a coal ere now!
Phil. Or raw, or roasted, what is that to us?
1 *Cit.* Ay, let it round until the spit do crack!
Give me more drink!—[*Knocks.*]—Sirrah! boy! rogue! more drink!

Enter Drawer.

Draw. Anon! anon, sir!
Speak in the Mitre, Christopher! What lack you, gentlemen?
2 *Cit.* Some drink, you rogue! some drink! And do you hear me?
The best i' the cellar! We trouble you but seldom.
Draw. Please you to walk up, gentlemen?
3 *Cit.* No; we'll take it here.
Draw. I wait upon you presently, gentlemen.
4 *Cit.* I've drunk enough, but I'll be rul'd! Whoop, Ambrose!
What—all-a-mort? [*Claps him on the shoulder.*
2 *Cit.* I am not satisfied!
But as a man would say, how do you? and so forth.
Phil. Why, what's the matter, man? Art thou that Greek
That knockst men underboard by scores, and cry'st
Have ye any more that must be drunkified?

Enter DRAWER, *and fills.*

Set out your hand, or hang you !—here's this to you !

4 *Cit.* I know what troubles him ! The Court is broke,
And most of 'um lie leiger * in his book !

Phil. 'Tis not all lost—'twill serve at last for waste-paper.
If that be all, give him his drink—fill 't up !

2 *Cit.* What was 't ?

Phil. Andronicus, his health !

2 *Cit.* Away with 't ! [*Leaves some.*

Phil. I must not bate you that !

4 *Cit.* Come, drink it off !
He's a brave person !

2 *Cit.* He's a man indeed—
He paid me honestly. Then down it goes
If it were a mile to bottom. Here's to thee, Greg !

3 *Cit.* With all my heart ! He kept a princely house :
One might have been drunk in his cellar with a good conscience—it cost a man nothing !

1 *Cit.* The most affable man
I never met ! You could not speak to him
But he'd be bare as soon as you.

4 *Cit.* He ow'd me
Some monies at his banishment ! I was paid,
And without sending for 't : Not many courtiers
Have such good memories.

3 *Cit.* A few such men
Would make tradesmen live. Bless him, say I !

Phil. So ! it begins to work. [*Aside.*

Enter two others, drunk and singing—Ta ! la ! la ! la ! la ! la !—To them a Fiddler.

Plague o' these fools !—they'll put it off again !
[*Aside.*

Fid. Please you, have any music, gentlement ? A

* Passive. Literally, an ambassador resident at a foreign court.

dainty, fine, merry, new song! There is none but I and my boy. Sirrah, come forth! Where are you? I have not lost you in the crowd, have I?

Enter a tall well-set Fellow.

Phil. A pretty child-chopper!

1, 2, 3 *Cit.* Ay, ay! Strike up—strike up!

4, 5, 6 *Cit.* Scrape, rogues, scrape! [*They play.*

3 *Cit.* But shan't we have a song too?

Omnes. Ay—ay—ay—ay—ay!

Fid. A merry drinking song, and 't like your worships?

Omnes. Ay—ay—ay!—that—that—[*he sings.*]—"Fill—fill up, and"—

Fill, fill up the bowl,
And about let it trowl,
'Tis a magical spell against sorrow!
It makes a man sing,
Hey! derry, derry, ding!
And ne'er busy his brains with to-morrow.

'Tis the beggar's ease,
And his charm against the fleas;
It recovers the man that did dwindle!
It makes a stiff giant
Both active and pliant,
And a cripple turn round like a spindle.

It cares not a straw
For the Justice or his law;
It fears neither spies nor reporters;
It makes all the house
Lie as snug as a mouse,
And a petticoat sleep without porters.

1 *Cit.* How now, brother? whence came you?

6 *Cit.* Even from where it was, or, as a man may say,
The more the merrier: we have been drinking
The best man's health in Europe.

3 *Cit.* Then here's to you—
The second best!
6 *Cit.* Who's that?
3 *Cit.* Andronicus!
6 *Cit.* 'Twas his I meant.
5 *Cit.* We cannot have 't too oft.
6 *Cit.* Come, then, away with 't!
[*They drink round.*
Phil. Now 's my only time.—[*Aside.*
What say you, gentlemen? You all confess
He is a noble person?
Omnes. As ever liv'd.
1 *Cit.* Wise!
3 *Cit.* Bounteous!
4 *Cit.* Valiant!
2 *Cit.* Everything!
5 *Cit.* And deserves everything.
6 *Cit.* And would he had everything!
Phil. Why, so; I see
You're understanding men, and may be trusted.
Look over this. [*He gives them a long roll.*
4 *Cit.* Here are a thousand hands.
Phil. Yes, ten at least!
I'm sure 't 'as cost my lord and me five days [*Aside.*
To scribble their ugly fists.
2 *Cit.* Let's see what is 't?

1 *Cit.* [*Reads.*] "The humble petition and address of the citizens and inhabitants of Constantinople,—Showeth," *etc.* Hang 't—give me a pen! I had rather set my hand to 't unsight and unseen than to trouble my head to read it over. [*Subscribes.*

4 *Cit.* Sure, there can be no hurt in 't; there are so many hands to 't.

Phil. You may be sure of that.
3 *Cit.* What is it, then?
Phil. Why, you congratulate his safe return,
And pray him he would assist the Emperor.
Alas, good Prince! he'll have a heavy trouble of 't!

5 *Cit.* Assist! hum!—that is as much as to say,
Assist—or so——

6 *Cit.* Ay, neighbour, ay; 'tis plain.

5 *Cit.* Not so plain as you make it, neither. Give me the pen! I cannot write, but I can make a G for John.

3 *Cit.* And I a K for Christopher.

6 *Cit.* I cannot read, but I can write—when I have written it any one may read it! [*They all subscribe.*

[*Nine others pass the stage.*

2 *Cit.* Hoop, holiday! What! 's hell broke loose? What are you?

Tai. Tailors, so please you, sir.

2 *Cit.* Oh! tailors! One man set his mark for you all.

Phil. They look like honest men! Come, gentlemen; subscribe, subscribe!

[*They all subscribe.*

Enter a seventh CITIZEN.

7 *Cit.* How now, my masters? Shearing of hogs? All cry and no wool? What's the matter?

2 *Cit.* Subscribe, subscribe!

Phil. Nothing but set your hand to petition.

7 *Cit.* For aught I know, it may be treason twenty years hence. Not I, beloved!

3 *Cit.* Not you? Why not you?—will you be wiser than the best o' th' parish?

4 *Cit.* And city too—will you?

2 *Cit.* Show him the President's hand there.

7 *Cit.* Oho! I'm satisfied.

Phil. Come, come; subscribe! [*He subscribes.*

2 *Cit.* But, hark you! how shall we get this presented?

Phil. The President's an honest gentleman, and loves the city: I hope he will do't.

2 *Cit.* Away, away! let's to him!

Omnes. Ay—ay—ay!

Fid. Please your worships to remember the music!

5 *Cit.* Music, you rogue! I'd have made better upon a gridiron!

1 *Cit.* Or I with a key and tongs.

2 *Cit.* Hang 'um—hang 'um! we have done with 'um!

Phil. There, sirrah! [*Gives him money.*

Fid. I thank your worship.

3 *Cit.* Hold, hold! let him do somewhat for his money before he goes. Has he subscribed?

4, 5, 6 *Cit.* No—no—no; he has not yet, but he shall.

Fid. What your worships please.—[*Subscribes.*]—Is there any more?

4, 5, 6 *Cit.* No—no—no! enough, enough, good Mr. Scraper. [*Exeunt, reeling.*

ACT III.—SCENE I.

Enter ANDRONICUS, *solus.*

And. It hits, and now my work's as good as done;
But I must cast more blinds, for fear it be
Too soon discover'd. One would not think how 't takes
That I have added fifty friars to pray
For the curst soul of Manuel! "See his revenge,
Good prince!" the people cry. 'Twas necessary.
Nothing established Cæsar's statues more
Than re-erecting those of conquer'd Pompey!
I must yet farther be their advocate
For liberty against restrictive laws,
And make whatever's their concernment mine.
Thus shall I steal the power, and the dull beast
Not dream it lost until it feel where 'tis.
Then 'twill be time, and not till then, to hew
Th' imperial cedar, and stop the people's mouths
With a few sticks and chips—'twill warm their hands
When t' other is forgot! The dog that fought
To save his master's wallet, when he could not
Defend it longer, ate for company;
And so will they. If not, necessity,

That has no law herself, shall coin one for it!
All things are lawful to their end: that war
Is just that's necessary, and those arms religious
Where a man cannot well be safe without them.
Then shall I triumph, when I make the Empire
Shrink at my weight and truckle under me,
Trample the world, and frighten fate to feel
A thread so stubborn as to twist her wheel!

Enter STEPHANUS.

How fares my lov'd Stephanus?
Ste. As ever;
Your highness' vassal.
And. Fie, my friend! we're one!
How does our friend Basilius?
Ste. He's well,
And better employ'd.
And. As how?
Ste. He's with his cousin,
A cunning sophister, that always followed
The rising sun! He now begins to find
It may be lawful. Give him but your hand
He shall be patriarch; my life! he brings
A text to make it out!
And. So; ply him there.
And put it to him what he thinks if an oath
Of being true and faithful to Alexius
Were set on foot. 'Twould be a handsome cloak!
Ste. But do more hurt than good; for, if you add
His successors,—as I believe you mean,—
We shall be ripe too soon, and easy smok'd!
And. Why? I shall be his successor, and then
The oath will reach to me.
Ste. That will be nothing,
Nor stand you much in stead. Suppose you were
Now Emperor, and 'twere now put about,
You'd find few boggle at it but such as could
Do you no hurt. These oaths are dangerous things:
They conceal enemies and make no friends!
One will be true enough without it; t' other

Will not regard it. He that's forced to take
An oath, straight makes a second not to keep it!
You're only sure of him whom, by believing
To be what you would have him, you make so.

And. But yet the greater number will swallow it.
Oaths are the same to them as rattles to children;
It makes the cheat pass easy—slide, as 'twere.

Ste. Howe'er, 'tis ticklish. Some cur or other
May find it out, and bark, and all the rest
Open for company. Then we shall have
Nothing but jealousies, distrusts, and fears;
News upon news, petition on petition;
Laws, liberties, religion, all at stake,
And will be lost, unless these geese, forsooth,
Cackle, and save the capitol!

And. Honest Stephanus!
[*Hugs him.*

Ste. Your actions will be table-talk; disputed
In barbers' shops and bakehouses; each slip
Be made a fault, and every fault a crime!
Then shall your oath be brought upon the rack—
Whether 'twere lawfully imposed, or you
Capable of receiving it; or, if so,
How far it binds. "No faith with tyrants!" says one.
"With robbers!" another cries. And then, how easy
'Twill be to make you one or both, especially
When they that give the sentence make the case,
I leave it to your highness.

And. My best friend!
[*Hugs him again.*
But somewhat must be done to blind the people.

Ste. Keep them but moving, they will ne'er mind you;
Do you but shake the tree, they'll pick the fruit,
And busy enough! But lest, when all is gone,
They should look up to see who 'twas that did it,
You must provide your mask; and of this kind—
None better than religion! Your highness
Knows how to wear it to the best advantage.
'Tis a rare servant, but a scurvy master!

And. Then you think best to let alone the oath—
At least not press it?
Ste. Yes; by any means—
You'll find an hundred safer ways.
And. We'll talk the rest within. These giddy fools
Are hunting out Basilius, and may chance
To 'light on me too soon!
Ste. I wait your highness!
[*Exeunt.*

SCENE II.

Enter PHILO *and* CITIZENS.

Phil. How say you, my masters? Who shall make the speech?
So many of us, and not one gifted brother?
2 *Cit.* Time was I could have done my part. The Prince—
And no disparagement—might have heard it too.
Phil. And ne'er the wiser. [*Aside.*
3 *Cit.* Troth, my pump is dry!
Phil. This is your drinking—I have often told you.
1 *Cit.* Have but a little patience! Yonder's one
Will end the controversy! Do but observe
How hard he wrings and squeezes. Somewhat's coming!
Phil. What!—he with that parenthesis about his mouth?
By no means, gentlemen; 'tis ominous—
Whatever comes between 't may be left out!
4 *Cit.* I'm satisfied; 'tis but a good speech lost!
Good master Philo, be that office yours.
Omnes. A Philo!—A Philo!—Philo!—Philo!
Phil. Ay, now the matter 's mended.
Omnes. Give 't him—give 't him!
[*They give him the petition.*
Phil. Well, if I must, what remedy?
Omnes. He comes!

Enter BASILIUS.

Phil. Save you, most worthy sir! I am commanded
By the inhabitants and citizens
Of this great city to present you this,
And beg your favour and assistance in 't.
[*Delivers the roll.* BASILIUS *reads to himself.*

1 *Cit.* Hang the rogue, how he trowls it out!

2 *Cit.* His tongue runs on wheels!

Bas. In troth, my masters, 'tis a noble thing,
And well advis'd—nay, and becoming men
That love their country! But I'm half afraid
He'll not accept it; he's so humble-minded,
You'll hardly draw him to 't! Howe'er, I'll try.

Omnes. We thank your honour.

1 *Cit.* I hope you will prevail.

2 *Cit.* I should be sorry else.

5 *Cit.* So should I that e'er I set my hand to 't.

Enter ANDRONICUS.

Phil. Stand off! he comes himself!
Long live your highness!

Omnes. Long live the founder of our liberty!

And. I thank you, gentlemen. But may I serve you?

Omnes. Long live the public Father!—Live Andronicus!

Bas. My lord, these gentlemen—both in their own
And friends' behalf—have made me promise them
That I'd present you this—[*delivers the roll.*]—Nor must your highness
Make me denial. Their request is short,—
That you'd be pleas'd to ease Alexius' years
By bearing half the burden of the crown.
Nor do I think you will disdain a part,
Though you deserve the whole. And thus, of old,
The Roman Senate to Marcellus join'd
Delaying Fabius*—age and youth together—
A wholesome mixture, where the one brought eyes,
The other hands—this, action; he, advice!

* Fabius, *Cunctator.*

Thus must the body of the Grecian State
Be wisely temper'd, lest we rue 't too late!

And. What kind of voice is this I hear? My friends
Either forget, or know not what they ask.
Joint Emperor! Were there no treason in 't,
I must not hearken to 't! Who would be clogg'd
With gyves, though made of gold?—for such are crowns—
Or stoop to take one up that knew the weight of 't?
Crowns are thick set with cares—for every gem
An hundred doubts and troubles! Nor are their ermine
More spotted than their fate; whilst privacy
Lies low, 'tis true, but yet that low is safe.
Thunder ploughs up the hills when valleys 'scape,
And rives tall cedars when the shrubs go free!
Sleep dwells in cottages, not thrones—content
In humble cells; whilst greatness is at odds
With everything, nay, and itself to boot!
Let others grasp at all, and by great pains
Aspire to greater! Let them vex the world;
They but disquiet themselves. He only lives
That's beneath envy and above contempt.
Be it enough that I have served my country
Thus long; that I have freed her from the yoke;
Broke all her fetters! You have had my youth;
Let me enjoy my age! 'Twere too severe
To have had one and yet deny me t' other.

Phil. That was well hinted, master. Excellent fox! [*Aside.*

Omnes. Andronicus! Andronicus! Long live Andronicus!

5 *Cit.* We've brought ourselves into a dainty noose.

1 *Cit.* Good sir, persuade him!

Bas. I must not leave your highness so.
Whom can Greece think more worthy than yourself?
Where should she pay most but where most is owing?
Let me prevail, my lord! This day shall be
Writ in a scarlet text, since hence we date
The happiness and new birthday of the State!

And. 'Tis strange, my friends, that you should press me thus,
And put my modesty to a blush! Can Greece
So far forget herself?—can Greece, so full
Of able Statesmen, Greece o'ershoot herself?
Who hath bewitcht thee? With what spectacles
Didst thou look on my merit, that th' 'ast made
So fair a letter in so small a print?
Andronicus deserve a crown! Alas!
Greece is mistook! I have one foot i' th' grave;
And can you think it sightly to behold
The other in a throne? No! Graves and thrones
Hold least proportion. You say you love me!
Show 't now, and dazzle not those eyes again
Which I thought shut to vanity. I am
Content, and what can Providence add more?
Not that I tell you this as I were lazy,
Or sullen, or refus'd to serve my country!
Far be it from me! No—we were not born
To live like hedgehogs, roll'd in our own down,
And turn out bristles to all the world besides:
Yet must we die t' ourselves; and so let me,
Whose age may challenge a writ of ease, and crave
Leave of the world to let me mind my grave!

Omnes. Andronicus! Andronicus! Long live Andronicus!

Ph. 'Tis all in vain to press him now. We'll find
Some other time, when he shall not deny us.

[*Exeunt with a shout. Manet* ANDRONICUS.

And. What is this giddy multitude?—this beast
Of many heads?—this thing *vox populi?*
It can do all—as much or more than fate:
Raise and pull down, make and annihilate!
Yet see, how easy 'tis to cast a gloss
Before those vulgar eyes—those leaden souls
Begotten in a dream! *Ex traduce*—
How natural is it for fire to climb!
And could they think a man—nay, more, a Prince—
Born near a crown, of such a frozen spirit
That Empire could not thaw? Come, come! I must

Play my cards handsomely; and though I yield—
As who would not?—make them believe it is
Through importunity, not my desire!
I'll slip the vizard first, then let it hang
Till it fall off of 'tself! Thus, while they woo,
I'll have my ends, and they beholding, too! [*Exit.*

SCENE III.

Enter CONTO, LAPARDAS, *and* DUCAS.

Cont. Observ'd you not the tumult? I've scarce heard
A fuller cry! I wonder what it means!
La. Where has your lordship been?—nothing, but treason,
Is more familiar! 'Tis a petition
To have Andronicus joint Emperor!
Du. And backt, they say, with twenty thousand hands,
Besides some great ones! But, to give him's due,
He has refus'd it. If he ha'n't, I'll swear
Mamalus was a witch!
Cont. Why, what of him?
La. His name slipt from me unawares. Good faith,
He guess'd at this, unluckily, long since!
But make no words of 't; it may do him wrong.
Cont. 'Tis spoken to a stone; yet, troth, I'm glad
He has denied it. Say he should be honest?
Du. I cannot see his drifts. Would he have took it,
He might have had it now ere it took air,
And we in no condition to prevent it.
La. What say you if we went and waited on him,
Took notice of the thing, and thankt his virtue?
Cont. I like it well!
Du. Then let us not delay it!
[*As they are going out they are met and stopt by* MARIA, CONSTANTINUS, *and* MAMALUS.
Mar. My lords, well met! But whither? You are posting
Who shall be first to kiss the rising sun?

La. No, no; there's nothing in 't. Besides, you, madam,
Know we've his honour and his oath engag'd!
Mar. Oh! w' hear you have! And yet I'll scarce believe,
Though I have reason to suspect, he'll break them!
Du. There is hope yet—he has refus'd the offer!
Mam. To make them hotter on 't. Good gentleman,
He's modest, and may chance to want entreaty.
Const. Perhaps the cry was faint and weak! There wanted
More curs to yelp, and hounds to mouth it out!
It was some time before he join'd with us;
But yet at last you saw——
Mam. I fear me, more
Than you'll be fairly rid on. Enemies
Are ten times easier kept out than thrown out!
Mar. But had this rabble no head? He is too cunning
To trust a giddy multitude!
Const. They say
It was the city president!
Cont. Most likely—
He's one that would be great, at any rate.
Const. Ay, here's the hand, but where's the spring that moves it?
Mam. The cobweb doth not cover the spider so
But I can see him work. This must be old
Basilius; I trace him by his cousin!
They two are hand and glove; only, one acts
What t'other's asham'd to own! That holy men
Must, like the holy language, be thus read backward!
Mar. But what would make him do 't? I'm sure my father
Preferr'd him well!
Mam. But can he make him Patriarch?
You'll say he's dead, and can't; then blame him not
To strike up interest with him that may.
T'other's forgot. Besides, ambitious men,
When they stand still, fancy they're going back.

Thus, much he has already only tells him
How much more's wanting; and what was a sum
In the desire, enjoy'd is but a cipher!

Mar. Prithee, Mamalus, do not draw the devil
More ugly than he is!

Mam. Nor you, good madam,
Believe him fairer! Don't we know the tree
By its fruit, and judge of men by actions,
Not fair pretences? You forget our proverb—
Remember to distrust! This easy faith
Has done more mischief than it e'er did good.

La. Had we believ'd your words, this had ne'er been.

Mam. As how, my leaky lord? These bor'd barrels!
[*Aside.*

La. Nay, be not angry, man! We are all friends,
And may be free! We'll live and die together!

Mar. No heats among ourselves, good gentlemen!
[ANDRONICUS *from behind the hangings.*

And. Yonder they are, i'faith! I'll stumble on them!
Now for a neat disguise, and all's my own!
[*A shout within.*

Mar. Hark! hark! What's this?

Mam. Ev'n the old rout again!
This will be somewhat at last, or I'm mistaken!

Enter ANDRONICUS, *as angry, and speaking to some within.*

And. Plague of these fools, and those that set them on!
What do they trouble me? Tell them I cannot,
Or if I could I would not! Have they none
To bait but me?

Mar. Save your good majesty!

And. My friends, and all! Is this the thanks you give me?—
This the reward I have? Who but a madman
Would serve his country? Who would warm a snake
That knew its nature? For such 'tis to me!
Was 't your design, when first you call'd me home,
To make me miserable that made you happy?

Who courted you? Did I? No! Heaven knows
'Twas otherwise! If not, you, madam, can
Be my compurgatrix. Nor think it strange
I talk this rate. Your ugly jealousy,
As closely as you carry 't, is cause enough.
Nay, I am right—I found it in your looks
Before this lady spake it. Is 't my crime
The people's mad?—or must my innocence
Suffer because they know not what they would?
You'll say, perhaps, I have been offer'd Empire!
But have I took it? That I might have been,
And am not, judge yourselves whether it speaks
My virtue more or your ingratitude.
Would he that told the people's heat had told you
My frosty answer: that had done me right!
But now I see good deeds are writ in ice,
And the least groundless jealousy in steel.
Let me remember once—but to forget it
Ever hereafter—I have serv'd you truly,
Done myself injury to be kind to you,
And wrought my own disquiet to lighten yours.
You know necessity first made me arm;
And, by whatever's good, there's nothing less
Shall make me keep it up! Then doubt not him
Whom you have tried. Could you believe I would?
Certain you could not!

La. My lord, I'm satisfied; and thank your highness
You took the pains to do 't.

Cont. The same am I.

Omnes. And all of us. [MAMALUS *skews his lip.*

And. Then pray continue so
Until you find me otherwise.

Omnes. We shall,
Your highness. [*Exeunt.*

And. Madam, I'll wait on you;
But I must chide you first! You've been unkind;
Good faith, you have. Distrust a friend? Nay, one
You knew so long, and might so well command!
I ha'n't deserv'd it.

Mar. Good my lord, forgive me!

I lov'd my brother well, and was afraid
What such a tumult might——

And. Hang them! D'you think
I'd ruin what you, the glory of your sex,
Took so much pains to save?

Mar. Nay, good my lord!

And. I'm yet too low. Th' 'ast a brave noble soul,
And such as might redeem a perisht world,
But that 'tis done already.

Mar. Nay—now—my lord!

And. I've done! But shall I never see the noble Cæsar,
Your husband, here? I'm sure the Empire wants him!

Mar. I would you could, but I'm afraid you won't;
His ague hath so shaken him in pieces!

And. I'm sorry for 't. He ne'er was well together. [*Aside.*
He has my prayers and wishes.

Mar. Thank your lordship. [*Exeunt.*

SCENE IV.

Enter MANUEL *and* PHILO.

Man. But tell me, Philo—prithee, tell me how
Thou cam'st in this great credit with my father?

Phil. Oh, sir, I've been his servant many years.
He bred me from a boy to what you see—
Trust and employment can do mighty things!

Man. How gatst th' into that trust?

Phil. As other men:
By seeming fool, yet such a one as might be
Fit matter for the knave; by bearing injuries,
And thanking them—at least, dissembling—
Till I had power to act a safe revenge.

Man. Suppose that never came?

Phil. Then I forgave them.

Man. I see th' 'ast studied the point. Prithee, teach me

Some of those little arts.
Phil. Call you them little?
As little as they are, they govern the world.
Man. 'Tis well 'tis ignorant how little governs it.
But on!
Phil. Since 'tis your pleasure, I shall. Who would
Grow to an oak, he must be first a twig,
Supple and pliant, bow with every wind;
He's long a growing up, but sure to stand
When t'other shows his roots. He must speak well
Of all in place, no matter what they are—
It is enough they're there.
Nature ne'er made so great a beast but somewhat
Might be said for it. Is the subject dirty?—
Wrap 't in clean linen. For example, now—
Is he a downright fool?—call him good-natur'd.
A babbler, sociable; a railler, witty;
If scoffing, pleasant; if malicious, subtle;
If vicious, affable; if foolhardy, daring;
If given to ribaldry, a merry gentleman;
All noise, a learned man; if he says nothing,
He thinks the more, and has a working brain;
If impudent, a handsome confidence!
They're very near allied, and only differ
I' the success. Is he thick-skulled and stupid?—
A modest man, and has an excellent wit,
But an odd art of keeping 't to himself.
What though the shop be thin?—the warehouse has 't.
Has he the Statesman's tread?—a wise man, no doubt.
If we perceive a river run dark and slow,
We straight pronounce it deep, and ne'er examine
Whether the mud at bottom be the cause.
Is he all apophthegm?—a shrewd man.
What matter though he want a trifling circumstance
Of sense and pertinence—what's that to us?
What hurt's in all this? Do not we call
Our pretty ladies civil obliging women?
And shall we be less modest to their husbands?
Man. How have I liv'd i' th' dark! I always call'd

A spade a spade; but now I see my knave's
Your thriving man.

Phil. Believe them what you please,
But treat them like honest men—t'other's so broad.
And what's your lordship better when you've done 't?
They know 't as well as you.

Man. Th' art a rare fellow!
Thou that hast this hast more.

Phil. Why, troth, not much!
He must swear everything, and, if need be,
Forswear 't again; but still beware it be
Done with a tenderness. He must own nothing
Laid by, nor boggle at anything cried up;
And for his conscience, he must split the hair
'Twixt techy and prostitute. The one
Flies in his face, the other makes him cheap.
Lastly, for his religion, since 'tis necessary
He have a show at least, chuse 't, as men bells,
By the sound, or we our magistrates, by th' poll.

Man. But does the world do this?

Phil. How think you, sir?
Do they eat, drink, or sleep?

Man. Wherever I come
I find it damn'd!

Phil. And reason good. The people
May chance to smoke it else. Who first discover'd it
Put teeth in the sheeps' mouths! You cannot fleece them
Now but they'll bite! No! he must still decry it;
But to believe himself, not worth his while.

Man. And dost not thou? What pity 'tis these parts
Should be thus lost in low, ignoble arts!—
Such little nothings! Leave them—I'll prefer thee!

Phil. Defend me from a lecture!—[*Aside.*]—'Tis no more
Than what my betters have done, and thriv'd by, too.

Man. Yet, let me beg thee, leave it. What is got
By such base means is but an empty blaze—
Crackles a while in talk, but quickly gone!
'Tis not too late for to be virtuous yet.

What's done already may have rather been
The vice of thy employment than thy nature.
What say'st thou, man?

Phil. I was ne'er obstinate.

Man. Let me instruct thee, then. And yet, Heav'n knows,
How much I want myself, yet I may serve
To light a candle to thee. Couldst thou but see
What virtue were, thou wouldst prevent my wish.
'Tis a continual spring and harvest both—
Bears fruits and blossoms, sows and reaps at once,
So quick is the return, and certain, too!
And as in equal temperatures the pulse
Beats true and even, so here she's still the same—
Not swol'n with good things nor cast down with bad;
Free, without cheapness; composed, without formality;
Calm, without dulness; active, without weariness;
And, in the want of everything, is all!
How sayest thou, Philo? Wilt thou have her, man?

Phil. No ready money, sir? Half one, half t' other,
Were somewhat like. I hearken to your lordship.

Man. Whose are the quiet sleeps but the virtuous?
Who valiant but they?—not brutish valour,
But such as dare die in cold blood.
Who honourable but they? Honour, without virtue,
Is what the people pleases, not our own.
Who are religious but they? Without it,
Religion's but a soul without a body,
A painted butterfly, a specious nothing;
Whilst join'd, they make a perfect harmony.
This is a virtuous man—fear neither drives him
Nor favour draws aside; he values not
The curled wrinkles of a tyrant's brow;
He's still serene, and tires as well the wit
As power of torture, and enjoys them too.
Such is his man's estate; and when old age
Has seized the outworks, he's secure within,
And is so far from wishing youth again,
He's only sorry that he e'er was young!
Come, I must make thee virtuous! Follow me! [*Exit.*

Phil. I cannot tell,
[*As he is going out* PHILO *speaks aside.*
But I half doubt myself.
One such a lecture more,—and good night, master!
Farewell, good, honest Philo!—How it sounds!
[*He startles.*
Had I a puling gizzard now, 'twere done;
But—soft and fair goes far. [*Exit.*

SCENE V.

Enter ANDRONICUS, STEPHANUS, *and* BASILIUS. *Shouts within.*

And. What would you have me do?
Ste. Troth, play no longer!—
Pardon the language,—they are all agog,
And may do mischief.
Bas. If you slip this minute,
You may wait long enough ere you get another.
If once they settle, all our labour 's lost—
They'll understand themselves. Besides, you're gone
Too far to go no farther.
And. You mistake me;
I am resolved upon it. What before
Look'd like ambition is but safety now.
I only stop'd awhile, as doubting whether
'Twere fit t' accept it yet.
Ste. What said the Lords?
And. Most satisfied; only Mamalus's face
Spake more than his tongue durst.
Bas. Puh! he's but one,
And may be made; at least be taken off,
By the old way—preferment, or his head.
And. But there are others, and not least concern'd,—
The sober party, that have stakes to lose.
The age is too refined for men to walk
Invisible. They ha'n't been dealt with yet.
Ste. 'Tis one o' th' greatest follies in the world

For to believe the world wiser than 'tis.
Call me a junto! They shall do it for you!
You'll ne'er want men until you want preferment.
And. That were to let them see I needed them—
Put a sword in their hands, and make myself
Less than I am, them more than they should.
Bas. How will y' avoid it? There is no other way
To fix and settle. Then you'll plead consent;
Nor will it be difficult to bring them to 't.
The people are like sheep—'tis better driving
A flock than one.
And. But say they should prove sullen?—
Unravel my title?
Ste. You must venture that;
'Tis easy turning them to grass again.
By all means let them meet, though they do nothing
But set the rates of tripes and pudding pies.
And. Well, be it so. And now, my friend, you may
Rally your rabble-regiment again!
Tell them—I accept it. [*Exit* BASILIUS.
Ste. I'll secure your highness
They shall not squabble for want of work! Myself
Has cut out more than they'll make up in haste.
Nor shall their speed be more than we think good;
Whilst, though wise men propose, fools must debate it.
[*Shout within.*
And. Now, how I love my genius!—[*hugs him.*]—
Let's keep here.
All will be well enough! And though I cannot
Make the deaf adder hear, I'll be sure this—
To charm him so, he shall not dare to hiss! [*Exeunt.*
[*Shouts within, proclaiming* ANDRONICUS.

Act iv.—Scene i.

Enter Alexius *and* Andronicus.

Alex. No longer cousin now, but dearest brother,
You're welcome to a burthen, and I'm glad
I've got so good a partner in the throne!

And. Great sir, I thank you, and—have been so used
To downright honesty—I believe you too!
It is enough to me that I'm your servant,
The partner of your cares and not your throne!
Yet who'd be great, when at the best 'tis but
A better sort of slavery, a handsome gaol,
And—what the worst of gaols is free from—envied?
Could you believe that in this little time
I should be struck at, and through your sides too?
What is my fault? If to have done them good
Be such, 'tis mine. If to have broke my rest,
That they might sleep secure, be crime, I'm guilty.

Alex. Alas! I'm sorry for 't, and cannot yet
Conjecture what you mean.

And. Please you, read this.

[Andronicus *gives him a paper.*

Alex. How's this?
Belgrade betrayed unto the King of Hungary?

And. It should have been; and had not I stalk'd with them,
It had been now too late to ask whose work 'twas.

Alex. What are the persons? They must be considerable.

And. And so they are.

Alex. But have you taken any?

And. Yes, divers; and on one a council of war
Has pass'd and sentenced. Please you, sign the warrant?

Alex. Gi' me 't; and, lest relation may sway me,
I'll ne'er inquire the name.—[*Signs it.*]—Yet let me see 't!

How now!—What's this?—My mother Empress?—
Hold!
Make me a Nero?—Take away her life
That gave me mine?
And. Have but a little patience,
And if I don't convince you, o' my honour
I'll give 't you back again. Consider it—
A frontier, a whole province in effect,
A little kingdom!—All the fate of Greece
Attends its fortune.
Alex. But we have it still.
And. What matter is 't? Then you believe no treason
Unless the Prince be kill'd?
Alex. But 'tis my mother!
And. Justice respects no persons, crowns, no kindred;
And fathers of their country know no mothers!
Alex. As if one could not be a Prince unless
He put off man! Come; you are too severe!
She is my mother!—Let a cloister serve.
And. Severe? Know I'm joint Emperor, and can
Do it myself, but that I would not rob you
The glory of the action. This will break
The neck of treason, when the age shall see
Such signal justice done upon a mother.
Alex. That shall not I.
And. Then let the Empire sink!
I'll never mind it more, nor break my sleep
To force a happiness on one that slights it!
Here—take your paper! but lest it be said
You did once well and straight repented it,
I thus dispose it. [*Tears a wrong paper and burns it.*
Alex. 'Tis all one. I thank you! [*Exit.*
And. 'Tis done! and your game's next! See—here's the warrant!
'Twas a wrong paper burnt! What excellent mortar
Blood makes! Rome batten'd in 't, and, from the ruins
Of Alba and the slaughter'd world, grew up
To what she was; and so must I the same.

'Tis not enough that I'm got up myself,
But I must beat down others—level all
That stand before or near me! I'm not safe
While young Alexius lives, or—which is worse—
Has a friend left him. He has many, and great ones,
And might be worth my fear could they but fix
Or know their strength. But there are only two
Considerable; that's Constantinus and Mamalus—
Honest and able both. For all the rest,
Would all my friends were what they think themselves,
My enemies, what they are! Yet, as they are,
They made me what I am, and may again
Crush me to nothing if I don't prevent them
By giving the first blow, and putting 't home!
Thus, thus it must. Nor can I sleep secure
Till they have slept their last, and fall together
Wrapt in one common fate. None ever rack'd
A grave to find the man he fear'd or hated.
The rest will follow. 'Tis but using well
The present time, and working on emergencies.
Things counsel men, and not men counsel things!

Enter MANUEL.

How now, my Manuel? Thus you see my pains
To make you happy!

Man. Would yourself were such!

And. Small time will do 't—Rome was not built at once!

Man. And better she'd continued cottage still,
Than built on rapine, or enlarged with blood.
The tears of orphans and the curse of widows
Rot not i' th' air!

And. Away, you fool! The fox
Fares best when he is curst. 'Tis a sure sign
H' 'as done his work. But to be serious—Tell me
Whether a man may not preserve himself?
Or whether all things that are tending to 't
May not be lawful, at least excusable?

Man. Thereafter, as they are; though this I'll grant you—

Peace without safety is a bare cessation,
No laying down of arms.
And. Th' 'ast hit the nail!
Come! you must help me. See this executed!
[*Gives* MANUEL *the warrant.* MANUEL *startles.*
What makes you startle? Let me have it done!
Man. Done! Were I satisfied o' th' crime—which yet,
The people say, was rather packt than proved,—
There's no such dearth of hangmen that your son
Need take the office.
And. Stranger to my blood,
And never true begot!
Have I for this run through so many hazards?
Ventured so far to make a villain great
That never had a soul above a dunghill?
See it be done, and quickly! or——
Man. I cannot;
And, which is more, I shall not! Disobedience
Is virtue here. If you suspect my courage,
Try 't yet again. Show me your enemy,
And, were he guarded with ten thousand devils,
I'll through and through but I will reach his head,
Or lose my own! But this—is such a thing,
Honour and conscience, justice, all forbid it!
And. What are those private toys to me? Kings may
Do what they list.
Man. But can they do 't by law?
And. By law, you blockhead! Doth not Justice sit
At Jupiter's elbow? What cannot power do,
And justify 't when done? He that can nothing
But what is lawful, reigns by courtesy.
Besides, what use of laws? Good kings may live
Without them; bad ones will not much regard them.
Had Alexander squared his actions
By common justice, he had never wept
The want of worlds. Or had Rome giv'n back
To every one their own, how had she sate—
Like Æsop's jay—stript of her pilfer'd plumes,
And fairly march'd to her first huts again!

Weigh crowns by th' balance, and you'll make fine work!
Preach laws to sword-men! Out! [*Exit* MANUEL.

At another door, enter STEPHANUS.

This squeamish slave
Will be my ruin, and his own in mine!
Welcome, my better self! You must see this
[ANDRONICUS *gives* STEPHANUS *the warrant for execution.*
Despatch'd, and quickly! If the people grumble,
Produce your warrant. Tell them how hard I stood
To have preserv'd her, but I could not do 't.
How says my Stephanus?

Enter PHILO.

Ste. I say—'tis done!
And. 'Twas my good angel's voice. Good luck attend it!
[*Exit* STEPHANUS.
Now, honest Philo! how goes your work on?
Phil. As well as heart can wish—the stag is lodg'd,
And my hounds ready.
And. But dost know them well?
Have they been enter'd, flush'd in blood before?
I hate the fearful hands.
Phil. Ne'er doubt them, sir.
There's not a man among them but has been
Kick'd out of all the sanctuaries in Europe.
Whoever speaks of young Alexius next
Shall only say, He was!
And. 'Twas bravely said!
Come—we have more to do! [*Exeunt.*

Scene II.

Enter Conto, Lapardus, Ducas, Constantinus, *and* Mamalus.

Cont. We have done well, my lords; we've made a rod
To whip ourselves! Right Æsop's frogs, i' faith!
We must be changing! Nay; 'tis well enough.
Lap. For why, my lord? I'm sure my thoughts were clear
As spotless crystal! Could I conceive one drop
Of blood within me traitorous, it should out,
Though 'twere that next my heart!
Du. The same were mine!
I only meant to use him as a purge
To carry ill humours, not our spirits, off.
Const. A fit comparison! We're purg'd indeed—
The remedy proves worse than the disease!
Mam. Ay; you o'ershot the mark! Ere he came in
He was your creature, but your master now.
Const. Where is this perjur'd villain? Sure he believes
The bottomless bag—that lovers' and traitors' oaths
Are lodged together!—[*Shouts.*]—The devil's in this rout!—
More shouting yet?
Lap. And more is like to be.
'Tis thought when fuel fails, they'll pluck down houses
To keep the bonfires up! Did not your lordship
See the instalment?
Const. No; but I have heard
'Twas very splendid.
Cont. Yes; as art could make it.
Mam. So 't should; the trappings of the President's horse
Is more than half i' th' government o' th' city.
Const. But have you seen no public acts of late?

The vizard is half off, the names transpos'd—
Andronicus first, and then Alexius!
Mam. And reason good. Should not the figure stand
Before the cipher? Cæsar and Bibulus!
One does all, t'other drinks all!
Lap. Could he yet stop,
There might be hopes.
Mam. Small hopes. Ambition
Is ne'er so high but she still thinks to mount.
That station, which lately seem'd the top,
Is but a step to her now; and what before
Was even beyond her wish, being once in power,
Seems low and cheap. If I mistake it not,
The Emperor yet lives; and though he is
But the bare shadow of a swelling name,
Can you believe Andronicus will brook
An equal in authority? Is Andronicus
No better known? Well, my good lords, what say you?
Please you to give me leave, and I'll propose
A short expedient?
Omnes. With all our hearts!
Mam. And you engage, however you dislike it,
Not to discourse 't abroad?
Omnes. Upon our honours!
Mam. Then thus: He's yet unsettled. Heavy bodies,
Once mov'd, retain a trembling ere they fix.
So here. The Empire's in a strange confusion,
And 'tis his interest to keep it so.
Now what I offer is this—that every one
Pick out his faction, and oblige it to him.
Get but so far into them as to please them,
You have 'm sure enough. The power to raise them
Follows of course. Then shall we fall upon him
Ere he have time to think, and break his neck
By the same hand that set it!
Const. I like it well;
But cannot judge it safe to trust a tumult
Unless we had a body to make a stand.

Mam. Nor will we want it—we'll but use the people
As a forlorn. And for the rest, what think you
Of Stephanus? I'll pawn my head I make him.
Const. Impossible! He was the chiefest person
Set t'other up.
Mam. But what has he done for him?
He's but the same he was; and, which makes for us,
Has equals, if not superiors, in favour.
I know his spirit can never brook it long.
Do you but give the word, I'll run the hazard.
Const. How say ye, my lords?
Omnes. Worthy Mamalus,
You have our hearts, and thanks, and wishes to 't!

Enter MARIA, *as in haste.*

Const. See! here's more news! I do not like the haste.
Mar. Help! help! my lords!—The Emperor and 's mother!
Omnes. What of them?
Mar. Oh! dead! dead! dead!—Murder'd!
That ever earth should bear so curst a traitor!—
Such a false, treacherous, perfidious slave!
And, which is worse than all, the people cry
A judgment on him for his mother's death!
Const. How!—what's all this? Good madam, divide your grief,
And let us bear a part!
Mar. I know not what 'tis—
Reports are various; but they say he sign'd
A warrant for his mother's execution
For a suppos'd betraying of Belgrade,
And since has broke his neck by a fall from 's horse
As he was hunting! There are others, again,
Say he was bow-string'd! Oh! this curs'd string,
That murders more than e'er the bow kill'd fairly!
That I could see him yet!
Then thus I throw off woman, and bury my tears
In my revenge! Come, lords! Let 't ne'er be said
There's nothing left us of our former greatness

But fame and ruin! Let it ne'er be spoke,
Greece is grown barbarous, and the merry Greek
Has drown'd the valiant!

Const. Most excellent madam!

Mar. Come, let's forgive—ourselves, I mean—that crime
Of ignorance and well-meaning. We that were
The stairs that helpt him up, our backs the steps
By which he climb'd, how are we trampled on!
Come, come, my lords! 'Tis time we look about us,
And ward the threat'ning blow! Let's but agree,
And our work's done! The tortoise is secure
Within her shell; if any part lie out,
It dangers all the rest! What says Mamalus?

Mam. What! But that he owes
Himself and his unto your highness' courage!
We had half drove the nail ere you came in;
But now 'tis riveted! There remains nothing
But that we thank your highness, and keep to it.

Const. Well mov'd! Let's on!

Mar. Do! and you'll find the lion
Is not so terrible as the painter makes him.

Lap. Du. Agreed! agreed! Let's on!

Mar. Bravely resolv'd!
Stars have their strongest influence in conjunction!

[*A clap or two of thunder.*

Const. Hark! hark!—the voice of Heaven! 'T 'as answer'd us,
And seal'd the enterprise! And when I fail it,
Let Heaven strike me as I this earth!

Enter PHILO *with a guard.*

Phil. Stand!—Treason!—Seize them!

Mar. Seize me! For what?

Phil. Oh! your highness,
The Emperor will discharge you presently.

Const. Unhand me, villain! Take that!

[CONSTANTINUS *knocks one of the guard down. After a short scuffle, all seized.*

Phil. So, so! Away with them! [*Exeunt.*

SCENE III.

Enter ANDRONICUS, *solus.*

And. Now I can say I live, and not till now.
I've elbow-room enough, and space to breathe:
I can look round me, too. There's not a tree
That stopt my prospect but I've levell'd it—
At least, am fairly onward. Not a mote
Hung in my light but I have swept it down.
Now, could the subtilest overgrown devil,
Whom age had render'd all experiment,
Done it more cleverly? These foolish lords,
Like Æsop's trees, have lent the axe an helve*
To hew themselves in pieces; and the people
Kindled a fire that shall burn them up.
And let it burn! This is my time to fix
And arm myself against the worst. Th' ascent
To thrones is slippery; the top, shaking;
The fall, a precipice! Men go not down
By the same stairs they climb'd! Yet what of that?
This must defend me!—[*Hands his sword.*]—Cæsar often sheath'd it,
But never laid it by!

Enter ANNA.

But see!—the Empress!
'Twere a good humour now for me, that kill'd
The husband, to make love unto the widow!
For once I'll venture.—[*He kneels.*]—Hail, renowned Empress!

Anna. What would this plague and mischief of our house?
What means he?

And. Duty, Royal madam, and leave
To drop a tear into this ocean! [*Rises.*
Alas! good Emperor! Who can be happy,
When careless fate shall spin a thread so fine

* A handle.

Only to snap 't in two again? Blest youth!
Had virtue, innocence, and all those graces
That build a Prince, and make him more belov'd
Than fear'd, done anything, th' 'adst been here still!
Or could that early majesty, or courage
Beyond thy years, prevail'd, th' 'adst not died yet!
But see our misery, that nothing can
Be happy long but Heav'n must envy it!
He was too good to live!

Anna. Would thou 'adst been so,
I had not lost him, then! Damn'd, cursed man!
How durst thou vent these lies, when thou art he
That didst contrive his murder, and his blood
Yet reeks upon thee?

And. Wrong not my innocence!
By all the virtues of your sex, 'tis false!

Anna. Thou liest!

And. I do not; 'twas a fall from's horse.
By this it was! [*Kisses her hand.*

Anna. P'th! I touch the hand [*She spits at him.*
That is besprinkled with my husband's blood?
The day shall sooner set i' th' east; the west
Shall be sunrising, ere I admit the hand
That took away my husband, kindred, Empire—
Nay, all; but, what's more dear than all, thy hate.
Which, to my sorrow, is the common case
Of all with me, but shall continue fresh
And green, when thy ill-gotten bays shall wither,
And thy perfidious conquests be forgot!

And. Call not my duty conquest. If you knew
With how much trembling I return'd again,
You would have pitied me, at least have judg'd
More favourably. I must change my key. [*Aside.*
But yet admit it conquest. He that did
That can do more. If still eternal hate
Lodgeth in mortal breasts, nor will it be
Reclaim'd though overcome, let conquerors
Keep what's their own, the conquered obey!

Anna. 'Twas thy ambition first began it all!

And. Say 't were! 'Tis not the justice of the cause,

But how it ends, is lookt upon. Success
Was always sainted.
Anna. Yes, i' th' devil's calendar!
And. Come, come, forget! And since I've sheath'd my sword,
Lay by your rancour!
Anna. Would my eyes were basilisks,*
That I might look thee dead!
And. They've done 't already!
And no less power than that that gave the wound
Can make the cure!
Anna. Then die, perfidious traitor!
And. Yet ere I do 't, let me, like dying men,
Make my confession! 'Twas I commanded
Your husband's death; nor can I quit myself
Of anything that you have charg'd me with!
Excuse 't I must and shall, or bring you in
As accessory!
Anna. Me! What means he, trow?
And. I love you, Royal madam! and with that zeal,
That to express it were to imagine
'Twere comprehensible, and make it nothing!
Were there ten thousand mischiefs more, each mischief
Clog'd with another million, I would through—
Value no hazard, laugh at blood and ruin,
Till I had plac'd me on that even ground
Might challenge your love! Now, madam, you have the cause;
Be merciful to me, or just to yourself!
Anna. What call you justice, then?
And. Either absolve me, or condemn yourself.
Anna. Was I the cause?
And. Your beauty was.
Anna. Would it had been blasted
Beyond the power of art!
And. Be not so cruel!
Consider who 'tis loves you, and what he did
Was for that love! The Emperor is dead,

* "Would they were basilisks to strike thee dead."
—SHAKESPEARE's *Richard III.*

And 'tis as easy to call back the day
That's past, as him! A living mouse is better
Than a dead lion; I am Emperor still.
Anna. But how? or by what means?
And. What matters that?
It is enough I am. Here! take that love
Which all the world would court! Nor think me old
Although 't 'as snow'd upon my head! Your beauty
Can raise new spirits, and my power shall fix them!
Anna. Let me alone—I hate thee!
And. But I love you!
Accept it yet, and keep that power and greatness
You ever had! Nay, I will double it!
I'll make yourself, and only you, the channel
To pass my favours through! The Empire shall
Be blest or blasted by your influence;
And the less world shall set its looks by yours!
Anna. Would it had ne'er seen thine!
And. Some angel help me! [*Draws his sword.*
Here!—[*Gives it her.*]—And I tell thee once again, I kill'd
Alexius—and to enjoy thee, too!
Revenge his death at least! And since I cannot
Live with thy love, let me die thy martyr!
Anna. I take thee at thy word. Repent, and die!
[*She offers.*
And. Repent?—the phrase of ignorance! That were
To doubt the action in its cause—your beauty!
'Twas I! Why doubt you? Strike! Strange that you'll neither
Revenge nor yet forgive!
Anna. Away, dissembler!
[*She throws the sword at him.*
Thou art not ripe for vengeance, nor shall
My hand anticipate thy fate! No! Live!
To let thee see how much I hate thee!—live,
Only to fall more infamous! [*Exit* ANNA.
And. What's here?
Love tricks? My life, she comes at t'other pluck!

SCENE IV.

Enter STEPHANUS, *solus.*

Ste. And must I still live this unmanly life?—
Still brook a rival? No! In Princes' favours
There is no middle 'twixt the top and bottom!
Their minds are large but various, and cloy'd
Sooner than others, easily o'erlooking
Their first election! Sure, the Emperor loves me!
I never wrong'd him in my thought. He does;
I'll ne'er dispute it further. But what is 't
Unless I could engross him? There's Basilius
Keeps even pace in's favour, and may in time
Get the start o' me if I don't prevent him!
No more! He falls! 'Tis here as 'tis in prospects,—
When others come on, we think ourselves go back!

Enter PHILO, *as going hastily over the stage.*

Whither so hasty, man?
Phil. I cannot stay;
I'll wait upon you presently again.
[*As he goes out he drops a letter.* STEPHANUS *takes it up.*

Ste. How now! More work? It is the Emperor's hand!
To Tripsicus! 'S heart!—a promoting rogue!
And can you stoop so low? Then I see anything
Will serve your turn. This letter may beget
Right understanding 'twixt us. Well, I'll read it!
[*He reads.*]—"Pray, mind what I hinted you last.
Affairs run high at present, but I shall weather them!"
Ste. Good! good! good!
"9, 41, and 85 meet at night. 200 will tell you where it is. Things are not yet ripe enough to own you publicly."
Ste. Better and better!
"You know your work—either bring the account yourself, or send it by 90. I had rather the latter.
—Your beloved friend, A."

A !—that's Andronicus! I'm sure the hand
Is all his own. Super-excellent!
I'faith! i'faith! and does the wind blow there?

PHILO *returns in haste.*

Phil. Dropt I no letter, sir?
Ste. You best know that
Yourself. What letter? or to whom directed?
Sure, Philo, you're in love; you're grown forgetful!
You know you stopt not here! Come, tell me true,
'Twas from your mis', and you're afraid another
May take the scent! Peuh! he'll but squeeze thy orange,
And thou may'st have 't again.
Phil. In troth, I'm serious!
And if it ben't within, am lost for ever! [*Exit* PHILO.
Ste. My pocket, th' 'adst hit right! Now for a trick
To kill two birds with one stone!—make me
A property!—an idle stale!—I have 't!
To see how luckily things hit! Andronicus,
Finding the city troublesome, as resenting
Alexius' murder, makes it his endeavour
To fetch off Constantinus to his party;
Perhaps to destroy me, too. Not unlikely;
But I shall miss my aim or I cross-bite him!

'Tis thus:—I smok'd the business, and, judging it a fit opportunity to ruin Basilius, went privately to Constantinus and struck up a friendship with him; and, as a first act of it, bade him have a care of Basilius, whose civil usage had no other respect than to betray him to the loss of his head, which,—to my knowledge, as I told him,—Andronicus had plotted, and would inevitably take effect unless he could turn the mischief upon t'other by making his escape. Whereupon, by my advice, he has possess'd Basilius of a seeming repentance for his former obstinacy, and that he is both able and willing to recover it by the discovery of a new plot. The thing takes. Andronicus has sent for him—I wonder he is not come yet; but if he does not give them the go-by, I'll lose my head. If he does, the work is done—Basilius destroyed, and, consequently, Andronicus disarm'd of the city by the falling of the power into my hands.

Now how I hug myself!
Who cannot make his port with a fore wind
Must use a side wind. Craft, where strength doth fail,
And piece the lion with the fox's tail! [*Exit.*

SCENE V.

Enter ANDRONICUS, *solus.*

And. And am I Emperor, and do my foes
Still live? or must I, that have dar'd so far,
Falter at last, for fear the multitude
May be displeas'd? Can wounded greatness sleep,
Or joy itself, when it beholds a sword
Hang o'er its head? No! Let me be safe,
Though the world tumble! Slow and fearful counsels,
Which narrow-hearted fools call caution,
Ne'er made Rome what she was! Who waits within?

Enter PHILO.

What! has Maria's doctor done his work?

Phil. As pat as wish—she's dead! and so's her husband.

And. Here! See these warrants executed! For Constantinus,
Let him alone till you hear further from me!

Phil. 'Tis done!

And. I like a man goes merrily on!
Are they not right? [PHILO *peruses them.*

Phil. Yes, yes! But if they were not,
I'd make them serve.—[*Aside.*]—Send me good luck! I've dabbled
So long in blood, that ten to one he serves me
As our musicians when the music's done—
Hang up the instrument! But I am in,
And must wade through or sink! [*Exit* PHILO.

And. So much for them—now for an after-game!

But that lies nearer home. Here are a brace
Of rogues, my lords in mischief! That's Basilius
And Stephanus, whom I kept hitherto
For a reserve, and thought t' 'ave sacrificed them
Unto a popular fury. But they're grown
Too cunning, and have stol'n the people from me.
Had they no other crime, this were enough.
Who puts off's hat unto the people, forfeits
His head to's Prince! Nor will 't be difficult
To compass theirs. They're jealous one of t'other.
I must foment it, and, by setting poison
To work 'gainst poison, rid myself of both!
I've instruments enough to fill their room
Less cunning and more tractable.

Enter BASILIUS *and* STEPHANUS.

My friends,
Most welcome! What's the news?
Bas. Little but that
The city's hush'd again.
And. I thank your care!
What would the buzzards have?
Bas. They know not what!
One's for a single person, another for two,
A third for neither, a fourth for liberty.
Oh! what a gallant thing this *Sparta vas!*
But what that was, the devil a bit they know!
'Tis hardly credible: There's not a tap-house
But 's a new polity—a small free state!
And there sit in judgment, and give sentence
Ere they agree the case.
And. What would y' advise me?
Ste. Let them alone! When the dull beast is weary
'Twill fall asleep! If not, grant them some toy
You meant t' 'ave done yourself. 'Tis the same thing
As you had given them all—they'll be as little
Contented if you had. They are not capable
Of having all or nothing granted them.
They neither brook a downright slavery,
Nor may be trusted with full liberty.

And for the rest,—carry an even hand,
You need not fear them. Wind your strings too high,
They crack; and let them down too low, they jar!
And. My worthy friends,—But is 't not possible
To find the hands that set the wheel agoing?
I'm sure the multitude are sots, and carry
Their brains in other men's heads.
Ste. I've heard of some:
But pitiful fellows!
And. As though a rogue
Might not bring in the plague! Have they no money?
Ste. I hope in a short time to give you a catalogue.
And. 'Tis but ill playing with these tools. I thank you!
And now I'll tell you news! Could you believe
That Constantinus should have tack'd about?
Ste. Nor shall I easily. The sky may fall,
But yet I wish my head ne'er ache till 't do!
And. O—you are too severe! What says Basilius?
Bas. Troth, I believe he will! And had you heard
Half our discourse, you must have judg'd the same:
I never met with larger promises.
And. I bade you bring him to me. Have you done 't?
Bas. I have; and left him with a guard without.
And. Go, fetch him in! [*Exit* BASILIUS.
Ste. And he shall fool you both! [*All this aside.*
Things jump as right as wish, and his escape
Must hit. Pray Heaven, he don't mistake the door!

BASILIUS *returns with* CONSTANINUS *and a* GUARD. STEPHANUS *points to the door.*

And. How now, my lord! Basilius has told me
You'd somewhat to offer me.
Const. I heard you were
Willing to speak with me.
And. How!—What's all this?
Bas. Why, he told me——
Const. Nay, if you can't agree,
I had as good be gone!

[CONSTANTINUS *makes his escape by a door, and claps it after him.* STEPHANUS *and* BASILIUS *pursue. Excursions of Guards. After some time, they force the door.*

Ste. Hold! Stop the traitor!
And. Where leads this door?
1 *Gua.* Unto the water, sir.
And. Nay, then, he's gone! Order a galley straight
To give him chase! Disperse! Stop ev'ry passage!
A thousand crowns to him that brings his head!
There must be more in this than barely chance—
'Twas a bold rogue that did it.

STEPHANUS *returns in a fury, with his sword drawn.*

Ste. Nothing but locks
And bolts? Sir, you're betray'd!

Enter GUARD.

And. Did you recover him?
2 *Gua.* No; he got boat ere we could reach the stairs.
And. But whither went he?
2 *Gua.* 'Twas so thick a fog,
And the boat so well mann'd, we quickly lost her.
And. Death and the furies! Am I then betray'd,
And myself made the instrument? Where's Basilius?
2 *Gua.* We left him fitting out a galley.
And. Hence!
Ste. Let me beseech your majesty; be not troubled!
Now you shall see I love you! If it be
A thing of chance, you'll hear no further of 't.
If otherwise, and he designs a rising,
The city is the scene. I'll get before him,
And raise the Guards! And, if your majesty
Thought it convenient, could seize the heads
Of the left mutiny. But then—Basilius——
And. And what of him?
Ste. May chance to take it ill—
There's some of them are his relations.
And. But are you sure to seize them?
Ste. Do I live?

And. And you dare act as high as I dare trust you?
Ste. Dare, sir! How think you? Dare I eat or drink
For fear of choking?
And. I am satisfied!
Seize him and all! 'Tis not our ancient friend,
But our new enemy.
Ste. It may be dangerous;
He is so popular.
And. Then knock out's brains!
Such as would own his cause when living will
Shift for themselves when once they see him dead.
Ste. Please you to leave 't to me. 'Tis time 'twere done.
And. Do what thou wilt—[*Exit* STEPHANUS]—and good luck follow thee!
Tell me of middle ways!—an even hand!
Who ever got a crown by evil arts
And manag'd it by good? That waking men
Should dream themselves away! Empire's preserv'd
By the same way 'twas got. I stand too near
A precipice to think of stopping now.
No! I must on! What I've already done
Is but the antimask to what I'll do.
When safety comes in question, there's no difference
'Twixt just or unjust, pitiful or cruel!
I'll break what will not bow—possess their hearts,
Or force them open! They that will not love
Shall at least fear my power. 'Tis decreed!
And this great beast must either bow or bleed. [*Exit.*

ACT V.—SCENE I.

Enter STEPHANUS *and* CONSTANTINUS.

Ste. Thus far, my lord, you're safe. But one pluck more,
And you may write secure!
Const. Nay; that I am

Is yours, and singly yours. But passing what
I cannot name too oft, let us consider
What must be done. 'Twere better die at once
Than be thus saw'd in pieces! Our wounds are
So far from being heal'd, they're hardly closed:
Nay, like sick men, we've rather lighted on
A new physician than a remedy.

Ste. 'Tis but too true, my lord! but 'tis too late
To spend ourselves in womanish complaints—
'Tis more than time 'twere done.

Const. But who shall do 't?
You know our friends are gone, or, what's as bad,
By having lost their eyes, unserviceable!

Ste. 'Tis our advantage; what we want in numbers
Will be supplied in secrecy. Great designs,
Like wounds, if they take air, corrupt. Besides,
These frequent slaughters make our game, thus have
Lost their authority, and rend'red him
As cheap, as funerals a physician!
And what is greater than all these, the city
Has ne'er a head!

Const. No! Where's Basilius?

Ste. He's gone the way of those that oblige tyrants
Beyond requital—he's strangled!
And now's our time to strike! Your lordship has
Good interest among the citizens,
And they're just ripe for mischief. I have agents
Now raising them to your hand, and shall be ready
To back you with the Guards. Make but a stand,
And all's our own! Isaacus Angelus
Is of the blood, and we'll proclaim him Emperor!

Const. But he's given up to privacy. Andronicus
Well knew 't, that suffered him to live so long!

Ste. I thought as much myself ere I went to him.
But now, he is so sensible of 's danger,
He catches at anything. This is our nick;*
For—I'm to tell you news—the Empress
Has, notwithstanding all her brave resolves,
Giv'n up t' Andronicus! Poor lady!

* Critical moment.

It will concern us to be quick. This action
Will rivet all unless we crush him now—
Now, while 'tis hot! Come, my lord! [*Exeunt.*

SCENE II.

Enter ANDRONICUS, *solus.*

And. Mischief of greatness! that has all to fear,
Yet knows not whom to trust. What desperate rocks
Must it run foul of, when to trust all or none
Is equally an error, and both fatal!
How am I fool'd! and by some bosom slave!
But let it pass; 'tis time must work it out.
I have enough at present to soothe the people.
Some crafty devil has buzz'd them in the head
With prophecies, the fond belief of fools,
But now and then the talk of wiser men!
Nothing but murmurs, news, seditious libels—
The common weapons of unmanly spirits—
It must not be dallied with! These hollow blasts
Bode no fair weather; these imperfect motions
Show somewhat's out of frame!

Enter STEPHANUS.

Ste. Safety to Cæsar!
The omen, to his enemies!
And. What is 't
Can need that preface? Speak!
Ste. A fearful comet
Sweeps the air!
And. Heav'n has done us right at last,
And grac'd our triumphs with its bonfires too!
If otherwise, and there be danger in 't,
'T 'as told its errand, and betray'd its end!
These toys astonish more than signify.
Ste. Nor is this all. Men talk as if an earthquake
Had overthrown some houses!
And. 'T 'as yet left
The palace standing! Have you more?

Ste. The statue
Of your St. Paul drops tears!
And. Mere change of weather!
Unless, perhaps, the general acclamations
May 've pierc'd its marble with a feeling sense
Of what we are. Tears are th' effect of joy
As well as mourning! But I thought my Stephanus
Had had more wit than to regard these fooleries;
They're natural, and ignorance of cause
Must make them miracles. He that regards
The crowing of a hen, a fox with young,
Hare, cat, or weasel crossing his way, a snake
Dropt from the tile, a black dog at his door,
A left hand magpie, or a right hand thunder,
Must never sleep! The very peasant, now,
Can half look through them!—and shall Empire fear
them?
Ste. Now, how it joys my soul to see your majesty
Thus yourself still; and to confirm you so,
Let me once say, be safe! I've charm'd the city
Into obedience; nor is there left
A head or hand that dare appear against you.
But though the flame be quench'd, there may, perhaps,
Some brands lie smoking! To prevent the worst,
'Twere fit the guards kept there—besides, 'tis good
To show the dog his whip.
And. My other self!
[*He embraces him.*
Keep up thy wonted courage, and make the Empire
Confess thou sav'dst it! If you can look so low,
You'll find a nest of slaves, that, like ill spirits,
Foretell the storm themselves intend to move.
Let not a mother's son escape! These villains
Are grown State mountebanks; nothing can pass
But they must raise some observation
Or use upon 't. And the dull beast conceives,
According to the colour of those rods
They cast before them!* Stephanus conceives me?

* See Shakespeare's *Merchant of Venice*, Act i. Scene iii., *voce* Shylock.

Ste. I do! and shall not sleep 'till I have giv'n you
Some fair account. [*Exit* STEPHANUS.

And. Farewell, my worthy friend!
So! he stands single now—he'll fall the easier.
He's grown too stubborn for me: I daren't displease him,
For fear he take a pet and set up another;
Perhaps himself. But I shall check him there:
He's only safe that has nought left to fear. [*Exit.*

SCENE III.

Enter a Rabble of CITIZENS.

1 *Cit.* Come, neighbour, come; it is not to be endur'd!

2 *Cit.* No, troth is it not! 'Twould make a man a whore to consider it seriously.

7 *Cit.* I told you this before—you might have hearken'd to a fool!

3 *Cit.* Ay, neighbour, would you had!

5 *Cit.* Hang would! let's be doing!

6 *Cit.* Ay, but what, neighbour? what?

4 *Cit.* Anything—anything! I am for anything!

Omnes. Liberty—liberty—liberty! [*A hollow.*

1 *Cit.* Why should this Andronicus lord it over us any longer?

2 *Cit.* He is a very tyrant, that's certain!

5 *Cit.* Troth, all I got by his government is, that where I had a little money before, now I have none at all!

6 *Cit.* Nor I neither! The devil might have danc'd in my pocket this twelvemonth, and not broke his shins against one single cross! Call you me this, assisting?

5 *Cit.* It seems, neighbour, it is not altogether so plain as you made it.

1 *Cit.* What say you, gentlemen? There's Isaacus Angelus, and, as I have heard say, has as good a title to the crown as another man!

2 *Cit.* Constantinus appointed us to have met him here. O' my word, they say he is a pretty gentleman!

4 *Cit.* I wonder they should stay so long!

6 *Cit.* Tell me of none of your pretty gentlemen! I am for liberty!

Omnes. Liberty—liberty—liberty! [*A hollow.*

1 *Cit.* But hark you, neighbours; we must have some government!

2 *Cit.* Time enough to think of that hereafter; let's destroy this first!

3 *Cit.* What think you of aristotocracy?

4 *Cit.* No—no—no! Oligasky for my money!

5 *Cit.* By your favour, neighbour, I should think demococracy!

6 *Cit.* And, with your favour too, why not anarchy?

2 *Cit.* Anything—anything but what we are!

Omnes. Liberty—liberty—liberty! [*A hollow.*

Enter PHILO.

Phil. Save you, gentlemen! What's the business? 'Tis not midsummer moon, I hope?

3 *Cit.* Suppose it be—what then?

Phil. Nothing, good gentlemen; but if it be, I hope it will not last all the year!

2 *Cit.* Then we shall have another in 's room; but what's that to you?

Phil. Pray, gentlemen, you need not be so stout! I could tell you news deserv'd a better face.

Omnes. What's that?—what's that?

Phil. The Emperor has thought upon a device, that no freeman of Constantinople shall ever want money unless it be his own fault.

5 *Cit.* That would do well!

6 *Cit.* Yes! O' my conscience, neighbour, would it!

Omnes. But how—but how?

Phil. Do but acquiesce a while, and you'll quickly see; whereas, if you disturb him in 't, you spoil all, and perhaps may repent it when 'tis too late!

2 *Cit.* Acquiesce, that's the word—huh!

5 *Cit.* Ay, neighbour, ay!—Acquiesce!

3 *Cit.* Troth, he speaks reason!

4 *Cit.* Marry, does he!

5 *Cit.* Our city orator's but an ass to him!

Phil. What say you, then, gentlemen?

2 *Cit.* For my part, now, I'll live and die with him!

3 *Cit.* And so will I; we may do worse!

Phil. Yes; I dare trust them for the first!—[*Aside.*] —But what's the matter? Has so good an Emperor but two friends among you all? Throw up your caps, and away with 't!

Omnes. One and all! one and all! long live Andronicus!

Phil. He is beholden to you, and I'll let him know as much! Farewell! good gentlemen. 'Twas a fair 'scape! [*Aside. Exit* PHILO.

Omnes. Farewell! farewell! Long live Andronicus! [*Hollow.*

1 *Cit.* Come, neighbours, come! We had as good be quiet. There will be faults while there are men!

3 *Cit.* Ay—ay—let's home—let's home! 'Tis good sleeping in a whole skin! [*As they are going off,*

Enter ISAACUS *and* CONSTANTINUS.

Const. Now, gentlemen, I see you're men o' your words!
'Tis but an easy risk, and all 's our own!
Can you remember your old Emperor,
Or his late murder'd son, and not acknowledge
The heir, the undoubted heir?

1 *Cit.* Ay, neighbour, ay!
'Twas this we came about.

2 *Cit.* Where's that rogue, Philo? Knock out 's brains!

Omnes. Ay—ay—ay! Where is he—where is he?

3 *Cit.* We cannot for shame now but proclaim him Emperor!

6 *Cit.* Oh, by any means!

Omnes. Long live Isaacus, Emperor of Greece!

Isa. It was so far, my friends and countrymen,
From my desires t'ave liv'd to see this day,

'Twas never in my thoughts: My privacy
Was all the Empire I or wisht or dreamt.
But since your joint unanimous consent
Has firm'd that title, which my birthright gave me,
I cannot but acknowledge it!

3 *Cit.* What's that he says? Long live Isaacus!

Omnes. Long live the Emperor!

4 *Cit.* Peace! hear him speak!

Isa. 'Tis not my business here to rip old sores,
Or to keep ope those wounds which, let alone,
Would close themselves. Yet, since the readiest way
To what we should be, is to know what we are,
Let me once ask you, what d' you call this place?—
Greece, or her ruins? You had once an Emperor,
A good one, too—I mean Alexius!
I will not say who murder'd him! He had
A sister; I do not say she was poison'd!
You had good laws; Andronicus made more—
I would he had kept either! I forbear!
Conto, Mamalus, Cæsar, Basilius,
Lapardas, Ducas, and a thousand more;
Some murder'd, others their eyes bor'd out! My way
Is not to speak against such as are absent.

Omnes. Yes — yes — yes — pray on! Long live Isaacus!

6 *Cit.* Peace! hear him speak!

Isa. Which of you all durst shake his head, and not
Believe it loose and might fall off? What though
You 'scap'd when others fell?—you were but kept
To close his stomach and be last eat up.
Yet let me give Andronicus his due:
He brought the city once again within
Her walls, whose suburbs, like the spleen, had swoll'n,
To the consumption of the rest o' th' body!
I would he 'd left inhabitants enough
To people that little remain'd! He built a chapel—
I would the devil had not set up the cross!
An aqueduct—I would the kennels had run
No other colour! One or two good actions
To blanch and varnish o'er a deal of ill

Is but the music to a tragedy.
But I forget myself: I never lov'd
To rake in dunghills. I only wish their author
Had his desert! Not that I bid you lay
Violent hands upon him; Justice will do
Enough but give her leave! And so I shall not
Detain you longer; only let me beg you,
If you meet Manuel, to preserve him safe.
His only crime is, that Andronicus gat him!

7 *Cit.* Ay, here's one spoke like an Emperor!

Omnes. Long live Isaacus!

3 *Cit.* Come, we lose time! Andronicus may chance to give us the slip!

5 *Cit.* But if we take him, we'll give it him!

Omnes. Follow—follow—follow!—whoop! [*Exeunt.*

SCENE IV.

Enter ANDRONICUS *and* STEPHANUS.

And. But did he land again?

Ste. I'm certain of 't.
I miss'd him narrowly; perhaps he may
Have taken sanctuary.

And. What?—Harbour traitors!
Demand him straight! if they refuse a search,
Force all the doors!—[*Shout within.*]—What means that hollow?
Some devil's abroad! Prithee go see what 'tis!
[*Exit* STEPHANUS.
Nothing but mischief still? No day-shine clear
Without a cloud? Ill follows ill, like waves,
One is no sooner past but t'other rolls.
Within there!

Enter PHILO.

Call me a lutenist, and let him sing
The song my Music sang me last! Make haste!
[*Exit* PHILO.

My head's disquieted; an old wizard's saw
Swims in my brains! 'Twas told me once I should
Live to be Emperor, and that I. S.
Should be my successor! No Delphian devil
Was ever more obscure!—I. S.—Isaurus.
But I've an eye on him. Whoe'er he be,
The devil was right; if not, 'twas our mistake.
But say—I. S.—Whom heaven intends to ruin
It first infatuates! There's Isaacus,
Whom hitherto I've rather scorn'd than fear'd,
Appears like something now! He must not live!
In vain we fell a tree if yet we leave
Quick roots behind. But what's the matter?
What makes the day post backward to the east?
Whence this unwonted night—these stars at noon?
Out with that dunghill stuff! See how it waves
And darts at me; but I'll fetch it down!
  Where be the sons of Titan? Let them come;
I'll be their captain! With this arm I'll pluck
Rocks from their standing, trees with roots and all,
Whole mountains with their Centaurs, and erect
A scaling ladder made of heaped hills,
Whose top shall touch the clouds! The world shall
    see
Ossa once more on Pelion; a third
Shall be Olympus, whose advanced chin
Shall knock the Heav'ns—if not, I'll throw it in!
[*He staggers, and falls into a chair.*

Enter a LUTE.

A Song.

Some have called life a stage play, that includes
    Nothing but scenes and interludes;
Others a month of April, where two hours
    Scarce pass without as many showers;
Others, again, a miscellane of years,
    Or chequer-work of hopes and fears.
But I'm confirm'd they were ordain'd by fate,
As hieroglyphics of a Prince's state.

One, while his genius is so kind, he'd swear
He's in an empyrean sphere;
So curst again by fits, the frozen zone
Is habitabler ten to one!
Strange kind of life! to have one's hopes be brought
To somewhat, and straight dash'd to nought.
When rais'd upon the pinnacle, 'tis all
To think, not whither, but from whence, we fall.

Since, then, our dappled fate is such, who can
Call himself blest and yet be man?
Ev'n crowns their crosses have; nor Cæsar shall
Write happy till his funeral.
More are our clouds than suns; our care and pain
Weigh down our bliss! Who's happy, then?
He, and he only, whom the womb doth smother,
And sends him packing from one grave to t'other.
[*Exit.*

Ha! what was that? Methought I heard a voice
And music! How 't 'as fix'd me! Plato, sure,
Was in the right—our souls are harmony.
I am myself again! What should I fear?
Who flies to shun his fate runs headlong on 't.
Heaven helps the valiant, and ne'er descended
To save that coward durst not save himself.
Since, then, the Empire knows not when 'tis well,
I'll make it sensible what power can do;
I'm but defendant, they provoke me to 't!
Nor can the world my blackest action blame—
Necessity has neither sin nor shame;
Mischief is never safe, but heap on heap
One must back t'other! They that stumble leap!
[*Exit.*

SCENE V.

Enter CITIZENS *and Rabble.*

Omnes. Hollow!

1 *Cit.* Where is this traitor that murder'd the Emperor?

2 *Cit.* Would I could light on him!—I'd have a leg or an arm of him! He hang'd my brother!

3 *Cit.* If every one he has wrong'd have but a little, I am sure a joint will not fall to your share.

4 *Cit.* Come, come! there will be enough for us all! Would we had him, though I were bound to give you mine.

5 *Cit.* What had we best do, neighbours?

3 *Cit.* Smoke the fox out of his hole!

2 *Cit.* Set fire on the palace!

4 *Cit.* By no means, gentlemen; 'twill destroy a deal of good pillage—That has done no hurt.

6 *Cit.* No—no—no! destroy all! You'll ne'er be rid of the wolves till you cut down the woods!

1 *Cit.* We had better sell them, and share the money!

6 *Cit.* 'Twill be too long a-doing, and others may get in.

Enter PHILO.

1 *Cit.* See, neighbour, see who comes here?

2 *Cit.* Even the very rogue that first betrayed us!

3 *Cit.* Down with him!

4 *Cit.* Stand!

5 *Cit.* Knock him down first!

Phil. Good gentlemen! But hear me——

3 *Cit.* No—no—no! Hear him?—That were a trick, indeed! [*They knock him down.*

2 *Cit.* So, farewell him! I have a boy at home will cry for him, I'm sure of 't!

5 *Cit.* Upon my conscience, neighbour, but my wife will do the same.

6 Cit. Hang him!—hang him! We lose time!
Let's about our work! [*Hollow. Exeunt.*

SCENE VI.

Enter ANDRONICUS *with his sword drawn, and a* SERVANT.

And. Ha!—Philo dead! These devils are everywhere.
Thou shalt not fall alone! What was you saying?
Ser. Another rout has seiz'd St. Sophy's temple!
And. Who heads them?
Ser. Constantinus! who has taken
Isaacus Angelus, and proclaim'd him Emperor!
And to them Stephanus, with all his Guards,
Is since revolted!
And. Then farewell my hopes!
But I am still Andronicus! Leave me!
[*Exit* SERVANT.
And is your anger such, ye powers? And can
What's least above stoop to contest with man?
Did ye of brittle clay his fabric rear
Only to dash 't in pieces? Bade ye him bear
His Maker's image in his brow to show
Ye reign'd above, he a small Jove below?
Only to show him happiness, and yet
Straight snatch it from him, or tumble him from it?
Had I submitted to a general fate,
It had been nothing! Had I seen my State
And Empire sunk before me, I had gone
Contentedly! But to fall alone—
Thus tamely lost! What boots it to complain?
Give me one battle! Heav'n be heav'n again!
One battle, and let me perish!

Enter three or four of the Rabble.

1 Cit. Here he is! Follow—follow—follow!
And. Villains!

2 *Cit.* Stand! [*He kills two or three, the rest run.*
And. Lie thou!

By another door enter SERVANT.

Ser. I'm sorry I came so late. Please you, great sir,
Retire a while, until the storm be past!
Your name's too great in arms to have it call'd
A cowardly flight. Then fall not out of season;
Reserve yourself for better times. I have
A galley waits your majesty!
And. Now Heav'n reward thy honesty! Lead on!
I know the worst!
Foolish despair is but occasion lost. [*Exeunt.*

SCENE VII.

Enter CONSTANTINUS, ISAACUS, *and* CITIZENS.

Const. Not find him yet? I warrant you we know him!
Stop all the passages, and desire Stephanus
To draw down with his guards!
6 *Cit.* All but that last
Is done already. I'll about it straight! [*Exit.*
Const. How?—Philo slain! He never did his master
A truer service.

7 *Cit.* And my good neighbours, Ambrose and Gregory. Alack, alas! Nothing certain in this life; to-day a man, to-morrow a cuckold, the next day dead!

3 *Cit.* Come, come! let's carry them off! But for that rogue, let him ev'n lie; he was a pestilent villain!

4 *Cit.* Are you sure he is dead? Does not the rogue counterfeit?

5 *Cit.* 'Twill do no hurt to see.

3 *Cit.* For the more certainty, 'tis good to be sure. [*Stabs him again.*

5 *Cit.* Well done, neighbour! You're in my mind. I scarcely believe a man dead as long as his head 's upon his shoulders. [*Exeunt.*

Scene VIII.

Enter Manuel, *solus.*

Man. 'Twould be some comfort yet I could but hear
My father 'scap'd their hands—I'm half afraid
He scorn'd to step aside. Ha!—what's here?
Alas, poor Philo! dead! Now I perceive
Thou hadst some honesty—thou lov'dst thy master:
'Twas more than I expected. What's this world
And all its greatness? It has rais'd up some,
But ruin'd more; and even those whom 't has
Most rais'd, 't 'as ruin'd most! What's all this toil
And blind pursuit, but like our children's following
A butterfly? Sometimes they cannot reach it;
Sometimes o'errun it; sometimes think they have 't,
But it slips through their fingers; and at last,
When, after all their offers, turns, and falls,
They've taken it, what is 't? Alas, poor fools!
Nothing but painted wings. 'Tis not my late
Experience taught me this—I ever found it!
Who could imagine to have seen my father,
So late the people's darling, now their hate?
But yesterday an Empire at his back;
Now scarce a hole to put his head! 'Twas Heav'n,
And I submit! But yet it lessens not
Their crime that were the cause. There's Stephanus!
False Stephanus, a traitor to both masters!
Were he my enemy, 't hadn't troubled me—
Nay, I'd forgiv'n him. But my friend, 'tis hard!

Enter Stephanus.

See! here he comes! Now Heaven forgive me!
I had a father till his treacherous faith
Bereav'd me of him. Father! methinks the word
Prompts me to something.
Ste. My good lord, be safe!
Safe as your virtue merits!

Man. What hast thou
To do with virtue? I ne'er suspected her
Until I found her in thy mouth. There!
[*He strikes off* STEPHANUS' *hat.*
Ste. Ha! Has your folly made you desperate?
Now would thy father and his daring soul
Perch'd on thy point! [*They draw.*
Man. The justice of my cause
May be enough to do thy work: My sword
In a child's hand, inform'd by that, with ease
Would reach thy treacherous heart! Words trifle time—
Defend yourself! [*They fight.*

And after some small time enter CONSTANTINUS.

Const. Hold! Stephanus, hold! Nay, good my lord,
Let me entreat you! [STEPHANUS *falls.*
Ste. How am I lost in sight of land, and all
My tow'ring hopes sunk with me! Heav'n is just;
I would, but cannot! [*Dies.*
Man. So may all treachery succeed! And if
T'ave been my own justiciar be a crime,
Forgive me—I had no other way; his treason
Had lost its name, and in the world's ethics
Had past for virtue else.
Const. Alas, my lord,
'Twas an unfortunate action! But since
'Tis done, preserve yourself. Pray, good my lord,
Withdraw a while, nor let your virtue fall
A prey unto the rabble.
Man. I always scorn'd them,
And shall not now, by showing of my back,
Make them believe I fear them!
Const. What's your courage
Against their numbers? Good my lord, withdraw!
Venture not gold to dirt. Pray, give me leave!
[*Calls a servant.*
Come hither! Attend my lord, and see him safe
Within my doors! I'll wait on you presently.

Enter another.

Ser. My lord, Andronicus——
Const. Well! what of him?
Ser. Had put to sea, and was now well-nigh reach'd
The other shore, when, of a sudden, the winds
And seas, as conscious whom they wafted o'er,
Check'd his full speed and beat him back again.
Yet he put out a second and third time,
But all in vain! The face of Heav'n was sullied,
The winds broke loose and clubb'd into a storm,
Till the poor galley, having lost her rudder,
Her oars unserviceable, and her masts
Spent by the board, came rolling on the back
Of an impetuous wave, and drove on shore,
Where he soon met a storm indeed! The people,
Having by this time utterly defac'd
Whatever bore his name or memory,
Fell foul of him, or rather he of them!
Had you but seen the hubbub!—One twicks his beard,
Another beats out an eye, a third a tooth,
A fourth cuts off a hand! No cruelty
He e'er commanded but was there again
Epitomiz'd on himself; and when at last
Their tired invention could inflict no longer,
Laden with dirt and obloquies, and crown'd
With garlic, they set him on a scabbed camel,
And in that odd procession led him to
The common gallows, where they hung up that little
They'd left of him! So fell Andronicus!
Const. May the same fate ever attend rebellion
And usurpation! And let the world
Hence learn on what a ticklish point they stand
Whose unjust actions and borrow'd greatness,
How speciously soever colour'd o'er,
Have no foundation but what's built upon
The people's favour! The uncertain people,
Constant to nothing but inconstancy;
Prone to affect, but without judgment still;
Hot-headed; envious; suspicious,

Yet credulous; frame whimsies to themselves,
And after fear them; now set up one, then t'other;
But deal with all as children with their dirt-pies—
First raise, then pash * them out!

Enter ISAACUS.

Isa. My Lord, you hear the news of Andronicus?
Const. Yes; and may treason never prosper better!
Isa. But I admire we hear nothing of Manuel.
Const. He's safe! and now an object of your mercy!
Isa. For why, my Lord? Is virtue grown a crime?
Const. Behold!—[*He shows him* STEPHANUS.]—I'll let you know the rest within;
But must assure your Majesty at present,
'Twas fairly done!
Isa. Shall my first letters, then,
Be writ in blood? Howe'er,—I pardon him!
It is enough to me he durst be virtuous,
When Cæsar, and that Cæsar his father, too,
Was otherwise. Bid him from me safe!
Const. I thank your Majesty!
Isa. But now, my Lord,
I must desire you look into the city.
The people, like the sea, keep rolling still,
Although the winds that rais'd them first be laid!
If they continue longer, there'll be nothing
Left them to spoil, and then perhaps they may
Consider and repent!
Const. I'll straight about it;
They have been up too long! 'Twere to be wish'd
This beast, the people, either never knew
Their strength, or always knew to use it right.
Isa. You may go farther, and, as you see cause,
Proclaim a general pardon! The more I spare,
The more are left me to adorn my trophy!
Promise them better days, and let them know
That though we're not in Plato's commonwealth,

* "With my armed fist
I'll pash him over the face."
—SHAKESPEARE.

To have whate'er's amiss at once remede,
Yet the first stone is laid, and I despair not
A hopeful superstructure! Rest and time
Will make your troubled waters clear again;
For what remains, a gentle hand will do' t.
Harsh, cruel Empires, like acute diseases,
Are rather sharp than lasting! That must dure*
When nations of their rulers feel secure;
So must that Prince who'd wisely govern here,
Trust in his subjects' love, not claim their fear.
[*Exeunt* OMNES.

* Continue.

THE END.

THE PROJECTORS.

The Projectors: A Comedy. By John Wilson.—Ætatem habet ipse de se loquatur.—Imprimatur, Roger L'Estrange, Jan. 13, 1664. *Lond. Printed for John Playfere at the White Lyon, in the Upper Walk of the New Exchange; and William Crook, at the Three Bibles, on Fleet-Bridge.* 1665. *4to.*

ALTHOUGH the editors of the *Biographia Dramatica* say that *The Projectors* "met with good success upon the stage," it has been questioned by Geneste whether the play was ever acted at all. "Neither the title page nor Langbaine," as he affirms, "give us reason to believe so;" adding, "the play itself seems badly calculated for representation;" while, at the same time, he acknowledges that "it is well written, but wants incident sadly. Suckdry, the miser, is an excellent character—a better character of that description is not to be found in any play: several of his speeches are translated from the *Aulularia of Plautus*. The scene in the third act between the women is founded on Aristophanes."—*See Account of the English Stage*, 8vo, Bath, 1832, vol. x. Mr. Halliwell's *Dictionary of Old English Plays*—London, 1860, 8vo—confirms the statement of the *Biographia Dramatica;* and Langbaine, although not specially commenting on this particular comedy, says, in reference to the author generally: "Whose muse has been applauded on the stage,"—inferring that all his plays had been acted. The supplementary volume of Langbaine contains this remark: "This play met with no great success."

The characters are well depicted, the dialogue is good throughout, and the interest is strong enough to warrant the piece being acted, at least in the days when it was written. Since then, so many writers have extracted its best parts, and turned them to their own uses, that, its freshness being thus gone, if it were brought forward in these times an audience would not accept it as a novelty. The "Miser" has not only been adopted by Sir Walter Scott in his *Old Mortality*, and repeated in his *Fortunes of Nigel;* but Mr. W. Harrison Ainsworth has again taken not only forcible possession of him, but has traded upon the incident in this piece, of the suitor for his daughter's hand disguising himself in mean habiliments, so as to make it appear that he was of a thrifty nature, and in accordance with the miser's own ideas.

It is uncertain whether Moliere's *L'Avare* was known to our author prior to his writing this comedy, there being doubts as to the precise date on which *L'Avare* itself was produced. In the memoirs of the life of Moliere prefixed to his works—Edit. Amst. et Leip. 1750—it is said to have been represented "sur le theatre du Palais Royal, le 9 Septembre 1668;" but this is qualified by a foot-note of the editor, who says: "On ne sçait pas precisément en quel tems *L'Avare* parut pour le premiére fois." The dates of the two pieces, however, in so far as has been stated, so approximate that it is difficult to determine whether Moliere or Wilson first brought the character of the "Miser" into comparatively modern notice; but the merit of this appears, if at all, to preponderate in favour of the English dramatist. It is clear that both of them took the idea from the *Aulularia* of Plautus, and both have frequently drawn upon that play not only for character, but for their language and incidents. Thomas Shadwell and Henry Fielding have in turn drawn from all these several sources for materials for their comedies, called, in both instances, *The Miser.* For the *Aulularia* of Plautus, the English reader is referred to the second volume of a translation "into familiar blank verse," by Bonell Thornton, Lond. 1769, 8vo.

Sir Gudgeon Credulous, in Wilson's comedy, bears considerable resemblance to Fabian Fitzdottrel, in Ben Jonson's *Devil is an Ass:*

"*Enter* ENGINE, *a broker, to* FITZDOTTREL.

Fitz. O, my fine Engine! What's the affair? More cheats?
Eng. No, sir! The wit, the brain, the great projeotor
I told you of, is newly come to town.
Fitz. Where, Engine?
Eng. I have brought him, he's without—
Ere he pulled off his boots, sir; but so follow'd
For businesses!
Fitz. But what is a projector?
I would conceive.
Eng. Why, one, sir, that projects
Ways to enrich men or to make them great,
By suits, by marriages, by undertakings,
According as he sees they humour it."

Meercraft is the projector, and among the projects he submits to Fitzdottrel, although designed as a satire upon the projects and monopolies of the time, there are many, then deemed improbable, which have since been brought forward in sober earnestness and have met with success.

At the end of the printed copy of the present comedy is the following note:—

"ERRATA.—Before the three first Acts you'll find Scœn. 1. Wherein the printer mistook his copy; be pleased to blot 'em: each Act being but one Scœne, and the stage throughout the whole play kept full.—The rest, being at most but literal, leaves to your favour."

THE PERSONS.

SIR GUDGEON CREDULOUS, *A Projecting Knight, Suitor to Mrs. Godsgood.*
JOCOSE, *A Courtier.*
FERDINAND, *His Son.*
SUCKDRY, *An Usurer.* }
SQUEEZE, *An Exchange Broker.* } *All in for Projects.*
GOTAM, *A Citizen.* }
DRIVER, *Jocose's Servant.*
LEANCHOPS, *Suckdry's Servant.*
SERVANT.

MRS. GODSGOOD, *A Widow.*
MRS. GOTAM, *Wife to Gotam.*
MRS. SQUEEZE, *Wife to Squeeze.*
NANCY, *Suckdry's Daughter.*

The Scene :—

LONDON.

PROLOGUE.

It is so hard to please, when things must be
Mouldy with age, or gilt with novelty;
That, in effect, 'tis but a cross or pile *
In all that's written, whether well or ill.
Nor have we ventured on this liberty,
That we suspect your judgements; no, they're free,
Free as that reason that inform'd them first,
And, were those common clogs of interest
Once shaken off, would be the same again.
What shall I say? Shall I entreat ye then?
A poor inducement, if ye will not do it,
Out of good nature let me bribe ye to it.
Ay! ——, now ye hearken; but mistake me not,
We give no money back, that were a plot
Upon ourselves; yet we have as good a shift.
Ye that would learn to thrive, we'll teach ye thrift;
And ye that would get more; why faith, for you,
We have, the Lord knows what, new projects too;
And you—I do forget myself. To run too far
May chance to cloy ye ere you see your fare.

* Head or tail. Chance.

THE PROJECTORS.

ACT I.—SCENE I.

Enter SUCKDRY, *solus, as coming from a journey.*

Suck. Now, send that all things be well at home. But, troth, I half doubt it, my mind so misgives me. It could not be for nothing, sure, that the rats ate a hole in my pocket last night, and a crow kept scraping and cawing at me this morning. Uh! my fears are out. This rogue has given me the slip, and is run away with my cloak bag.

Enter LEANCHOPS, *with a cloak bag under his arm.*

Oh, Leanchops! Art thou come? I profess thou didst half fright me. This London is so villanous a wide place, I was afraid I had lost thee, and must have been at the charge of crying thee. Art thou come, rogue?

Lean. As you see, sir; but, it seems, must thank this for your care and my welcome. And yet I'll undertake it might have slept safe on a dunghill for anything that's in 't.

Suck. Away, sirrah! I have often told you of your surly proud heart; sirrah, sirrah! he that scorns a little shall never be master of a great deal. No more, I say, but stand forth, and let's see whether we have lost anything by the journey.

[*He takes out a roll, and reads.*

"Lazarus Suckdry!" Ay, God wot, a poor man,—as poor as Lazarus. I must be contented. Here I am. "Zachary Leanchops!"

Lean. Here, sir.

Suck. 'Tis well; let's on. "*Item*, one horse, three shoes and a half, two stirrups, one saddle, one bridle, one girth, one crupper, and half a saddle-cloth!"

Lean. All safe and forthcoming.

Suck. Very well. Observe—"One doublet with a new pair of foreskirts, one pair of breeches with a blue codpiece point, one pair of stockings."

Lean. Without feet, sir.

Suck. No matter, no matter; 'tis not seen. "One pair of boots, one spur and spur-leather, one pair of gloves, one basket-hilt sword, one girdle hanger, one hat, one band, one coat, one jump,* and one switch."

Lean. All in view.

Suck. "*Item*, in the cloak bag, one Sessions' suit and cloak, one pair of blue stockings with orange-coloured garters and roses, three shoes, one comb with five teeth, one razor, half a washing ball, and a piece of a glass." Let me see, is it fast? All safe—ha?

Lean. As you left it. He deserves to be damn'd after it that would venture a hanging by stealing any of 't. [*Aside.*

Suck. Come, Leanchops, come! this place is a little too public. We'll look over the rest when we come home.

Lean. Unless we chance to meet a ragman by the way, and then—rags to rags and rubbish to rubbish. [*Aside.*

Suck. Follow me, and have a care—here comes a couple!

Enter JOCOSE *and* DRIVER.

One does not know what they may do. Have a care, I say; have a care!

Joc. Mr. Suckdry, your servant! Welcome to town.

Suck. Thank you, good sir. Uh—uh! he believes I have money in my cloak bag. Would I were well rid of him! [*Aside, walking.*

Joc. How do you? You do not look well. Let me give you a glass of wine; 'twill comfort your heart.

* A waistcoat.

Suck. Wine! uh—uh! I dare not; my doctor tells me 'tis naught for me. I was right—he thinks I have got money, and would make me drunk, to steal my cloak bag. Uh—uh! [*Aside.*

Joc. Come; it shall cost you nothing!

Suck. Another time. Uh—uh! This rogue Leanchops has smelt out my gold at home, and told him where it lies buried. Uh—uh! [*Aside.*

Joc. What ails you, sir?

Suck. Uh—uh! sick! A fit of the colic. I must home.

Joc. But perhaps I have somewhat to say to you may deserve your stay. You have a daughter?

Suck. A poor girl, God wot. What of her?

Joc. Call her not poor; she that is virtuous and handsome is rich enough.

Suck. Ah, sir; but every man is not of your opinion. Alas! poor child! she wants a portion. There's something else requir'd besides virtue and handsomeness. This may bring admirers, that sweethearts; but 'tis money, money that gets the husband!

Joc. Let not that trouble you. I have a son, and though I say it, a handsome fellow; one that, throw him where you will, shall live in the world.

Suck. But I can give nothing with my daughter. Poor wench! she's a right philosopher; she carries all she has about her. Good sir, do not abuse our poverty. Uh—uh!

Joc. Nor do I. Here's my hand; I'm in earnest. What say you?

Suck. I have told you already; she has no money.

Joc. And I have answered it. Shall we bring 'em together?

Suck. For that as you please; you know her portion. Uh—uh! I am sick, and cannot stay to talk it longer now. Farewell, sir! This is a trap to catch my gold; but he may be mistaken—old rats are not so easily taken as young cats think. Uh—uh! [*Aside.*

[*Exeunt* SUCKDRY *and* LEANCHOPS.

Joc. Farewell! My son and I'll see you within a few days.

Dri. But, with your leave, sir, I hope you are not in earnest.

Joc. No? but I am. And if I can but compass it, shall think it the best day's work I ever did in my life. This fellow, as poor as he seems, tell him but of a good mortgage, shall lend you ten thousand pounds upon 't at a day's warning, and yet would have the world believe him to be a poor man. And such, in troth, he is, since he dares not enjoy what he has; for, o' my conscience, were he now sick in earnest, he would rather die, to save charges, than be at the expense of a glister.

Dri. A man would wonder at it; yet such I've heard of.

Joc. But beyond him, I think, few. I have had this design in my head a long time, and made him many a mortgage, and kept touch with him at his day, merely to beget an opinion in him that I had great dealings in the world, when yet I have found enough to do to keep my head above water.

Dri. Do not despair, sir; but think how I may be serviceable to you, and see what I'll do. A mountebank's zany shall not be at more command, nor half so nimble, as I'll be industrious.

Joc. I do believe thee, and perhaps may have occasion to try you sooner than you think of 't.

Dri. Never too soon, nor nothing too much, to serve so good and bountiful a master!

Joc. Well, then, to be serious. I have a great while gone the plain downright honest way, but I find that begets nothing but laughter; and therefore I'm ev'n resolv'd to follow the rest of the world—that is to say, feed the humours of fools; and if they will set up windmills in their heads, contribute my assistance to cut out the sails. When saw you Sir Gudgeon Credulous?

Dri. Very lately; but so big with contemplation, there was no coming near him. 'Tis true he cried, "How does your master? Remember me to him!" gave me the state nod, and—*exit.*

Joc. 'Tis such a political hocus, such a frippery of shreds and parings, that I can liken him to nothing better than a tailor's cushion,—no two pieces of the same colour,—to-day this, to morrow that, the next a third thing; but what that is, no man knows. 'Tis past all men's understanding, and his own too; for, to speak truth, he never had more than a man might well truss up in an egg-shell, and room to spare. In a word, I may say of him, as 'tis said of nature concerning monsters, he was produc'd, not intended.

Dri. Nor have you mistook your character. I have known him a mathematician, a pol,* a star-gazer, a quack, a Chaldean, a schoolman, a philosopher, an ass, a broken grammarian, and most abominable poet, and yet sick of all—but the ass; and now at last, if I mistake him not, a most confident ignorant projector.

Joc. And that he may thank me for. I saw he was past the remedy of a mortar, and if I should have pretended to a miracle, to have reduc'd him, 'twould have been hardly believ'd; and therefore I ev'n let him alone, and, as I saw occasion, work'd him to my own purpose. Methinks you might be useful to me in 't.

Dri. And will. I am your servant; command it.

Joc. Here dwells hard by one Mistress Godsgood, a rich widow, to whom I have made some long pretences; nor had they been, as I am told, altogether successless, if this coxcomb's estate had not hung in my light. She believes him what he is, an ass, but yet a golden ass, and cries that's enough to cover his other faults. Now, could I flay him of that fine skin, I need not trouble myself to make him ridiculous, and consequently do mine own work.

Dri. And truly he's in a fair way to 't. And now, give me leave to tell you, you could have thought of nothing wherein I could have serv'd you better.

Joc. I know thou hast been bred a scholar, and thy invention not ill. But canst thou cant?

Dri. How think you, sir? Suppose I should tell him

* Query, a polemic? *i.e.* a disputant, a controversist, or, it may be, a preacher.

I had studied the Emporeuticks, Lemnicks, Camnicks, and Plegnicks; could demonstrate the *minimum quod sit* of Homocrecious and Heterocrasious; and, stripping Materia Prima to her smock, discover the most private recesses and occult qualities of Ignicadrillica, Metallorgonica, Euricatactica, and Hydropanta Pressoria? Do you believe, I say, he would be able to understand more of it than I do myself, which is just nothing? If you call this canting, let me alone with him!

Joc. Excellent! Then, to subdivide them into as undemonstrable, yet seemingly probable, projects. We shall make such sport!

Enter FERDINAND.

Dri. And yet good money, I warrant you, sir. But see, my young master! yet, methinks, not so merry at heart as we are.

Joc. Now, Nando! what news with you? Thou art as spruce as if thou hadst been with thy young widow, yet look'st as heavy as she had turn'd thee to lead. How goes it?

Fer. Why, faith, sir, I just came from her.

Joc. And what? How did she receive thee?

Fer. So, so—the city way; but at last I had laugh'd her into a pretty good humour, till, as the devil would have it, in dropt her uncle, and quite damp'd all with a noise of jointures and I know not what—a disease, I think, I shall be last troubled with. To be short, she did in effect tell me she was handsome, and would never marry but to better her fortune.

Joc. Let her go! let her go! If thou wilt not be wanting to thyself, I'll put thee upon a better, and one that shall never cheat thee by pretending to be richer than she is; for, in a word, she is not worth one groat!

Fer. What do you mean, sir?

Joc. A good wife, and, for aught I ever heard, may make a virtuous wife.

Fer. No ready money, sir? Methinks half one half t'other were somewhat like.

Joc. Let not that trouble you. Her father is rich, very rich, and has no other child to leave his estate to, and shall rather put her off to an ordinary fortune with nothing, than give an hundred pounds to marry her to the best estate in London.

Fer. And who may this be, good sir?

Joc. Old Suckdry's daughter.

Fer. I could like it well; but how is it to be done?

Joc. Not with that tossing feather, lewd periwig, lac'd band, flaunting linen, embroider'd belt, wide slops, shop of ribbons, and vile porte-canons!*

Fer. Why, sir, you have seen them all before!

Joc. Nor am I angry with thee for doing as other people do. No; I had rather have thee comport thyself to every man's humour—with old men, severe; with young, jocund; with the humoursome, morose; with women, galliard; with thy companions, pleasant; and with a niggardly rascal, more sordid than himself—at least appear so. And so would I have thee treat this fellow.

Fer. If that were all, I could easily follow your directions.

Joc. And you may not repent it. Go! be rul'd by me. Strip all this trumpery; 'tis enough to fright him. Should he see thee now, he'd swear the feathers were more worth than the bird. Go, I say, and get me some little odd hat, but quite out of fashion; a diminutive band, no cuffs, hair shorter than your eyebrows, at most not beyond your ears; close breeches, greasy gloves, Gresham shoes, leather shoe-ties; and for your cloak, no matter if it be of another parish,—he'll like it the better.

Fer. My acquaintance would laugh at me.

Joc. Get thou the money, and laugh at them, boy! Then, for your discourse,—get me together all the base, ill, sordid tricks of a covetous wretch, and deliver them as morals; wonder at the ignorance of the age,

* Or 'canions;' rolls at the bottom of the breeches immediately below the knee. They were sometimes indented like a screw; the common ones were called *straight canions.* See *Strutt*, ii. 148.

that knows not those honest thrifty rules, or, if it do, its shame in not practising them.

Fer. Well, sir, I see you are in earnest, and for once I'll try what I can do. But I doubt——

Joc. Do; and ne'er doubt it. About it straight while 'tis hot, and leave the rest to me!

Fer. You have commanded, and I shall not dispute. But if I bring it to pass, I may well swear miracles are not ceas'd! [*Exit.*

Joc. Come, let's be gone! Thou knowest the plague's in the city, and if I stay longer, 'tis odds but I may be infected.

Enter SIR GUDGEON CREDULOUS.

Dri. I hope, sir, you do not fear Sir Gudgeon Credulous?

Joc. O no! he's a good preservative against it.

Dri. I told you he was as big as he could hold. Do you not observe, sir, how hard he wrings his brows, to the manifest hazard of disblocking his periwig? Will you not speak to him?

Joc. Presently. Let's view him a little!

Sir Gud. It must take without doubt, and the profit be infinite; no man knows what. But for the manner of doing it:—this way? no; it may be certain, but 'tis too far about the bush. That way? no; for though it be the shorter cut, we may yet be too hasty in the experiment. T'other way? neither; the charge will too vast. Hang charge! we shall quickly fetch 't up again. All I fear is, the thing will be so considerable, it may chance to be begg'd from us; and against that there's no other fence but to swear 'tis worth nothing. That was well thought on. Then, after this, comes my widow! I shall be but too rich!—One Jupiter! there could be no less than ten Jupiters lords of my nativity!

Joc. Sir Gudgeon Credulous! save you! I see there's hopes of the business, you mind it so well. Have you made any experiment?

Sir Gud. Yes; but I do not find it altogether answer expectation. However, 'tis but early days yet.

Joc. Pray be very curious in it; and Driver, to whom I have committed the management of my interest, shall assist you. I must tell you he's no ordinary artist.

Sir Gud. Better and better! Then he has seen it?

Dri. Seen it, sir! If I should tell your worship all I have seen, I should despair of the work; 'twould so put you out of patience!

Sir Gud. Good Driver! And how? and when?

Dri. Did not I tell you; you would not have patience? Good sir, let things do themselves—one minute's over haste is enough to put us a twelvemonth back; for it fares here as with the philosopher's stone, the least error in the work and we must begin all anew.

Sir Gud. Honest Mr. Driver, I will be rul'd!

Enter GOTAM, *a note-book under his arm.*

Got. 'Tis he! I have his name here fast in my book in good black and white. Let me see—E, F, G, H, I, J, J—Jo, Jo, Jo—Jocose; here 'tis—Jocose, page 150. "Mr. Jocose, for himself and wife, £108, 7s. 9d. *ob.*" A good round sum. Would I had it! I could be content to bate him the single money!

Joc. But hark you, Driver! thou seest this pagan cousin of mine, and know'st his business? Prithee put him off with some whim or other.

Dri. I warrant you, sir; leave him to me!

Joc. Cousin! your servant. I was just sending my man to speak with you; but he knows the business, and can tell 't you as well as myself. Come, Sir Gudgeon; I'll wait on you! [*Exeunt* SIR GUDGEON *and* JOCOSE.

Got. Your servant, sir; I thank you.

Dri. Now, Mr. Gotam, you may see what 'tis to have a friend at court. You thought, I warrant, my master had forgotten you.

Got. Why, truly, sir, this money has been due a pretty while—long before his wife died, I am certain.

Dri. No more of that! Suppose he put you on a business shall make you for ever, and be worth ye; thou hast hardly faith enough to believe, what!

Got. Ah! good Mr. Driver; as how, I pray?

Dri. Why, thus: My master, you know, has great friends, and therefore doubts not but by their assistance to procure a patent of privilege to engross a business solely to himself. I must confess it will scarce amount to more than a copyhold project.

Got. What do you mean by that?

Dri. That is to say, it will not exceed ten thousand pound a year. And I can assure you, if ever there were an ingenious invention, 'tis this; and in this my master intends to take you in with him, and let you go what share you please. You shall do no worse than himself!

Got. Ah, sir, my cousin is an honest gentleman, and I have had long experience of his love! How do ye call it?

Dri. 'Tis an ignick, hydrelick, and hydroterrick invention, consisting of heat without fire or smoke! And certainly nature and art melted down into the same body could not produce such another diacatholicon that shall equally serve to all purposes,—roast, bake, boil, wash, brew, dry malt, hops, wheat, oats, and generally everything else, as I told you before, without the help of fire or smoke! Now, sir, you know the business, and may consider of it.

Got. Consider! I apprehend it already, and find it too great to be dallied with. Why, it will destroy all the woodmongers upon the river, and reduce them to their first dung-boats again! How have you done touching the charge?

Dri. Truly you have hit upon one of the main points, and part of the reason why my master made you privy to it. For, as on one hand we must take in some sharers to lessen the charge, so on t'other it behoves us to consider how many we may admit, for fear of diminishing the profits!

Got. Most true! we'll carry 't on between ourselves. It will fall to my turn to be churchwarden this next year, and then I shall have the custody of the parish stock. If that will serve you, command it; we shall be able, I hope, to fetch it up again before my time be out.

Dri. By much. But the business is now on foot, and must not stand still for fear of spoiling, and therefore we must be provided of present money; because, you know, some fees must be scatter'd among servants and clerks, and some other will go to making of trials. Things will not come without charge!

Got. You say right! And now I think on 't, I may be able to bring in my neighbour Squeeze, the Exchange broker, and by his means old Mr. Suckdry and Mrs. Godsgood. There's money enough at an hour's warning, if one could tell how to get it!

Dri. Pray, about it, and I'll see you to-morrow. If you go forth, leave word where I may find you. Farewell! I must follow my master. The knight and he are gone to see a proof of what I told you.

[*Exit* DRIVER.

Got. Farewell! but mum. Certain I rise with the right end upward to-day, I have had such good luck! I shall be an alderman, I see, in spite of all three-halfpenny stars! I think a brass jack-line would hang as well o' my shoulders as on another man's—certain it must. But see, my wife!

Enter MISTRESS GOTAM.

This hyterridinctido will be news to her,—i' faith will it! Sweetheart! well met!

Mrs. Got. I had as lief ha' found you at home. The main chance goes well forward in the meantime, and you never in your shop! God held! a beggar I found thee, and a beggar thou'lt leave me!

Got. Nay, wife, I have good news for thee. I have been with my cousin!

Mrs. Got. And has he paid you the money? I am sure 't has been due ever since my first husband's time!

Got. 'Tis sure enough! not too hasty, wife; we are beholden to him. You know he took notice of me at court, show'd you the privy lodgings, got you a place at the play, gave you a bottle of the king's wine and a court tart, and sends us venison twice in a season, wife!

Mrs. Got. Better he had sent his money, and I could have got t'other myself! Marry gip! this is one of your old excuses. You think you have got a wife can maintain you, and now, forsooth, you must walk like a gentleman! Sirrah, sirrah, look out and mind your business, or I'll make you look out!

Got. Good faith, I do.

Mrs. Got. Yes, among your gills too much! What was that you said to our maid t'other night in the kitchen, when you thought I was abed? I heard you. You mought* have come up a pair of stairs higher if you had pleas'd. I don't wonder now she 'as lost her stomach!

Got. This is nothing but thy jealous head.

Mrs. Got. Jealous! Come up here! You can be merry enough abroad when you are amongst your flirts, but at home you're as sad and lumpish as a gibb'd cat! I can tell you the reason,—thou art sad because thou canst not bury me! I half doubt the ratsbane you bought t'other day was not altogether for the rats! Do you understand that, gentleman?

Got. Not I, in troth.

Mrs. Got. No, you won't! you can understand your gossips well enough! 'Tis a fine thing you must be perpetually hopping after them; and I, forsooth! I cannot walk in the fields with a friend, but, whoop! the house is too little for you! My first husband was another kind of man; my finger could not ache but he I woo's!—nothing was too good for me. When will you say, "Dear wife! honey wife! sugar wife! how dost thou? Dost want anything? Would'st have a new gown? Go abroad? Walk to Islington? See the bears? Go whither thou wilt, do what thou hast a mind to, I am not jealous?" Here was a husband!

[*She cries.*

* Might, must.

Got. Prithee, have done! I told thee I had been with my cousin, and have good news for thee!

Mrs. Got. As what, I warrant?

Got. What! Such as shall make thee a lady within this twelvemonth! My cousin and I are engag'd in a business cannot be less worth than fifteen thousand pounds a year honestly! Now, wife, where's your loving husband?

Mrs. Got. Whatever I say in my passion thou art—— 'Tis but only to make thee better! But hark ye, my dear! sha'nt we not keep a coach then?

Got. A coach! Yes, and eight horses; and our country house new built! Come, follow me! and I'll tell thee the rest within, which I would have thee communicate to your friend Mrs. Godsgood, and bring her in for a share, while I do the same to my neighbour Squeeze, the Exchange broker! Come!

Mrs. Got. Anything, good husband! I'll be thy best wife! [*Exeunt.*

ACT II.—SCENE I.

Enter LEANCHOPS, *solus.*

Lean. Well! o' my conscience there was never so unlucky a fellow as myself! Service, do you call it? Certainly, if damnation be only *pœna sensus*, that were a fitter name for it! Here I live with a master that has wealth enough; but so fearful, sad, pensive, suspicious a fellow, that he disquiets both himself and every one else! Art, I have heard say, has but seven liberal sciences, but he has a thousand illiberal! There lives not a more base, niggardly, unsatiable pinchpenny, nor a more gaping, griping, polling,* extorting, devouring cormorant! A sponge sucks not up faster, and yet a pumice gives back easier! The sign is

* Thieving, cheating.

always with him in the clutches; and a kite's pouncke truss* not more readily! He shall watch you a young heir as diligently as a raven a dying horse, and yet swallow him with more tears than a crocodile! He never sleeps but he seals up the nose of his bellows, lest they lose breath, and has almost broke his brains to find the like device for his chimney and his throat! A gamester has not studied the advantage of dice half so much as he a sordid parsimony, which yet he calls thrift; and will tell you to a crumb how much difference there is in point of loss between a hundred dozen of bread broken with the hand and cut with a knife! The devil's in him, and I am as weary of him as of our last journey, which both of us perform'd on the same horse! As thus:—In the morning, about two hours before him, out gets Peel Garlick, he jogs after, overtakes me, rides through the next town and a little beyond it, leaves palfrey agrazing for me and marches on himself. In like manner I get up, overtake him, ride on, and leave him on this side the next town, and so order our business, that he rides out in the morning and into the inn at night, and through every town by the way. Nor need we fear any man's stealing him! Smithfield, at the end of a long vacation, can't show such another wall-ey'd, crestfallen, saddle-back'd, flat-ribb'd, gut-founder'd, shoulder-pitch'd, spur-gall'd, hip-shotten, grease-moulten jade, besides splint, spavin, glanders, farce, stringhalt, sprains, scratches, malander, and wind-galls innumerable! Like the fool's hobbyhorse, were it not for the name of a horse a man had as lief go afoot; and thus we jog on in grief together. But hold! I hear him—somewhat's amiss!

Enter SUCKDRY.

Suck. Undone, undone! whither should I run? whither should I not run? Stop there! Whom?—what?—where?—I know not! Leanchops!

* Pouncke—*i.e.* 'pounces,'—the talons or claws of a bird of prey. 'Trussing,' in falconry, is the hawk soaring up with any fowl or prey, and then descending with it.

Lean. Sir, what ails you?

Suck. Oh! a lost undone man! What a deal of misery a day brings forth! I have lost my money, and what should I live longer? Hunger and poverty will be my end!

Lean. How much have you lost, sir?

Suck. I believe thou knowest as well as I. Ah! a whole half-piece! gone, gone, gone, and I undone! I believe thou hast found it! Open your coat! let's see your right hand! your left hand—both hands—your third hand! Ah, no hopes! undone, undone!

Lean. Pray, sir, search! Perhaps it may be about you; you have many pockets!

Suck. Impossible, impossible! Uh!

[*They search, and find it in a dirty cloth.*

Lean. Why, see now! may not you be asham'd to use me thus—and for nothing too?

Suck. Asham'd! What should a poor man do with shame? Get in! get in!

Lean. 'Tis past three of the clock, and I have eat nothing to-day!

Suck. This rogue's mind is nothing but his gut! A good thrifty servant, that minded his master's profit, would have gone to the cook's and cheapen'd every joint, tasted all, but bought none, and made a good meal on 't! One would think, sirrah, you might not be asham'd to do what your master has done before you! Get in, I say, and look to the house!

Lean. There's no fear that any one will carry 't away; and, for anything in 't, there's nothing but cobwebs!

Suck. What's that he mutters? No marvel, sirrah, if for your sake I am not made an alderman! I will have the cobwebs preserv'd; they are good for a cut finger! Get in, I say! How the slave stirs! If I come to ye, I'll mend your snail's pace!

Lean. One were better be hang'd than endure this life!

Suck. How he mumbles the devil's *paternoster!* Sirrah, get in! and stir one foot till I call ye and thou hast as good have broken thy neck! So; he's gone!

[*Exit* LEANCHOPS.

And I'll go visit my gold! I am afraid I have spoken in my sleep, or dropp'd some word or other that may discover it, or that this rogue has eyes in his poll, and observ'd where I buried it; but if he has, I'll so dig 'um out! I have reason enough to suspect it—men speak more heartily to me than they were wont, are more free in their salutes, stop and talk with me, shake me by the hand, ask me how I do, whither I am going, what's my business, if they may serve me, and the like! Nay, Mr. Jocose t'other day would have giv'n me wine, and proffer'd his son should marry my daughter—without a portion, too! Ah—ha! I do not like when rich men speak kindly to a poor man; they offer bread with one hand, but carry a stone in t'other! But I lose time!—my gold, my gold! This must be the place! All's safe, and I'm alive again! All hail!—[*A board sinks, and his bags are discovered.*]—Thou that givest form to everything! thou sun of life! thou guardian that protectest us! thou regent of the world, that disposeth of all things as thou best pleaseth, and without whom human society would quickly fall in pieces! For, whatever else may be call'd the girdle, I am sure thou art the buckle that hold'st it together! There! rest in peace, my better angels!—[*He covers it again.*]—And while I call ye mine, let the world frown, laugh, point, or hiss—one glance of yours is worth it all; and I shall want nothing but too few arms to hug myself! I shall be courted by every man, welcome everywhere—at least from the teeth outwards; for in this world gold seasons and relishes everything, and men are received, not for the ass's, but the goddess's sake! 'Tis like having a handsome wife—every man is, or would be, your servant! Ho! Leanchops! Leanchops!

Enter LEANCHOPS.

Lean. Your pleasure, sir?

Suck. I am going abroad, Leanchops! Shut the door after me, bolt it and bar it, and see you let no one in in my absence. Put out the fire, if there be any, for fear somebody, seeing the smoke, may come to borrow some! If any one come for water, say the pipe's cut off; or to borrow a pot, knife, pestle and mortar, or the like, say they were stole last night! But hark ye! I charge ye not to open the door to give them an answer, but whisper 't through the key-hole! For, I tell you again, I will have nobody come into my house while I'm abroad! No; no living soul! Nay, though Good Fortune herself knock at a door, don't let her in!

Lean. She'll have care enough of that herself. She has been often near us, but I think there is a cross upon the door—she ne'er came in yet!

Suck. Sirrah, sirrah, hold your peace, and do as I bid you! 'Twould better become you to know more and speak less! See it be done!—[*Knock within.*]—See who's at door; but let not one in till you have brought me word! [*Exit* LEANCHOPS.

What a misery 'tis to be thought rich—one or other is perpetually haunting him; while the poor man yet is rich in this, that he's troubled with none of it! He fears neither thieves nor quartering of soldiers! He is exempt from rates and parish duties! He sleeps securely without bolts, and is subject to no man's envy! Every man's trencher is his table, every place his own country, and lives in peace with all men but the justice, the constable, and the beadle!

Enter LEANCHOPS.

How now? Who was 't?

Lean. Mr. Squeeze, your Exchange broker! He would fain speak with you!

Suck. O! let him in by all means. He is a good man, and never comes empty-handed! Make haste before he be gone, sirrah! [*Exit.*

This rogue will never learn wit! One would have thought he had liv'd long enough with me to have been able to distinguish persons! I must ev'n discard him; 'twill save charges!

Enter SQUEEZE, SIR GUDGEON CREDULOUS, MRS. GODSGOOD, *and* GOTAM.

Squ. I'll show you the way, gentlemen! I have some interest in my pocket for him, and will pay him that first; 'twill make him more supple! I was just coming, sir, to wait on you with some money that I had receiv'd for you, and met with these gentlemen coming to me about a like business, and I ev'n brought 'em with me. 'Tis—— [*They whisper.*

Suck. O, they are welcome—they are welcome! and chiefly yourself! It came in good time, for I profess I had hardly a groat in the house!

Got. How? Then our business is done already! What's worse than ill luck? [*To* SQUEEZE.

Squ. Please you to tell it over? The overplus is for continuance. [*He whispers it.*

Suck. Don't speak so loud! I understand you! [*Goes aside and counts it.*

Squ. Let him alone awhile; let him handle the money! He means he has never a groat he would spare by his goodwill! [*They whisper.*

Suck. 'Tis all right and well, only here's a Parliament sixpence; pray change it!

Squ. How was I mistaken? There, sir!

Suck. Hark you, neighbour! what's their business?

Squ. Such as you never dealt in before—the most ingenioust invention was ever yet found out! I'll undertake, after the first year, you may make cent. per cent. of your money every three months, besides a certain bank ready upon all occasions!

Suck. Say you so, good Mr. Squeeze? As how—as how?

Squ. They'll tell you that themselves. You know Mr. Gotam?—he has been always held a sober man!

Suck. Indeed has he, and well to pass. He is of the livery, and in a short time will be master of his company. He married the Widow Mince! I knew her first husband; he was a thriving man!

Squ. Marry was he! But the business is of so

great a concernment that 'tis not one or two ordinary men's purses are able to carry it on. The other is Sir Gudgeon Credulous, a worthy wise knight, and in his own country of the peace and *quorum.*

Suck. He seems no other.

Squ. There is a gentlewoman, too—one Mistress Godsgood!

Suck. O, I have heard of her! A rich widow?

Squ. That she is, o' my knowledge—I deal for her. All persons concerned; but the main wheel of the work is Mr. Jocose! Faith, sir, I'd have you come in too! As poor a man as I am, I am resolv'd to go in five hundred pounds!

Suck. But what shall you come out, neighbour?—what——

Squ. No man knows what! You had best speak to 'um.

Suck. How much would they have from me?

Squ. That shall be as you please, whether anything or nothing; only at present they would borrow of you two thousand pound!

Suck. Two thousand pound! Do you know what you say?

Squ. Yes; £2000! You are too quick for me—I meant upon good security.

Suck. Oh, that alters the case! Life is frail, man is mortal, but good security may do much! What is the security?—Citizens or country gentlemen? You know my way,—I must have a judgment at least!

Squ. Pray talk with 'em yourself.

Suck. You're welcome, mistress! Sir Gudgeon Credulous, I understand? And you, Mr. Gotam? Your business with me?

Sir Gud. The same, sir! I thought Mr. Squeeze had inform'd you!

Got. If he has not, we shall.

Suck. Why, truly, he has given me a small touch of 't.

Sir Gud. Then thus, sir,—we are all persons jointly concern'd in the same business, and we look upon the whole charge, what is past and to come, may amount to £9000—somewhat under a year's profits! Of this, I am out already £4000; the Widow Godsgood advances £1500 more; Mr. Gotam, £1000; Mr. Squeeze, £500; and, to make up the sum, we would borrow of you £2000, upon good security!

Suck. Alas, sir! £2000!—I am a poor man—£2000 and I are not so near of kin but we may marry to-morrow! But if your security be like, and you'll be civil to me, I have some friends! Pray, sir, what is your security? [*Spoken whiningly.*

Sir Gud. Would the Court of Aldermen were as good! Security!

Enter LEANCHOPS.

Lean. Sir, there's a gentleman at door inquires for you!

Got. For me? It may be Mr. Jocose. Pray, desire him to come in! I am glad he found me out! Now you'll be able to see the very guts of the business!

Suck. What share goes he?

Sir Gud. Alas, sir, none! 'Tis enough for him that the invention was, and the patent will be, his! There's reason in all things!

Enter DRIVER.

Oh, Mr. Driver! Where's your master?

Got. Where's my cousin?

Dri. He intended to have been with you himself; but being unluckily taken ill of the gout, he sent me to your house, where I heard of your being here.

Suck. A good rich disease! I warrant I shall ne'er be troubled with 't!

Dri. All that he bade me signify to you was, that the work went well on, and only wanted more workmen and more materials!

Sir Gud. We are about it now, and have provided very well for the time. And now you are come, pray save me a labour, and let this gentleman understand the business.

Dri. Which, sir? That of the Plegnic Screw, the Handquern, or the Horse-Wind-Water-Mill?

Sir Gud. Ha, ha!

Suck. Have you more than one?

Sir Gud. Divers, divers—which is the reason of the excessive charge! Though, troth, 'twas more than I knew before!—[*Aside.*]—But the more the merrier! Prithee, let's have that that is now in operation. I think you call'd it the *Metallorganicum Ignicadrillicum!*

Dri. You mean that of a constant heat, without fire or smoke?

Sir Gud. The same—the same!

Suck. How is 't possible?—which way?

Dri. Tell you that, and tell you all! Every art has its occult quality, which, once demonstrated, would cease to be a secret, and some other might chance to get between us and home! However, since here are none but friends, and all well-willers, I will give ye some small hints of 't, which, to be short, is singly effected by a new kind of motion,—for, you know, motion is the cause of heat,—and this, meeting with matter ready dispos'd, shall either work naturally by itself, or, in cases extraordinary, by an antiperistasis; and be not only equi-sufficient, equi-cheap, equi-excellent, as all minor projects pretend to, but more cheap, more sufficient, and super-excellent, which, when we are better acquainted, I will easily demonstrate!

Suck. I'll promise you, if this be able to be made good, 'twill save abundance of wood and coals!

Dri. That's least! What say you to this? *First,* There can be no danger of firing; for, as I told you before, 'tis done without fire! *Secondly,* You are not troubled with smoke, the greatest enemy to man's health! *Thirdly,* No soot shall fall into the pot, nor fat be lost in the fire! *Fourthly,* It shall so preserve the radical moisture, juice, and substance of hops and malt, that whereas now they retain in a manner only their fixed salt and excrementitious dead substance, this shall so conserve their balsamical spirits that the brewer shall be able to afford twelve-shilling beer at half-a-crown a barrel, and get more by 't than he does now! *Fifthly,* As you well observ'd, no charge of fuel! *Sixthly*—which one were enough by itself—It is an invention, or rather a new marvellous art, useful to all and injurious to none, and such as, besides the eternizing our names to posterity, shall give us at present honour, fame, friends, wealth, and, as a consequent of that, everything!

[*The rest whisper, while* SQUEEZE *and* SUCKDRY *discourse.*

Squ. What think you of this, sir?

Suck. O' my word, no contemptible business! I hear he has more on foot—and why mayn't we get one to ourselves?

Squ. Perhaps you may; and the lending this money may be a good introduction to t'other!

Suck. Don't you think they would take half money and half jewels?

Squ. Perhaps they might; but then you must enlarge the sum, or they may want money to carry on the work!

Suck. You say right! What's their security?

Squ. O' my conscience, if you would but stand upon 't, they'd go near to mortgage to you a third or a fourth part of the clear profits!

Suck. Softly! Don't talk of a fourth! I'll make 'um believe I will have a moiety; though, rather than fail, I could be contented with less!

Squ. If I might advise you, sir—— [*They whisper.*

Dri. Why, truly, to tell you truth, we have made very few proofs of the rest; but if you will call at my master's, I'll give you that account of 'em may be worth your trouble! There will be enough for you all!

Sir Gud. But hark ye, Mr. Driver, don't you bob me off with a third-rate project now!

Dri. Sir Gudgeon, that you should think so!

Suck. Do you propose it to 'um! [*To* SQUEEZE.

Squ. I shall, sir! Mr. Gotam, you know we propounded £2000 for Mr. Suckdry? I have done the work, and he shall be contented with a third part of the profits for security. I hope you will consider me in my share? [*Aside.*

Got. And all the reason in the world! You hear, gentlemen, what he says?

Sir Gud. I would have him secured. But I would not, though, leave a twenty-shilling piece in pawn for a groat!

Suck. Alas, sir! 'tis none of my money—'tis my friend's, and I'll account truly between you both. If you intend honestly, you cannot give too great security.

Dri. You may do it; I'll undertake my master shall not oppose it.

Sir Gud. Then get ready the writings. I hope we shall have a good account in a short time!

Suck. As soon as you please!—I'll about it straight. We may be all made, and send us but good luck!

Sir Gud. Well, sir, farewell for the present!

[*Exeunt all but* SUCKDRY *and* DRIVER.

Suck. Farewell, good gentlemen! But stay, Mr. Driver—pray stay! Let me speak with you! Methought you were saying your master had a great many other projects? Surely—surely, he must be a very rich man?

Dri. Why, faith, sir, he is well enough, tho' he be at a great deal of charge; for now and then an engine breaks, and an experiment fails! Should all take right, he would be too rich; but that's almost impossible! He that will get must now and then venture to lose! This is our comfort—the first good hit pays for all miscarriages!

Suck. That's well! But pray, tell me, what children has your master?

Dri. One son, sir, and that's all. I have often ask'd him why he toils himself to leave so great an estate, when the tenth part of what he has already would serve my young master and to spare!

Suck. No ill sign!—I like him the better. But dost

think he was in earnest when he propos'd a match between his son and my daughter?

Dri. Yes, truly; if he said it, you may believe him. But, alas! what should my young master do with all that wealth you two are like to leave him?

Suck. Keep it—keep it—and breed more! Prithee, tell me, dost think thy master would settle a good swinging project upon him in possession?

Dri. Yes, truly, I believe he may.

Suck. Then, hark you! pick me out a good round one, and it may not be the worse for thee! 'Tis the first part of falconry to hold fast; and if thy young master has that good quality, I dare trust him for the rest, or he may quickly learn it!

Dri. I shall be glad with all my heart to be an instrument in the business! And now, upon second thoughts, I think your daughter may make an excellent wife for him!

Suck. Your reason, good Mr. Driver?—your reason?

Dri. Because I have so often heard him protest against your great matches, as he calls 'em, and compares 'em to an ill pudding—all blood and no fat.

Suck. I'll be sworn a hopeful young man! But tell me—prithee, be true to me!—what kind of wife does he most affect, if he might have his choice?

Dri. What? Ev'n a good honest man's daughter, that shall bring him no charge, nor put him in fear of being eat out by her kindred! One that shall never send her husband on a how-d'-ye, or keep more coaches in town than he has ploughs going in the country! One that shall not spend his Michaelmas rents in Midsummer moon, and cost him more in sails and rigging than the hull's worth!

Suck. 'Tis a hundred pities but thou were supervisor-general of the female sex!

Dri. Faith, sir, I car'd not much if I were—I should be the better able to serve my friends; but this is not all!

Suck. Prithee, on! I like it well.

Dri. One that is not haunted with perfumers, lace-men, milliners, silkmen, jewellers, mercers, exchange men, seamsters; and, heyday! and can be contented with her husband's tailor! One that understands not the way of smooth-chinn'd pages, and can find both lackeys and women in a single chambermaid! One that was never read beyond *aquafortis* and tinning-glass, and is as much gravelled at Spanish paper and talk as a country vicar at an Hebrew pedigree! One that has no aunts nor she-cousins to visit, and goes not above thrice a week to the drawers for new patterns! One, to be short, that is all herself, and thinks it no scorn to be her own seamstress and tirewoman!

Suck. Say'st thou me so, my heart? And if I ha'n't a girl that fits him, she is not like her father! Come, Mr. Driver, be but assistant in striking up this match, and thou shalt ne'er know what it may be worth thee! Come!—A man must promise at large though he perform at leisure—hope makes men diligent!

[*Aside. Exeunt.*

ACT III.—SCENE I.

Enter JOCOSE, FERDINAND, *in a Precisian habit, and* DRIVER.

Joc. Ay, this is something! I protest I should hardly have known thee myself! But one thing—I do not like this hat; 'tis so high crown'd, he'll swear 'tis mere waste, and three ounces of stuff might have been well sav'd!

Fer. That may be quickly mended, either by getting another or circumcising this! It lies under the band, and will ne'er be seen, or if it should, he'll like it the better.

Dri. Ne'er doubt it, sir! It must take, for I have read him such a lecture of my young master's frugality that he is out of all patience till he see him; and if you can but outcant him now, the work's done!

Fer. That must be left to chance! and yet, 'tis not impossible but I may make my party good with him. Have I liv'd in Genoa, where the Jews come laughing in and go crying out, as having met with greater Jews than themselves, and do you think I shall not be able to deal with him? I warrant ye!

Joc. Well said, Nando! A good confidence is half the thing!

Fer. But when must this robbery be?

Dri. I expect him here instantly, though not purposely, about this business; for my design was to have it come on, as it were, by the by, and of itself!

Joc. What other business has he?

Dri. Oh, sir, to see how the main work goes forward. Besides, he expects you should settle a good lusty project upon my young master, and I am wide of the mark if he is not hammering at another for himself! And to tell you truth, so they are all!

Joc. Now, send that thou hast not engag'd us further than we shall be able to get off fairly!

Dri. Pray, sir, trust me! Have I desired you to appear in 't? or been wanting to 't in anything myself?

Joc. Well, I refer it to thee. But must you have all the sport? Were 't not possible that I might at least laugh inwardly?

Dri. I was just making it my request to you that you would so dispose yourself as to overhear the discourse, and perhaps it may not be unworth your while. For the men, having consider'd that two heads are better than one, have communicated it to their wives, and ask'd their advice in the point; and they are so agog upon 't that they must have their projects too, and amongst them you'll find your widow! I never saw things hit more luckily; 'tis impossible but you must carry her!

Joc. Do you expect 'em here?

Dri. I wonder they stay so long, and when they come what they will say!—[*Knock within.*]—That knock may chance to be theirs!

Joc. Take the occasion of leaving 'em alone, for perhaps they may be more free amongst themselves than if either of us were present!

Enter SERVANT.

Ser. Sir, here are some gentlewomen that inquire for yourself or Mr. Driver!

Dri. It must be them!

Joc. Desire 'em to walk in! [*Exit* SERVANT. Do you tell 'em I am a little busy, but you'll go and acquaint me with it! You shall find me in that window! [*Exit* JOCOSE *and* FERDINAND.

Dri. So—and now for the good women! But what to say to 'em, tell he that can—he must be better read in these books than I am!

Enter MRS. GODSGOOD, MRS. GOTAM, MRS. SQUEEZE, *and* NANCY.

Dri. Ladies! your servant! And had you not commanded the contrary, I had sav'd you this trouble by waiting on you myself!

Mrs. Got. No, sir; 'tis our own business, and we thought least notice might be taken of it by discoursing it here!

Mrs. Squ. Yes, indeed, 'twas all our opinions! Only, I must confess, the widow here would have preferr'd a little state before convenience!

Mrs. Gods. But since I was overrul'd, pray, sir, where's your master?

Dri. I'll let him know you are here, and he'll wait on you presently!

Mrs. Got. I think this gentleman would be able to do our business as well!

Mrs. Squ. Yes, truly! He looks like a likely man!

Mrs. Gods. However, if Mr. Jocose were present too, 'twere no whit the worse.

Dri. Be pleas'd to repose yourselves a while, and it will not be long 'ere my master wait on you!

Omnes. Your servant, sir! [*Exit* DRIVER.

Mrs. Gods. Come, neighbours! I think it were not

amiss if we agreed among ourselves what we would have before they come!

Mrs. Got. Now, truly and indeed, 'twas well mov'd!

Mrs. Squ. I like it well; pray begin!

Mrs. Got. Trust me, not I; but I'll do as good, I'll put in now and then. Pray, Mrs. Godsgood!

Mrs. Gods. However you mistook me, I meant it so. Pray, madam—no pray, forsooth!—will you?

Mrs. Squ. Not I, indeed! How say you?—The widow?

Omnes. The widow—the widow!

Mrs. Gods. Then, in obedience to your commands, and may this present meeting be happy and prosperous to ourselves and the whole commonwealth of women, and that we propose those things that may be for the common good and dignity of the sex. You cannot be ignorant how much your husbands have encroached upon you, or, to speak truth, how much we have all lost by letting the men engross all business to themselves, without so much as asking our advice, as if we, forsooth, were no part of them, and made to no other end but to sit at home and prick our fingers!

Mrs. Got. Ay, indeed, a public grievance.

Mrs. Squ. The more's the pity.

Mrs. Gods. Pray, sisters, has not every pitiful corporation its counsel, the meanest parish its vestry, and our very fumblers their common hall? And shall women only lose their privilege?—shall we alone do nothing?

Mrs. Got. Had we no more wit than to be rul'd by our husbands, we shouldn't; but for all that, we now and then do our parts, and sometimes, too, more than comes to our shares.

Mrs. Squ. Thank themselves that won't be quiet when 'tis well!

Mrs. Gods. Pray, no interruptions in the middle of a speech; there will be time enough for all! Nor would I set up a new thing,—only revive an ancient and laudable, though somewhat antiquated, custom.

I have heard of an old emperor, somewhere or other, that ordain'd that, as he had his council of men, so his wife should have hers of women, which should be independent, and without appeal to t'other!

Mrs. Got. Marry, away with him!—an old man!—what should we do with him? And I have heard of a place, too, where they hung up the men, after they come to threescore, as things past their labour, and consequently useless!

Mrs. Gods. Yet, again——

Mrs. Squ. No more of that, good sister; for, if I mistake not the story, they were more severe upon us, and burnt us for witches at forty!

Mrs. Gods. Heyday! Pray, sisters——

Mrs. Squ. Peace—silence!

Mrs. Got. With all my heart! No offence, I hope?

Mrs. Squ. None on my part, I assure you!

Mrs. Gods. More still! This council, as I told you, whether in jest or earnest it matters not, they call'd the She Senate; and this is that which our present interest should prick us forward to restore! Nor let it be any rub in the way that women are forbid to speak in public, that being meant of a congregation of men, and I speak only of an assembly of women; for otherwise, if we were ever to hold our tongues, to what use were they given us? Those tongues, I say, that if they might would speak sense as well as their own, and upon a good occasion could be as loud! Think you, I warrant, they were given us to no other end but to lick our teeth and cheapen eggs? I think not! And why should we not use 'em, then? No doubt but we may, and perhaps, too, to as much purpose as the men; for could we look into their councils, 'tis ten to one but we should find many things ourselves would have been asham'd of! How common is it with them to be five days in wording the question, and as many more e'er they can put it right, and perhaps at last make nothing of it; whereas we are plain downright —we think what we please and speak what we think! How does this consultation thwart that, a third both, a fourth all, as if they met only to justify the proverb, so many men, so many minds; whereas we, if the reins were in our hands, if we did not manage them better, I am sure it could not be worse!

Mrs. Got. Well open'd! Pray, proceed!

Mrs. Gods. I think this enough for introduction. The next thing I would have consider'd is, of what persons this council should consist?

Mrs. Got. Of whom but women?

Mrs. Squ. All that will—what else?

Mrs. Gods. That would be rather a tumult than a council!

Mrs. Got. And to select a few and exclude the rest would be—what d'ye call it?—the men have a hard word for 't—oli—oli—oligar—fie upon 't, I can't hit it! Oil and garlic I think they call 't; 'tis either that or somewhat near it—a very mark of tyranny!

Mrs. Gods. Pray, no more interruptions! If you do not like it, refer it to another time. And first, if I might advise, I would have no maids of this council!

Nan. No maids! Why, I pray? Were you never one yourself, or was it so long since you have forgot it?

Mrs. Gods. Pray, give me leave! I say no maids, because we may happen to speak that among ourselves that may not be fit for them to hear!

Nan. Goodly—goodly! as if we could not tell how the market went, though we neither bought nor sold in 't!

Mrs. Got. Well said, little gentlewoman! Stand up for your privilege!

Mrs. Squ. I warrant they are not so ill bred but they know what's what as well as ourselves! How say you, Mrs. Nancy? Do not you know a pudding from a cart wheel?

Nan. I think I do!

Mrs. Squ. Did not I tell you so?

Mrs. Got. But how will you know which are maids and which not? Do not all go for maids till they are married?

Mrs. Squ. And are not some afterwards? What think you of those that have overgrown old fellows to their husbands? May not they be call'd maids, though, perhaps, much against their will?

Mrs. Gods. However, for honour's sake, we'll think 'em otherwise. But my meaning was, that none be receiv'd but such as are, or have been, married!

Mrs. Got. Well distinguish'd! And yet, perhaps, it might be no hurt if they sat behind the hangings, though they gave no voice; 'twould make 'em the abler against they came to 't themselves!

Mrs. Gods. For that, as you please. But, pray, no more interruptions! The next, I would have none admitted that have been shod round; and amongst them I would place such as are past fifty, who, like old garrisons, are fit for nothing but to be slighted, and the rather, too, to make room for others!

Mrs. Got. And good reason. Pray, on!

Mrs. Gods. Then, I would have none admitted that had not first purg'd herself by her corporeal oath that she had never made her husband a cuckold; unless she be very ugly, and that in such cases it be taken for granted that she has not!

Mrs. Got. Now out upon 't!

Mrs. Squ. This widow, I see, would make a very tyrant!

Mrs. Got. Confess, and be hang'd!—I am for none of 't!

Mrs. Squ. Nor I neither. Here's a fetch with all my heart!

Mrs. Gods. At least you may qualify it by proviso, that if it be done to oblige a gentleman, she may, notwithstanding, etc.

Mrs. Got. That alters the case a little. But I am clearly for throwing out both.

Mrs. Squ. And so am I—at least for laying the debate aside till a full house.

Mrs. Gods. What you please—I do but offer. Next, that if any discover the secrets of the house abroad, that such person or persons have their tongues committed to a three days' silence, without bail or main price!*

Mrs. Got. Insufferable!

Mrs. Squ. A tyranny never heard of before.

Mrs. Gods. Pray have patience! Next, that none be permitted to speak irreverently of their husbands, inasmuch as, be the men what they will, the wives' honour depends upon theirs—to traduce them were but, in effect, to disgrace ourselves!

Mrs. Got. Oh! worse and worse!

Mrs. Squ. Abominable, and not to be endured!

[*They walk and fume.*

DRIVER *and* JOCOSE *appear above.*

Dri. You see, sir, how hard your widow's beset. I think 'twere not amiss if you reliev'd her!

Joc. And so I will. She's better qualifi'd than I expected. Follow me!

Mrs. Got. Not speak irreverently, as you call it! Do you think it reasonable that my sham-legg'd Monsieur should say what he please of me, and I nothing? Or fit, I woos, that he be ever rambling abroad, when, though I say it myself, I am as able a woman for the matter of the point of that as any woman in the two next parishes! And I must sit still and blow my nails, forsooth!

Mrs. Squ. Or that mine should be perpetually abusing and striking me? I am sure he has so pommell'd me about the head that I am hardly able to bear a cup of drink, as they say! For, look ye, d' ye see, when I am troubled, I go to the Salutation with two or three neighbours or so, and call for our gills of sack apiece!—alas, you know it is not much!—and then we sit and chat over it; and look ye, d' ye see, I am now and then troubled with a rheum in my side, and go lame a little, and then when I come home my rogue says I am drunk, and stink of *aquavitæ;* when, alas, 'tis well known 'tis mere grief—mere grief makes me in that condition! Aa! you don't know this

* Delivery into the custody of a friend, upon security given for appearance.

husband of mine: he were a very devil but that he wears his horns! And is this to be borne, think you?

Joc. Hold a little—not yet!

[*To* DRIVER *offering to enter.*

Mrs. Got. No, by my troth, is it not! Come, come! serve him as I did mine! He struck me t'other day, and I set out my throat as loud as I could that he had murdered me for what I had; and as the neighbours came in, I made 'em believe I was in a swoon, and held him so long in suspense that from that day forward I got the staff into mine own hand! Ah! my poor first husband—he was a man of a thousand! I could have made him believe the cow was made of wood! But how d' ye think I brought him to 't? Even by complaining first, and pretending he did this and that in his drink, which he, good man, never thought of; and, if ever he denied it, 'twas but bringing my maid to witness, and I was sure to be asked pardon.

Mrs. Squ. Ay, here were a woman for the chair!

Mrs. Gods. With all my heart.

Mrs. Squ. Then for the quorum,—if two women and a goose make a market, I see no reason why three may not make a council, at least to determine, tho' not to hear.

Mrs. Got. I agree with you;—and truly I think so we should all. But for this widow,—she 's insufferable! Come, neighbour Squeeze, I see we must be well advis'd whom we trust the chair with: she may in time betray our liberties.

Enter JOCOSE *and* DRIVER.

Joc. Madam, your servant! Methought I heard you somewhat hot; couldn't you agree?

Mrs. Got. No indeed, sir, nor is it likely.

Mrs. Squ. Truly, I think 'twere not amiss if we entreated this gentleman to take up the business.

Mrs. Gods. You could not have thought better. Pray, sir, will you give yourself a small trouble to oblige us?

Joc. Alas, madam, 'tis too large a parish for me! however, I shall look upon your entreaties as commands. What may it be?

Mrs. Squ. Why, thus, an't please you.

Mrs. Got. No, pray let me!

Joc. Hold! suppose we walked in, we should be less subject to disturbance. Will 't please you, madam?

Omnes. With all our hearts.

[JOCOSE *leads off* GODSGOOD, *they follow*, DRIVER *manet.*

Dri. Call you me this matrimony? Help the good man, say I, for I am sure they need it; and yet certain there must be some little, I know not what in't, that I am ignorant of, or they would not be so hot upon't, that like bold seamen, having 'scaped one wreck, they dare yet venture on another. Whatever it be, I envy it no man; bless him with it, say I. I had rather believe my share of it than run the experiment; for, as far as I have ever observed, between a quiet and an unquiet woman there is only this difference, that he that has the first rides an ambling horse to the devil, and he that has the second a trotter.

Enter SIR GUDGEON CREDULOUS *and* GOTAM.

Sir, your servant!

Sir Gud. Honest Mr. Driver. And how? what news? Ha' you been as good as your word?

Dri. Yes, sir, here are some!—and you may take your choice. [*Shows his bag.*

Sir Gud. Aa! Mr. Driver, you were ever my friend. But prithee satisfy me by discoursing the reason of them, as why some are more lucky in their hits than others.

Dri. You must know, sir, that inventions came by degrees, but have ever had this ill fortune to be fatal to the first inventors, who have only discovered a new shore to shipwreck their persons on it, or bury their fortunes in it.

Got. How shall we do then?

Dri. Well enough! We have this advantage, that

others have gone before us, and broke the ice to our hands. However, we must not be so hasty as to expect all things should be done at once. No! Nature makes no leaps, and Invention, which is the handmaid of Nature, must but follow her and take pattern from her.

Sir Gud. Nay, I grant ye, time perfects everything; nor can it be thought that our invention should be so absolute, as that it were impossible to be improved.

Dri. You have hit the point, and learnedly. However, for demonstration:—The spade and shovel were primitive inventions, and from thence came theplough; in like manner from the rake, the harrow; from the pestle and mortar, all sort of mills, whether horizontal or plegnick, horse, hand, wind, water, or otherwise; from the wheel-barrow, carts and coaches; from the scraping of a hen, letters; from pease-hulls in the kennel, the invention of shipping; and from a kite's tail, the rudders to 'um. I should have mentioned another thing, which, how simple soever at first, 't has been since improved to a wonder.

Got. As what, good sir?

Dri. Why, thus: You know men originally lapt water like dogs, but finding that a little troublesome, they soop't from their hands; from thence came wooden dishes, thence earthen pitchers, thence black-jacks, thence flagons, thence cans, thence horns, thence pewter cups, thence glasses, and, as an *eumechanic* from the whole, silver and gold tankards.

Sir Gud. I'll be sworn thou hast cut out the business notably.

Got. Marry has he!—a shrewd fellow. But hark you! have you remembered me?

Dri. Presently! I was just coming t' ye; and shall only tell you, by way of prolegomena, that inventions are of two sorts, to wit, either such as are destructive to human society—as the invention of walking invisible, and making ships and boats sail in the air as well as on the water, which we call *Cacamechana*—or such as are advantageous and useful; and of this kind,

I think I can show you as much choice as any man, whatever he be.

Sir Gud. I must confess I am for those,—let's see!

Got. Ay, ay!—Those, those!

Dri. You see, gentlemen, I am not shy to you; I dare trust you to peruse my papers!

[*They turn over his papers.*

Sir Gud. Aa! good Mr. Driver, what are these?

Dri. Let me see!—most excellent things! You know, sir, we Englishmen chiefly buzzle our heads about two things, that is to say, religion and trade; and truly you have luckily hit upon both,—the one is a project for a divinity mill, that shall go by any wind, and never stand still.

Sir Gud. But of what use?

Dri. Marry, to grind controversy, and that so fine and subtle, it shall hardly be perceptible, and, I'll undertake, make more proselytes than ever did Chaucer's Friar with his shoulder-blade of the lost sheep.

Sir Gud. Lay that by! I'll fit you a chapman. T'other!

Dri. Why, this—'tis the height of art! An emporentick invention, of making cloth without wool.

Got. How's that? Cloth without wool! Make me but that good, and write your own conditions.

Sir Gud. With your favour, sir, I was in before you. Pray, go on!—how is it to be done?

Dri. Why, thus:—I shall discover all.

Sir Gud. Not to your friend, good Master Driver?

Dri. Then thus: you must gather the atoms into a glass well ground, and then thread them upon a fine imperceptible loom; and, when they are once wove, 'tis easy milling them to what consistence you please.

Sir Gud. But how shall we do for this loom?

Dri. Did you never hear of Vulcan's net?—You must take copy by that.

Sir Gud. Cry y'mercie! good Mr. Driver, this shall be mine. I have a glass, as one would say, made for the purpose,—a most excellent optic; it shall make you an atom show as big as a quarter-staff.

Dri. Alas, sir! the thread will be too big, and fit for nothing but to thrum coverlets; whereas my design in't was to alter the affairs of Christendom, by breaking the Spanish trade of fine wool, and the Dutch new manufactures.

Sir Gud. I apprehend you!—the price?

Dri. Why, troth, sir, it will not go under five hundred pound and a quarter share.

Sir Gud. No more! I'll give thee a note to my goldsmith, honest Mr. Driver.

[*He goes aside and writes.*

Got. Here—here! Mr. Driver. What are these?

Dri. A rare invention for the sealing of butter, without the charge of butter prints;—the same for gingerbread.

Got. Go on. This!

Dri. This—a whirligig for draining the sea for treasure-trove. But to this there belongs another—oh! I have it,—a device to stop up the rivers, that they shall n't run in till the work be over. But this will be a work of time and charge.

Got. However, the profit will answer it.

Dri. Here are others would do as well, or better;—you grasp at too great things;—an invention for the making books sell at treble the rate they would have done otherwise.

Got. As how, good sir? My brother shall be in for this.

Dri. By a fine new title and picture before it; or if that fail, getting 'um suppressed, and somewhat else which I shall only tell the bookseller himself. A new engine for the better sowing of wheat and setting of leeks. A proposition for the farming the excise upon Jews' trumps and town tops.

Sir Gud. Not forgetting nine-pins and shovel-board tables, I beseech ye.

Got. As how, I pray?—can that amount to anything?

Dri. Almost incredible! there's a great mystery in 't;

for look you, sir: do but consider how many more boys than men there are, and then make the conjecture. Where's this?—Oh! here!—Be happy. Here's an invention will do thy work:—thou may'st even shut up shop, or do what thou wilt.

Got. I can turn it over to another, which will be all one,—what is't?

Dri. Why, 'tis a project to incorporate the goldfinders, and makes 'um turn saltpetre-men; for, besides that the materials will be exceeding cheap, the learned, upon experiment, have found it makes the best gunpowder by reason of its nitrous quality, and the refuse, most incomparable soap; an invention must necessarily destroy the trade of potashes, and consequently bring all the soapboilers in London under your girdle.

Got. I'm satisfied! Not a word to Sir Gudgeon;—let's shake him off, and you and I'll drive the bargain by ourselves. Pray, sir, use me as kindly as you can, and I promise to consider you better as the profits shall arise.

Dri. Well, sir, I shall not press too hard upon a young beginner. I hope you'll be as good as your word.

Got. If I am not——

[SIR GUDGEON *gives* DRIVER *a note.*

Sir Gud. Here, sir! If to-morrow be anything fair, I'll begin the experiment, and perhaps make some small essay this night upon the moon.

Dri. I know not what excellent quality your glass may have above others; but, if I might advise you, I would defer it to the dog-days.

Sir Gud. The goodness of my glass will supply a small defect. I'll tell you what,—but you'll happily believe it,—I have discovered with it a flea in the Bear's tail, and a louse in Caput Algol—*Anglice*, Medusa's head. 'Tis but trying.—Come, I am out of patience till I set it on foot. My service to your master; I cannot stay to talk with him now. Farewell!

Dri. Your servant, sir! [*Exeunt severally.*

Act IV.

Enter SQUEEZE *and* DRIVER.

Dri. Good Mr. Squeeze, no more!—I am so full of business I can hardly tell which to set about first.

Squ. But I am afraid these will scarce turn to account.

Dri. How!—not turn to account! Is the sole engrossing of all love letters, whether in verse or prose, within the realm of England, dominion of Wales, and town of Berwick-upon-Tweed, so cheap in our eyes? Besides, that unimaginable project of procuring a fifth term and the multiplication of offices, according to the augmentation of suits, so slight with you? O the boundless avarice of insatiate men!

Squ. Nay, good Mr. Driver!

Dri. What! Nothing content you, unless you fine for Sheriff the first year? Gi' me 't again.

Squ. Pray, sir, are you angry because my wit is not so ripe as yours? Great things are not so easily apprehended. Suppose I offer'd that of a fifth term to the Inns of Court and Doctors Commons, do you think they would advance anything considerable upon 't?

Dri. Think! About it, and be thankful. We shall have you now once in a twelvemonth not know your old friends! But if you do, it shall be a warning to me how I ever——

Squ. What d'ye take me for? Pray, no more. Fare you well! [*Exit* SQUEEZE.

Dri. Your servant!—So, so; the wheels go merrily round. And now for my main game, Mr. Suckdry. If I can but squeeze that sponge into my young master's pocket, the work's done. Let me see!—[*Noise within.*]—He must not take me unprovided. Hark! 'tis he. [*He turns over his bundle.*

Enter SUCKDRY.

A project for the reprinting of *Tom Thumb* with marginal notes and cuts; and that every man within this kingdom buy it of the patentee at the rate of twelve pence, or come up to town to show cause why he will not.

Suck. Good! I won't disturb him yet.

Dri. Another, for raising sixpence upon every thousand of bricks; and twopence a joint for every joint of meat that shall be dressed on Fridays and Saturdays.

Suck. Excellent! This fellow will be rich; he minds his business.

Dri. That every usurer pay twelve pence per pound out of all interest money towards charitable uses, and that the patentee have the disposing of 't.

Suck. Oh! he'll spoil all again. [*He starts.*

Dri. Who's there? Mr. Suckdry! Your servant. You see I am at work for you; but this is not the business I have design'd for you. Hmh! 'tis come at last. Here 'tis! A thing shall bring you in a vast deal of money without any charge besides the primary charge.

Suck. As what, good Mr. Driver? What?

Dri. Why, 'tis a wooden horse, so contriv'd with screws and devices that he shall out-travel a dromedary, carry the burden of fifteen camels, run you a thousand mile without drawing bit, and, which is more than all this, not cost you twopence a year the keeping.

Suck. Ha! ha! he! I'faith, i'faith! prithee on! Is there no difficulty in the work?

Dri. The greatest will be to set him agoing. But I think I have sufficiently provided for that. I'll tell you how I have ordered it. Turn one pin, he shall trot; another, amble; a third, gallop; a fourth, fly: and all this perform'd by German clock-work! Don Quixote's Rosinante was an ass, Reynaldo's Bayart a mere slug, and Clavellino the swift a very cow to him.

I might mention Alexander's Bucephalus, the Cid's Bajeca, the Moor's Zebra, Rogero's Frontino, Astolpho's Hippogryphon, Orlando's Briliadoro, the Muse's Pegase, the Sun's horses, and Zancho's Dapple; but they are not to be nam'd the same day together. One thing more I could tell you; but——

Suck. Good Mr. Driver, out with it! No buts among friends, I pray.

Dri. 'Tis but shoeing him with cork, and he shall tread as firm and strike as true a stroke on the water as he does on land; and, which is more, care for neither tide nor weather, and run in the wind's eye! A device must of necessity break the packet-boats, and consequently engross the whole dispatch for Ireland, France, and Holland.

Suck. And do you think you could prevail with your master to part with this horse?

Dri. Yes, certainly, for his son's good. Though, as I told you before, he has more already than he knows well how to spend.

Suck. No more of that. Prithee, let me speak with him. He shall have bags, daughter, devil, and all!

Dri. I'll wait on you again immediately.

[*Exit* DRIVER.

Suck. Not cost a man twopence a year the keeping! So—so. 'Tis an excellent shaped horse, and must be good. Why may not I improve this project now, and make him carry as much on his back as the Trojan horse did in his belly; at least, as many citizens and their wives at once as the great bed at Ware will hold at twice? 'Twas well thought on.

Enter DRIVER *and* FERDINAND.

Dri. This is my young master, sir! will you please to be known to him?

Suck. A towardly young man. Save you, sir!

Fer. Your friend and Ferdinand. Pray, no compliments.

Suck. An humble young man, and sparing of his very words. I'll try his temper. With your favour, sir, I have long desir'd your acquaintance, and, having a further inclination to continue it, I must crave leave to ask you a few questions.

Fer. The fewer the better. As near as I could, I would not waste either time or breath.

Suck. Excellent! Pray, sir, what do you take to be the greatest virtue in the world?

Fer. Thrift!

Suck. Short, but pithy. Admirable! But might not I be so much beholden to you as to give me your reason for 't?

Fer. It would better become me to learn from you. However, since you desire it, I shall tell you what first mov'd me to it.

Suck. I am beholden to you. Pray, begin!

Fer. Then truly, sir, I find it founded upon nature. The sun, the moon, the stars are sparing of their light, and do not always shine. The earth is barren in some places that it may be fruitful in others. And the sea has its ebbs and neaps, as well as flowings and spring tides. And, in a word, from the beginning 'twas ever so.

Suck. Excellent again! Let me not interrupt you.

Fer. Nor is this all; it has been the general practice of all times. The golden age, to save charges, were clad in skins, drank water, eat acorns, and, to show their innocence, wip'd their noses on their sleeves. The philosophers, they were sparing; the Brahmins went naked; Diogenes liv'd in a tub; Pythagoras on carrots and cabbage; Plato wonder'd a man could eat two meals a-day; and Epicurus, whatever we think of him, was as great a Prince with a toast in the dripping-pan as a fat citizen with his shoulder of mutton and capon. The Stoics were abstemious to a miracle; and, if ever they exceeded, 'twas never at their own charge. Nor have they walked alone, the learned tread hard after 'um; for either, like the ancient Druids, they commit nothing to writing, or if they do, 'tis so close and enigmatical that nobody can pick anything out of 't. But I burden you?

Suck. By no means. Good sir, on!

Fer. To come nearer home, we all cry up charity, and, no doubt, do well in it; but who makes any use of it? at least, any more than needs must? We bless, 'tis true, but without a cross; and, for good works, we do no more than will just serve, if yet that, for fear of supererogating. Pray tell me, was it for nothing, think you, that we found a late style of the keepers of the Liberty? or that the keeper of a park had his name to no purpose? Surely no! The age is arriv'd to that height of thrift, that they find more's got by selling their bucks than by eating them themselves, or giving them their friends.

Suck. Right! I have not found more thrift,—no, not in Spain or Italy.

Fer. And now you mention Spain, give me leave to put off my hat to that venerable name! The Spaniard!—the frugal Spaniard!—that shall make you five meals upon one hen, feast his family with three pilchards, and carry a pound of mutton in triumph on a skiver! But I forget myself: I am sure now I weary you; yet, if you have ever so much time to spare, read but Sir Jeffery Dropnose his discourse upon save-alls, or his new method of skinning of flints, and perhaps you may not think your time ill spent.

Suck. Ha—ha! What was that? Books—books?

Fer. Yes, sir, a good thrifty author, and well received.

Suck. Uh! Have a care! No books, I beseech you. They cost money. Read men—read men! Hang these liberal sciences! this is no time for 'em. Study thrift—study thrift! 'Tis strange, you, that are so great master in the theory, should be so much out in the practick! Let me read to you.

Fer. With all my heart, and I readily embrace it.

Suck. 'Twas well said. And first, for your person. Have nothing about you that may be spar'd—nay, though it be not worth a farthing; for if you would but seriously consider how much one poor farthing, use upon use, in 200 years amounts to, you would not lay it out upon waste. Next, eat little, drink less, and sleep much, to save fire and candle-light; and, if ever you are sick, be your own doctor, and never exceed above a halfpenny worth of senna. Then for your clothes: Make no new, but beg an old suit as for a poor friend of yours; but fit it up for yourself, but short and close, lest your wife, taking example by you, run out as much in train.

Fer. But suppose, sir, I kept her always in mourning, would it not do well, think ye, to save linen and washing?

Suck. Very good, and well observ'd. And, hark you! never let her be too forward in making baby-clouts; perhaps the child may be still-born, and then there's so much sav'd. And since you have nam'd mourning, let me advise you, never give any upon your will; they'll then mourn indeed. And for your wife, make her no more new clothes than needs must. As long as the cat's skin is burnt, you shall have her keep home; let it be once sleek'd, and she's presently a caterwauling. Then for your housekeeping: Be ever exact in keeping fasting-days and holiday eves; for, besides that you comply with the discipline of the church, you save your own purse. And for your provision: Be sure to buy the worst of everything, as rotten eggs, mouldy wheat, stinking beef, and the like; for, besides that it is much cheaper, your family will eat the less, and for that reason also, let your meat be either blood-raw or over-roasted, and as near as you can dine late, that they may have no stomach to supper.

Fer. Then, sir, if you'll give me leave——

Suck. Good leave have you. Proceed!

Fer. If your friend come to dine with you, ask him, by way of prevention, when he'll be so kind as to come and dine with you. But if he chance to surprise you, treat him not, but tell him you'll make no stranger of him. Either he has an appetite, or he has not. If he has, hunger's the best sauce; if he has not, 'tis all lost. If he be your friend, he'll be contented with what you have; if not, 'tis too much.

Suck. Or rather take pattern from the prudent Dutch: Tell him your house is visited, and so carry him to the next inn, and there eat upon his purse. Two men's meals well sav'd! But one thing more which I had quite forgot. If ever you should chance to keep servants, change 'em often; they are generally diligent in their new clothes. And for their service, let every one perform two offices at least; following herein the example of the same thrifty Dutch, with whom, generally, one and the same person supplies the several offices of chaplain and barber.

Fer. How unfortunate am I, that have been so long a stranger to such excellent morals! Pray, sir, oblige me once more.

Suck. Ha! ha! he! Shall I turn prodigal in my old age?

Fer. Of counsel you may, sir; it costs you nothing.

Suck. Well-well-well,—since I must:—make the ant your pattern for laying up, and the limbeck your example for giving it out again,—the limbeck!—peace be with him that first invented it—the limbeck, I say, that, be it never so full, gives back again, but drop by drop;—which that you may the better do, let me advise you, first, to avoid law-suits, it being like a sheep's flying for shelter to a bramble, where commonly he leaves the better part of his fleece behind him;—next, give no money to servants, it being in effect a paying for your entertainment, and as little, upon hopes of return. Ingratitude reigns! Then, never fish with a golden hook for fear you lose it, or that the profit do not countervail the hazard and charge. But this I would have you: when you have any business doing, let your hand be either fumbling about your little pocket, or playing with some gold. Ah! it makes a man so nimble when he believes it will be his presently. But, when 'tis done, give him ne'er a groat; only shake him by the hand, invite him to your house, and tell him your wife and he are town-born children. Let him say what he will when you're gone; you've sav'd your money, and the loser may be allow'd the liberty of speaking. Let the world call it sordid, or what they please. He that can do this may be presum'd to be content with it, and consequently happy; for happiness consists in nothing more than in being content. *Populus me sibilat, at mihi plaudo.* A good saying, and the only piece of all the poets I ever understood. And, hark ye! if thou marriest my daughter, it shall be the posey of her wedding-ring.

Fer. How, sir! Marry your daughter? Why, I scarce ever saw her!

Suck. No matter, no matter; she shall be rul'd by me.

Fer. Alas, sir! charge of children will come on; and, I have heard say, a wife's as chargeable as an old tenement; 'twill cost you half your rent to keep it wind-tight and water-tight.

Suck. Well, well, well! thou shalt be at the charge of repairs during my life, and, after my death, shalt have all—all I have—all, all, all!

Dri. Troth, sir, my young master is bound to you. Come, sir, speak comfortably to the old gentleman.

Fer. I can only thank you, sir, and tell you that I am wholly at your dispose.

Dri. Why, that's well said.

Enter JOCOSE *and* MRS. GODSGOOD.

Suck. Mr. Jocose!—in pudding time! Do you remember what you said to me touching your son and my daughter? Truly—truly, I like the young man so well, that if I had twenty daughters he should have 'em all,—all, body and bones,—and all I have after my death,—ay, truly, every groat, unless it be four old Harry groats, which I have thus dispos'd in my will, viz.: one groat to the poor of St. Giles's and St. Andrew's, Holborn, to be equally divided amongst 'um; a second to the hospitals of St. Bartholomew's, Christ Church, and St. Thomas, to be equally divided as before, provided always that, within the first six months after my decease, they set up my name amongst their benefactors; a third to charitable uses in general, to be disposed as to my executors shall seem meet; a fourth towards my funeral expenses,—I think there will be no great need of a sermon. A man must do some good, you know.

Joc. And may he never thrive that shall go about to subvert so pious an intention! And now for my son: you have my consent.

Suck. I thank you. But, d'ye hear, Mr. Driver?—don't you forget the horse now. No more, but mum.

Dri. I apprehend you, sir. Your nod's enough!

Suck. Come, son,—for that must be thy name now,—come, go home with me! And, good Mr. Driver, let it be your care to get us a gentle reader, he will not expect so much as another. But for the clerk, you may let him alone; one of us can say Amen as well as he. There's so much sav'd!

Dri. It shall be done, sir!

Suck. Farewell, good sir! We'll make no wedding of it. Tailor's lists and blue points shall be both garters and favours.

Fer. So much the better. Your servant!

[*Exeunt* SUCKDRY, FERDINAND, *and* DRIVER.

Mrs. Gods. Send them good luck!

Joc. And none for me, good widow?

Mrs. Gods. O, by any means. Your project deserves it.

Joc. Am I unkind to you, then, that I'd have you take your money again? No; you are rather beholden to me, that have not made those advantages of you that, had I lov'd your money better than your person, I might have done.

Mrs. Gods. In that respect I must confess I am. But pray tell me, how came this humour about?

Joc. You may best answer that yourself. You know I lov'd you, and could not be ignorant but that I look'd upon Sir Gudgeon Credulous as a block in my way, which, once remov'd, I might have the better hopes of kissing the mistress myself. Pray, what did you most fancy in him—his person, his parts, or his estate?

Mrs. Gods. I was never so greedy to expect all three. I could for a need have excus'd the two former, to have been well secur'd of the last.

Joc. A right widow!

Mrs. Gods. You men, alas for you! you never mind those little things of estate. You are above ordinances; you are altogether for virtue!

Joc. Not so far neither, good widow. A little of both does no hurt; they do as well together as ill asunder.

Enter SIR GUDGEON.

But see! your haberdasher of small projects.

Sir Gud. Yours, sir! Madam, who thought to have found your ladyship here?

Mrs. Gods. Can you blame me, that am so far dipt in your projects, to inquire at least how things went?

Sir Gud. You might have trusted that to me. I dare warrant you a good return, and in few days. A little time must needs make us either Princes or beggars—I hope the first.

Mrs. Gods. But suppose the latter?

Sir Gud. 'Tis not to be suppos'd. Let me tell the widow of mine, Be happy.

Mrs. Gods. 'Tis the thing we all wish. But how came you to be so confident of a sudden?

Sir Gud. Because 'tis impossible we should be otherwise. The work goes pleasantly on. And, hark ye, widow! I am resolv'd to present thee a piece of scarlet, for thy own wearing, shall not have a lock of wool in 't; and yet good substantial cloth.

Mrs. Gods. But who makes it, Sir Gudgeon?

Sir Gud. What matters that, so you have it? I am promis'd an artist shall do wonders.

Mrs. Gods. A small philosopher, I hope?

Sir Gud. 'Tis not material whether he be or no. I love to trust every man in his way. What care I whether my tailor be a good musician, or my coachman be able to con a ship? It is enough to me that he perform what I intend him for. For my own part I am so well assur'd of the thing, that I could wish I were no knight, but had staid to have been made a lord for altogether. And so let me say to thee once again, widow of mine, Be happy!

Joc. For that of happy, be so as long as you can. But pray take me along with ye: no longer widow, nor yours, I beseech you.

Sir Gud. How's this? Who dare say the contrary? He were better——

Joc. Have broken your worship's pate. With this lady's leave, that dare I; or if you will not believe it—pray, madam, lend me your busk.

Sir Gud. Mr. Jocose! 'tis impossible! I never thought you would have serv'd me thus.

Joc. And why not? Would you engross all to yourself? He projects, and she projects too. Good, Sir Gudgeon, there's conscience in everything!

Sir Gud. 'Tis well you are my friend; but don't ye presume too far.

Joc. Further than this lady I shall not; and yet so far, with her good favour, I ever shall.

Sir Gud. But you may come short home. You know the necessity of attending more grand affairs lies upon me; but——

Joc. Does the fool prate? [SIR GUDGEON *runs out.*

Mrs. Gods. Nay, Mr. Jocose!

Joc. I obey! And now, madam, I leave it to your own judgement how much I was out in my character; and if there remains anything to your further satisfaction, pray let me know it.

Mrs. Gods. I'll consider of it within. [*Exeunt.*

ACT V.

Enter MRS. GOTAM *and* MRS. SQUEEZE *severally.*

Mrs. Squ. Mrs. Gotam, well met!—whither so fast?

Mrs. Got. Marry, to find out this rogue that has abus'd my husband! I tell thee what, Squeeze, he and his staffmen have made such a stink in our house, that all the neighbours are up and cry, A wedding, a wedding! I have been this half hour a shaking the bride laces off my petticoat.

Mrs. Squ. Why, what's the matter?

Mrs. Got. Hang him for a fool! He cries 'tis a new way of making gunpowder; but, when he's in a condition of receiving it, I'll ring him such a peal! I'll gunpowder him!

Mrs. Squ. And mine's as bad on the t'other side. He's so full of business, he's even mad! He talks of nothing but sonnets, madrigalds, acrostics, love letters, wedding posies, and I know not what! Well, if thy husband's project be the beginning of love, I am confident mine's the end of 't.

Mrs. Got. O that these men must do all things by themselves, and never advise with their wives till it be too late! But I'll make my gentleman know a piece of my mind before I have done with him.

Enter GOTAM, *sputtering.*

Mrs. Squ. Peace, peace! here he comes!

Got. Uh—hum—puth! 'Ta'd need be profitable, I am sure 'tis not very toothsome.

Mrs. Got. And whither, gentleman, whither so fast? Your wife's nothing with you! But I've a crow to pluck w' ye. Where's my coach and the eight horses you talk'd of, and the new dining-room to our country house? D'ye think to rob me thus?

Got. Nay, good wife—dear honey—they're all a coming! Do'st not see what pains I have been taking, and all to make thee a lady! Prithee, 'tis all for thee; good faith it is!

Mrs. Got. Marry, fough! all what?

Got. Whatever I bring to perfection. Thou must have patience; 'tis but an embryo yet.

Mrs. Got. Pray leave me off your brewing, unless it were to better purpose. I was finely helpt up when I married you, and refus'd more likely men every way, and such as would have maintain'd me like a woman. But the devil ow'd me a good turn!

Got. Nay, dear wife, thou art always in this key. What encouragement can it be to a man when his wife believes nothing but what she should not?

Mrs. Got. Say! speak! what should I believe, or what should I not believe? you'll teach me, will you?

Got. No, good wife; but we may hear one another though.

Mrs. Got. I've heard too much. Thou lets every one lead thee by the nose, and make thee an ass and a beast. And I could find it in my heart to make thee too—(look better to your business). Come, come! where be the keys of the chest? give them me!

Got. What to do?

Mrs. Got. What to do with my own? Why, was it not all mine? and dost thou grudge me my own? Go, go! try thy experiments with what thou broughtst thyself, unless they were better or more likely.

Enter MR. DRIVER.

Got. Mr. Driver!—Never in better season.

Dri. Why, how now, Mrs. Gotam?—sitting in judgement upon your husband?

Mrs. Got. If I do, 'tis my own husband, and one that, if you please, sir, has been fool'd enough by you.

Got. Nay, wife, you won't spoil all? The gentleman is a civil gentleman, and an excellent person in his way.

Mrs. Got. I'll excellent ye both! What fine project is this you have put my husband upon? Had your master no one to fool but his own flesh and blood?

Dri. What does your wife mean, Mr. Gotam?

Got. Alas, sir, if you liv'd at our house you'd never ask that question. 'Tis her ordinary exercise to keep herself in breath.

Mrs. Got. I'll breath you! Must you abuse me too? Remember this, gentleman!——

Dri. But may not I know whence all this heat?

Mrs. Got. You know but too well; and as you have

brought him on, pray bring him off, or I'll make the house too hot for you and your master too. I'll powder you!

Dri. And why?—how goes it forward?

Got. In plain troth, sir, between ourselves, I half doubt the woman's mad. She has thrown all the tubs about house, and rais'd the neighbours about our ears!

Dri. And you think you've done a wise action now, to discover in one minute what some men might have studied their whole lives for, but never found?

Mrs. Got. Indeed, sir! And do you believe there was anything in 't?

Dri. It matters not whether there were or no; your own folly will best teach you.—[*He tears a paper.*]—There, there's the counterpart of your articles, and to let you see how much I scorn to take advantage of you, I discharge you of all monies due by virtue of 'um.

Got. You've done well, wife! you've made a fair hand on 't!

Mrs. Got. Nay, pray, sir!

Enter SQUEEZE, *singing.*

Dri. Not a word more! I ha' done with 't.

Squ. And wilt thou gang with me, my Jo?
And wilt thou gang with me?
Now for thy daddy's benison,
I prithee now gang with me.

Dri. Ay, here's your diligent man; he has traverst Scotland already. Now, Mr. Squeeze, how goes all affairs?

Squ. Why, as a man may say, on wheels. I had no sooner set up my bills, and hung out a large label, with this inscription in capital letters—

Young men advance, and maidens eke draw near,
Here dwells Love's epistoliographer!

I say, I had no sooner hung it out, than my house was too little to hold the company! O' my conscience, I think Wapping, Ratcliff, and East Smith-eld were never so drain'd since the last great show. I'll undertake, 'twould have made two gingerbread women for ever.

Dri. See here, Mr. Gotam, see what industry can do! And yet I valu'd your device at least fifty per cent. more than this.

Got. I'm an unlucky fellow! This a man gets by making his wife acquainted with his business.

Mrs. Got. Nay, prithee sweetheart, let's home again! I'll try to recover all.

Got. Impossible! or, if it weren't, the neighbours have smok'd it. O, Mr. Squeeze! what luck you have!

Squ. My faith, I do pretty well, and at small expense. I'll be sworn the Packet of Letters, Familiar Epistles, Academy of Compliments, and two or three of the new poets, is the greatest charge I have been at; and I am confident I shall, in a short time, be able to bring it into a lesser compass, by printing some blank copies of the several kinds that shall indifferently serve to every occasion.

Dri. A pretty device and well found out.

Squ. But the main thing I built on troubles me. You remember the fifth term?

Dri. And what of that?

Squ. I have offer'd it to all the Inns of Court, Chancery, and Commons, and none bids me anything for 't; for they that have anything to do cry four is enough, and they that have not, though they shrug their shoulders and look smilingly on 't, yet, whether it be that t'others keep 'um so low, or that they fear they'd in a short time engross this too, though they seem to wish well to 't, yet they bid me not a farthing.

Dri. No matter; you'll find enough in this. You must not be too covetous.

Mrs. Got. But, good Mr. Driver, will you assist us at least in the soap business?

Dri. They go together: make one, and t'other follows. But I'll meddle no more in 't; I am too full elseway.

Got. Pray consider of 't, and we'll take a turn or two in the garden the while; perhaps I may light upon some new proposals. Mr. Squeeze, shall I beg your company?

Squ. With all my heart! [*Exeunt all but* DRIVER.

Dri. Well, I am gone so far, but how to get clear again, there's the question. I brought it on, and I hope my master has by this time thought of some device or other to bring it off.

Enter SIR GUDGEON.

Sir Gudgeon Credulous! your servant.

Sir Gud. Oh, Mr. Driver! how have you serv'd me? I have been trying your experiment at least forty ways, and I'm sure my glass is as good as any in Christendom; but the devil of a thread can I make hold, 'twas as rotten as dirt. An old black, died out of a rotten scarlet, and that too burnt in the dye, is iron to it.

Dri. Sure, sir, your mistaken.

Sir Gud. No, no, no! 'tis but too true.

Dri. Or did not take the right way.

Sir Gud. Oh no! I was exact to the thousandth part of a hair.

Dri. Or perhaps overdid your work, and so calcin'd 'um. O' my conscience, if the truth was known, this was it. And yet 'tis strange, so grave a philosopher, that has written so profoundly of cobwebs and perry, should be so much out in his first rudiments!

Sir Gud. I know not, but 'tis as I tell you.

Dri. You see what 'tis when men cannot be contented to do, but they must overdo. 'Tis well I did not trust you with the business of malleable glass, suppressing mountebanks, and enlarging the city charter. If I had, 't 'ad been all one.

Sir Gud. How's that, good Mr. Driver? Pray let's hear 'um; they may make amends for t'other.

Dri. No! no more. I'll never trust a man again that can't go by himself. One of your years and intellectuals, and not read without a fescue! *

* See Davenant's Works, vol. ii. p. 104.

Sir Gud. Come, come, let's try to recover 't again.

Dri. Never, never! I know, though I han't seen your work, you have spoil'd the design; for things of this nature are so nice and kickish, the least error renders them irretrievable. A man had better fix mercury in a blowing mill than offer to think on 't.

Sir Gud. What remedy then?

Enter JOCOSE *leading* MRS. GODSGOOD.
SIR GUDGEON *walks.*

Dri. Patience, Sir Gudgeon, patience!

Sir Gud. Hugh! patience! And had I more, here's that would exercise it all.

Joc. And now no longer widow, be as merry as a good husband can make thee.

Mrs. Gods. I have but your own word for 't, and yet hope I shall have no cause to repent the action.

Joc. 'Twas well said! and I'll promise thee, as near as I can, I'll give thee none. But see, Sir Gudgeon Credulous! He's come to give thee joy.

Sir Gud. Joy! choke 'um! [*Aside.*

Mrs. Gods. Save you, Sir Gudgeon! you've been a great stranger. I see I might have even done what I would for all you——y' are a kind suitor!

Sir Gud. She jeers me too! Is it not enough to have injur'd me, but you must tell me so?

Mrs. Gods. I injur'd you! forbid it. Pray how goes on our common business?

Sir Gud. All evaporated! Gone—gone—quite lost!

Mrs. Gods. Why, as I understand you, there was to be neither fire nor smoke in 't.

Sir Gud. I know not. The devil was in 't! and my new drape—quite defunct.

Mrs. Gods. And do you think it was kindly done to engage me in such a business?

Sir Gud. 'Twas no more than what I did myself. But I see, now it is too late, that I am merely tricked out of my money, my widow, and all. But somebody shall dearly rue it.

Joc. That's not I, Sir Gudgeon, is it?

Sir Gud. No matter whether it be or no. There are other bodies in the world besides yourself.

Joc. Yes, that there are. There are bodies politic, as London and Westminster; and bodies simple, as Sir Gudgeon and his participants.

Sir Gud. D'ye hear this, Mr. Driver? I shall order you, i'faith, if there be any law between the mount in Cornwall and Berwick stairs.*

Dri. However, sir, I am to thank you that you have been pleas'd to lend me some money to defend the suit.

Sir Gud. Well, look to 't! I say no more.

[*He offers to go out,* JOCOSE *stops him.*

Joc. No departing in wrath, good Sir Gudgeon! One does not know what you may do to yourself; you had better stay a while and take a little advice with you. Go, go down into the country, and awe your poor neighbours with my lord's nod, or his whisper in your ear at parting. Study longitude and the philosopher's stone, the north-west passage and the square of a circle. So brave a Sir Poll trouble himself with trifles? By no means—no, no! Embark for the Indies in a cock-boat, or to France on a mill-stone; plant a colony in *Terra Incognita*, or settle an intelligence with the Emperor of Utopia. These were fit for Sir Gudgeon!

Hæ tibi sunt artes!

Sir Gud. Well, sir, well! 'tis your time now.

Joc. Or, if you love the smoke o' the town better, enter yourself a virtuoso, and sit in judgement on every man but yourself. Never open your mouth with less than a cabal, and yet speak little, for fear you be understood. However, let your sententious tooth-pick speak for you, that you could say more if you durst trust the company, or were not under an oath

* *I.e.* between Land's-end and the most northern point in England—her Majesty's "good town of Berwick-upon-Tweed." "Berwick stairs" may be meant for "Berwick walls," or, perhaps, for the barbican of the old ruined castle of Berwick, which, resembling stairs, is still standing (1873), and runs down to the margin of the Tweed.

of secrecy. Sir Gudgeon beat his brains about ordinary matters? Fie, fie!

Enter SUCKDRY, *hugging himself.*

Sir Gud. You do well, sir.

Suck. Not cost a man twopence a-year the keeping? —O rare!—Mr. Driver—

Joc. See! here's another of your brethren. Prithee, Driver, entertain him while I look to the knight.

Sir Gud. So, keep me a prisoner too? you fear nothing.

Suck. Well met, well met, Sir Gudgeon! I sent you home the boy and the girl.—Ha? [*To* JOCOSE.

Joc. They are within.

Suck. But hark, Mr. Driver! A word. Ha' ye fitted out the horse yet?

Dri. And over-fitted too. What's worse than ill luck? Certain we are bewitch'd!

Suck. As how—as how—as how, Mr. Driver? No hurt, I hope, good Mr. Driver?

Dri. Yes, faith, sir! but it could not be helpt.

Suck. What? what? what? what? what, I pray?

Dri. Why faith, as he was coming full speed down Highgate Hill, he tript upon a stone, fell, and broke his leg short off!

Suck. Uh! undone for ever! No good to be done with him now? Speak! ha?

Dri. Why, truly, he may be made serve again—to the Court of Guard, or so—but, I fear me, not without some charge.

Suck. Uh! charge! What a fool was I to be so forward in this match, till I had seen what would come of t'other!

Dri. How, sir! is my young master so cheap with you already?

Enter FERDINAND *leading* NANCY, *both in rich apparel.*

Suck. Why, that's some comfort yet. He'll save it up again by little. Oh, Driver! what's this I see? Surely this house is the land of visions. My daughter in beaten satin! Hold me! I faint—I faint! Uh!

Fer. Come, my dear! And now no more of your No pray I thank ye's. 'Twas well carried.

Nan. While I was at my father's, blame me not if I obeyed him; and, now his election has made me yours, I hope I shall not so mistake the person as to pay you less.

Fer. That's a pretty rogue!

Nan. O my father! Good sir, help!

Fer. Certain he never gat her; nay, were she not my wife, I'd swear it! What's the matter? Stand off and give him air!

Suck. Uh—hu! my son and all!—and all to be daub'd! Is this the thrifty gentleman? Uh! how apt is even the best ground to run into weeds! Uh—uh!

Fer. Come, pray, sir, do not disquiet yourself, or judge me by my outside; 'tis the way to be mistaken a second time.

Suck. Is this founded upon nature?—this the habit of the ancient philosophers? It had not been amiss, if, while they pretended to instruct others, they had yet taught themselves.

Fer. Let me supply that defect, if yet you doubt it.

Suck. This the keeping your wife in mourning, to save linen and washing? This the burnt cat's skin we talk'd of?—defend her from what follows!

Fer. Pray, sir, hear me! and though I did a while put a force upon my nature to humour you, be not now disturb'd that I am yet at last come to myself again.

Suck. Uh—uh! he believes these things are death to me, and will murder me, though it be but to scatter that little which with so much pains I have rak'd together!

Fer. Do not misconceive me; 'tis my desire you may live and enjoy what you have. The earth, though she conveys the water through her veins, is allow'd yet to suck in as much as may refresh herself.

Suck. I was right: he is resolv'd to break my heart.

Fer. Pray, sir, hear me! and set not up your rest on that which, simply considered, is not that blessing the world takes it for. No; wealth not enjoy'd is but a dead heap of muck, and the same unactive lump in the chest it was in the mine. Were you master of all the most mighty could wish; did you not only possess riches, but tread on them; should fortune cover you with gold, and were your wealth as boundless as your eye; yet, had you not a heart to use 't, you would but from thence learn to covet more, and those false desires having no limit would become as infinite as error.

Suck. Uh—uh! no mercy!

Fer. Let me prevail, good sir. You cannot but hear a man that pleads against his own interest. You have enough; why should ye deny yourself at least a moderate use of it? Why should ye be fearful to approach it, and yet be jealous of others—like the sensitive plant, shrink at the touch, and cramp into a convulsion? Why should ye use your wealth, as anglers their little fish, only to bait for more? Or why degrade yourself from that sphere wherein nature set ye by a voluntary sale of yourself to slavery? In a word, why should you possess that with pain which others behold with envy?—such as, in itself, rather threatens than profits, and, thus obtain'd, becomes not the end, but change of misery. Come, pray, sir?

Suck. How shall I believe him? He said as much on t'other side erewhile. Give me leave!

[SUCKDRY *offers to go out,* JOCOSE *stops him.*

Joc. I'll be his security. Pray, stay a little! all will be well.

Enter SQUEEZE, GOTAM, *and their Wives.*

Oh, gentlemen, you're welcome! Now, Sir Gudgeon, what think you of reconciling all interests?

Sir Gud. You're in your own house, you may do what you list.

Joc. No more of that, I pray. I must have all

friends, though to my own loss. And therefore, to be short, let me tell you, Sir Gudgeon, that, finding you so inclin'd to projects, I thought you might be instrumental to mine, and I have compassed 'um. This—[*he points to the Widow and* NANCY]—for myself, and that for my son: for anything beyond that, I am wholly a stranger to 't. For I ever look'd upon projectors like the dogs in the fable, that burst themselves by endeavouring to drink up the pond, that they might the easier come at the carcase that floated on the middle of 't.

Mrs. Got. And do you think to carry 't off thus? Dost look like a sheep-biter, and seest thyself laugh'd at? [*To her Husband.*

Joc. Pray, gentlewoman,—with your good patience a little,—the use may chance to be more comfortable than the doctrine. For once I'll be the author of an ill court precedent; you shall all have your money again.

Sir Gud. Say you so, Mr. Jocose? Now, send us more such courtiers! Come, gentlemen, we will be friends before his mind alter; 'tis ten to one but he had been too hard for us.

Got. Indeed might he have been.

Suck. And so he has been for me.

Squ. I shall lose nothing by 't.

Joc. What say ye, gentlemen? d'ye like my motion?

Sir Gud. Ay, ay! Mr. Suckdry shall be ruled by me.

Suck. That's more than you know, though.

Omnes. Come! pray, sir!

Sir Gud. 'T'as taught us wit.

Joc. And I hope you'll consider your tutor Driver.

Sir Gud. Well, well, leave him to me!

Joc. And so you're pleas'd?—and you, and you, and you? And I hope [*They answer several.*

The same of you,* since now at last you find,
Who ploughs the clouds shall only reap the wind.

[*Exeunt* OMNES.

* The pit.

EPILOGUE.

PLAYS are but morals, and the ancients,
That first wrapt truth in tales, had their intents.
Full well they knew nothing discover'd vice
Like its own picture : so we hope of this.
How ill Suckdry appears ! How oddly those
That grasp at shadows, and the substance lose !
Take you the moral right, and say: The stage
Then does its work when it reforms the age.

BELPHEGOR:

OR,

THE MARRIAGE OF THE DEVIL.

Belphegor: or, The Marriage of the Devil; A Tragi-Comedy. Lately acted at the Queen's Theatre in Dorset-Garden. By Mr. Wilson.—"Prodesse potest aut delectare."—Licensed, October 13, 1690. *London, Printed by J. L. for Luke Meredith, at the Angel, in Amen-Corner,* 1691.

It is probable that the fiction of *Belphegor* may be traced to some monastic legend or ancient *Fabliaux*, from which the two tales on the subject, ascribed to Machiavel and Straparola, have been constructed. Indeed this is asserted in a note to the tale in the French translation of the latter, to which we shall afterwards have occasion to refer. The intention of both writers was to show that the sharp sting of a woman's tongue is quite sufficient to subdue the devil, whenever it is her pleasure to give his Satanic Majesty the full benefit of it.

In the olden time, the saints usually came off victorious in their battles with Belzebub. St. Dunstan once settled matters very speedily with a devil, who had slipped into his cell while he was piously engaged in completing a chalice, and, peeping incautiously over Dunstan's shoulder, he exposed his nose to the eyes of the saint, who, seeing his advantage, turned round, suddenly seized it with the red-hot tongs he was using for the sacred utensil, and held it so tight, that the fiend roared so loud and so long that the whole adjacent country was in a state of alarm for hours. Hone, in his useful and entertaining *Every-Day Book*, has given a woodcut of this interesting occurrence, copied from an original engraving, under which were these verses—

> "St. Dunstan, as the story goes,
> Once pull'd the devil by the nose
> With red-hot tongs, which made him roar,
> That he was heard three miles and more."

After reposing on his laurels for many centuries, St. Dunstan was raised from his grave by the unknown author of *Grim, the Collier of Croydon*, a drama of the latter days of Elizabeth, or commencement of the reign of James I.*

St. Francis was a still more potent adversary of Satan. His wonderful career will be found in the *Alcoran des Cordéliers*,† a work "tant en Latin, qu'en Francois," taken from the great book *Des Conformitez, jadis composè par frére Barthelemi de Pise, Cordelier en son Vivant*, and illustrated by Picart. Two of the engravings represent the conquest obtained by the

* His presence was deemed necessary to watch the proceedings of the court of Satan, which had deputed Belphegor to the earth to ascertain whether the scandals circulated in Pandemonium relative to the fair sex were well founded.

† Amsterdam, 1734. Two volumes 12mo. There was a copy of this very rare and curious work in the *Bibliotheca Stanleiana*, 1813, No. 658.

saint over the devil and his imps. The first is thus described: "S. Francois et son compagnon trouverent une bourse, que le Diable avoit mis la pour le tenter; mais sitot que le compagnon eut touchè a la bourse le Diable en sortir et tout disparut," a striking instance of the power of the saint, when his mere personal presence protected his companion from the "glamour" of the evil one.

The second engraving represents the saint, who, after having, in the month of January, vanquished the devil in a thicket (*buisson*), gathered twelve red and the same number of white roses, and, proceeding to carry them to the church, found the ground covered with silk tapestry. He had an angel on each side. In the back part of the print, Francis is placed in the middle of the *buisson*, whilst the devil in despair reluctantly takes his departure; two heavenly beings in the sky view everything with infinite satisfaction.

St. Francis was too exalted in mind to indulge, even with Belzebub, in vituperative discussion. Shunning female society, and resisting the temptations of beauty, he was ignorant of the wondrous power of a female tongue, and would never have credited the flight of Belphegor by its means.

The temptations of St. Anthony are well known. For twenty long years he was persecuted daily. Armed with his crucifix, he vanquished the arch-fiend, whose *effigies*, copied from the original painting by Salvator Rosa,* of itself was sufficient to strike terror into the bosom of the boldest combatant. The saint, of course, was triumphant, and so completely established his superiority, that the fiends, upon hearing *the voice* of Anthony, fled as fast as Belphegor did when he thought he was about to be afflicted by the voice and presence of his wife Imperia, as Wilson calls her.

La Fontaine has introduced Belphegor into his collection of tales and novels. According to his biographer, Monsieur Auger, "Sa femme, nommée Marie Héricart, fille d'un lieutenant au Balliage royal de la Fertè-Milon, ne manquoit ni de beauté ni d'esprit; mais elle etoit d'une humeur exigeante et fierce, et l'on croit generalement qu'elle est original de Madame Honesta dans le conte de Belphegor. Ce qu'il y a de certain, c'est que La Fontaine se conduisit avec sa femme a-peu-pres comme Belphegor avec la sienne, c'est-à-dire, s'eloigna d'elle le plus souvent, et pour le plus de temps qu'il lui fut possible."† It is very probable that this conjecture is correct.

The *Contes et Nouvelles* were printed some years before the appearance of Wilson's drama on the same subject in 1690. La Fontaine died upon the 13th March 1695, in Paris, at the age of sixty-four, Wilson having survived him. Fontaine ascribed

* Hone's *Every-Day Book*, p. 114.

† *Vie de La Fontaine. Œuvres complètes de La Fontaine*, à Paris, 1814, 8vo. Tom. I. f. xi. Printed by Crapelet.

the tale to Machiavel, whereas Wilson, who prefixes an abridgment of the fiction, is uncertain whether the Florentine or Straparola was the writer.

In the translation by "Pierre de Larivey, Champenois," into French, of the *Tredici Piacevoli Notti del S. Gio. Francisco Straparola da Caravaggio*, *The Marriage of the Devil* is the fourth tale of the second night, and in several respects resembles the story ascribed to Machiavel.

Larivey, in the following note upon the tale of Straparola, says: "C'est, comme tout le monde sçait, le Belphegor de Machiavel. Le Doni, pourtant,—fuillet 89 de sa seconda Libraria de l'edition du Marcolini en 12mo, à Venise 1551,—dit que cette nouvelle, après avoir eu cours sous le nom de Machiavel, a été depuis imprimée parmi celle du Brevio à Florence, ensuite dequoi il la raportè tout au long, telle que l'auteur, dit-il, l'avoit originairement ecrite. Ce qui a toute la mine d'être une suposition du Doni. Un chanoine de Saint Martin de Tours m'a dit que dans un vieux manuscrit Latin de la bibliothèque de cette églíse, l'istoire du mariage du Diable se trouvoit redigée en ciuq ou six lignes."*

At what time the version of *Belphegor* ascribed to Machiavel was first printed has not been ascertained, but the tale by Straparola will be found in the edition of his novels printed at Venice 1578, page 57. Of this work there was a still earlier edition—San Luca, 1557—in the sale catalogue of the valuable library of Colonel Stanley,† which was sold by auction in 1813, realising the sum of £8215, 11s. 6d.

With the exception of the *History of Florence*, Machiavel's works were translated into English from the Italian,—London, 1663, 12mo,—by Edward Dacres, and dedicated by him to James, Duke of Lenox, Earl of March, etc., Lord Great Chamberlain and Admiral of Scotland. In this translation the story of Belphegor is not found, although it contains all the other works then known to be his. In the folio edition, said to be the third, printed London, 1720, but which was "licensed February 2, 1674," *Belphegor* is the last article but one, and is followed by what is called "Nicholas Machiavel's letter in vindication of himself and writings." This is believed to be a forgery. It was translated by the celebrated Marquis of Wharton, the author, as is generally believed, of *Lilliburlero*. Bishop Warburton says, that having had access to the Wharton papers, he found the first proof of the letter corrected by the future Marquis. This was the edition of 1680.

The resemblance of Machiavel's *Belphegor* to *Grim, the Cobbler of Croydon*, is so very marked, that some notice of the drama may not be unacceptable. The first scene is in the "Devil's Dormitory," where St. Dunstan enters, properly armed

* Tom. I. f. 9. Amsterdam, 1725.
† Sold for £4.

with his beads, book, and crozier, and informs his auditors, that after the lapse of many hundred years, he had been brought back by Envy to

> "Show myself again upon the earth;"

he then gives an account of himself, his high position, his services under seven great kings, whose reigns he epitomizes, when "on a sudden," the Holy Man, in the middle of his autobiography, is overcome with sleep, and "layeth him down." Whereupon "lightning and thunder" commence. The curtain is drawn "on a sudden;" and Pluto, Minos, Æacus, and Rhadamanthus are discovered, "set in counsel" to judge the case of Malbecco's ghost, which stands before them guarded by furies. The unhappy spirit had committed suicide by throwing himself headlong from a rock, driven by his wife to the rash act. He furnishes the judges with a catalogue of his sufferings, assuring them at same time that they were just

> "What the world is plagued with every day."*

Pluto, in a state of astonishment, exclaims:

> "Can it be possible, you lords of hell,
> Malbecco's tale of women can be true?
> Is marriage now become so great a curse,
> That whilome was the comfort of the world?"

Minos and Æacus both express opinions confirmatory of Malbecco's statement, when Rhadamanthus counsels that

> "Your Grace should send some one into the world,
> That might make proof, if it be true or no."

To this proposition Pluto at once agrees, and it is resolved that Belphegor should be sent to visit the earth in human form, in order to test the truth of Malbecco's accusation. Disguised as Castiliano, an opulent merchant, he visits the earth, and from his personal experiences reports that there had been no exaggeration in the ghost's justification; he was but too happy to escape from earth and resume his comfortable position as one of the cabinet council of Pluto. Malbecco having thus established the truth of his charge, is sent back to plague the earth as the demon Jealousy. Pluto having dismissed his visitor to the realms above, thus concludes the play:

> "And now, for joy Belphegor is return'd,
> The furies shall their tortures cast away,
> And all hell o'er, we'll make it holy-day."

The decision meets with general approbation, and the play concludes, as it began, with thunder and lightning.

The story of Malbecco will be found in the *Fairy Queen*,†

* Dodsley's *Old Plays*, vol. x. Lond. 1827. p. 191.

† *Spencer's Works* by Todd. London, 1805, 8vo, vol. v. page 5.

but greatly altered by the author of the drama. The name, says the learned editor, "is derived from *male*, and *bacco*, a cuckold or wittol; *becco* signifies likewise a buck-goat."

The scene of the drama having been laid in England, before the Conquest, the author may perhaps have founded it on some legend or tradition of that country, as otherwise it is difficult to understand why St. Dunstan was introduced, or had anything to do with the experiment of Pluto and his council to ascertain, through the instrumentality of Belphegor, if ladies on earth were as bad as they were understood to be in Pandemonium. The Continent would, for such an investigation, have been more suitable than the island of Great Britain. It induces a suspicion that the author may have been indebted for this part of his plot to other sources than those afforded by Machiavel and Straparola. St. Dunstan's assertion that he had been dead some hundred years was an unnecessary fiction, as he was a prominent character during the Saxon rule, and died in the year 988, not very long before the battle of Hastings.*

Geneste says that *Belphegor* was brought out at Dorset Garden, and was licensed October 13, 1690. He remarks that the plot is professedly taken from a novel by Machiavel; but, as before observed, Wilson himself tells his readers that he is uncertain whether the story was by Machiavel or Straparola. Wilson, he continues, "has added an underplot which is rather dull; the comic scenes are good. The plot being so much out of the common road, some explanation of it should have been made in the prologue; it was perhaps for want of this that the play was unsuccessful." It appears from the prologue that *Belphegor* was the next new play after the *Prophetess*.

The *Prophetess* can hardly be called a new play, as it was only an alteration of Fletcher by Betterton, after the manner of an opera. There was one singularity about it—the prologue was after the first day suppressed, probably in consequence of two offensive lines by Dryden alluding to the machinery used, and the quantity of singing—

> "Never content with what you had before,
> But true to change, and Englishmen all o'er."

No authority has been given as to the want of success of *Belphegor*, and the conjecture that it was occasioned by the want of an introductory explanation can hardly be accepted as a sufficient reason, as Fontaine's tale, which had been recently published, and with which the reading public must have been familiar, superseded any requirement of the kind.

The tragi-comedy of Wilson has great merit, and is worthy of a high place amongst the dramas of the times in which it was written. It is original and full of interest, and the characters are well drawn, especially the "Demon Merchant" and his

* 10th October 1066.

grasping wife, the fear of whose tongue had the immediate effect of compelling his flight from the body of the Princess he had possessed, and forced his return to the fiery regions from which he had emanated. In the hands of a skilful dramatic writer, we are inclined to think that Wilson's *Belphegor*, with considerable purification of the dialogue, aud a judicious alteration of some of the scenes, might, in the present time, be successfully put on the stage, and received with that applause which Geneste says was denied to it on its original performance in 1690.

Straporola's tale, as translated from the original Italian by Pierre de Larivey into French, will be found in the Appendix, as well as that by Machiavel, from the English edition of his works in folio, London, 1720.

MATCHIAVEL—whether the original were his own or Straporola's, for both lived near the same time, and both played with the same story—gave me the Argument of the ensuing play, the substance of which is briefly thus :—

The Argument.

It having been observed in hell that the souls of such as came thither generally complained that their wives sent them, it was at last resolved that some one of themselves, as by lot it fell, should, for the better discovery of the truth thereof, repair to the earth, take upon him some human figure, and, for his better encouragement, carry with him a round sum of money in his pocket; subjected, nevertheless, to all the conditions of humanity, and, in the first place, to marry a wife, and live with her ten years, if possible, and after that to return, and make them a true account upon his own experience.

This lot fell to Belphegor, their old general, who, assuming a brisk young figure, settles in Florence, under the name of Roderigo, and quality of a merchant newly come from the Indies, and marries a lady of greater blood than fortune, whom he so loves in earnest, that she finds it, and seeks all occasions of squandering his estate, which yet he as readily complies with, because it pleases his wife. However, the trade of a merchant goes forward, and his adventures at sea fall nothing short of her extravagance at home.

This, and other accidents, make him incur debts; and, as other men in like cases, he takes up money to support his credit, till at last, his ships at sea being all lost, what with his creditors pressing him on the one hand, and his wife's uneasiness on the other, he fairly breaks.

And now, being subjected to all the conditions of humanity like those of other men, he flies, and takes sanctuary with one Mattheo, a neighbouring vineyard-keeper, tells him his condition, and that if he'll shelter him from the bailiffs that are in close pursuit of him he'll make him a man for ever. In short, Mattheo does it; and, expecting the performance of his promise, Roderigo tells him that he is not what he appears to be,—a man,—but a very devil, and gives him some pregnant instances of it. However, to show him what a gentleman of a devil he had met in him, he further tells him that as soon as he parted from him he would instantly possess such a great lady, and that nothing should remove him till he came, and therefore bade him be assured, and make his terms, and so leaves him.

Nor was he worse than his word, but immediately possessed the said lady, and suffered himself to be dislodged from her by Mattheo; as also of a second, —with this caution, nevertheless, that if he put him to it a third time, he should find him his mortal enemy.

On this, Belphegor makes a trip into France, and possesses that King's daughter, but not sooner than the report of the two former ladies had reached that Court. Whereupon the King sends several messages, with large promises of reward, to Mattheo, to come and dispossess his daughter, which he as often shifts; till at last, the King, having gotten him into his hands, tells him that unless he dispossess her he will certainly hang him. To be short, Mattheo puts on a bold face, and accosts Belphegor; but, finding all to no purpose, throws himself upon the King's mercy in favourably accepting his endeavours, and demands a large stage, with all sorts of music and pomp imaginable, and that the lady be brought upon it; to be sure, withal, that when he threw up his cap that they all strike up together with a general shout. And this, said he, with some other ingredients he had, would, he doubted not, but deliver the lady.

In fine, all things being accordingly prepared and ready, the lady is brought upon the stage, and from one thing to another, they at last quarrel, and Mattheo throws up his cap, which is seconded with a full shout; at which the possessed lady starting, and demanding the meaning of all that noise, Mattheo tells the devil in her his wife had found him out, and was just coming up-stairs, on which the lady gives a spring at him, and drops, and Belphegor leaves her.

Thus far Matchiavel, whom I have chiefly followed; saving that, where he runs his fable from one country to another, I found myself necessitated, for preserving the unity of time and place as much as it would bear, to fix the scene in some one place, and accordingly changed it from Florence, etc., to Genoa; and this the rather, partly in that the women in Genoa have a greater liberty than in other parts of Italy, and partly that the dukedom of Genoa, being elective from two years to two years, I might make way for a cross walk of virtue, and thereby divert the tediousness of a single walk—a path, I must confess, not so generally trodden, yet even in that the less subject to sloughs or dust.

To this purpose, I fancy Imperia, the wife of Belphegor, had a sister Portia, of as high virtue as herself was void of it, married to Montalto, a noble Genoese, who had sunk his fortune in serving the Republic, which yet, unknown to him, had been generously restored by another nobleman, his friend; and thence endeavour some short characters of friendship and gratitude,—of a woman that sweetens her husband on all occasions of discontent; one whom no accident of fortune can move, nor injury, how designed soever, provoke to an indecency: and of a man in him that weathers his troubles with an evenness of mind; one whom his country's ingratitude cannot tempt to a revenge, and so little affecting his own grandeur, that when the Senate had at last elected him duke, he modestly refused it.

And having wrought all together the best I could, I absolve the whole. Of which yet, because I may not be so competent a judge myself, I here give it as I wrote it, and leave it to my unbiassed reader to determine whether it might not have expected as much justice from the house as it found from the actors.

PROLOGUE.

On the occasion that the Play fell to be acted next after the "Prophetess." *

Bold was the man that first put out to sea;
Nor less advent'rous he that writes a play;
Both have their hits: Some scud before the wind,
Others lie by, and others lag behind.
And what's the fate of plays?—the bare success
Of any one makes the next comer less.
The market's cloy'd; some like not this, some that,
And, as in surfeits, would they know not what!
So when the *Prophetess* has fed your eye,
From pit and box to upper gallery,
What may our *Devil* of this night expect?
Our Author once was half afraid, neglect;
Till he bethought him the best remedy
For a pall'd stomach was variety!
What made the poets gods so oft below?—
Or what Apollo so unbend his bow?—
Or what makes you leave a fair wife at home
For a grass-girl, or some odd homely Joan?
What but diversion? And so I'm bid say,
He's in good hopes you'll not forejudge his play.
But stay! Let's see whom 'tis he must accost!
'Tis not the wits he fears; they're ever just.
And for those that can only carp, nor care,
While they keep pushing, how themselves lie bare;
Those that speak well of nothing but their own,
And damn or save merely for faction;

* *The Prophetess*, a Tragical History, by Beaumont and Fletcher, revived and printed (1690) by Mr. Dryden under the title of *The Prophetess; or the History of Dioclesian*, with alterations and additions after the manner of an opera. Represented at the Queen's Theatre.

Those that bolt what they please, no matter how,
And carry 't off not by their brains but brow!
If any such are here, 'twere well they knew
Rome's greatest wits were the best natur'd too.
But if this will not do, he justly thence
Brings his appeal to you—the men of sense!
And if he must be pelted, begs this boon—
Let him that has least wit throw the first stone.

THE PERSONS.

MONTALTO, . *A noble Genoese, who had impaired his fortune in serving the Republic.*
GRIMALDI, . *One other Nobleman, his friend, who, unknown to him, relieves his estate.*
RODERIGO, . *A Devil, disguised under that name and person — his proper name Belphegor. Given out for a Spanish merchant come from the Indies.*
FIESCHI, . . *Nephew to Grimaldi; Gallant to Imperia.*
MARONE,. . *An upstart Officer of St. George's Bank; speaks evil of mankind, admires Roderigo for his wealth, and vilifies Montalto.*
MATTHEO, . *A Vineyard-keeper.*
PANSA, . . *Servant to Fieschi.*
DON HERCIO, *A Bravo.*
CRISPO, . } *Two Puggs, Servants to Roderigo. Crispo,*
MINGO, . } *his valet; Mingo, his page.*
PICARO, . . *The common Executioner.*

PORTIA, . . *Wife to Montalto.*
IMPERIA, . . *Her Sister, Wife to Roderigo.*
JULIA, . . *Niece to the Duke of Genoa; a Demoniac, possessed by Belphegor.*
BIANCA, . . *Woman to Portia.*
QUARTILLA, . *Matrona to Imperia.*
SCINTILLA, . *Woman to Imperia.*

SERVANTS. OFFICERS. WATCHMEN. JEWS. WOMEN.
BELZEBUB and PUGGS. BOYS. RABBLE.

The Scene:—

G E N O A.

BELPHEGOR;

OR,

THE MARRIAGE OF THE DEVIL.

ACT I.—SCENE I.

A stately room in RODERIGO'S *house.*

Enter RODERIGO, *followed by* CRISPO *and* MINGO.

Rod. We spirits, uncompounded essences,
Not manacled or immur'd with walls of flesh,
We can dilate, condense, or limb ourselves,
As like us best—assume what colour, shape,
Or size we please. And I have taken this:
My servants, that; my name below, Belphegor;
Here, Roderigo. My quality, a merchant
Come from the Indies. O, most happy lot!
Who would believe that void and formless mass,
That fluid infinite, had e'er produc'd
Such an harmonious order? It strikes wonder
And ecstasy! [*He turns to his servants.*
And what think ye of this world? Is not this better than toasting the soles of your feet?

Cris. The air, I must confess, is somewhat better; but for the people, not a doit to choose.

Min. I fancy them the worst of the two, and more fond of the place than ourselves.

Rod. Can ye blame them? They know what they are in this world, they know not what they may be in the next.

Cris. Yet live here as if they expected no other! And so exquisitely practis'd in cheating one another, that the best of us is a mere novice to them.

Min. Not a skip-kennel but gives you three tricks for one.

Cris. And for their masters—could you believe it, sir?—I met with a signior t'other night, most devoutly, with his beads in one hand and the other in my pocket!

Rod. Why didst not beat him?

Cris. I did but challenge him for 't; and the rogue had the impudence to kick me for taxing a person of his honour!

Min. I believe both our assumed bodies were damn'd cowards while they lived here. For my part, I had rather take ten kicks than so much as look back to see who gave me one of them.

Rod. But sure, the women treat ye better?

Cris. As judge yourself. It is not long since I had a concern with a signiora, and, just as I had stript and was going to bed to her, slip went the trap-door, and down dropt Crispo into the common shore!

Min. And mine has given me such a remembrance of her love, that, as young soever as my figure speaks me, I can hardly speak knitting-needles without endangering the bridge of my nose. And when I tax'd her for it, had the impudence to ask me how she could give it when she still kept it herself?

[RODERIGO *smiles.*

Rod. But how d' ye find mankind in general?

Cris. Still slandering us:—As drunk as a devil—As mad as a devil—As poor as a devil—As dull as a devil—and what not!—when yet there's not so much difference between us as would turn a pair of scales.

Min. And then perpetually playing fast and loose with us! Ever and anon giving their souls to the devil; yet at last bequeathing them another way, without the least thought of the pre-conveyance to us. And therefore, I beseech ye, give me leave to return to my old quarters.

Cris. Not forgetting thy excellencies, poor Crispo.

Rod. Villiachoes! And must ye throw up your cards when they play into your hand? Peace, and be thankful! all this but makes our game. Go, humour them! for we're restrain'd, and can do nothing without themselves. They hold the candle to us. The mud's their own: we only shake the vial and stir it up—and so, look out, and sharp!—

[*Exeunt* CRISPO *and* MINGO.

Now to my own affair:—

[RODERIGO *takes out a paper and reads.*

"At the Pandemonium or Common Council of the Infernal Lake. Present—Lucifer, Abaddon, Belzebub, and others, the high and mighty lords, potentates, and princes of the Grand Abyss.—Whereas, upon taking our yearly audits, it has been observ'd that the souls of such as arrive generally agree that their wives sent them: And whereas the said Board had formerly ordered, that for the better discovery of the truth thereof, some one of their body, as by lot it should fall, repair to earth: And whereas the said lot fell to Belphegor, Generalissimo of the Asphaltic Lake,—Resolved as followeth:

"1. That the said Belphegor forthwith take upon him that province, and that a million of ducats be assign'd him, not as advance, but his full complement."—And well enough, no ill encouragement.

"2. That for the better carrying on of the said service, himself (and two other spirits assigned him as servants) be at liberty to assume and actuate what bodies, and settle in what part of the world, shall like him best."—And I have done 't.

"3. That upon his first choice of his place of residence, he immediately marry a wife, and live with her ten years if possible; after which, pretending to die, that he return, and upon his own experience make affidavit of the pleasures and calamities of marriage."—And I have done that first. A desperate service, no doubt! [*He smiles.*

"4. That he lose all qualities of a spirit (unless,

perhaps, upon some last exigence), and become in all things as a man; subject to all the conditions of humanity—poverty, imprisonment, passions, fear, hate, love."—

Were there ten thousand more, that sweetened all:
Love!—There's no passion but what's founded on 't;
Men fear for what they love—desire, hate, envy,
And all because they love themselves. But mine
Carries a nobler tincture; and I love
To that degree, I've half forgot the sex.

[*He changes his voice.*

And, but that she has little odd humours, and perhaps, too, some fits of her mother; O Origen! I'd release thy kindness, and never accept other heaven than here.

But see! she comes!

[IMPERIA *and attendants cross the stage, as conducting her sister* PORTIA *to her coach. They bow at distance. He points after her.*

Such was the infant morn, when it first brake,
And blush'd, to see the Chaos left behind her.
Thence I felt passion first: what else I view'd
Wrought in my mind no change, no fond desire;
But there, I am transported.—I, that was
High proof 'gainst all things else, there, there alone,
Weak, for to me whate'er she wills is fate.

[IMPERIA *returns, sola. He runs to her.*

Sure Nature was asleep when thou stol'st forth,
And all the graces she design'd an age
Crowded themselves together, and made thee.

Imp. And are not you a fine gentleman to coax your poor wife? Alas, poor fool! she cannot choose but believe ye.

Rod. Couldst thou but see my heart, thou wouldst.

Imp. You can't dissemble, not you—you are—marry —that you are. [*She strokes him.*

Rod. At least would be, whate'er I thought might please thee;
And were the world at my dispose, 'twere thine!

Imp. No doubt of it. Witness the necklace!

Rod. I had forgot——

Imp. And so you do everything that concerns me.

Rod. See! I have brought thee a better.

[*He gives her a necklace.*

Imp. But I long'd for t'other. The set of Neapolitan horses, too; but I'm your wife. There!—[*She throws it away.*]—Pray bestow it where you intended it! I could observe that eye of yours as my sister pass'd you. [*He offers to embrace her. She turns him off.*

Rod. Fie! my Imperia, fie! Wilt thou be always thus?

Imp. And much you care whether I am or not. One would think a woman of my quality——[*She puts finger in eye.*]—I know not why so many good women die, but wish I were dead too, that I might trouble you no longer!

Rod. No! I'll die first, that thou mayst have another.

Imp. No marvel, truly,—I live so well with you!

Rod. She cries! By heaven she cries! Poor innocence!—My life! my soul! my Imperia! thou shalt have anything—we'll come to articles.

Imp. And long you'll keep them.

Rod. By this kiss, for ever!

[*She receives it still sobbing.*

Imp. And shall I have the necklace I long'd for?

[*Sobs.*

Rod. Thou shalt, my dear!

Imp. The set of horses, too? [*Sobs.*

Rod. I would they were better for thy sake. Thou shalt!

Imp. The brooch of diamonds would be very becoming, and the locket.—[*A half sob.*]—Now, 'twas so pretty!

Rod. That and whatever else thou wilt!

Imp. The pearls, too, were large, round, oriental; and the pendants so delicate—I fancy how I should appear in them! [*She comes into a pleasant humour.*

Rod. Less than thou truly art; but thou shalt have them!

Imp. And—[*she strokes him*]—do what I will?

Rod. What pleases thee sha'n't be amiss to me; only be kind, and love thy Roderigo!

[*They strike hands upon it.*

Imp. A match, a match! I will.

[*Makes a low reverence. Exit.*

Rod. Some tetchy mortal, now, would have quarrell'd; but we old experienc'd devils know better things. [*He walks.*
And live with her ten years, if possible? Mistaken fools, 'tis possible! I will live with her, and that for ever! [*It thunders.* A HEAD *rises.*

Head. Thy articles, Belphegor, thy articles!

Rod. And what of them? The Casuists are clear in the point; they may be shifted for advantage. Sue them!

Head. But is there not a public faith even among devils?

Rod. It may be broke for empire; why not for love, then, that commandeth empire? It may, and shall! Begone!

Head. Be witness, thou inviolable Styx!
Thou 'ast broken thine, and I pronounce thee mutinous.

[*Sinks.*

Rod. That I could reach the slave I'd make him know
I fill my orb myself, and make my circle
Without a borrowed light! [*Another thunder.*
Squib on! and say
I am more proud in my Imperia's love
Than when, as thunder proof, I once bestrid
That vast convex of fire, and leading up
The embattled legions of apostate cherubs,
Plough'd the parch'd earth, and made the affrighted deep
Shrink to its last recess!

Enter IMPERIA *running.*

Imp. O, my dear! heard you not the thunder? I'm so afraid!

Rod. Of what?—Of thy own shadow?

Imp. How can you be alone?

Rod. Yet meditating on thee; that very thought were company enough.

Imp. O, but confess; you look as you were disturbed.

Rod. And thou so near? Impossible! Or were it so,
The sight of thee would reconcile my passions,
And give me to myself. [*She strokes him.*

Imp. But won't you tell me true? Are you not well?

Rod. How can that man be ill that's happy enough
To pity Cæsar? And such am I in thee.
[*He embraces her.*
Here will I fix my empire—here I'll reign,
And reign alone! [*He leads her off. Exeunt.*

Scene II.

A stately room in Grimaldi's *house.*

Enter Grimaldi, Marone, Fieschi, *and* Pansa.

Gri. You cannot say but that he paid you honestly.

Mar. I wish I could say I were as well satisfied. I never found such honest payments rais'd an estate. If ever I deal more on single interest, may I lose my principal!

Gri. Who'd have expected even that, at least [you'd have] taken it from one so honourable, that has perish'd his own fortune to save the public?

Mar. These honourable rags are such fine things! How, I pray, do you find the price current? Does the frippery deal in such lumber? I think not. Good sir, keep your whipt-posset for your better friends, and give me more substantial fare.

Fies. His virtue might deserve better language; and it may be a question, if it had not been for him, whether the State had been at least what it now is!

Gri. And true! When the sun could hold no longer, and the moon slept, his eyes have been our sentinels.

Mar. But what money has he got with all this? or what share in the government? Simple merit lords few men's horoscopes.

Gri. Greater than both—the conscience of worthy actions.

Mar. What credit has it in the bank? For my part, I can boast I have kill'd mine. And, if you'd hear me, could show you a man has done nothing of all this, and yet even the senate will confess him wise, prudent, virtuous—everything; and that he is not one of themselves, I believe it more his own fault than theirs.

Gri. Who should this be?

Mar. What think ye of his brother-in-law, Roderigo? There's a man for ye! and, to my glory, he calls me friend!

Gri. But whence this meteor?

Mar. Whence e'er he came, he darkens all our stars.
You'd swear he were descended of the Goths,
Or had been at the siege of Constantinople!

Gri. Some Moor or baptiz'd Jew?

Mar. Be what he will—
Turk, Pagan, or Infidel—would I'd his wealth
With his religion! He's a Castilian!
Were I that man!

Fies. You'd take 't for an affront
His Catholic Majesty should call you cousin.

Mar. And yet you hear me not complain. I've that
Which finds me friends, or makes them!—That one thing
That can do all things! How it makes a door
Or shut or open.

Fies. Or yourself, perhaps,
Snore o'er your cup, or find a fly in the ceiling.

Mar. That matters not. I'm sure it breeds compunction
And fellow-feeling in a man of office—

Makes and remits offences—even Justice
More deaf than she is blind. And who would want it?
Gri. That would Grimaldi, and every man whose soul
Is not compos'd of the same dirt he treads.
Want it! I mean, rather than have 't on terms
Dishonourable or sordid.
Mar. But do ye think
Any one's morals can reform the world?
Don't they all thus? and, which is more, Court, follow,
Adore the rich, and spurn the unfortunate.
Gri. And I as much the world.
Mar. But say that world
Spurn you again? Did ever wise man choose
Him for a friend that was deprest by fortune?
Rats quit a falling house, and men a party
When they perceive it going.
Gri. Where's honesty and honour all this while?
Mar. Nay, if you come to that, farewell kingdoms!
Nor is it mine to question them. Your servant!
[*Exit* MARONE.
Gri. Well, Fieschi, and what think'st thou?
Fies. As is his name, such is the slave himself!
Who'd expect other from a dog but snarling?

Gri. His soul is sense; and as he has no knowledge of virtue, he has no use of it. But how have you dispos'd Montalto's matter? Is it so order'd that it be not known from what hand it came?

Fies. 'Twas the last thing I did. I left the writings in a seal'd box with Bianca, who has assur'd me she'll watch an opportunity, and convey it into her lady's closet!

Gri. As well as I could wish, good man!
He could have sooner perish'd than told me—
Told me, his friend—he wanted me! Who sees
His friend's distress, and stays till he's entreated,
He comes too late. 'Tis an extorted kindness,
Lost ere it comes, and shows he wanted will
T'ave done 't at all. But this Marone sticks in my stomach!
Whence truly is he?

Fies. Pansa, I think, remembers the first plantation.

Pan. That do I, sir, from the time he first came to town in second mourning—that is, in a livery as ragged and tatter'd as an he-goat; his hat right beggar's block, no crown to 't; his doublet and breeches so suitable, that in a dark morning he'd have mistaken one for t'other; his stockings without feet or ancles, like a chandler's drawing-sleeves; and those, too, he durst not trust off his legs, for fear of crawling away. In a word, a thing made up of so many several parishes, that you'd have taken him at first sight for a frontispiece of the resurrection.

Fies. Thence he came in as a sub-subcollector, and thence into St. George's Bank; and now, being in his nature insolent, this imaginary reputation has made him intolerable.

Gri. And for his other qualities, I know somewhat myself. He never forgave beyond the opportunity of a revenge, or spake well of any man but to his greater disadvantage. A pretty gentleman! but, 'tis pity—

Fies. Nay, worse! shall play both the devil's parts of tempter and accuser; provoke his friend into a freedom of talk, and then inform it.

Gri. Enough! and for fear of any mistake make another step to Bianca.

[*Exeunt* FIESCHI *and* PANSA, *Manet* GRIMALDI.

And this man thrives? O Lucian, thy gods! The groans of deprest virtue and loud laughters of exalted folly gave first name to the fortunate islands,* where men slept themselves away in the melancholy contemplations between virtue and success.

To him enter MONTALTO *and* PORTIA.

You have prevented me—I was just coming
To give you joy. The senate have at last
Consider'd your services!

Mon. And sent me a gewgaw,

[MONTALTO *takes out a chain and medal, and shows it.*

An empty nothing! Pth!

* Supposed to have been the Canary Islands.

Gri. 'Twas never intended
Beyond a mark of honour, and a pledge
Of future kindness!
Mon. He's a beast that serves
A commonwealth; for, when he has spent his blood
And sunk his fortune to support the pride
And luxury of those few that cheat the rest,
He straight becomes the object of their scorn
Or jealousy.
Gri. How oddly my friend argues
Against himself! Have you not served the State
These twenty years? And can you think it wisdom
To quarrel now? Or now, when reasonably
You might expect the fruit of all your hazards,
Arm them against you? Virtue, merit, worth,
Ne'er wanted enemies; make not you more!
Mon. When they behold themselves through their false optics,
They swell a gnat into an elephant;
When others, how they turn the glass, and lessen
A mountain to a mole-hill!
Gri. Are you the only man has been so serv'd?
Who deserv'd better for a lawgiver,
Than Solon? or captain, than Thrasibulus?
Or orator, than Demosthenes? Yet Athens,
Ungrateful Athens, banish'd the two first,
And slew the latter! Unto whom owed Rome
More than to Manlius, who, when her capital
Was grown too hot for Jupiter, preserved it?
Or what might not Camillus have pretence to,
Who, when she was reduc'd to her last stake,
Push'd it and won it? What should I mention?—
Rutilius, Scipio, Hannibal, Themistocles—
Men famous in their age—yet they fell—
Fell where they most deserv'd.
Mon. How my blood curdles at it! And methinks
I feel a kind of currishness shot through me,
And want no property of a dog but fawning,
Tho' necessary to a rising man.
Por. Is this that fortitude, my Montalto,

This that heroic virtue you taught me?
Sure 'tis not the Montalto I have seen,
When victory sat perching on his helm;
Or that Montalto, when, opprest by numbers,
He lost the day, and yet brought home more glory
Than if he had been conqueror; yet still,
Still the same even temper—unconcern'd
At loss or vict'ry!

Mon. Would it not heat a man
To view his wounds, which, like so many mouths,
Speak out his wrongs the louder?—t'ave consum'd
Himself to warm ingratitude?

Por. The fruit
Of worthy actions is to have done them;
And every man that will may give 't himself.

Mon. How can I stand my breast against a torrent
Of adverse fortune?

Por. 'Tis your greater glory
To stem that flood. How 're you beholden to her,
That she could pass the herd and single you
To combat her?

Mon. But she has cut my sinews.

Por. The more your honour! I have heard you say
That a Roman was more glorious in his scorch'd
Than armed hand. Do not distrust yourself,
And you must conquer her! The constant man
Is master of himself and fortune too.

Mon. Bless me! Thou glorious woman, never made
Of common earth, I am concern'd for thee!

Por. To the world's fondlings be their world! With me,
My own Montalt' outweighs the apparition,
The airy dream, which, when they think a substance,
Grasp at it, they awake and find it nothing!
Sure, had it anything worthy our love,
It were a mind that can contemn it.

Gri. Brave woman!
And who might'st bring philosophy to manners.

Por. If you call this philosophy, 'tis what
Its first inventors meant it, ere our pedants

Had made it rather difficult than great.
Come, my Montalto, come! and let th' example
Of others' virtue now engage your own:
Their glory your imitation.

Mon. Thou hast o'ercome, my Portia, and I'll try
If that content the larger world denies
May be found in ourselves. Even poverty,
If it can be content, has lost its name.
He never has enough that gapes for more;
Opinion was never rich, nor content poor.

Gri. Now, how I love this rugged honesty!
Like the first matter, 't 'as all the seeds of good,
Only wants form and order. [*Exeunt.*

SCENE III.

The FIRST SCENE *again.*

Enter QUARTILLA *and* SCINTILLA.

Qua. Believe me, our signiora has manag'd her affair, and if I understand anything of the world, well.

Scin. As how? Pray instruct me against the good time.

Qua. Sh'as brought my Don on's knees; 'tis all now as she'll have it.

Scin. That all? A mighty business! Ha'n't they been married two years? and does not he love her, and she know it? Few women but would have done as much; besides,—and 'tis every day's experience,—even the wisest men, when they once come to love in earnest, turn generally half-witted.

Qua. You are to be instructed indeed, Scintilla. He is good-natur'd and does love her; but there are many stubborn fools in the world, and a woman need have all her wits about her to keep her own. But to get ground, I know it may be done, but not so easy.

Scin. I warrant ye, do but bring him to the right

manage at first, humour him in everything you can't hinder, and the rest follows; 'tis not the point whether she loves, but whether he believes so. There's your art: to get him play himself into the noose, and be proud of 't too.

Qua. Well, well, the world is strangely alter'd since my time. Young girls then were not wont to be so knowing, but now they are even able to teach us.

Enter PANSA.

Pan. Now, grannum, and my pretty convenience!

Qua. Grannum, with a murrain t' ye!

[PANSA *colls* SCINTILLA.

Nothing down with you but squab-pigeons!—A likely fellow if a woman durst trust him, but men now-a-days are so deceitful. [*Aside.*

Scin. Get ye to Bianca! I'll tell her—you do so mousle one.

Qua. Fie, Signior Pansa, fie! is there no more but fall on without so much as a short grace? I'm sure it was not so——

Pan. The year you lost your maidenhead; and that was so long since, you have by this time forgotten you ever had one.

Qua. Away, knave, away!

Scin. Yet she'll not turn her back to you now.

Qua. Nor a better than himself.

Pan. No anger, I beseech ye! After the dull rate men made love formerly, I should look upon a petticoat as one of the most defensible spots in Christendom—so many scarfs, curtains, portcullises, counterworks, and what not; but, now that we'ave a shorter cut of surprise, sapping, downright storm, or springing a mine, up goes scarf, curtain, portcullis—and, hey da!

Scin. Well, Pansa, thou'lt never break thy heart for love.

Pan. Love!—'tis a kind of colic; as long as ye keep it under girdle ye may linger on with 't, and well enough; but if it once get breast-high, the whole mass is infected, and I can only say, as physicians of their dying patients, his time is come, cover him up, and send for a parson.

Enter BIANCA.

Qua. Come, Scintilla! 'tis as thou saidst, here she comes. He's a filthy man, e'en leave them together.

[*Exeunt* QUARTILLA *and* SCINTILLA.

Pan. B'w'ye, grannum! And now, my best girl, thou hast not forgot, I hope?

Bian. I wish I had. My lady was abroad this afternoon, and I laid the box as you directed; but, when she came forth, she gave me such a look, ask'd me who had been there, and particularly named your master.

Pan. Never the worse; she could not have done less. But thou hadst the grace to deny all?

Bian. D'ye take me for a fool? But this I told her, —a gentleman I never saw before brought it, and pray'd me to lay it in her closet, as I had done, and I hop'd without offence; if otherwise, I was sorry.

Pan. And that clear'd all again?

Bian. Quite contrary! I saw fire in her eyes, yet trembled, and could hardly speak. At last, she commanded me to find you out, and that you let your master know she must speak with him.

Pan. Must, my she secretary?

Bian. Yes, must, and out of hand. And if I lose my place by the bargain, I have spun a fine thread.

Pan. Fear nothing; or if thou should'st, my master's a gentleman, and my bed will hold two.

Bian. You men consider nothing.

Pan. And you women too much. I tell thee, my master, the knight, shall make his amour to thy lady, the princess, while I, Pansa, the squire, put it in practice with thee, Bianca, the damsel.

Bian. Well, now, and that's so fine! but when will ye bring me some of those books? Beshrew me, but I should have broken my heart long ere this if 'twere not for them.

Pan. Thou shalt have anything — my heart, my all!

Bian. 'Tis not the first time you told me so. Ay, but——

Pan. D'ye think I am bound to find ye fresh oaths every time?

Bian. When shall I see ye at our house?

Pan. To-morrow, without fail. And is not this better than putting all to the last? And what's that but singing a psalm under the gallows?

Bian. But be sure, now, and find out your master presently, and send him to my lady!

Pan. Doubt not of either.—[*Exit* BIANCA.]—'Tis the best-humour'd thing—a jolly pug, and well-mouth'd —none of the first or second rate, I must confess; he that sees her by day would hardly break his neck to come at her by night. However, she's good merchantable ware, and well-condition'd; and, how shy soever she now and then makes it, serves my turn when a better's out of the way. [*Exit* PANSA.

ACT II.—SCENE I.

The FIRST SCENE *again.*

Enter RODERIGO, *solus.*

Rod. My private instructions were to pervert and enlarge the kingdom of darkness. Nor have I been idle. I thought Marone might have given me some pains, but he was mine at first, and has engaged to me for his brothers of the bank; but this Montalto I much doubt, or rather fear him.

Enter MARONE.

My friend! welcome, my better half! we're now concern'd, body, soul, interest.

Mar. And when I fail ye, I'll turn a new leaf, and build hospitals. But what progress have ye made with Montalto?

Rod. He's rugged, and will neither lead nor drive but his own way; and therefore I question whether we had not better let him alone.

Mar. But he is poor and lofty; despair him not. This gold, 'twill make a man do anything; I never yet found man or woman that withstood it long.

Rod. I would you'd feel his pulse, and I'll advance the money.

Mar. That shall be least in the case, and I'd willingly undertake it, but that, as you know, there's no kindness between us; and for me but so much as to appear in it may render it suspected, whereas from you, his brother-in-law, his friend, it can't but pass.

Rod. I yield; it shall be so!

Mar. Then, if you find him cold, I'll discover it myself. Tell me of's virtue!—a rattle for children! I hate it perfectly, and him for it. Why should any man pretend to more than comes to his share?

Rod. Now let me hug my genius! and whom I love so well, that, were I not sped already, I'd go no farther than your family.

Mar. Between ourselves, give her a fig, and see if I don't fit ye to your wish.

Rod. O by no means; you run too fast!

Mar. You need not be asham'd of her; we are descended from Marius, and have had some crown'd heads of the house, tho', I confess it, somewhat long since they have had any sceptre in their hands.

Rod. I judge it by yourself.

Mar. Nor, to tell ye truth, can every man say so much, or would, perhaps, be willing to hear all that may be said of his. And that's the reason why so many of the ancients were descended from the gods; for, when their birth was so obscure that they were asham'd to own it, the jade the mother, or some blind poet, found out a god to father the bastard. What, I pray, were Bacchus, Hercules, Romulus, and several others? Story lies, or their fathers were of the doubtful gender, and their mothers of the common. But this by the by. And, because I hear somebody coming, I'll withdraw, for fear it happen to be Montalto.

[*Exit* MARONE.

Rod. Devils, do they call us? Poor devils, where have we been bred? This one, Marone, may shame us all, and, had I done no more, is worth my journey.

Enter MONTALTO.

Health and his own wishes to my brother!
Mon. The same and more, were 't possible, to you.
Rod. But I'm half angry—angry with myself—
That this alliance is not yet made friendship.
Mon. No man shall court it more. And such a one
As loves the man and not his fortune—such
As can hide anything but his love, and whose
Mistakes shall be of weakness, not design.
Rod. Now, how you speak, my soul! This empty world
Is hollow, false, ungrateful; and men live
As if 'twere made for them, they for themselves.
Mon. 'Twas ever so.
Rod. Witness those mangled officers,
Maim'd soldiers, wooden-legg'd artillerymen,
Spies and intelligencers out at heels—
Some showing their wounds, others numbering the battles they have been in and the estates they have lost; some muttering libels, others modelling a reformation, and not the least part of them studying where to get a meal upon reputation.

Mon. And yet there's not a private soldier but glories in his wounds, as having received them in defence of his country.

Rod. And no doubt but they call them worthy deeds, but I say they are deeds worthy of repentance; and such are all services paid to the ungrateful. To go no further than yourself, what have you got by all yours?

Mon. The satisfaction of having done what I ought. Virtue is theatre enough into herself!

Rod. You have said well and worthily; and, because he that is pleased with another's good increases his own, give me leave, brother, and now friend, to propose to you an honourable advantage.

[MONTALTO *bows to him.*

But it requires secrecy, and I must have your word for 't.

Mon. I know not what it may be.

Rod. You're at your liberty if you don't like it.

Mon. You have my word.

[IMPERIA *is seen peeping in.*

Rod. Then thus: There is a prince, whose name must be as yet conceal'd, is so sensible of your merit and this republic's ingratitude, that he has order'd ye ten thousand pistoles, as a small pledge of his future favour; and I'll advance the money.

[MONTALTO *starts.*

Mon. Ten thousand pistoles! and from a prince unknown! And what must I do for all this?

Rod. Kings have their reasons to themselves, too deep for private men to fathom. Who knows but he may have a design upon Italy?—this, or some other place? and, which is further in my instructions, has pitch'd on you as general for the expedition?

Mon. How are you sure it has not taken wind?

Rod. Not a man on this side the Alps knows it besides ourselves.

Mon. Or that your king will keep his word, more than Genoa has hers?

Rod. I have the money in the house. He's coming!

[*Aside.*

Mon. But is not this to betray my country?

Rod. Give it another name, and do 't! Who ever scrupled a safe revenge? Success will call it justice.

Mon. Upon my country?

Rod. But ungrateful country. That only is my country where I am well! And what think you?

Mon. That you have said too much for me to hear.

I lend a hand to slave my country? No!
That won't Montalto, the disoblig'd Montalto;
Virtue forbid the thought! Tho' she may've lost
Th' affection of a mother, she's my mother;
And, as she bears that name, I must and will
Support her, or lie buried in her ruins!

Rod. Howe'er, I doubt not but I'm safe; your word,
The great credentials of mankind, secures me.

Mon. Unlawful promises oblige to nothing
But a repentance; and to keep mine here
Would be a double crime, and break those laws
Of piety and faith my country claims.

Rod. Country!—A thing of chance, no choice of yours;
Your mother might have dropped ye anywhere! But if
You break your word, you violate your honour;
And that's your own.

Mon. Perish for me that honour,
Life, estate, everything, so she be safe!
And so, my sister-in-law's husband, no more friend,
I'll not resolve ye what I'll do; but know,
'Twas not within my word not to prevent ye. [*Exit.*

Rod. Bubbled! by this good light, merely bubbled! and when, one would have thought, I had him—all to nothing! Sure, sure, our masters lie under a great mistake, and mankind were once the ancienter devils, and invented that sham of their wives sending them only to frighten us from vent'ring among them.

Enter IMPERIA.

I hope she did not hear me. [*Aside.*

Imp. And what, if I may be so bold, have my wise brother-in-law and you been projecting? When d'ye set out?

Rod. For what, my dear, or whither?

Imp. Why, for the Indies in a cock-boat, or France on a mill-stone! I hope you'll go by the north-west passage, and take a bait by the way, to hear the meremaids sing! Your friend, my sister's husband, would make a special general for the expedition! Ten thousand pistoles will do no hurt; you have it in the house, and may advance it.

Rod. Betray'd too !—[*Aside.*]—But why this to me? Prithee, my dear——

Imp. Methinks you're very familiar.

[*She turns him off.*

Rod. Nay, my best wife, do but hear me !

Imp. Wife? marry! You think I cannot read your thoughts in your looks? You must be plotting, must ye?

Rod. If to raise thee to grandeur be plotting, I'm guilty ! One successful work *à-la-mode* is a surer game than a thousand good works.

Imp. I smell your design; it is to ruin me. I was once told by a cunning woman beggary would be my end, and you take the way to 't.

Rod. I have enough—ne'er fear it.

Imp. Yes, and are free enough of it to every one but me; and there it goes from your heart.

Rod. Thou know'st the contrary; it is but ask and have. Dost want anything?

Imp. As if a woman must have nothing but what she wants and asks! My family were never wont to ask.

Rod. And I've been kind to them for your sake. I have honourably bestowed two of your sisters.

Imp. They could have done 't themselves.

Rod. Sent a brother of yours into the Levant; another for France; a third into Spain; and am now making provision for a fourth. So that, in effect, I have married a tribe, to enjoy one.

Imp. Yes, to twit me with it.

Enter DON HERCIO.

O signior! that you had come a little sooner! Our spouse and I have been at jingle-jangle. He knows I love him, and that's the reason.

Her. Hough!—jangle with you! I hope, sir, you did not lift a finger; if you had——

[*He cocks his hat, and struts.*

Imp. I'd given him two for one. [*She points at him.*

Rod. And who are you?

Her. *Soy hydalgo come il re!* My name—Don Hercio Zanzummim Gogmagog, lineally descended from the Dukes of Infantado, Trinidado—or somebody else. And if you had——

Imp. No, there was nothing like it.

[RODERIGO *startles.*

Her. I only say, if he had, my great, great, great, great-grandfather's ashes—his that gave the Sultan the lie, and took the Cham of Tartary by the whiskers royal—would blush to see any of his posterity not true to honour. You say he did not, and I'm satisfied. But if he had, or durst but offer 't—Voto!

Imp. Come, signior, I'll be his security.

[HERCIO *leads* IMPERIA *off.*

Rod. She has her bravo, too! Cowardly devil that I was not to draw upon him! Yes, and fright my wife, who, which is some sign of love, did not aggravate it. Well, go thy ways, thou hast thy frolics! yet it shall go hard but I will hit thy humour.

[*Exit.*

SCENE II.

A noble room in MONTALTO'S *house.*

Enter PORTIA *sola.*

Por. My husband is convinced, and so am I,
The action, in all its circumstances,
Must be Grimald's; for 't can be none's but his.
And yet I'm racked between the two extremes
Of friendship to him and my just resentments
To his false nephew. All unknown to us,
The generous Grimaldi has restored
My husband's fortune: his degenerous nephew
Has taken this occasion to renew
His long rejected love.

Enter FIESCHI, *as at a stand, and gazing on her.*

Fies. Her virtue, sure,
Has wrought impossibilities, and added
New graces to her person, as if infinity
Could be increas'd.

Por. I sent for ye, Fieschi;
But it had been more honourable in you
Not to have given me cause. Your worthy uncle
Has, to his frequent obligations,
Added a fresh—I need not tell ye what.

Fies. And 'tis his satisfaction that he wanted
Neither the will nor means of doing it.

Por. Debts are discharg'd with payment. Benefits,
Pay what we can, there will be still arrear.
But, for his nephew to profane that friendship,
I could be angry—verily I could
And would, were 't not to make another's ill
My own affliction.

Fies. Blame your virtue, then!
Montalto loved it; and the selfsame cause
That absolves him absolves Fieschi too.
He rested not in speculation only;
And shall I turn philosopher?

Por. I'm his,
And only his, and therefore barred to you.

Fies. But nature's free, and walks not by restraint
But choice.

Por. And I have mine.

Fies. She never coined
Those bugbear words of honour, jealousy;
She ne'er impaled free woman, or designed
A thing so excellent for one's embrace.

Por. Enough! When that I ever heard ye, was as
Much against my will as the concealing it
Against my duty. No; a virtuous woman
Takes no more liberty than what she ought.

Fies. At least blame love, not me. I've often rais'd
Your great idea in my soul, and, as
A diamond only cuts a diamond,

Set your own virtue 'gainst yourself; yet still
Love gets the upper ground, and pours upon me:
So weak a fence is virtue against love.

Por. We still excuse ourselves. The fault lies not
In virtue, but our resolutions.
Could we once make our actions work up
To our intentions, the work were done.
There—take your idle whatsoever it be!

[*She takes out a long white box, and throws it toward him.*

I knew the hand too well to open it.

Fies. And will you still torment me with the sight
Of a forbidden good?

Por. Not good to you,
Because forbidden. If you're wise, begone!

Fies. You've said it, and I obey.

[*He is going off, as forgetting the box; she kicks it after him; he takes it up. Exit.*

Por. But take your box wi' ye.
Sure I have done some evil, and the guilt
Sticks on my brow. It must be so, or he
Had never offered this amour to me.
Be't what it will, this I'm sure, my will
Had nothing in 't; yet how poor and cheap
Do even the appearances of evil make us!

Enter GRIMALDI *and* MONTALTO *hand in hand.*

Mon. Your repeated obligations
Deprive me of my liberty.

Gri. In exchange, take mine!

Por. The only injury you ever did us;
For it has put us on the necessity
Of living and dying ungrateful.

Mon. A benefit too great to be received.

Gri. Not for a friend to give.

Mon. But what return
Could ye propose?

Gri. 'T has overpaid itself.
To have done well, in hopes of a return,
Is the most sordid usury. Alloy

Does but embase the coin; and such a thought
Had derogated from the majesty
Of friendship, and been interest.
Mon. But does not
Equality make the lasting friendship?
Gri. Of minds, I grant it. Friendship cannot stand
With vice or infamy. Degenerous mixtures
Seldom outlive the birth. And as ours was
Founded on virtue, like a true-built arch,
May it grow up until it knit at top,
And bid defiance to the shocks of fortune.
Por. Thus you o'ercome us every way.
Mon. Teach me
What 'tis to be a friend; one without whom,
As a man can't be happy, 'tis not his least
Unhappiness he never knows his friend
But by being unhappy himself. A friend!
My earthly God!
Gri. As you are mine, no more!
Come, let's enjoy this salt of life—this all
That gives it relish, and without which life
Were but a dull parenthesis of time,
The world a wilderness, and man the beast.
I've wanted company in a crowd. Blest friendship!
Thou girdle of the world! Had I been heathen,
I'd sacrificed unto no other goddess. [*Exeunt.*

SCENE III.

The FIRST SCENE *again.*

Enter IMPERIA, QUARTILLA, *and* SCINTILLA.

Imp. To say otherwise were to belie him; and, as all men have their faults, the worst of his that I know is that he loves me too well.

Scin. And such a fault may be easily borne with.

Quar. Thou'rt a mere chicken, girl! there may be as great a mistake in loving a woman too well as in loving her too little. What would I care for a man should court my little finger, look babies in my eyes, sit and admire me? That was not the fashion of my time; men were men then.

Imp. And there, too, he's likely enough—truss and well knit. But why this to me?

Quar. Your ladyship was wont to allow us this harmless freedom.

Imp. Or, if I don't, you'll take it.

Quar. Without offence, then, what diversion have ye?

Imp. As pleases my husband; and I have neither eye nor ear to anything else.

Scin. And a friend would study as much to please you.

Imp. I should think one husband were enough for any modest woman. Are there naughty women?

Quar. Marry forbid it! Or that they should not be content with one eye, one hand, one leg.

Imp. But one's husband, tho', is the best friend.

Quar. And the worst company. Fie, madam, you'll ruin the sex! Husband, say ye? A mere thing—a cover-slut of custom!

Scin. Has not every well two buckets?—every ship two anchors? Or did you never see two cocks cruckling about one hen, and her all the while picking of straws to make her own nest?

Quar. Well said, my fine girl! Thou may'st come to something in time.

Imp. How these jades hit my humour!—[*Aside.*]—O—but—would a woman—a virtuous woman—a woman of honour——

Quar. Do anything but say her prayers.

Imp. Besides—the injury.

Scin. To what?—or whom? You lose nothing, sell no household stuff, nor waste goods.

Quar. Or if the main house fall, do but keep up the dovecot, and you'll ne'er want pigeons till ye dam up the loovre.*

* "Loover or lover," an opening at the top of a dovecot.

"A loover or tunnel in the roof or top of a great hall to avoid smoke."—BARET, 1590.

Imp. But you know I seldom go abroad, and for me to receive visits would make my husband jealous.

Scin. That all?

Quar. Or can he be so ill-natured, as, when his own belly's full, to deny a beggar his leavings?

Imp. But people will be apt to talk of a body.

Quar. For what?—For going to church? Can't you pretend a vow of devotion and chastity for three days a week?

Imp. And suppose he make the like for t'other four?

Scin. How willingly, now, would she be persuaded into her own desires!—[*Aside.*]—You're young, and the town's full.

Imp. You could not set up, then, with partridge and quail for the year round?

Scin. No, by my troth, could I not; and yet I've but a puling stomach.

Imp. There's somewhat in 't. What's everything we do but a mere circle of variety, or grand oleo dish'd up several ways to sweeten the wearisomeness of one pleasure by another? What's imagination or desire, when once attained, but surfeit? Fish of four days old—away with 't!

Quar. Your ladyship takes it very naturally. Don't the men say of us—women—and women—and more women—but still women?

Imp. And shall woman—nature's last hand, to show what she could do—she alone walk by herself?—To one dark lantern?—She shut her windows to the sun, to pore over a farthing candle? Which of themselves does it?—and shall I?

Scin. No, madam! if the men ring the changes, I know not why we mayn't shuffle, and cast knaves again.

Imp. Well fare, honest Mahomet! We read of no couples in his paradise—and yet young juicy girls, plump, balmy, and never above fifteen.

Quar. Beloved fifteen!

Imp. And eyes!

Scin. More sparkling than the diamond.

Imp. I should have thought the cow's eye better. A demure look keep its own counsel, and a little seeming innocence cheats a man into a fondness. The sparkling eye may hit a straggling fool; but 'tis the melting, 'tis the dying eye that sweeps whole ranks. Let's see—[*to* SCINTILLA]—set thine!—Hold—there—there was a look! So—that again!

Enter FIESCHI, *as consulting somewhat to himself.*

Fies. What! practising against the ball? I fear me I may have disturbed ye.

Imp. Not at all, unless it be with your new gravity. But whence—whence this starched face?—or why?

[*She beckons off* QUARTILLA *and* SCINTILLA.

[*Exeunt.*

Fies. Besides my former disappointments, it is not many hours since I left your sister Portia—but the same chagrin still. Like the Parthian, she kills by flying.

Imp. Alas, poor Fieschi, thou'rt smitten! I thought how ye loved me, and have found it.

Fies. You wrong me; there's nothing might have taken in that sullen fort but I've attempted—made all the approaches love backed with interest could contrive, but all in vain.

Imp. The necklace cost me twelve hundred ducats.

Fies. That you had seen with what scorn she kick'd it after me!

Imp. That all?—she shall have a better jewel.

Fies. To as much purpose. A rock is not more immovable.

Imp. Yet I have known a rock blown up.

Fies. Her virtue is as firm as her face charming.

Imp. Away, ye fool! I have too many charms of my own to suspect another's.—'Tis not her beauty, but virtue, quarrels me—that half-faced virtue that has its faults as well as others, but a better way of hiding 'em.

Fies. Be 't what it will, 't 'as conquered me; and,

were 't not for my prior love to you, I must have doted on her.

Imp. False man! And, when I think upon the thing I'd curse, I'll name Fieschi. [*She seems to weep.*

Fies. Be merciful, and kill me, or forgive me! I'll yet attempt her—I will!—but—she's your sister.

Imp. What's that to my command? Only conquer her, and wear myself and fortune. That nature had made me a man! Consider—I'll return instantly! [*Exit.*

Fies. If ever man had a wolf by the ears, I have one now. If I renew my attempts on Portia, and carry her, I hazard the friendship between my uncle and Montalto; and, if I don't, I lose Imperia. Of all devils, defend me from a woman's devil!

Enter IMPERIA, *with bags of gold in her lap and a casket of jewels in her hand.*

Imp. There!—[*she drops the bags, and gives him the casket.*]—There's more gold and richer jewels, and, as a farther pledge, this—[*a ring*]—and my heart. Not yet resolved? Away! [*She strokes him.*

Fies. I was meditating some new contrivance. 'Tis done!

Imp. There spake my better angel.

Fies. But say——

Imp. More but's? Has she no she friend, no woman?—and while I think on't, you may trust Bianca—yourself no wit, or these no rhetoric. [*Pointing to the bags, etc.*

Fies. Once more, 'tis done, as sure as fate had sealed it! And if Pansa has wrought up Bianca, as I once designed it, you'll say 't yourself. [*He leads her off.*

SCENE IV.

MONTALTO'S *House.*

Enter PANSA *and* BIANCA.

Pan. They're all abroad, then?

Bian. Whether they are or not, you're out of hearing. But what does your master mean by all this? I overheard them when he was last here; but never let him look to come again.

Pan. Not without thee, Bianca.

Bian. I've had enough of it already—my lady has not given me a good look ever since.

Pan. Patience, my beloved! time and patience——

Bian. Will do no good with her. Besides, you men are so inconstant; if ye had your wish to-day, you'd have another to-morrow.

Pan. And are not you women the same—as fond of an old sweetheart as a brisk widow of her third husband?

Bian. E'en thank yourselves that taught us.

Pan. Sick of everything but a new face.

Bian. Your own picture to a hair.

Pan. And so fickle, fickle, fickle—a man knows not where to have ye.

Bian. Beshrew me, now, but that's a fib! where to have you 's the question—once fill your belly, and ye drop off.

Pan. And there, I must confess, you have the 'vantage; you stick the closer. And perhaps, though I spake too soon, what have we got here?

[*He strokes her stomacher.*

Bian. Nothing of your's, I'll secure ye. I shall be married a Tuesday next.

Pan. Still my good merry girl! But say he find it?

Bian. You men think you have all the wit, but I can tell ye some women come two, three, four, and sometimes five months sooner than ordinary of the first child; but for the rest as right as others. You're all for nine months at least, but I have known a nimble fellow not married above eight weeks and his wife has brought him a couple—and so like the father, too!

Pan. Still the same merry rogue!

Bian. But hark ye, tho'—where are the books you promised me?—I can't sleep for thinking of 'em.

Pan. And thou shalt have them in a day or two.

Bian. O what a dainty thing it is to see a man here to-day and a thousand miles off to-morrow!—mow giants by the waist, conquer armies, overrun kingdoms, and all for the love of some distressed princess he never saw; whilst she, poor lady, apprehending it by instinct, sits bemoaning him in some castle grate, and, if she can borrow so much leisure from her grief, records his doughty deeds to posterity in window cushions and coverlets.

Pan. And then, when, over the heads of forty or fifty thousand men, all slain by his own hand, he cuts his way to her chamber, O! what sighs, looks, half words, and I know not what! till, the lord of the castle having reinforced his guards, surprises him ere he can recover Morglay, and from his lady's arms conveys him to a dungeon, where he's fed with nothing but horse biscuit and puddle water, till, being fortunately released by some enchanter, his friend, he's dropt in an unknown desert, whence, within three days, he becomes master of a great kingdom, and within four more by some private mark proves the rightful heir of 't.

Bian. There were a man for me! I hate your sots that turn hermits, and can live seven years together on nuts, blackberries, and acorns. They lovers! O that I were a man, that I might ha' been a knight! or, being as I am, some little odd princess.

Pan. And I have much of thy humour about me; for never had any man greater desire of wealth and command than myself, and that only to eat well, drink lustick,* care for nothing, and have my flatterers as other men. But come, Bianca! though I cannot make thee a princess, I can put thee in the way shall make thee as fine as a princess. Two hundred pistoles would do no hurt, I take it.

Bian. Ay, marry! but where's the money?

Pan. Thy master now and then lies at his country house, and, do thou but give my master the opportunity of getting into your lady's apartment some such night, and I'll secure it thee.

Bian. To what purpose? I'm sure he will do no good.

Pan. Do thou thy part, he'll venture that;—two hundred pistoles is money.

Bian. And, truly, to speak my heart, I've often wonder'd how she can be so unkind. [*She hugs him.*

Pan. Goodnature, thou must! and, to let thee see he's in earnest, he has sent thee fifty in hand.—[*Gives her a purse.*]—Come, come! there are certain critical minutes when a woman can deny nothing.

Bian. But shall I be sure of the rest?

Pan. If thou hast it not, never trust Pansa more!

Bian. Well, then, you speak in a lucky hour, for my master goes out of town to-morrow, and an hundred to one if he return that night. Let your master and you come about midnight, and you'll find the street door unlock'd, and me ready to receive ye. But be sure, now——

Pan. That thou should'st doubt it!

[*Exeunt hand in hand.*

* "Lustick," according to Halliwell and others, means "healthy, cheerful, pleasant." The word does not appear as a noun.

Act III.—Scene I.

Of Roderigo's *House.*

Enter Crispo *and* Mingo, *wiping their faces.*

Cris. Here's a clutter, with all my heart! Why, sure, this master of ours is either running mad, or never thinks of returning!

Min. Here was a palace as well furnish'd as the Duke's itself—such hangings, pictures, carpets, plate, and everything suitable; but it seems they were not rich enough! We're all new from top to bottom!

Cris. For my part, my back's almost broke with luggaging, and I think thine's not much better. Would 'twere her neck that has been the cause of all!

Min. Yet what would not a man do that loves his wife?

Cris. Commend me to our old home; we have no wives there. And I've observed here, those that so gild this pill of matrimony, to make it go down the easier, never take it themselves.

Min. The truth is, neither of us need be fond of the sex. But every one is not our Imperia! A wife, if you have money, will help to get more.

Cris. Or rather spend what you have.

Min. If you're at home, she'll bear you company.

Cris. Or rather scold ye out of doors.

Min. If you're abroad——

Cris. Perhaps cuckold ye ere ye come home! But how now, Mingo, have ye forgot your knitting-needles?

Min. Nor your trap-door—mere accidents!

Cris. I tell thee, brother of mine, a devil of clouts would ha' more wit; and I'm afraid our master has spoil'd thee.

Enter Roderigo.

Rod. So, so, ye have done well; ye have done more in a few hours than a dozen lazy blockheads would ha' done in a week. Yet, methinks, the rooms might have been better perfum'd!

Cris. We reserv'd that till last.

Rod. Never the worse! Is the music come?

Min. They only wait your call.

Rod. Go, then, and be sure everything be in order!

[*Exeunt* CRISPO *and* MINGO.

My wife and I are friends again, and to confirm it I've promis'd her a ball, and can't but laugh to think how she'll be pleased with the preparations I have made for 't. She's but taking the air, and can't be long ere she return.

Enter IMPERIA; *she runs to him.*

Imp. O my dear! and am not I a good wife, now?
That thou'dst been with us at Duke Doria's garden!
The pretty contest between Art and Nature.
To see the wilderness, grots, arbours, ponds,
And in the midst, over a stately fountain,
The Neptune of the Ligurian Sea,
Andrea Dorea, the man who first
Taught Genoa not to serve! Then to behold
The curious waterworks and wanton streams
Wind here and there, as if they had forgot
Their errand to the sea.

Rod. Thou set'st off this
So well, I fancy thou'dst design a fairer.

Imp. Dear husband, try! And then, again, within
That vast prodigious cage, to see the groves
Of myrtle, orange, jessamine, beguile
The winged choir into a native warble,
And pride of their restraint. Then, up and down,
An antiquated marble or broken statue,
Majestic even in ruin!

Rod. It pleases me
To see thee pleas'd!

Imp. And such a glorious palace!
Such pictures, carving, furniture! my words
Cannot reach half the splendour. And after all,
To see the sea, fond of the goodly sight,

One while glide amorous and lick her walls,
As who would say, Come, follow! but, repulsed,
Rally its whole artillery of waves,
And crowd into a storm. But when, my dear,
Will ye fancy me such a retirement?

Rod. When I, like him that rais'd it, can command
The spoils o' th' rifled ocean, thou shalt!

Imp. Thou'st ever a fetch for what thou'st no mind to! How can a woman love ye?

Rod. Do but consider; the house we now live in is little inferior to a palace, and might become my better.

Imp. A mere hole! and that so damp, musty, and raw!

Rod. You ne'er complain'd of it before. However, fire and perfumes will rectify the air.

Imp. Yes, to put a woman into fits!

Rod. Bating that palace, there's not a house in Genoa better furnish'd! and, for pictures, I dare almost vie Italy! Come, and I'll show thee!

[*He offers to lead her out.*

Imp. What, those in the gallery? I saw 'em as I came in: mere sign-post work!

Rod. How! Titian's Venus sign-post work?

Imp. A downright country Joan!

Rod. Raphael's Paris and the three goddesses?

Imp. A bumpkin and his milkmaids!

Rod. What think'st thou, then, of Guido Rheni's Rape of Lucrece?—Michael Angelo's Leda?—or Corregio's Jupiter and Semele?

Imp. Enough to make a modest woman look through her fingers!

Rod. Would'st thou have nobler actions? What say'st thou to Carrachio's Perseus and Andromeda?—Pietro Testa's Iphigenia?—or Mola's Curtius?

Imp. What Mr. Dawber pleases.

Rod. Or, if thou lik'st hunting, there's Tempesta's Acteon!

Imp. E'en keep it to yourself! For my part, I would not put such an affront on my friends as to have them seen in my house. Pictures, d'ye call 'em?

Enter CRISPO.

Cris. Sir, the company are now lighting at door!

Imp. And why not madam, saucebox?—[*She strikes him.*]—Your servants must disrespect me too! Entertain them yourself for me.

[*She is running off; he stops her.*

Rod. Nay, wife, my dear wife! what will our friends say? For thy own sake, if not mine, be civil!

[*She presses to go off.*

Imp. Say what they will, shall I humour a husband that can deny me anything? You'd as good let me go, or I'll spoil all. Let me go, I say!

Rod. Thou shalt have anything. Here, take the keys of all I have, and please thyself!

[*She takes them grumbling.*

Imp. You can make me do what you please, that ye can.

Rod. I'll wait upon our friends!

Enter PERSONS *in masquerade.*

Known or unknown, be pleas'd!

[*They seat themselves; music begins.*

Do but observe this air!—[*to* IMPERIA.]

[*A dance of all but* RODERIGO *and* IMPERIA.

Imp. Scraping, you mean! I'd 've made as good on a gridiron.

Rod. Softly, my dear!

[*The dance ends; they seat again.*

Imp. And such a stringhalt dance.

[*After a small interval, another music.*

Enter a BOY.

He sings.

Were I to take wife,
As 'tis for my life,
She should be brisk, pleasant, and merry;
A lovely fine brown,
A face all her own,
With a lip red and round as a cherry.

Not much of the wise,
Less of the precise,
Nor over reserv'd, nor yet flying;
Hard breasts, a straight back,
An eye full and black,
But languishing as she were dying.

And then for her dress,
Be 't more or be 't less,
Not tawdry set out nor yet meanly;
And one thing beside,
Just, just so much pride
As may serve to keep honest and cleanly.

Imp. Whoo—ho—ho—hoo! here's a voice and a song! I thank ye.—[*A noise within, as of some dishes breaking.*]—You'd have you can't tell what!

Enter QUARTILLA.

Qua. O madam! your monkey has got into the next room, and overturn'd all your cupboard of china!

[*She runs off in a fury.*

Imp. Or I had done 't myself, to spite my Don.

[*Exit.*

Rod. I beseech ye, gentlemen, let this make no disturbance. I hope you'll take share of a short regale!

Omnes. Alas, poor Roderigo!

[*Exeunt maskers; manet* RODERIGO.

Rod. Poor, henpecked devil, they might have said! The very boys will pelt me!—[*He walks.*]—But is this Belphegor? this the once Generalissimo? Yes—[*he makes a shrug*]—but subjected to all the conditions of humanity; and I must be contented as well as others, at least till I get my keys again; for, to say truth, my ships are longer out than was expected, and bills come thick upon me. Some of them, too, begin to be importunate! My comfort is, they're three rich cargoes, and any one's return will pay for all. [*Exit.*

Scene II.

Of Montalto's *house.*

Enter Pansa *with a dark lantern, conducting* Fieschi.

Pan. She's as good as her word! The door was unlocked!

Fies. And I may trust her?

Pan. My life ye may! for she ever made it a matter of conscience to take a gentleman's money and do nothing for 't.

Enter Bianca.

Bian. What shall we do, sir? Our master's return'd, but in his own apartment. Consider!

Fies. It must be, and why not now?

Bian. Then follow me close and softly! and do you, Pansa, stay here till I return.

[*Exeunt* Bianca *and* Fieschi.

Pan. And if it hits, I'm made; and who knows but I may marry the jade myself for all her Tuesday next? O but—but what? To be a cuckold! And how many are there in the world yet live contentedly? But—your own cuckold—forestal the market—antedate your own fortune! and what of that? I am not the first has done 't, and sha'n't be the last. This I am sure, I am the less deceiv'd. Whate'er it be, two hundred pistoles and my master's kindness will make amends for all.

Bianca *returns.*

Now, Bianca, I was thinking, what if thou and I should join jiblets in an honourable way? What think ye of matrimony, Bianca?

Bian. No, Pansa, no! for though I love ye well enough, you shall never twit me with anything of your own knowledge; but for old acquaintance, I'll recommend ye. She is——

Pan. The very mop of modesty! But what has she?

Bian. Enough for you, and to spare. The truth is, not above sixteen or seventeen thousand ducats ready money, and as much more after the death of her grannum. But, for virtue!

Pan. The Lord knows what! But say she won't ha' me?

Bian. I'll put in a good word for ye. This for your comfort; she'll sip Verdua—privately, though—and then, so good-natur'd.

Pan. That's half the work; for I never knew the devil at one end but his dam was at t'other.

[*A noise within as of a falling down-stairs.*

Bian. Here, Pansa, here!—[*She puts him in a closet, takes his lantern, and exit by one door.*

Enter FIESCHI, *running, by another. He falls, and drops his dagger.*

Fies. Where am I? Blind fortune assist my blinder self! [*He recovers, and exit by the door he first came in at.* BIANCA *peeps in with her dark lantern, sees the dagger, takes it up, and gives both to* PANSA, *then likewise peeping.*

Bian. There! bolt the door t'ye, while I look out another way. [*Exit.*

Enter MONTALTO *with a case of pistols, in his nightgown, by the same door* FIESCHI *ran in at.*

Mon. The last noise lay this way. Within there, ho!—[*He knocks.*]—What's here? Methinks I see a faint glimmering of a light within that closet.—[*He endeavours to open the door.*]—Bolted within, too? Nay, then!—[*He fires at the door,* PANSA *slips the bolt, glares him in the face with his dark lantern.* MONTALTO *fires at him and closes with him. Both fall.* PANSA *stabs him, and by that means gets from him, but not without the loss of his dagger. Exit* PANSA *by the same door as his master.* MONTALTO *rises.*

Enter SERVANTS, *with lights and swords, undressed.*

1 *Ser.* Thieves, thieves! Waken my lord! he may be kill'd in's bed.

2 *Ser.* Hold! there he stands! He bleeds! A handkerchief, to keep the wound from air!

Mon. What needs this noise? One of ye stay with me, another get me a chirurgeon.

3 *Ser.* I run, I run! [*Exit.*

Mon. The rest look about the house! 'tis almost impossible he should escape.

3 *Servant returns.*

3 *Ser.* The street door, my lord, is open.
[*He runs off again.*

Mon. Nay, then, the bird is flown. However, see what servants are wanting or out of bed. That men knew when to put on arms!

[1 *Servant sees a dagger on the floor, takes it up, and gives it* MONTALTO. *He starts.*

1 *Ser.* Here's some one's bloody dagger.

Mon. And I know whose; I gave it him.
That was unkind. [*He throws it carelessly.*

Enter PORTIA, *in a nightgown.*

Por. My husband bloody! What have I done, good heaven? Now pity me, and press me not with more than I can bear, or give me strength.

[*She staggers; 1 Servant supports her.*

Mon. Do not thou stab me too!

[MONTALTO *breaks from the other.*

'Tis but a scratch, and thy Montalto lives.
Stay! stay, my Portia!—yet one minute stay,
And take me with thee!

[*He runs to take the dagger; 2 Servant prevents him.*

2 *Ser.* She begins to stir, sir!

[MONTALTO *runs to her and shakes her.*

Mon. Return—return! At least but give an eye,
And see who calls thee back!

Por. My hovering soul

Was on the wing, and nothing but that voice
Had check'd its flight.

Mon. Do not torment thyself;
Thou may'st accuse, but canst not alter fate.
Heav'n, earth, all things have their period.

Por. But Portia has resolv'd she will be Portia
In not surviving you.

Mon. Respite till then.
Ev'ry wound is not mortal; or, if 'twere,
Who comes to his last period dies old.
If I've liv'd well, it's enough; if ill, too long.
Life's measur'd not by years but actions.

Por. But to be thus rent from me!

Mon. If I must leave the town, what matter is 't
What port I go out at? or which way I die?
Death has a thousand roads, but all of them
Meet at the journey's end! How happy, then,
Is man, that he can neither lose his way
Nor pass it twice.

3 *Servant returns.*

3 *Ser.* The chirurgeons, sir, are coming!

Mon. Bring them into the next room! Come, my dear; I hope there's no danger. However, happen what will, it sha'n't surprise me. [*Exeunt.*

Scene III.

Roderigo's *house.*

Enter Roderigo, *with letters in his hand.*

Rod. 'Tis what I feared! My Levant merchant taken by the Turks, my Frenchman sunk at sea, my Spaniard lost at dice, and, what's worse, my credit is at stake, my cash in my wife's hand; and if she prove cross, there's no more to be said—I must break.

To him DON HERCIO.

Her. I am a gentleman, sir, and the King's no more. [*He struts.*

Rod. Heaven maintain it, sir.

Her. Maintain me! I have an estate somewhere beyond the mountains in my own country, and where a pigeon-house once stood; which, were it standing,—as it is now fall'n,—well stock'd with pigeons, and removed to Madrid, might be worth to me a brace of thousand maravedis yearly!

Rod. That is to say, about twenty shillings English.

Her. Maintain me! [*Cocks and struts.*

Rod. Your pardon, sir.

Her. Yet think it no dishonour to converse with our Jews in black hats here. Somewhat below me, I must confess, but I am now and then serviceable to 'em, and they thank me.

Rod. I remember ye, sir. Your commands to me?

Her. That's as you please. You are, signior, a man of fortune, which makes them envy you. In short, 'tis given out your ships are miscarried; and now, one taxes this, another that, a third your cattamountain, my relation, your lady!

Rod. Alas, poor fool! must she suffer too?

Her. I was once about to have made them eat their words; but prudence, as sometimes it should, interpos'd. Upon the whole, if you pay 'em not forty thousand ducats, you'll be arrested ere night.

Rod. Neither my ships nor that will much affect me.

Her. The more's my joy. But since they are such scoundrels, name me the man ye do but doubt, and —he's dead!

Rod. By no means, signior. However, as an acknowledgment of your respect, be pleased——

[*He gives him a small purse.*

Her. I beseech ye, sir—what d'ye mean?—nay—[*but takes it.*]—Now could I quarrel you myself in that you dare not trust my honour; but I can take nothing ill from so noble a patron, and when you have any such occasion, let me oblige ye. [*Exit.*

Rod. Her relation, he said!—A worthy one! And yet it may be true as he says; and who knows but he might be sent to set me? My last comfort is, I have cash enough in the house, but the keys of it hang at my wife's girdle.

Enter IMPERIA.

Never more welcome, tho' to unwelcome news!

Imp. Your ships, you mean? 'Tis everywhere!

Rod. I'm happy yet in such a partner of my cares; all will do well again. Lend me thy keys!

Imp. For what, I wis'?—Your wife, it seems, is not fit to be trusted?

Rod. Thou knowest the contrary;—but I have some bills charged on me that require speedy payment, or they'll be protested; and then, where am I?

Imp. Ev'n where you please; but keys you get none of me—the fool has more wit.

Rod. I shall be ruin'd else.

Imp. Better you than I—she'll provide for one.

Rod. I have enough to bear forty such losses.

Imp. Yes, in your great iron chest. Away, you pitiful Don!—With what face could ye cheat me with a parcel of stones and brickbats instead of coin? Was this the treasure—these the doubloons ye talk'd of?

Rod. I tell thee, woman, 'tis all good silver; and more gold than the best of thy family thou so much tattlest e'er saw together.

Imp. My family, gentleman? I was finely hope up, when all the pride of Italy courted me, to marry a Tramontane, a beggarly Don,—Don Roderigo Castiliano, the first of his house and the last of his name!—blot my blood with your damn'd Morisco! That Moletto face might have forewarn'd me. But alas! poor me—I loved! [*She puts finger in eye.*

Rod. Thou hast a prince incognito in me.

Imp. The devil I have! Ha, ha, ha!

Rod. Provoke me not, for fear thou find'st me such.

Imp. And what would my poor pug? I have a charm shall lay ye, good sir devil—a circle shall cool your courage.

Rod. Give me my keys, I say!

Enter a WOMAN *with a bandbox.*

How now? who's this?

Imp. Who should she be?—my tire-woman! She brings me knots, gloves, ribbons, points, everything.

Rod. And now and then a letter in the bottom o' th' box.—[*He puts his hand in the box, finds a letter, she snatches it from him, and throws it back; the tire-woman takes it up, and exit running.*]—Mighty fine! And from whom, I pray?

Imp. What's that to you? Jealous! o' my conscience, jealous! I see a mousled hood, rumpled tippet, or tumbled petticoat would not down with you!—my Lord Dick or my Lord Tom stick in your stomach. Jealous, my life! jealous! Know, Tramontane, jealousy is the effect of weakness; whereas he that's virtuous himself believes the same of another.

Rod. Give me my keys, I say again, and that letter! or—— [*He takes her by the sleeve.*

Imp. But shall I have 'em again?

Rod. Upon my honour, thou shalt! I'll only take what will serve my present occasion.

Imp. Shall I indeed, La?—[*She embraces him.*]—And will ye never be angry with your wife again?

Rod. All, all's forgotten.

Imp. Well, then, I'll try for once.—[*She whips out his sword and beats him about the stage; and as she hears company entering, she drops the sword and takes to her handkerchief.*]—Murder! murder! help! murder!

Enter five or six women.

Sure all women ha'n't such husbands.

1 *Wom.* Now, fie upon him for a villain!—beat his wife?

2 *Wom.* Draw upon a woman?

Rod. Do but hear me!

3 *Wom.* That were wise work indeed.—[*Third woman takes up the sword; all fall upon him, and beat him down, and having well pommelled him, they go up to* IMPERIA *and exeunt with her.* RODERIGO *rises.*

Omnes. I hope you are not hurt—[*to* IMPERIA.]

Rod. Nor all men, sure, such wives. What shall I do? Debts threaten me abroad—my wife's at home; stay here I cannot, and return I dare not.—[*He walks.*]—And live with her ten years, if possible,—that blest parenthesis, if possible!
But yet, to fall thus tamely—be outwitted,
And by a woman! By the drowsy Lethe,
Cocytus, Acheron, or whatever worse
Than fables ever feign'd or fear conceiv'd,
I'll make her know me better—make her know
What an Italianated devil can do. [*He gives a stamp.*
Ho! Sacrapant! Adramelech!

Enter SERVANT *with a letter.*

Ser. I am told, sir, it requires no answer.
[*Exit* SERVANT. *He reads.*

Rod. "Your house is beset with bailiffs—consult your safety—haste, if you're wise." How I command, how the dull slaves obey!
[*Another stamp. A hollow voice between the scenes.*

Voice. What would Belphegor?

Rod. Attend me without! What shall a poor devil do?—but—might not friends take up the matter?—yes—and your house beset. I'd come to any terms, but the letter said haste. I have a loophole yet—but never more to maintain my figure. Haste was the word; but must I leave thee? I will yet stand it—men and their wives have quarrell'd and been friends again.—[*A noise, as of the clatter of a door, is heard within. He starts, runs his head against the wall, recovers, and exit.*
They're got into the house.
The best of 't is, I have not far to go.

Scene IV.

A street.

Enter Crispo *and* Mingo, *by cross doors. They meet, jostle, and lay their hands to their swords.*

Min. Signior Crispo? Mio multo illustre!

[*They make their drunken scrapes, and embrace.*

Cris. Min' here Mingo? Vostre tres humble. That comrades should know one another no better!

Min. And which becomes us least of all others—us, that should unite against the common enemy, mankind.

Cris. Thou'rt right. And now, that we're pot-valiant, what think'st thou of a frolic?

Min. And kill the next we meet.

Cris. My very thought. A match!—[*They shake hands.*]—Our master will not hear of our return; and, if I'm hang'd, 'tis what I would.

Min. And better far than living under the dominion of this superdevilified Imperia.

Cris. Poor Belphegor! I have known him somewhat in my time, but now so sotted on her, he's not himself; and all this to please her that will be pleased with nothing.

Min. How one may be mistaken! I remember, while he courted her, almond-butter would not melt in her mouth—so innocent, she'd have blusht t'ave seen her own hand naked—and a voice so low, she could not hear herself. But not three days married, ere, like an alarm clock, the house rang of her.

Cris. I'm sure I bear her marks. Time was I could have bolted through a key-hole, cut capers on the point of a needle, giv'n the double somersault on a pin's head, felt no more blows than a sack of wool; but now she 'as beaten me to mash.

Min. And made me mere gut-founder'd. And I'm afraid, our master, return when he will, will make but a ragged accompt of it.

Cris. My only hopes are, he'll be weary in time, and leave her behind him; for if e'er she come among us below, we break up house for certain.

Min. A lion, they say, runs from a cock; and well may the devil from a crowing hen.

Cris. I am glad to see this amendment, friend Mingo, and hope now you are not so matrimonially inclin'd as once you were.

Min. I tell thee, Crispo, I know not what to make of 'em. Some are so skittish, no ground will hold 'em; others so resty, one can bring 'em to nothing; and others, again, like a rattle at a dog's tail, run where you will and it still follows ye.

Cris. When all's done, there's nothing like an honest private friend; and, between ourselves, I have such a piece.

Min. As mine, I warrant ye—so loving!

Cris. So careful of her honour, yet so obliging!

Min. As if I did not know your old Flora—a mere rag of a jade; I wonder thou durst venture on her, for fear of navel-gauling.

Cris. And, I think, you have not much reason to brag of your greasy tripe-wife. For my part, I hate bog-trotting,

Min. What need this reservedness among friends? Upon honour now—who shall say first?

Cris. And wound reputation!—fie!

Enter MARONE *and a large* WATCH. CRISPO *and* MINGO *run; the* WATCH *follow.*

Mar. You may believe, neighbours, there's somewhat more than ordinary that I am here in person. Every man would not have done 't. But see, who are those fellows running there?—follow, follow! There is a dangerous plot now brewing, and I know who has a finger in it up to the elbow. Follow—follow 'em!

[*Exeunt.*

Scene V.

Enter Mattheo *and* Roderigo *as in a vineyard;*
Mattheo *a spade in his hand.*

Mat. I have heard of your quality and great losses —but your wife, say you? Alas, poor gentleman! I lost mine about a month since, and, tho' I have no great reason to brag, find a miss of her.

Rod. I'll change with ye—my living wife for your dead wife.

Mat. Not too much of that neither—I had one before, and she was well enough. But this last!— such a—I'll tread lightly on her grave, for fear she wake.

Rod. And what difference found ye between a good wife and a bad one?

Mat. I said not she was good, but well enough; tho' I think the difference be much the same as between a wild rabbit and a tame rabbit. However, at last I found the way of beating the devil out of mine.

Rod. And I should ha' thought there was more danger of beating him in. But, sir, you don't consider the catchpoles; they follow upon a fresh scent. Do but preserve me from 'em, I'll make ye a man for ever.

Mat. Nor shall you repent the putting yourself under my protection. Look ye, sir—[*He takes him to the scenes.*]—You see those parings of vines! creep under them, and I'll cover ye up.—[Roderigo *creeps,* Mattheo *covers him.*]—When they are gone, I'll give you notice. A handsome fellow, and wears good clothes! If it miscarry, I have little to lose; and if it succeed, I'm made for ever.

Enter Officers; *they beat about.*

Pray, gentlemen, don't trample my vines. Who are ye?

1 *Off.* We are the State's officers, in quest of a gentleman we are sure took this road.

2 *Off.* And cannot be far behind him. At your peril be it if you conceal him.

Mat. My house is open to ye.

3 OFFICER *enters;* MATTHEO *digs.*

1 *Off.* Prithee be honest to us, and thou shalt snack.

2 *Off.* We can afford him forty ducats—and that's more than thou'lt get in haste by digging.

Mat. Forty ducats, gentlemen, would do me a kindness.

1 *Off.* And if we take him I'll be thy paymaster—I'm sure thou knowest me—and I'll be true to thee.

[*He gives his hand.*

Mat. Signior Bricone, if I mistake not?

1 *Off.* Thou hast me right, and therefore doubt not thy money.

Mat. Well, then, he is——

[MATTHEO *describes* RODERIGO'S *person and clothes.*

2 *Off.* The same—and if he's about thy house, show him us, and here's thy money down.

[*He pulls out a bag. Third officer returns.*

3 *Off.* There's nothing within!

Mat. I rather wish he were; but d'ye see that blind road, on the left hand of my vineyard as ye came?

1 *Off.* And were I to have fled for my life, I'd have taken 't myself.

Mat. There did I see such a person, and one other with him, ride by about an hour since. And now I better consider on 't, he was the great merchant that lost some ships t'other day.

Omnes. The same, the same!—to horse, to horse!

Mat. Ride hard, and ye can't but overtake him.

[*Exeunt* OFFICERS, *running.*

They're gone, and Roderigo's wishes follow 'em. He told me he'd make me a man for ever, and I hope he'll be as good as his word, and not lick himself whole again by non-performance. Ho, Signior! the coast is clear; you may advance.

Enter RODERIGO, *stalking and looking about him.*

Rod. I fancy I hear them still—hark ! what was that ?

Mat. Nothing but the wind among the leaves. I have perform'd my promise, and you're safe, tho', if you overheard us,—as you needs must,—to my disadvantage.

Rod. I did, and doubly thank you; nor shall it ever be said that I forgot mine. But first, 'tis requisite that you understand my condition. Know, then, I am not what I appear to you—but, in few words, a very devil.

Mat. A devil !—[MATTHEO *starts*]—and afraid of bailiffs ?

Rod. Yet so it is. I was sent to earth by special command, subject, nevertheless, to all the conditions of humanity, but more particularly oblig'd to marry a wife.

Mat. Keep your wife to yourself; I have no mind to cuckold the devil.

Rod. And now, what with her insulting, peevish humour, my losses at sea, my correspondence failing, and creditors pressing, you see to what condition I'm brought.

Mat. Is't come to this ? The sham won't pass on me. Come, come—uncase !—[MATTHEO *goes about to strip him.*]—A man for ever ! A devil would ha' been more honest.

Rod. Have but a minute's patience, and if I don't convince you of what I told ye, and you don't find me the most ingenuous, grateful, and as gentleman-like a devil as you could wish, I am contented you deliver me up to my creditors. And, without your consent, part from ye I will not.

Mat. 'Tis civil, tho'. [RODERIGO *gives a stamp.*

Rod. Ho ! Sacrapant, Adrameleck, Paganuccio, Fortibrand !—[*Music is heard, spirits rise ; they dance an antic about* MATTHEO, *and exeunt,* MATTHEO *all the while trembling.*]—Fear nothing ! they sha'n't hurt ye.

Mat. Fear nothing, said ye? I'm not yet secure but my soul may slip out at the wrong end.

Rod. I've shown you what I am; and now consider, what devil of a thousand would not such circumstances have tried? But to my promise!—[*A noise within; he starts.*]—Huisht, huisht!—My wife!—that wife, whom now I dread more than ere I doated on her.

Mat. A tittle-tattle of mine; I know her voice!

Rod. My promise, I was saying. You know the Lady Ambrosia?

Mat. And what of her? She's rich; and do you but make a match for me there, I'll release you your promise.

Rod. I am no go-between; but this I'll do—as soon as I leave this place I'll instantly possess her, and, on the faith of an oblig'd devil, will never leave her till you come and force me from my quarters. And so, you know how to make the terms.

Mat. But which way must I go about it?

Rod. Sputter anything, and that shall do't; and besides, good brisk nonsense, with a little balderdash, and the gravity of a graduated goose to set it off, will give ye the vogue among the greater number, who, like Socrates' children, take more after the mother than the father.

Mat. My noble patron, I see you are in earnest; and, because you and I must be better acquainted, your name, I beseech ye, and quality in the other world?

Rod. Belphegor, Generalissimo of the Subterranean Forces; but this condition of humanity has so discompos'd me, that I'm asham'd to own what I was.

Mat. Generalissimo! A friend at court may, if he please, stand a man in stead. But pray, sir, what do ye do below?

Rod. Much after the rate ye do here—ever speaking well of ourselves and ill of others. And for friendship, as we profess not much, for what we do we observe it as little as yourselves.

Mat. A wise people! But how do men get thither? Have ye no standing porters to attend the service?

Rod. By no means; no man comes thither but of himself, or his wife's sending. I won't deny but when a devil meets a man with his skates on he may give him a push forward. But, I'm uneasy!

[*He looks over his shoulder.*

Mat. There's no danger. What kind of people are ye?

Rod. A hotch-potch of all tongues, nations, and languages. We speak the Lingua Franca, keep open house, and never shut our gates to any that had either wit or money; and that's the reason we have so many wits and usurers among us.

Mat. And no women?—for, notwithstanding all, I am no profess'd enemy to the sex.

Rod. They're the best customers we have; they seldom come alone with their own lading. Some bring more, some less; not one in ten without a liver and a gizzard—two friends at least, besides followers.

Mat. But have ye no divines, physicians, lawyers? What have ye?

Rod. Of that, when we meet next.

Mat. And you'll forget, you will.

Rod. Upon parole, I won't.—[*They shake hands.*]—With this further—whenever you hear of any lady possess'd, be sure it is your humble servant, and no other. [*Exeunt severally.*

ACT IV.—SCENE I.

Of RODERIGO'S *house.*

Enter IMPERIA, QUARTILLA, *and* SCINTILLA.

Imp. Our gentleman, it seems, is gone to take the air, and I can look about me now, without asking leave.

Quar. He took so little with him, I wonder we hear

nothing of him; his proud spirit will come down in time.

Scin. But to run away in such a hurry!

Imp. That last note I sent him did the business.

Scin. What made a gentleman of his wealth and credit go off so soon?

Imp. I was privy to none of his actions; however, so foresaw it as to secure his estate to myself.

Scin. And with your ladyship's leave, are you not bound in honour to set him up again?

Quar. If I thought he might not be troublesome, I'd persuade my lady to take him home again, and keep him in pocket money, for her own credit.

Imp. No, no! I'd better remove privately, and secure what I have; and that the rather, for if ever I heard anything in my life, I heard his tread in my chamber last night.

Scin. So have I fancied a man in bed with me, but when all came to all, 'twas nothing but a nightmare. However, madam, remove where you will, a man is some credit to a house, and ours, methinks, seems naked without him.

Quar. These girls never consider; we should have him rummaging the next bandbox again.

Imp. Oh, thou rememb'rest me!—[*She takes out a letter broken open. Reads.*]—"Terrachina! The thousand crowns I formerly presented your ladyship emboldens me"—ha, ha, ha! my Lord Lack-land! There!—[*She throws away the letter.*]—Tell her that brought it I have forgot the token, and he must send it again, or 't won't do. [QUARTILLA *takes up the letter.*

Quar. Now, out upon him! Had he the impudence to believe other? No, madam, you have it seven years yet good to take; and after that, you may truck, barter, or, at worst, give.

Enter FIESCHI. IMPERIA *beckons them off.* *Exeunt* QUARTILLA *and* SCINTILLA.

Imp. Ye may keep within call. And now, Fieschi, we have no more excuses, sure? And how?—was my sister complaisant? Has good nature yet brought her about?

Fies. Judge of me as you think I deserve. I had found all open approaches as troublesome as fruitless, and therefore resolv'd on stratagem. To this purpose, I follow'd the hint you gave me, and engag'd her woman to give me the opportunity of getting into her apartment, which not many nights since I attempted; and, tho' no one knew the house better than myself, yet being in the dark, it was my misfortune to mistake his apartment for hers. Montalto heard me, and sprang out! I, as well I might, fled, and by another mistake fell down-stairs; he pursu'd! I recover'd the fall, and got off.

Imp. As, to give ye your due, you had ever the discretion to save one.

Fies. I thank your ladyship! In short, my servant, endeavouring to make up with me, engaged Montalto, wounded him, and got off himself; and, I know not by what accident, is since taken, or you might have been sure I'd waited on you sooner.

Imp. Would thou wer't in his room! A pretty story!—and I believe 't? No, thou silly nothing! 'Twas thou that hired'st thy servant to kill Montalto, to make room for thyself. You were there?—The same was I. I've heard the story—a mere invention of your own, to excuse yourself and cheat me.

Fies. You do me wrong; that my design miscarried is not my fault!

Imp. You might have laid it better!
Did I command ye to a night adventure?
I bid ye murder? No; my spotless honour
Cannot be blasted by a villain's tongue!
Send me the jewels and the gold I lent ye,
Or you will rue the time that I send for 'em!
And so, as far as honour, still command me;
Further than that, your humble servant!

[*Exit* IMPERIA.

Fies. Hey day!—perfidious woman! and I the fool,
To think there ever was or could be other.

How, like Egyptian temples, do they at distance
Strike reverence and admiration!
How beautiful! how glorious! Approach 'em,
And view the god—you find a cat, or ape,
A weeping crocodile, or perhaps a goat!
Forgive me, virtue, but a just revenge,
And I'll abjure—that fair defect of nature—
The very sex, and never think on 't more,
But as men do of debts and sins, to curse 'em!
[*Stamps.*

And now for that revenge. My servant's in hold, and I know not how soon it may be my turn, but that I think him honest, and Montalto, as 'tis said, in no great danger. Help me, invention!

Enter QUARTILLA.

I have it!

Qua. I thought my lady had call'd; however, I am glad to see your worship so well. I have often tasted of your bounty, and would be glad it were in my power to deserve it.

Fies. Thou hast an honest face, and I ever found thee trusty.

Qua. And shall, I hope, continue so. And for my face, 'tis all as you see!—let them be beholden to slops that want 'em.

Fies. Nay, there is somewhat in it; for Signior Guido is so concerned for thee, thou'lt scarce believe it.

Qua. Indeed, sir! I am beholden to him for his well-wishes!

Fies. What wilt thou say, now, if I make it a match between ye?

Qua. Ha—ha—ha! But how shall we live together?

Fies. He has an hundred ways of getting money, only, like other men, an hundred and fifty of spending it, besides drinking; but a wife will take him off that.

Qua. And a discreet woman will bear with a small fault.

Fies. Well, then, there is a small job which thou may'st and canst, if thou wilt, do for me; and that once done, let me alone for thine.

[*He chucks her under the chin.*

Qua. And if I don't, never trust woman again, for my sake.

Fies. Your lady—but thou'lt laugh—and I are all to pieces.

Qua. Marry forbid it! Why, I have known ye play together like two kittens, and as often told ye playing commonly ended in earnest. If that be all, I bring ye together again, and she'll love ye the better.

Fies. To move it to her were to set her the farther off. But thus—tell her there's an outlandish prince new come to town, and that he's so enamour'd of her that he intends her a rich damask bed and cupboard of plate, which he'll send in to-morrow, and wait on her himself at night! Now, this prince will I personate; let me alone for the disguise.

Qua. Impossible! She stands upon her honour! She receive a night visit, from a stranger, and by her own consent? Besides, your tongue will betray ye.

Fies. Tell her the prince understands no Italian, and therefore she need not speak to him, nor take more notice of him than if he were her husband. And we shall have such laughing next morning. Come, thou must! [*He gives her money.*

Qua. What contrivances you men have to betray poor women! Well, then, if you'll run the hazard, send in your present to-morrow, and come yourself at midnight; because we are to remove in a day or two, for she fancies the house is haunted.

Fies. I'll venture that too! only do thou thy part.

Qua. You are resolved, and be it so; in the mean time you shall see how I'll work her—we women can do much together. But I'd almost forgot—what's your prince's name?

Fies. Il Principi Polacco!

Qua. Then say, and hold Polacco. You'll find me ready! [*Exit* QUARTILLA.

Fies. What fools a man must sometimes be beholden to! And if I am not even with her ladyship, I'll forgive her. That once over, I will endeavour, by some worthy action, to expiate my past folly! [*Exit.*

SCENE II.

Of RODERIGO'S *House.*

Enter MARONE, IMPERIA, *and* QUARTILLA.

Imp. 'Twas a sad accident, and, I fear me, more than a bare chance! I hear you took th' examinations?

Mar. The friendship, madam, I ever ow'd your husband might have commanded more; the rest Signior Grimaldi has appointed to be taken here!

Imp. And what d' ye think?—was my poor sister? I love her with my soul!—Is there anything reaches her?

Mar. Directly nothing, but a single uncertain evidence—her servant Bianca. Tho', to deal freely with ye, I suspect it; men of my station can see day at a little hole—letters make words, and circumstances things!

Imp. Alas! alas! tho' yet my private thoughts don't contradict ye. What would she have done had she had my beast? But he was my husband, and, the more unfortunate me, I lov'd him! But pray, what ground have ye?

Mar. Enough, if not too much! Montalto's estate—however, it went in my name—was dipped in the bank for thirty thousand ducats; Fieschi pays the money; his servant gave Montalto his wound; and whether your sister and Fieschi were absolute strangers, I leave it to your ladyship.

Imp. I am afraid y'ave gone too deep!

Mar. I'll not give a rush for that man that cannot pick anything out of nothing—at least bring it in by an innuendo! Men of business, madam, are not so much to seek as the world takes them.

Imp. And, truly—I tremble while I speak it—I wish there was no design of taking off a husband, to make room for a gallant!

Mar. My conscience tells me y'ave hit the nail!

Imp. And shall I own that sister? Virtue forbid it!

Enter GRIMALDI *and* PORTIA.

Grim. According to my appointment, I am come! yet thought it not altogether unfit that this lady, who is most concern'd, should hear the matter.

Mar. And pray, sir, how goes it with our friend Montalto? Is there no hope?

Grim. Yes, truly; and, as far as I conjecture, the greatest danger of his wound lies in the chirurgeon's hard words. All of them agree it fortunately slanted on a rib.

Por. This worthy person inform'd me it was his desire the examinations might be taken here, which made me willing to come myself.

Imp. And that, perhaps, too soon for somebody's credit!

Por. Whose e'er it be, I can hear it with more grief than trouble.

Imp. Peradventure your own, or some one's else—who knows?

Grim. I beseech you, madam—[*to* IMPERIA.]—What mean ye?

Por. How ill this had become another!

Imp. If any modest woman might have resented an husband's injuries, I ought not to have sat down with Roderigo's to me; but when I consider'd he was my husband, that name soon covered all; I pray'd no gallant's aid!

Grim. What's here?—The devil washing his face! O woman! what can'st thou not? [*Aside.*

Por. What virtuous woman ever did?

Imp. Recollect yourself; I never doubted your wit!

Por. Add patience to my innocence, good heaven!

Grim. No more, I beseech ye! and pray, sir, how d'ye find it?

Mar. I met a person t'other night incognito, whom, not giving me a good account of himself, I committed: he's now without.

Grim. And being informed that Bianca was found in her clothes at that late hour when this accident happen'd, I thought fit to examine her; and all I could get from her was, there were other-guise persons concern'd than thieves. I sent her t'ye.

Mar. The same she says to me, and more. She's without too!

Grim. Let's have her in!

Mar. Within, there! bring in Bianca! But were 't not convenient that Portia withdrew?

An OFFICER *enters, and exit again.*

Por. She can say nothing shall shame me to her.

Returns with BIANCA.

Grim. Now, Bianca, you remember what you've said? Who were those other-guise persons?

Bian. My lady will be angry!

Por. Speak boldly, woman! Let truth come out, tho' I perish!

Bian. Fieschi and my lady had made an assignation, and I was privy to it. But it seems my master, sitting up later than ordinary, and Fieschi making some noise, my master rushed upon him, and in the scuffle receiv'd that wound from him.

Grim. Fieschi! I'll cut him from my blood!

Imp. My sister! Her virtue, sure, knew better things!

Por. And does, Imperia! My innocence is above scandal.

Grim. And no one with him but himself?

Bian. Not that I saw or heard.

Mar. Take her back again!

[*Exeunt* OFFICERS *with* BIANCA.

The other, perhaps, may tell you more; I've kept them asunder, and neither knows of the other's being apprehended.

Grim. It was discreetly manag'd; bring him in, Fieschi!—Villain! Whom shall a man put faith in?

Enter, by another door, an OFFICER *with* PANSA.

His servant, too! What mischief, sirrah, have your master and you been contriving?

Pan. None, I yet hope; however, come what will of me, I will declare the truth! About three nights since, Bianca and I had appointed a meeting at her master's house. When stealing by his apartment, it was my misfortune to make a stumble; he hears me —I fled; he pursued—I got into a closet; he sees a glimpse of my lantern and fires thro' it—I got out and glar'd him in the face; he fires a second pistol and closed with me, and having no other possibility of escaping, I was forc'd to that unfortunate stab, which yet I put not so home but that he wrench'd my dagger from me.

Grim. This agrees word for word with what Montalto told me. I wish, tho', I could have seen the dagger!

Pan. It was my master's, who having left it carelessly on his table, and I, considering there might be danger in the streets, put it in my pocket, and with that dagger made the blow!

Imp. Where was your master?

Pan. Had he been there, it is not to be thought I'd take another's guilt upon myself!

Grim. This cloud will break by degrees, and I am glad we're got so far into 't. Take off your prisoner!

Mar. Or rather, confront him with Bianca!

Grim. Well thought of; bring her in again!—[*She is brought in again.*]—You said ere while that you saw no one but Fieschi; and Pansa says 'twas himself only, and that by appointment between you two.

Pan. By this token, that she, hearing the noise, put me into the closet, and bade me bolt it on the inside.

[BIANCA *stutters.*

Bian. If th'ast a mind to hang thyself, do. Yes, he was there, and I believe with a design of robbing the house!

Grim. Prithee, speak truth! Whoever was there, did your lady know anything of it?

[*She stands confused; at last kneels.*

Bian. Good madam, forgive me; you're innocent!

[*She howls.*

Grim. Take them away, and keep them severally!

[*Exeunt* OFFICERS, *with the prisoners.*

Por. And now, sister, judge favourably of me—
Poor me, whom nothing but a quiet conscience
Had kept from sinking. This is the true joy,
And this we give ourselves—this makes us bear
A mind above our sex. Fortune may clear
The visage; only this can fill the soul!

Mar. Your servant, sir! and occasion offers I'll wait on ye. [*Exeunt* GRIMALDI, *leading* PORTIA, *by one door,* MARONE *and* IMPERIA *by another.*
Manet QUARTILLA.

Qua. And now, when all's done, Fieschi for my money! He's scarce half rid of a surfeit and yet vent'ring on the same dish again. He has a passion for her, that's certain; or otherwise, a love fit at this time were inexcusable! Well, his present is sent in, and that so noble, I am afraid he does not intend to come often.

IMPERIA *re-enters.*

Imp. What's all that luggage in the other room?

Qua. A damask bed, with massy fringe and everything suitable!—besides a rich cupboard of plate!—and no other name for 't but luggage. I wish your ladyship had such another to-morrow, we'd find it house-room.

Imp. I must confess it noble; but whence came it?

Qua. No Terrachino, I dare warrant ye. It is the humble present of the outlandish Prince new come to town, Il Signior Principi Polacco; your ladyship understands the rest. But did ye know how I enhanc'd the affair,—husband, relations, reputation, honour, and to all this your utter averseness,—you'd say I was no fool!

Imp. Is he handsome?

Qua. What matters that?—his present is. However, to satisfy ye, he's as handsome a man as the best of us need wish to lie board and board by; for my part, I could sink by his side.

Imp. When will he be here?

Qua. At midnight, and you'll be asleep!

Imp. But to a man I never saw!—how shall I look next morning?

Qua. Just as you did before; or, you may, if you think fit, cry out your women has betray'd ye; nobody will hear ye! Tho' yet, if ye should, he understands no Italian.

Imp. Thou shalt supply my place—all petticoats are sisters in the dark.

Qua. I would it were not to wrong your ladyship. Come, madam, no more words! do you but leave him one side of your bed, he'll find the rest himself.

Imp. Well, we'll further consider it within.

[*Exeunt.*

SCENE III.

The Vineyard.

Enter MATTHEO, *solus, in a black velvet coat; a tipped cane; turning up his moustaches, strutting, and viewing himself.*

It is the same! of a better edition, tho'; and truly, to give the devil his due, he has shown himself much a gentleman, which is more than I'll say of every man. I have already dislodg'd him from two great ladies; and if it holds but one year, how shall I dispose of this good fortune? My boy—an arrant crack-rope, father's own son—I'll breed him to my own new trade, and send him abroad to take his degree! My daughter—let me see, she shall marry some count or other!

Enter GRIMALDI.

But hold! who knows but here may be another customer? and if so, I must stand off, to raise the price. [*Aside.*

Grim. Our duke, sir, is so well assured of your more than ordinary faculty at exorcism, that the Lady Julia, a niece of ours, being at this time a demoniac, he sent me to pray your help, and further assure you of as large a reward as yourself could wish, or the obliging a prince may merit!

[MATTHEO *puts on a starched gravity.*

Mat. I shall be proud, signior, if my poor talent might contribute anything to his serenity's or your service. How far have you proceeded?

Grim. Tried all that religion or physic could propose!

Mat. Have ye erected a scheme to know under what direction the lady lies, and what kind of devil it is that possesses her?

Grim. I think not!

Mat. The reason I ask ye is, because there are diversities of devils,—some so easy, gentle, quiet, ye may do what ye will with 'em; others, again, so sullen, refractory, cross-grain'd, that neither threats, enchantments, nor devotion itself will do any good on 'em.

Grim. I leave it wholly to ye!

Mat. Then the first thing I'll do shall be to erect one, both as to the horary question and the matter itself; and, when I've done that, I'll make a step to the lady as incognito, and give ye my judgment of it.

Grim. And credit me, it shall be gratefully acknowledg'd! [*Exit.*

Mat. So, so, here's more money coming! A count, did I say? we'll better consider it.

Enter RODERIGO *behind him, and gives him a tap on the shoulder.*

Thy fist, my Mephistophiles! And what?—thou'st left the Lady Julia asleep to see a friend?

Rod. Thyself, thou mean'st; but how cam'st thou to know it?

Mat. You see how I improve by your acquaintance; 'twas kindly done. And now your parole; what sort of people have ye in the other world?

Rod. What not?

Mat. Have ye any divines among ye?

Rod. Why, truly, we were once afraid of 'em, and were ever and anon making laws against 'em; 'till at last, finding we were more afraid than hurt, we left them at their liberty to come or go. But for the schoolmen, we ever shackle them, for fear they make as much disturbance there as they have already done here.

Mat. Any physicians?

Rod. And they, too, for several years together, had sent us so many on their errand that we grew jealous of them, as that they design'd a party; till, coming to a better understanding, we have ever since not denied 'em house-room, for past services.

Mat. Any lawyers?

Rod. What should they do there? The poor devils have no money, and the rich will part with none, and yet we want not their company too; but alas! let 'em get what estate soever here, they bring not a groat with 'em, as not doubting but to raise another among us; but there the case is alter'd.

Mat. Have ye any poets?

Rod. Of pretenders, not the least number. And even there, too, some few who, regarding glory more than profit, in studying to divert others, slipped their opportunities and lost themselves.

Mat. Have you any philosophers?

Rod. What—they sell hawks' bells and rattles?

Mat. The same.

Rod. We are with them like Rome of old with their figure-slingers, ever banishing 'em but never rid of 'em; however, we reckon them among the virtuosi.

Mat. What are those virtuosi?

Rod. They study nature—as why a fly should have six legs, and a dromedary but four; why a cat when she's pleas'd holds her tail on end, and a dog wags his; why crabs go backward, and the like.

Mat. And very useful inquiries. What painters have ye?

Rod. The truth is, we had once banished 'em for painting us more ugly than we are, till Michael Angelo's Day of Judgment complimented us with a Master of the Ceremonies; and Parmasano and Carrachi with their improvements upon Aretine,—pieces, I assure ye, of as much service to us, as their others of devotion had like to have done us mischief.

Mat. But what becomes of tyrants and others, those common pests of mankind—a sort of men we read of in old story, though I think the race be wholly run out now?

Rod. 'Twould make ye laugh to see 'em, — one cobbling of old shoes; another heeling of stockings; a third rubbing the sweat in hothouses.

Mat. Have ye the pox there too?

Rod. Millions of millions; for they that bring it not with them are sure to get it on their first landing.

Mat. Well, thou'rt a merry devil, and I must say an honest devil. But hark ye, I must beat up your quarters once more.

Rod. What?—never have done?

Mat. You know I deliver'd ye from the talons of the law, and then you told me what a grateful gentleman devil you'd prove. Prithee, oblige me this once, in quitting the Lady Julia, and I release thee of all demands whatever.

Rod. And I have paid ye sufficiently.

Mat. But I'm concern'd in this beyond a retreat. Prithee this once, or I must say too thou art not that grateful devil I expected.

Rod. How, sirrah!—tax me with ingratitude? Have ye forgot 'twas I that made your fortune?—I that gave ye the occasion of that aphorismatical cane, and reform'd your greasy chamois into silks and satins? And are ye now grown insolent? I'll make ye know I can take back as well as give; or otherwise, call me the most pitiful, poor-spirited rascal of a devil.

Mat. Nay, let's not part in anger. A word with ye.

Rod. As many words as you please; but no more stark love and kindness.

[*They whisper.* MATTHEO *takes him by the collar.*

Mat. Now, sirrah, too; and since nothing else will do it, I'll e'en return ye to your wife.—[*They struggle.* RODERIGO *sinks under him, and leaves a dead body.*]—Now shall I be hang'd for killing this rascal. There's no more to be done but cut off his head and bury him; and then, perhaps, wanting a retreat, he may quit the lady of himself. I'll run for a hatchet, and do it. [*Exit* MATTHEO. RODERIGO *springs up with a hollow laugh.*

Rod. Hoh—hoh—hoh! [RODERIGO *runs.* BELZEBUB *rises with horror.* MATTHEO *returns with a hatchet, trembles, drops it, and crowds himself up to the wall.*

Belz. Whither, Belphegor? Hold!

Rod. My old colleague and friend, Belzebub!

Belz. Which I abjure. We've heard of ye, thou poor,
Thou pitiful, hen-hearted, sneaking devil!
Thou general? A scandal to the name!
Where's all that fable of the giants' war
Thou hast so often boasted as thy story?

Rod. And 'tis my glory yet.

Belz. In chimney-corners!
Thou ever threw'st Ossa on Pelion!
Away, thou changeling! No; thy best pretence
Is the degenerate offspring of their gore,—
Their earth-born gore,—and all thy former soul
Is dwindled to a glow-worm. Thou a devil?
A very shame t' us all!

Rod. The inclination
Follows the temper of the body; and I
Was out in mine.
Belz. Thou mightest have chosen better.
How many brave bandits were there hang'd yearly
That durst have trod the utmost brink of space,
Have fought the devil on a precipice,
Brav'd fate, and stood a second and third thunder!—
And thou to take such a tame, snivelling slave!
Rod. Men have no windows in their breast, and what
Could I judge of a carcase? He was handsome,
And so a step to get a wife, which you well know
Was the first thing I was obliged to do.
Belz. And thou hast got one with a vengeance! Mistaken fool! As if women knew not what a smock-face meant! They take him for one of themselves, only that nature mistook him in the coinage. If ever they loved anything, it was a rough-hewn fellow that knew what was fit for 'em, and let 'em have it; but never their wills. If they once get that bit between their teeth, they run away with ye.

Rod. I was to become in all things as a man, and did no more than what other men did. And if your Grand Cabal knew 'em so well, why was I sent hither?

Belz. As an honourable spy. Thou hadst the world before thee; every lap * was thy chapel of ease: nor wert thou bound to residence.

Rod. And yet to marry one.

Belz. As those other men, for fashion sake. You may easily believe we design'd no breed. But where lay the obligation of loving her more than other men their wives? But to doat on her—'tis thy eternal blot!

Rod. There had been no quiet without it.

Belz. Unthinking sot! could there be any with it? If so, what makes thee shifting thus? What's become of your million of ducats?

* "I'll make my haven in a lady's lap,
And 'witch sweet ladies with my words and looks."
SHAKESPEARE.

Rod. My wife has either spent or cheated me of 'em.

Belz. Beast of a devil! Must we torment the bowels of the earth, or from our treasure of the ocean, the spoils of wrecks and tempests, furnish thee? Thy folly, or thy wife's, never to be satisfied—I know not what?

Rod. Ye left me to myself, and I was guided by others. What counsel ever drew his own conveyance?

Belz. But thou, contrary to all rules of practice, hast given thyself physic.

[RODERIGO *steps forward to him.*

Rod. As his penance, then, even take the doctor.

Belz. Stand off, thou less than man, and unworthy the name of devil! I hate a trimming devil. Keep off!

Rod. You are no competent judge; you were never married yourself. I submit all to Lucifer.

Belz. And, when your time's expir'd, you shall be heard.

Rod. But if either my wife or creditors catch me in the meantime, I must and will return at all adventures.

Belz. That at your peril! and remember I tell it ye. [*Sinks.* RODERIGO *goes up to* MATTHEO, *yet trembling, and takes up the hatchet and lifts it at him.*

Rod. Now, sirrah! remember for what you brought this hatchet. But I'm a gentleman. Live, and trouble me no more! [*Exit with it.*

Mat. A fair escape. But what shall I say to Grimaldi, though? Why, he's a noble person, and if I tell him the truth, he may, perhaps, be satisfied—at least for a while. And if I don't outwit my devil at last, I give him leave to brain me. [*Exit.*

SCENE IV.

Of GRIMALDI'S *house.*

Enter GRIMALDI *and* MARONE.

Mar. 'Tis the most I can gather. Pansa stands firm to his first examination, and Bianca more and more clears her lady.

Grim. Nor can anything please me better but that, my friend's getting up again.

Mar. Would I could say as much of Roderigo!

Grim. For why, man?

Mar. He's broke, and run away.

Grim. What?—He that darkened all our stars? Impossible!

Mar. Too true.

Grim. Yet how you magnified him.

Mar. His great dealings and punctual payments might have cheated any man as well as me.

Grim. Was the sum considerable?

Mar. Two hundred thousand ducats at least.

Grim. 'Tis a wonder no more follow him; for it is often with merchants as nine-pins, hit but your first and second right, and 'tis odds but two parts in three tumble.

Mar. That, I'm afraid, shall I, for one! He owes me ten thousand ducats; and, when I went to his lady this morning, she told me he had left her a beggar.

Grim. And yet, you know, he was wise, prudent, virtuous, and once your glory; he called ye friend, and shall a little dirt part ye? Come! your credit will set him up again.

Mar. If it would to the gallows, I'd venture as much more.

Grim. Your friend! You wouldn't, sure?

Mar. My friend! A very rogue—a mere cheating, beggarly, bankrupt rascal!

Enter a SERVANT *to* MARONE.

Ser. Roderigo, sir, attempting to have got home last night in a disguise, was met by the bailiffs, who secur'd him, and coming to him this morning, found him dead.

Mar. Nay, then, farewell my ten thousand ducats! —if yet that were all.

Ser. And there were found in his pocket some papers purporting a design of betraying this city, wherein you seem concern'd; upon which the Senate have issued warrants against you, and seiz'd your house and goods, for moneys, as 'tis said, due to the bank.

[MARONE *starts and tears his hair.*

Mar. Roderigo!—my papers!—the bank! What shall I do?

Grim. Consult your virtue! A virtuous man is ever present to himself, and proof against the worst of fortune.

Mar. Virtue!—Cold comfort.

[*He runs off.* RODERIGO *meets him.*

Rod. I was at your house, to have adjusted some accounts between us, and they directed me hither.

[MARONE *embraces him.*

Mar. Roderigo! I'm o'erjoyed! They've belied my friend. We'll never part!

Rod. Content!

[RODERIGO *takes him in his arms, and sinks with him.*

Grim. Defend me, heaven! What's this?

[*He walks.*

Enter SERVANT.

It has half bereft me of myself.

Ser. A gentleman, sir,—they call him the devil-doctor,—desires to speak with you.

Grim. I would he had come sooner. Bring him in! —[*Exit* SERVANT.]—Sure hell's broke loose this year.

Enter MATTHEO, *his head broken.*

The dreadful object's not yet digested.

Mat. I was with the lady according to my promise,

but, like a dog by a glover, the devil smelt me out from all the company. *Ecce signum!*

[*He points to his head.*

Grim. I'm sorry for 't; but the duke will send ye a healing plaister.

Mat. And I more sorry that the lady lies under such an ill direction. Strange configurations—the planets in their detriment, retrograde and malevolent; nor do I remember to have seen a worse aspect of heaven. Saturn and Jupiter, sir——

Grim. No canting, I beseech ye! I believe it.

Mat. And for the spirit that possesses her, there has not such an ill-contriv'd, capricious, hectoring devil broke loose these three last centuries. I believe the fathers are sensible of it.

Grim. The truth is they have had a hard tug with him.

Mat. He is *perversus hæreticus.* Bell, book, and candle—he danced a jig to 't; and for holy water, he made no more of it than I'd have done of a bottle of Montefiasco. Upon the whole matter, I judge him some devil of quality; and then I have no power over him. All mine are poor devils.

Grim. This will not do. If you please to free her, it will be well accepted and better rewarded. If not, be sure the duke will have ye in the Inquisition, and make ye set forth by what new way, unknown to the Church, you have delivered the two former; or, who knows, inquire *de vita et moribus*, and hang yourself.

Mat. Will ye, then, hear me without canting, and I'll discover all?

Grim. Hear ye I will! but promise nothing.

Mat. I ask no more. And who d'ye think this devil is? Even Roderigo, our late great merchant!

Grim. Convince me of that, and thou say'st somewhat.

Mat. The story is too large to tell you now; but thus, in short, 't was by compact between us for a prior service,—of which I'll give ye an account anon, —and on that score, and no other, was it that I freed those ladies of him.

Grim. Then thou may'st the better do this.

Mat. I once thought it. But, since you spake to me, we met, and I propos'd to him the quitting the Lady Julia as the last kindness I'd demand of him; and he not only refus'd me, but profess'd himself my mortal enemy. And if this—[*pointing to his head*]—be the token of a friend, I leave it to you.

Grim. I am inclined to believe thee; for 'twas not a minute before you came but he was here, and gave me that evidence of what you say. I'll never desire to see 't again. But what shall we do with the duke?

Mat. Do not despair! I've yet a trick shall do the business. Get me a large stage, with a full throng of people, fifes, flutes, cornets, trumpets, sackbuts, drums, kettle-drums, hautboys, and bagpipes; and let the Lady Julia be brought on the stage well attended; and when I throw up my hat, let 'em all strike up together! and, when I cry advance, let a lady in a veil, whom I'll appoint for that purpose, enter with another shout; and this, with some other ingredients that I have, will, I doubt not, send him packing.

Grim. Appoint your time and place! all shall be ready.

Mat. I leave that to your pleasure.

Grim. What think you of to-morrow, and the duke's great hall for the place?

Mat. None better; and I'll attend ye there. [*Exeunt.*

Act V.—Scene I.

The Street.

Enter Fieschi, *solus.*

Fies. It takes, as right as wish. Quartilla was just to her hour; and in the dark I shuffled my Signior Principi's hand into hers instead of mine, and there's no doubt but she has put them together. He's a brawny fellow, and like enough to please her; but, for fear the jade should be fond of him next morning, he has his lesson not to answer her anything but broken gibberish. The Jews sent in the bed and plate on Roderigo's account, as new furniture for his house, and, as I am told, are resolv'd to seize it. And, if my Signior Principi has not deceiv'd me, we shall have rabble enough about the house presently. I'll take a turn or two to see the issue. [*He walks.*

Enter JEWS.

1 *Jew.* I say 'twas your folly, brother, to send it hand over head.

2 *Jew.* We have had greater dealings with him, and his payment was ever good.

1 *Jew.* But men may not be the same at all times. It was considerable, and you should have inquir'd.

2 *Jew.* You knew his broker; and I saw the goods deliver'd.

1 *Jew.* But he was broke before.

2 *Jew.* How could I know that?—Men don't proclaim it.

1 *Jew.* Had we been bitten by a snap, 'twere somewhat; but by a prodigal fool! The town will laugh at us.

Enter OFFICERS.

2 *Jew.* Let's not make it worse by talking. Come, gentlemen; stand close, and as the door opens, enter!

[*He knocks;* FIESCHI *comes up.*

Fies. 'Morrow, gentlemen! You're early men.

1 *Jew.* Business must not be neglected.

Fies. And if I mistake not, your attendants speak where it lies.

2 *Jew.* It is too late to conceal it now; we're miserably cheated!

Fies. What?—beaten at your own weapons! Roderigo, sure, is a man of estate and credit.

1 *Jew.* Time was he might have commanded all we have; but now—the bird is flown.

2 *Jew.* Gone, as a man may say, *in fumo!*

Fies. He left enough behind, unless his wife has sold it.

1 *Jew.* There's the danger! Knock harder!

[*Another knock.*

Fies. I have no small concern with him myself, which brought me hither, too, though not so well provided. But—[*he whispers them*]—if ye can, I'll give ye—— [*Again.*

2 *Jew.* When we have serv'd ourselves, we're yours.

Enter DON HERCIO.

Her. What rude hand profan'd this sanctuary?

Fies. And who are you?

[FIESCHI *takes him by the arm, while the rest enter.*

Her. I'm the righter of wrongs, and undoer of injuries—heart of steel, and arms of brass!

Fies. And what figure do you make in this house?

Her. Only engag'd in Roderigo's absence; and, like the dragon of old, I watch the golden fruit till his return. Still true to honour, and will fight her battles!

Fies. As thus—with that baboon's snout?

[*He wipes him over the face.*

Her. Voto! Had it been under the ear, y'ad measured your length.

Fies. Sirrah, begone! and take to your old trade of knitting caps and making hair buttons, tooth-picks, and false dice, which you learnt of your comerogues of the galleys.

[JEWS *and* OFFICERS *run out again,* QUARTILLA *following with a paring-shovel.**

Qua. Why, villains! rogues! Jews! Is there no consideration of a lady's honour?

1 *Jew.* Keep her honour to herself, and give us our goods.

Qua. And thou, Polacco?—Oh me! [*To* FIESCHI.

Fies. I hope your lady had a good night of it.

Qua. Thou devil incarnate!

* Paring-iron: an instrument to pare a horse's hoofs with.—PALSGRAVE. Paring-spade: a breast-plough.—YORKSH.

Enter Boys *and* Rabble, *whooping.*

Boys. Picaro! Picaro! make haste, Picaro!—execution stays for ye!

Qua. What was that?—Picaro!

[Picaro *appears above.*

Pic. I'm but buttoning my coat, and will be with ye instantly.

Boys. Come down! come down! There will be no sport till you come.

[Boys *hollow;* Quartilla *lays at them with her paring-shovel; they take it from her.*

Qua. Ah, rogue! art thou there? Have we refus'd Velasco, Tedesco, di Parphar, di Laco?

[*She wrings her hands.*

Fies. The devil and all!

Qua. And now to be sham'd by the common hangman!

Enter Picaro *in a white cap, sleeves, apron tuck'd round his waist, and a large knife stuck in it.*

Boys. Picaro! Picaro! Picaro! Picaro!

Qua. Is this your Principi Polacco? *Poveraccia! Poveraccia, peccatrice me!* I could eat thee!—[*to* Fieschi.]—Thou a gentleman? You said you'd make a whore of me, too; but why don't you, sirrah?—why don't ye? [*Clapping her hands at him, and crying.*

Fies. The fool raves! And so, Picaro, I hope you lik'd your bed-fellow?

Pic. So well, sir, I owe ye another job, and that for nothing—she was such flesh and blood!

Her. And shall I see honour thus trampled on, and yet wear trusty steel on thigh? Let me come at the rogue? I'll pink his doublet, and make a sieve of 's skin.—[Boys *hollow round him, and twitch him behind. He draws; they tie a cracker to him.*

Her. Rogues! scoundrels! tatterdemallions!—[*He whets his point on the floor. They fire the cracker, and hollow.*]—I say, rogues! dogs in doublets! were ye more renown'd than Palmerin of England, or valiant than his cousin D'Oliva; more undaunted than the twelve peers of France, or greater bullies than King Arthur's Round Table men; more adventurous than Valentine and Orson, or invincible than Don Bellianis of Greece; nay, were the whole mirror of knighthood contracted in ye, I'd make ye know——[*As he is ranting*, PICARO *and another slip the paring-shovel between his legs, hoist him on their shoulders, carry him round the stage, and exeunt, the boys hollowing. Manet* FIESCHI.

Fies. 'Twas somewhat sharp, but just; her treachery
Deserv'd no better from me. And now no more
But a long, long farewell to everything
That looks like woman, till some worthy action
Compound for my past folly. To repent
Is the next step to being innocent.
Men are no angels! Somewhat must be indulg'd
To passion, error, or mistake. The best
Are not without their faults; and the fairest life
Has some leaves in it to be read without favour.

[MARONE *is thrown upon the stage.* FIESCHI *helps him up.*

Marone! sure 'tis he! 'Twas said the devil had carried him away, and now, belike, has thrown him back as not worth keeping.

Mar. Where am I? or whence came I? O Signior! I have wonders to tell ye. Roderigo is a spirit—a very devil!

Fies. And make you a good use of your escape from him.

Mar. I will, I will! and never more oppress any man; but having got clear of the Senate, what I once said in scorn I'll now perform in earnest—I'll build an hospital.

Fies. To lodge those yourself first beggar'd.

Mar. Give what I have to charitable uses.

Fies. That is to say, you'll sleep upon 't, and look out for another mortgage next morning. Charity, you know, begins at home.

Mar. Respite your censure till you hear my story. That I had hearkened to your good, virtuous uncle!

Fies. Whom, under my present circumstances, I'll never see. If ever man lost his reason in a petticoat, 'twas I,—the poor, unfortunate, mistaken Fieschi.
[*Exeunt.*

SCENE II.

A great Hall.

Enter GRIMALDI *and* MATTHEO.

Grim. You're a man of your word.

Mat. And pray, believe I made not those scruples out of any repugnancy, or want of will to serve ye; but that, in case my endeavours answer not my desires, you might judge the more favourably of me. Are all things ready?

Grim. They are! and if you want nothing, I'll go for the lady.

Mat. I only wait her. But be sure you follow the directions I gave you.

Grim. They shall be observ'd. [*Exit* GRIMALDI.

Mat. And now assist me, thou great patron of mankind, Impudence! I have some ends of Latin myself, besides a bushel of hard words I learnt from others, if I can hit 'em right. However, like them, I'll trowl it off boldly, and enough of it; nor shall that trifling circumstance of sense and pertinence be any rub in my way. Ha'n't I heard a man quote the books he never read, and cited authors that never were? And ha'n't it past? What should hinder it?

GRIMALDI *returns with* JULIA *in an elbow-chair, well attended.*

Jul. Are you there? I'll conjure ye! Unhand me, villains!

Mat. And you, too, nor man, nor devil—*semibovemque virum, semivirumque bovem.*—[*He whispers her.*]—Belphegor! dear Belphegor! you know I once serv'd ye at a dead lift. Come, be yet civil, and depart! if not, this is the last time of asking.

Jul. I forbid the banns! both parties are not agreed. Have I gravelled so many doctors, to turn out now for a pitiful *vinerollo?* Let me come at him!

Mat. Then know, foul fiend, *conjuro et commando tibi*, by St. Hugh's bones, St. Luke's face, and *ventre St. Gri;* and by all the occult qualities of salt, sulphur, and mercury, I once more command and conjure ye, that ye make me direct answer touching yourself, your tatterdemallions and puggs, and forthwith depart this lady, with all your signatures, tricks, trinkets, and trumperies, from the crown of her head to the sole of her foot, under the pain that I releage and confine ye to your dismal lake for a thousand years yet more than were ever decreed ye.

Jul. The rogue's pleasant, and I'll humour him. [*Aside.*

Mat. Tell me I say, and conjure ye as before, what are ye?

Jul. Shame fa' him that speers and kens sae weel.

Mat. Your name, I say?

Jul. Monsieur Devile; Don or Signior Diavolo; Meinherr Tifle; Herenagh Mac Deul; or Sir Duncan, in the devil's name.

Mat. What's here?—Philippus, Aureolus, Theophrastus, Paracelsus, Bombastus of Hoenhayim? How many are there of ye?

Jul. Ten hundred thousand ton!

Mat. Of what order?

Jul. Like other bodies aggregate, of none, nor ever reducible under any.

Mat. At least, your superior's name?

Jul. I never own'd any.

Mat. Tell me, I say, and *jubeo*—Is there *absoluta potentia asmodei, sive cujusvis alii*, or a *vitium corporis*, as say the learned? What made ye first possess her?

Jul. Look on her, and answer yourself—she's young and handsome!

Mat. So was your wife, sirrah! and yet——[*She*

falls into a fit.]—This will work presently.—[*Aside.*]—How long have ye been there?

Jul. Much about the time you crack'd a commandment with your tailor's wife.—[MATTHEO *starts.*]—Are ye concern'd, gentleman? Ha—ha!

Mat. Bring me the *flagellum dæmonum!* I'll taw ye.

Jul. Or rather give yourself the first discipline, and I'll help to lay it on. Ha—ha—ha!

Mat. Once more, I say, turn out, or by the *phoberon phoberotaton, ton de apomeibomenos,* and *heautontemorumenos—Smyrna, Rhodos, Colophon, Salamis, Chios, Argos, Athenæ*—I'll——

Jul. What, my new conjuror—what? Hoh—hoh!

Mat. I'll lead ye about the country, like a bear, by the nose; make ye turn spits, like a dog in a wheel; and if that won't do 't, have ye chain'd, like a flea in a box. And therefore, despatch, and let me know what sign you'll give of your departure.

Jul. Thunder—thunder—thunder! As thus, rascal!

[*She flies on him.*

Mat. I'll have ye bound over for bloodshed and battery.

Jul. I fear no justice under heaven.

Mat. I'll bring ye into th' spiritual court, and have ye excommunicated!

Jul. I am no member of your church; or, if I were, I have no money to pay fees.

Mat. I'll have ye burnt in effigy, with brimstone, galbanum, aristolochia, hypericon, and rue, in a more terrible cap and painted coat than the Inquisition yet ever thought of. And, if all this fail, I'll send ye back to your wife.

Jul. You told me so once before; but now, I hope you'll stay till you catch me. Yet I don't like the rogue. [*Aside.*

Mat. Then I'll bring her to you.—[*He throws up his hat. Wind music is heard, with a shout without.*

Jul. What would this peasant be at? I have more than once view'd all the pomp of heaven, nor am I ignorant of what's most formidable in hell. But what means this? Prithee, Mattheo, what is it?

Mat. Are ye come to your prithee, sirrah? Either march off civilly, or know that, will or nil, you shall! Alas, poor Roderigo! your wife's in chase of ye, and is just coming up-stairs. Advance, Imperia!

[*The same music is heard. A lady in a veil enters, with shouting.* JULIA *springs at him, and falls as dead. It thunders. All startle.*

Jul. 'Tis she! she 'as found me out.

Mat. Fear nothing! the work is done. And now, take care of the lady.

Grim. I'll see it done. And, having made the duke laugh, it shall be my next business to see you gratified.

[JULIA *is carried off. Exeunt all but* MATTHEO.

Mat. And if I get no more, 'tis no great matter; I have lin'd myself pretty well already. And now, all things consider'd, I think myself happy enough that I have 'scaped hanging at last; and if, in spite of my stars, I set up as a doctor, who can help it? [*Exit.*

SCENE III.

MONTALTO'S *house.*

Enter MONTALTO, *in a nightgown,* MARONE, PORTIA, *and* ATTENDANTS.

Mon. I heard it from my friend, and must confess
Not without some surprise. I've here and there
Read of the devil's power to condense
A cloud, t' assume and actuate a body;
But never came near the experiment till now.
Where were ye in that absence?

Mar. I remember
No more of that than how I was thrown back.

Mon. You would do well to make a scrutiny
Into yourself, and where you guess the cause,
Unlearn that first.

Por. And if you chance to find

You have oppress'd the poor, make restitution,
And by what's past correct what is to come.

Mar. I'd once such thoughts; but when I consider'd
I only took what law had given me,
I thought there was no such great haste or need.

Por. The greater the oppression, when law
Is made the stale to 't. This of Roderigo,
For aught you know, was given ye as a caution.

Mar. And had there been no malice of his own,
I should have thought so; but he ow'd me money,—
Ten thousand ducats,—and, o' my conscience,
Thought to have frighten'd me to a release;
And if I've giv'n him one, I'll plead *per dures.*

However, this I'm resolv'd—that, and other the like debts, I'll give 'em all to pious uses. But for restitution—alas! my estate's but small, and I cannot.

[MONTALTO *smiles.*

Mon. That is, you will not; nor, perhaps, repent
The late intended treachery to your country.
A virtuous man, like Sceva, in the breach
Combats an army singly for her safety;
Inseparably they stand and fall together.
Cato would not survive his country's liberty;
Nor did that liberty outlive Cato.
Make me think better of ye. Yet begin;
Delay is just so much time lost.

Enter GRIMALDI *and* MATTHEO.

Grim. My doctor, here, has giv'n him a third remove.

Mat. And I hope there will be no occasion of showing him round.

Grim. He'll tell ye the story within; and not unworth your hearing. In the mean, I cannot too often congratulate your recovery.

Mon. Nor I acknowledge your friendship.
I'll tell ye news—good news! for there's nothing
We must not share. Methinks I am become
Another man, and this small quiet pleases
Beyond the noise of crowds. Now I can see

The great ones heave like moles, and at next turn
Heave out themselves; another, mushroom-like,
Spring in a night and cropp'd ere noon; a third,
Snatch at a booty, which a fourth strikes from him,
And unconcern'd myself.

Grim. True happiness
Lies not in greatness but an honest mind,
Not fram'd of accidents, nor subject to 'em—
A serene breast, and such a life as is not
'Sham'd to live, nor yet afraid to die.

Por. And yet how does the world turmoil itself!
How do they play away their days, and trifle
Their time in parts till they have slipp'd the whole!
One business breeds another; hope, desire;
And that makes room for more. How they afflict
Themselves and envy others! Restless in war,
And ev'n in peace unquiet! Compass with care
What they possess with more anxiety!

Mon. To them that love it, be 't; I neither like
The merchandise nor price. What is 't to him
That can't dissemble?—him that cannot flatter?—
That's not ambitious by indignities
To rise to dignities and lose himself?
Whereas retirement, as it costs us nothing,
Is much the shorter cut to heaven itself.

Enter IMPERIA *and* QUARTILLA *as distracted.*

Imp. Help—help me, sister! Can ye forgive me? You can't—you can't! Whither shall I run? He'll ha' me—he'll ha' me.

Por. You never injur'd me; or if you had, I have, as I ought, forgot it.

Qua. Our house is more than haunted!

Imp. Sister—sister, I've married the devil! See! where he stands!

Por. Bless the poor miserable woman! good heaven!

Qua. His eyes as big as pumpkins—[*she starts*]—and a mouth like any baker's oven! Let me alone, good devil, and take my lady—she's younger flesh!

[*She starts up and down, and shrieks.*

Imp. See! see!—the house cracks!—the walls are coming together!—that beam was shot at me!

Qua. I'm your old servant, Quartilla! Good devil——

Imp. There, too, the ground opens!—I'll at him, though! Dost thou yet brave me?—Time was thou fear'd'st me more!—I'll give ye back your keys!—Dost thou yet—yet——

Por. I see nothing, sister. Pray, walk in with me; my innocence dares speak to him.

Imp. There, there—the greater devil—Fieschi!

Por. Poor afflicted woman!—her hurt imagination conceives anything. Pray, go in with me! I'll bear ye company.

Imp. No—no; I'll out at that window!

Enter RODERIGO. *All are surprised.* IMPERIA *and* QUARTILLA *shriek and run off.* PORTIA *follows.* RODERIGO *makes up to* MARONE. *He gets behind* MONTALTO. MONTALTO *steps out.*

Mon. Horror! Be man or devil, I'll know what thou art! [RODERIGO *gives back.*

Rod. Thy virtue is beyond the power of hell. Be safe! and if you have not heard my story, there's one —[*he points to* MATTHEO]—can tell it ye. And so my embassy is at an end perforce.

Mat. And your creditors may speak to ye upon even terms.

Rod. No more of that. On what account I first assum'd this body, you—[*to* MATTHEO]—know; how I liv'd among ye, ye all know; and why I went off so soon, my wife best knows. In short, I have found earth the greater hell, and, being obliged to no more than my own experience, must declare that men's souls are in the right, and 'tis their wives that send them thither; and, for myself, promise ye I'll never again repent me at so dear a rate. [*Exit.*

Mon. Stupendous! And the more I consider it, the more I'm at a loss. My first surprise is now astonishment.

Grim. I'm of opinion his two servants, that were

taken up the other night, may be the same as their master, and therefore I order'd Picaro to bring them hither, as if they were to be put upon the rack. Perhaps they'll tell ye more.

Mon. It can be no hurt, tho' nothing yet appears against 'em.

Grim. I would I could say as much of my unfortunate nephew that was; and whom Imperia's last words unwillingly brought to my memory. Can ye, as I have, and ever will, forget him?

Mon. And more than that, I have forgiv'n him! do you the same. He is not naturally vicious, and who knows what his future actions may be? Whatever were the injury design'd, it was to me. My Portia is safe, and I'm reveng'd enough. The dismal object once again!

Enter RODERIGO, *plodding. All the company again surprised.*

Rod. But stay! Suppose——

Mat. Are you come again? Nay, then, advance, bailiffs! [RODERIGO *starts. Recovers, and goes up ruffling to him.*

Rod. Beware, sirrah, how you fool once too much! Suppose, I say, my term being not a full third part expir'd, they'll not receive me below! Why, I must find somewhere to put my head. For the women, I bar 'em, bye and main.* Who knows but I may have better luck among the men? I have, I must confess, learn'd some wit among ye; and according to your frank, open, wonted simplicity, I'll tell ye my design —cross-bite it if you can.

Mat. That could I, sirrah, if I durst.

[*From behind* MONTALTO.

Rod. I'll buzz fears and jealousies among citizens, factions among country gentlemen, grumblings among younger brothers, heart-burnings among courtiers, and sedition among the common people. But suppose, again, my citizen's wife work her husband into a good

* Terms in dice-play.

trade?—my country gentleman be made a justice of the peace?—my younger brother become an elder brother?—my courtier stumble on a good office, or be taken off with a feather in his cap?—the common people get another opinion by the end?—and, at last, necessity force every man to comply with what he is? Then am I but where I was; and, as I said before, in the greater hell. And therefore, gentlemen, till we meet again, *Bueonos nochios!* [*He sinks on the stage.*

Mon. It yet amazes me!

Mat. Do not believe him; it is not the first time he has shown me that trick.

Enter PICARO, *with* CRISPO *and* MINGO *manacled.*

Pic. I have brought them, sir, according to your commands; but if I may be believ'd in my own trade, the first stretch will pull 'em in pieces.

Grim. However, give 'em the question. What are ye?

Cris. The same our master was. And since our master, as I see, has giv'n us the slip, what have I to do but follow him?

Min. The same will trusty Mingo. Tell us of racks! As I came whole among ye, be assur'd I'll not hazard a joint to satisfy a world; ev'n take 'em all together.

Cris. And mine to boot.

[CRISPO *and* MINGO *drop, and leave dead bodies.*

Grim. 'Tis what I thought. Those bodies were assum'd. See if you know 'em; perhaps they may have pass'd your hand. [*To* PICARO.

Pic. As likely as not.—[*He turns them.*]—Why, truly, sir, it is no country work, and whoever did it need not be asham'd of 't. Once more—the knot is in the right place; and now I better consider it, 'tis all my own work. This Roderigo, I remember him; his name was Scabbalucchio, a Neapolitan bandit—I made his passport for t'other world about four years since, but a more cowardly rogue I never saw. He hung on arse more than a bear going to a stake; and was three-quarters dead ere he got half the ladder.

But for the other two, I know no more of them but that it was my work too; and for plain work, I dare justify it.

Grim. Well, take them off, and throw 'em together into some hole or other! [*They are dragged off.*

Mar. And let 'em lie till I inquire after them.

Grim. And beware you how ye venture another trip to *terra damnata!*

Mar. But the mob, I'm told, are got into my house, and rifling what the bank has left.

Grim. 'Tis natural to 'em, when they cannot cudgel the ass, to vent their rage against the pack-saddle! Go, make your peace with the Senate; and for the rest, time may obliterate your oppressions, and the next age forget their fathers were undone by ye.

PORTIA *re-enters.*

Por. Poor, comfortless woman! she's fall'n asleep at last.

Mon. I think 't would do well to send her and all the women to the *Convertiti!*

Grim. And for Pansa, I'll secure him the galleys! And now, sir, give me leave to tell ye in private what yet I have in charge from the Senate. Our duke having absolv'd his two years' government, the Senate is at last become so sensible of your merit, that they have elected you Duke in his room. A more solemn message will suddenly attend ye.

Mon. Tempt not your friend with a fair gilded pill,
All bitterness within. I am content,
And what can Providence add more?
Cæsar himself, the master of so many,
Is yet the servant of more.

Por. And why should my Montalto seek elsewhere
What he may give himself? If ever ambition
Were justifiable, 'tis the ambition
Of being rather good than great.

Grim. Let snakes and worms, the emblems of self-love,
Circle themselves into themselves, while nature

Minds more the preservation of the whole
Than any single birth. Your country calls,
And you must once more serve her.

Mon. Why should I waste my small remain of life
In blind pursuit of what can only serve me
To furnish out an epitaph, yet must
Subject me to the world and lash of fortune?

Por. Fortune! Who'd trust her that has ever heard
A triumph turn'd into a sacrifice?
Or a swoll'n favourite, whom the same day
Saw worshipp'd by the Senate and ere night
Torn piecemeal by the people?

Mon. No, Portia!
We'll find some nobler object—one on which
She has no empire.

Por. There spoke Montalto!
And let the world, from his example, learn—
Crimes may be fortunate while virtue creeps,
And, like a flower oppress'd with morning dew,
Droops its neglected head; but it will rise—
Rise under the dead weight, when t'others shall,
Like mighty ruins, break themselves on what they fall.

[*Exeunt omnes.*

EPILOGUE.

Spoken by IMPERIA.

All is not done: there's yet a word or two
For th' author; and, fair ladies, first to you—
You, who're the making or the marring powers;
For most men's watches ever went by yours.
From you he hopes he need not fear a frown;
For what is Portia's virtue but your own?—
Your own transcrib'd, and what—if ye must know
The truth—he only copied off from you.
  But for myself—for once ev'n let me pass,
And tho' the face mayn't please ye, spare th' glass;
Ye can't but say, I made the Devil an ass!
Contraries by their contraries appear;
Were you all 'like, where were the good or fair?
There were no fund for wit were all men wise;
And fools would want their representatives.
  Faith, ladies, take it favourably! and then,
He thinks he's more than half secure o' th' men.
For you that have good wives can't disapprove
That in another which in them ye love!
And you that have got bad ones cannot call
The copy ill that hits the original.
What tho' at home ye dare scarce tread for fear?
Y'are out of hearing now, and may laugh here!
And you that ne'er had any of your own,
May view the ground before the match be run.
  Sure, some of ye will be pleas'd; and if so,
Give me your hands upon 't. And seal it, you
Fair ladies, with a smile; 'twill clear the air,
Make it a starry evening, and all fair.

APPENDIX.

I.—THE MARRIAGE OF THE DEVIL.

THE tales of Straparola are so little known in this country, that the following translation of the fourth fable of the Second Night, *de Les Facecieuses Nuits de Straparole*, by "Pierre de Larivey-Champenois," from the original Italian, may not be unacceptable to our readers, particularly as Wilson refers to the author in his preface to *Belphegor*.

The edition of Pierre de Larivey, from which it has been extracted, was printed at Amsterdam in 12mo, 1725, and is in two volumes. There was an earlier translation by "Guillaume Roville" in 1615, the preface to which is reprinted by De Larivey; it is of uncommon occurrence, and we have not been able to obtain access to a copy. It is not to be found in Colonel Stanley's sale catalogue, probably the richest collection of Facetiæ ever brought to the hammer in this country.

Le Diable entendant que les maris se plaignoient de leurs femmes, épousa Silvie, & print pour compère Gasparin Bonci, & ne pouvant plus durer avec sa femme, entra ou corps du Duc de Melphe, puis son compère Gasparin l'en jelta hors.

La legereté & peu d'entendement, qui se trouve pour le jourd hui en la plupart des femmes; je parle de celles qui sans aucune consideration se laissent aveugler les yeux de l'entendment, tâchant d'accomplir leurs desirs effrenez me donne occasion de raconter à la noble assistance un conte, non point par ci-devant entenduë. Et jaçoit que vous la trouviez assez briève & mal façonnée, si est-ce qu'elle donnera à vous autres femme quelques instructions, comme j'espere de n'être point si fâcheuse doré-navant à vos maris: Comme vous avez été jusqu' à present. Et se je vous semble un peu trop piquant, ne m'en accusez point, car je suis humble serviteur de toutes vous autres, mais addres-sez-vous à Madame, qui malâché la bride de pouvoir raconter, comme vous avez aussi entendu, ce qui me sera plus agréable. Il y a douc assez long temp, gracieuses Dames, que le Diable aiant eté abruvé des grosses noises & questions, que faisoint journellement les mariez contre leurs femmes, délibera de se marier. Et pour ce faire, il print la forme d'un beau jeune fils, & de bonne grace, garni de deniers & possessions, & le fit nommer Pancrace Stornel. Etant déjà seme le bruit d'ice lui par toute la ville beaucoup de Courratiers le vindrent trouver, lui presentant en mariage de fort belles femmes avec gros deniers, & entr' autres lui fut presente une fort belle & honête Damoiselle, nommée Silvie Balastre, laquelle étant eu la grace du Diable la print pour sa bien-aimée épousée.

On ne pouroit estimer les magnifiques nôces, avec les triomphes, parens tant d'un côté que d'autre, qui furent invitez à ce festin. Le jour des épousailles il print pour son compere de l'anneau Gasparin Bonci, & les pompes des nôces finies, il mena sa chere épouse en sa maison. Peu de jours, après le diable lui dit : Ecoutez ma femme Silvie, que j'aime plus que moi-même, vous pouvez assez facilement connoitre de quelle affection je vous aime, comme vous en avez pû faire l'experience en beaucoup de manieres. Puis qu'ainsi, est donc vous me ferez une grace, qui sera facile à vous & à moi agréable. La grace que je veux de vous est, que vous me demandiez à present ce que vous pouvez imaginer soit de vêtement, comme perles bagues, & autres choses qui appartiennent aux femmes, car j'ai déliberé pour l'amour que je vous porte, de vous contenter de tout ce que vous me demanderez, voire valût-il un Roiaume, sous cette condition, que pour l'avenir vous ne me molesterez plus pour telle occasion, mais que tout cela suffise pour tout le tems de vôtre vie, & donnez-vous bien garde de m'en demander plus! Car vous n'aurez jamais autre chose de moi. Silvie aiant demande tems de répondre à cèla se'n alla trouver sa mère qui s'appelloit Anastasie, laquelle étant déjà assez âgée étoit pareillement bien fine & russée, & lui reconta tout ce que le mari lui avoit dit en lui demandant conseil fur cela. La mère qui sçavoit fort bien joür son personnage en telles matieres, aiant entendu sa demande, print la plume & du papièr & commença à écrire tout ce qu'une langue n'eut pû raconter en deux jours, puis dit à sa fille. Tien, retourne t'en à ta maison & dis à ton mari qu'il te fournisse de tout ce qui est escrit en ce papier, en se faisant tu feras contente de lui. Silvie s'etant partie d'avec la mere, se'en alla vers son logis où elle se present a devant son mari, & lui requit tout ce qui etoit contenu en son memoire. Pancrace aiant lû & diligemment consideré le contenu sa demande, lui dit tels propos, sçavez vous bien qu'il y a, ma mie Silvie, regardez bien qu'il n'y défaille rien de ce que me demandez, afin que vous ne vous plaigniez pas après de moi, car je vous avertis que se vous me demandez après aucune chose, elle vous sera refusée, & ne vous serviront de rien vos prieres ni larmes & soupirs. Pensez donc bien à vôtre cas, & regardez bien qu'il ne vous faille rien. Silvie ne sçachant autre chose que demander, dit, qu'elle se contenoit de ce qui étoit ecrit au papier & quelle ne lui demanderoit plus rien. Tant y a que le Diable fit faire de beaux vêtemens garnis de grosse perles, bagues & autres richesses, les plus belles & les plus triomphantes, qui furent oncques vûës. Outre plus il lui bailla de belles coëfes sem'ees de perles, les aneauex, ceintures & autres choses encore en plus grand nombre qu'il n'y a voit au memoire. Ce qui seroit impossible de raconter. Or Silvie se voiant ainsi bien vêtue & si bien accoûtrée, qu'il n'y avoit point d'autre femme en toute la cité qui lui ressemblat, en celas s'en tenoit toute glorieuse, & ne se pouvoit imaginer de demander, aucune chose au mari vù qu'elle se sentoit garnie de tout ce qu'il lui étoit nesscessaire. Advint qu'il se prépara en ce même tems un magnifique triomphant festin, où furent invitées toutes les plus fameuses & honorables Dames qui se trouvassant, & entr' autres, Madame Silvie ne fut pas oubliée etant des plus belles nobles, & plus apparentes de toute la cité. Alors les Dames changérent toutes les façons d'habillemens en d'autres, non point encore accoûtumez, tellement que leurs accoutremens étoient si differens des premiers qu'on ne les connoissoit aucunement. Elle n'étoit pas fille de bonne mère, comme on fait encore pour le jourd'hui, celle qui ne trouvoit une nouvelle façon pour mieux honorer le festin, chacune femme tâchoit de tout son pouvoir de surmonter les autres en nouvelles pompes & magnificences. Cependant les nouvelles vindrent aux oreilles de Madame Silvie, que les bourgeoises de la ville trouvoient nouvelles façons d'habits, pour honerer la féte triomphante, tellement qu'elle se vint à imaginer que les vétemens qu'elle avoit fait faire n'etoient plus bons, ni convenables pour le tems, parce qu'ils etoient faits à l'antique, & lors s'usoient accoutremens d'autre maniere, au moien dequoi elle tomba en si grande mélancolie & depit, qu'elle ne pouvoit manger ni dormir, & n'enténdoit-on autre chose par la maison que soûpirs & plaintes, que se départoient du plus profond de son cœur.

Le Diable qui sçavoit tout ce que sa femme avoit au cœur, fit semblant de ne'n sçavoir rien, & s'aprochant d'elle, lui dit. Qu-avez-vous, Silvie? que vent dire que vous êtes ainsi fachée. Ne voulez-vous pas aller à ce festin? Silvie voiant l'occasion de répondre, prit un peu de hardiesse, & lui dit; comment voulez-vous, mon mari, que j'y aille? mes habits sont tous faits à l'antique & ne sont pas comme ceux que les autres Dames portent. Voulez-vous qu'on se mocque de moi? vraiment je ne le crois pas. Alors le Diable lui répondit; ne vous ai-je pas fait faire tout ce qui vous étoit necessaire pour tout le tems de votre vie? Comment me demandez-vous quelque chose maintenant? Mais elle répondit n'avoir aucuns vêtemens de telle façon, se plaignant grandement de son malheur; tellement que le Diable lui dit. Or sus, que se soit pour jamais demandez ce que vous voulez, il vous sera octroié pour cette fois, & si vous me demandez aucune chose pour l'avenir, soiez assûré qu'il vous adviendra chose dont vous serez, mal-contente. Silvie tout joieuse lui demandu tant de choses qu'il seroit impossible à d'écrire. Le Diable sans guéres retarder contenta pour lors sa femme en ce qu'elle lui demanda. Bien-tôt après les Dames commencerent à trouves nouvelles façon d'habits que Silvie n'avoit point; & pour autant qu'elle ne pouvoit comparoître entre les autres Dames qui avoient façons sur façons, nonobstant qu'elle fut richement accoutrée & garnie de toutes sordes de bagues, s'en fâchoit grandement & n'osoit le manifester à son mari, à cause qu'il l'avoit déjà contentée par deux fois, de ce qui ce pouvoit sonhaiter en ce monde.

A la fin le Diable la voiant ainsi triste, & saçhant bien la cause toutes-fois feignant de ne'n sçavoir rien, lui dit. Qu'y à t'il, ma mie Silvie? qu'avez vous à être si triste? Alors elle prit un peu de hardiesse, & lui dit. N'ai-je pas occasion d'etre fâchée vû que je suis sans habits à la nouvelle façon, tellement que je n'oserois comparoître entre les autres femmes que je ne sois mocquée & montrée au doigt. Ce que retourne a grand reproche de yous & de moi, joint que la sujétion où je suis étant avec vous avec la fidéletie que j'ai envers vous ne merite point une telle honté & scandale. Alors le Diable émû d'un dépit qu'il avoit, lui dit: Dequoi avez-vous en faute etant avec moi? Ne vous ai-je pas déjà contenté par deux fois de ce que m'avez demandé: dequoi vous plaignez-vous donc? Quant à moi je ne scais plus que vous faire, je vous veux encore contenter de vôtre désordonné désir, toutes-fois je m'en irai si loin que vous n'aurez jamais nouvelles de moi.

Et de fait après lui avoir donné de toutes les sortes d'habits de soie selon, le tems, & l'aiant du tout contentée se partit sans prendre congé d'elle, & s'en alla à Melphe ou il entra au corps du Duc en le tourmentant â prement. Le pauvre Duc se trouvant ainsi maltraité en étoit merveillesement fâché, & n'y avoit en Melphe homme de si bonne & si sainte vie qui lui pût chasser du corps. Or advint que Gasparin Boney compère de Monsieur le Diable, fut banni de la cite, pour quelques excés par lui commis; tellement que afin qu'il ne fut point prins et puni par justice, il se partit de-là & se'n alla à Melphe, pour autant qu'il ne sçavoit aucun metier, sinon joüer & trompes un chacun; incontinent le bruit fut semé par la ville de Melphe, que c' étoit un homme expert & métable a toute entreprise honorable, & néan-moins il étoit du tout inutile. Ainsi que ce Gasparin joüoit un jour avec quelques gentilhommes de Melphe, & les aiant attrapez avec ses piperies, ils se fâchérent grandement, & si la crainte de la justice ne les eut divertis ils l'auroient facilement tué. Toutefois ne pouvant plus l'un diceux endurer tel outrage, dit en lui même. Je t'en punirai d'une telle sorte qu'il te souviendra de moi tant que tu vivras, & sans plus retarder laissa ses compagnons, & s'en alla trouver le Duc, auquel aiant fait un grande reverence, dit ainsi: Tres excellent Duc & Seigneur il y aen cette ville un nommé Gasparin, qui se vanté partout de sçavoir chasser du corps des hommes, les esprits de quelque qualitié qu'ils soient ou terrestres, ou aërez: Au moien dequoi il me semble qu'il seroit bon que vous en fissiez l'experience, afin que suffiez deliveré d'un tel tourment. Le Duc aiant entendu ces propos, envoia incontenent querir Gasparin lequel entendant le vouloir du Duc s'en alla par devers lui, sitôt qu'il l'eut regardé en la face, il lui dit: Seigneur Gasparin, j'entends que vous faites profession, & vous vantez de sçavoir chasser les esprits; quant à moi, comme vous voiez, j'en ai un au corps, & si vous m'en déliverez, je vous promets, Seigneur Gasparin, de vous faire un tel present, que vous serez heureux tout les tems de votre vie. Gasparin qui n'avoit jamais oüi parler de telles choses fut tout étonné niant fort et ferme de s'en être jamais vanté. Le Gentilhomme qui n'etoit guéres loin de-là s'approacha, & lui dit: Ne vous souvient-il pas maitre, que vous me dites telles paroles & telles, & Gasparin assûroit qu'il ne'n etoit rien. Etant ainsi tous deux en ce débat, l'un niant & l'autre affirmant. Le Duc leur dit: Or sus, faites un peu de silence, quant à vous mâitre Gasparin, je vous donne trois jours de terme pour penser à vôtre cas, & si vous me déliverez de misere, je vous promets de vous donner le plus beau château qui soit en mon päis: et pourrez disposer de moi à vôtre vouloir, comme de vôtre personne propre; autrement soiez assûré que d'aujourd'hui en huit jours, vous serez pendu & éntranglé entre les deux colonnes de mon palais.

Gasparin aiant entendu le vouloir de Duc, fut merveilleusement fâché, & s'etant parti de sa compagnie, commença à penser jour & nuit comment il pourroit chasser cet esprit. Le jour de l'assignation venu, Gasparin retourna vers le Duc, & l'aiant fait entendre sur un tapis en terre, commença à conjurer le mauvais esprit qu'il sortit de ce corps et qu'il ne le tourmentàt. Le Diable que se reposoit alors en ce corps à son plaisir, ne lui répondit autre chose, mais enfla si fort la gorge au Duc qu'il se sentit quasi mourir. Gasparin réïterant encore sa conjuration, le Diable va répondre: Mon compére, vous avez si bon temps, & je suis bien à mon aise & vous voulez que je me parte d'ici vous me tormentez en vain & ainsi se moquoit du compère. Etant venu Gasparin pour la troisiéme fois à le conjurer, en lui demandant beaucoup de choses, & l'appellant toûjours compére ne pouvant imaginer qui c'etoit, à la fin il le contraignit de dire quel il etoit. Alors le Diable va repondre: Puis que je suis contraint de dire la vérité, & vous manifester qui je suis; sçachez que je suis Pancrace Stornel, Mari de Silvie Balasrie, ne le sçavez-vous pas bien? Pensez-vous que je ne vous connoisse? N'etesvous pas Gasparin Boncy, mon trescher compére? Ne sçavez vous pas bien combien de triomphe avons fait ensemble? Helas, mon compére! repóndit Gasparin, que faites-vous ici à tourmenter ce pauvre homme. Je ne le vous veux pas dire, répondit le Diable, allezvous-en je vous prie, & ne me fâchez plus; car je ne me trouverai jamais mieux que je fais à present. Alors Gasparin lui fit tant de conjurations, qu'il fut contraint de raconter par le menu la cause pourquoi il s'étoit parti d'avec sa femme, & entré à corps du Duc, tellement qui Gasparin lui dit comment mon compére, mon ami, ne me voulez-vous pas faire un plaisir. Quel plaisir? dit le Diable. Otez-vous de ce corps ici, répondit Gasparin, & ne le tourmentez plus. Mon compére, dit le Diable, vous me semblez un grand fol de me demander telles choses, car je trouve un si grand plaisir ici dedans, que je ne sçaurois imaginer d'avantage. Alors Gasparin dit, je vous prie par la foi de compere qui est entre nous deux, que me fassiez ce plaisir, pour le present, car si vous ne vous partez d'ici je perdrai la vie; en ce faisant vous serez cause de ma mort. Le Diable répondit, il n'y a point pour le jourd'hui de plus méchante & abominable foi que celle d'un compere, & si vous en mourez ce sera votre dommage & non pas le mien. Je ne desire autre chose que de vous voir abîmé au plus profond d'Enfer; vous deviez être un peu plus sage, & tenir la langue entre les dents; car un bon taire ne fut jamais écrit. Dites-moi à tout le moins, répondit Gasparin, que fut celui qui vous mit en si grand travail. Aiez patience, dit le Diable, car je ne puis, & si ne le vous veux pas dire. Otez-vous seulement d'ici, & n'attendez point d'autre reponsé de moi. Et ainsi tout dépité laissa le pauvre Duc plus mort que vif. Mais après qu'il fut un peu revenu, Gasparin lui dit, Seigneur Duc prenez courage, car vous serez bien-tôt déliveré. Je ne veux autre chose de vous pour le present, sinon que demain au matin vous fassiez venir au Palais, tous les Musiciens & joüeurs d'instrumens, & que toutes les cloches de la ville sonnent, & qu'on tire toute l'artillerie des boullevards, en signe de joie & triomphe, & tant plus il y aura grand bruit, tant plus j'en serai content. Puis laissez faire à moi.

Le Matin en suivant, Gasparin s'en alla vers le Palais, & commença à conjurer l'esprit du Duc, & cependant qu'il le conjuroit, on commença à ouïr, trompetes, timbres, tabourins, bassins, cloches, artilleries, & tant de sortes d'instrumens de musique qui sonnoient en un méme tems, qu'il sembloit quasi que le monde düt rüinor. Or ainsi que Gasparin poursuivoit sa conjuration, le Diable lui demanda que signifioit telle diversité d'instrumens, & si grande confusion de sons, que jamais il n'avoit oüi. Ne le sçavez-vous pas bien, répondit Gasparin. Non! dit le Diable. Est-il possible, répondit Gasparin, parce que nous autres qui sommes envelopez en ce corps humain, ne pouvons sçavoir ni entendre tout, à cause que cette matiere terrienne est trop grosse, je vous le dirai en peu de paroles, si vous mecoutez sans molester ce pauvre Duc? Dites le moi, je vous prie, dit le Diable, & je vous écouterai volontiers, vous promettant dè ne lui donner point de fâcherie. Alors Gasparin lui va dire; sçachez mon compére, mon ami, que le Duc voiant que vous ne le voulez-pas laisser, & que ne cessez de le tourmenter, aiant entendu que vous avez laissé vôtre femme pour le grand tourement quelle vous donnoit, il la envoié querir, tellement que toute la cité fait fête & triomphe pour sa venuë. Ce qu'entendment le Diable, lui va dire: O méchant compére, vous êtes plus fin & plus rusé que moi! Ne vous dis-je pas hier qu'on ne trouva jamais compére que fût loial à l'autre. Vous avez éte l'inventeur & celui que là fait venir. Mais j'ai en si grand horreur & ai en si grande haine le nomme de ma femme, que j'aime mieux demeurer au plus profond d'Enfer que de la voir près de moi. Au moien dequoi jeme veux partir dici, & m'en aller si loin que vous n'aurez jamais nouvelles de moi. Et aiant dit cela, avec un enflement de gorge, & tournant les yeux en la teté, & autres signes épouventables, il se partit du corps du Duc; tellement q'aiant laissé une grande puanteur, le Duc fut délivré du tout de cet esprit. Bientôt après, le pauvre Duc revint en son premier état, & recouvra ses forces accoûtumées, & ne voulant pas être ingrat, fit appeller Gasparin & le fit Seigneur d'un fort beau chateau, en lui donnant grande quantité de deniers & serviteurs pour la servir, & en dépit des envieux, le bon Gasparin vécut longuement en felicité. Et Madame Silvie voiant ses beaux vétemens bagues & annéaux être convertis en cendre & fumée, mourut bientôt après misérablement & comme desesperée.

Ce conte fut racontè par le Trevisan, avec grandes merveilles et fut grandement louée, mémement pas les hommes avec ris excessifs. Vrai est qu'elle déplût quelque peu aux Dames, tellement que Madame oiant les Damoiselles murmurer assez bas, & les continuez ris des hommes, commanda que chacun mît fin à ses propos, que le Trevisan commençat son Enigmé; lequel sans prendre autre excuse envers les Dames de ce qu'il les avoit si vivement piquées, commença son Enigmé.

Enigmé.

Mes dames nous avons une chose entre nous
Belle en perfection si onc beauté fut belle,
Qui sans langue, sans mains, pieds ni chose telle;
Parle, touche, chemine & se montre à tous coups,
Sans yeux elle regarde, & nous contemple tous,
Ce ne'st qu'entendement, et n'a point de cervelle,
Elle peut tout sans vous, & vous rien sans icelle,
Car de nötre puissance elle tient les deux bouts.
Toûjours elle nous suit, compagnant nôtre vie,
Qui sans son bon secours nous seroit tôt ravie,
Elle est fidéle, aimant en toute extrémitié,
Des long-tems avant nous, dedans nous elle est née,
Elle ne craint la mort n'y étant destinée,
Ainsi vive elle vit en toute etrernité.

L'obscur Enigmé raconté par lé Trevisan donna bien à rêver aux assistans, & chacun mettoit peine en vain de lui bailler la vraie intérpretation, tellement que le Trévisan, voiant que leurs opinions étoiant bien éloignées de la verité, dit: Messeigneurs, il ne me semble pas convenable de tenir longuement en suspens cette honorable compagnie. Si vous trouvez bon que je vous en die mon opinion, je vous la dirai volontiers, ou bien j'attendrai la résolution de quelque gentil esprit. Tous d'une voix le priérent de l'interpreter. Alors le Trévisan va dire que son Enigmé ne signifioit autre chose, si non l'ame immortelle, laquelle est esprit, & n'a ne téte ni pieds, ni mains, & fait toute opération, & où elle est jugée, soit au ciel ou à l'Enfer, elle vit eternellement. Cette docte exposition de l'obscur Enigmé plût merveilleusement à toute la notable compagnie. Et pour autant qu'il étoit déja passé une grande partie de la nuit, et que les coqs commençoient à annoncer le jour ensuivant. Madame fit signe à Vincende qui étoit la derniere en song rang pour diviser en cette seconde nuit, qu'elle dût finir la nuitée avec quelque plaisant conte. Mais elle qui étoit devenue toute vermeille au visage par couleur naturelle quelle avoit, non point par une honte, mais plûtôt par le couroux, & dépit qu'elle avoit conçûde ce conte auparavant raconté, dit telles paroles contre Trévisan : Seigneur Benoît j'estimois que fussiez plus paisible, & que tinssiez plus le parti des Dames que vous ne faites, mais comme je ne puis comprendre par le conte de vous recité, vous leurs êtes fort contraire. Car si que me fait penser que vous vous sentez outragé de quelq'une qui étoit possible trop indiscrette en sa demande. Toutefois encore ne dévriez-vous pas si âprement blâmer les autres, car combien que nous soions forgées d'une matiére, si est-ce qu'on en voit tous les jours, une plus gentille de meilleur esprit que l'autre. Déportez-vous donc de plus les blâmer en telle mániere. Car si elles vous mettent une fois la dent dessus, vos sons & chants ne vous serviront de rien. Quant à moi, dit le Trévisan, je n'ai point fait cela pour faire tort à la moindre, ni pour me venger de ses paroles, mais pour instruire les autres qui se mariorant, aprés moi, dêtre plus modestes vers leurs maris. Or bien, quoi qu'il en soit, dit Damoiselle Vincende, je ne m'en soucie guéres, & moins ces autres Dames y presentes. Mais afin qu'il ne semble point que par mon silence je vueille tenir le parti des hommes, & être contre aux Dames, j'en veux raconter un qui vous donnera grande instruction, & aient fait la révérence, commença à dire.

II.—THE MARRIAGE OF BELPHEGOR,

BY

NICHOLAS MACHIAVEL.

Of this ancient legend there are two English versions. The first of these is to be found in the "Works of the famous Nicholas Machiavel, citizen and secretary of Florence, written originally in Italian, and from thence newly and faithfully translated into English." This translation was licensed upon the 2d February 1674, and the third edition, "carefully corrected," was printed at London, 1720—folio. The translator's name is not given, but a curious statement made by Bishop Warburton might induce a belief that it may have been no less a person than the first Marquis of Wharton, the reputed author of the celebrated political ballad of Lilliburlero.

The Bishop says, that having had access to the Wharton papers, he found the *first* proof of the translation of the letter said to have been written by Machiavel,—"to Zanobius Buondelmontius in vindication of himself and his writings,"—carefully corrected throughout by the Marquis for the original folio edition. It comes immediately before the letter. It is from this version that the tale has been now reprinted.

Machiavel was at a later date translated by the Rev. Ellis Farneworth, M.A., Vicar of Rosthern, in Cheshire, who also translated the *Life of Pope Sixtus V.*, and Davila's *Civil Wars of France*. The first work was published at London in 1762, in two volumes 4to. It is now much esteemed, although on the original publication it met with little patronage, and very many copies were disposed of as waste paper, which has made the remaining copies difficult to procure. "Belphegor's Marriage" occurs in the second volume, page 165. The older translation has been selected as the one which we may presume was used by Wilson.

According to the *Biographie Universelle*, Straparola was born towards the end of the fifteenth century, and died after 1557—the year in which the first edition of his tales was given to the public. Machiavel is generally believed to have departed this life in 1530, and it is understood that during his lifetime he was not known as the author of the "Marriage of Belphegor." This much is certain, that the tale was not included in the edition of his works published 1550. On the other hand,

Straparola's version of the Devil's Marriage appeared whilst he was in life. Though both tales originate out of the inquiry instituted by his Satanic Majesty as to the treatment of husbands on earth, they vary considerably in detail; and it may fairly be assumed that the authors in both instances took their text from some ancient manuscript chronicle or from tradition.

It is recorded in the ancient Chronicles of Florence, that a certain holy person, whose life was the admiration of that age, falling one day into a trance, had a very strange apparition. It seemed to him that the souls of married men, that came trooping in great numbers to hell, cried out all of them as they passed, that their marriage was the cause of their misery, and their wives the occasion of their coming thither. Minos, Radamanthus, and the whole infernal privy council were amazed at the clamour. At first they could not believe there was anything in the business; but at last, observing the same complaints continually multiplied, they thought it fit to make Pluto acquainted. Pluto, understanding the report, without imparting anything to his wife (who had taken physic that week, and kept her chamber), resolved the matter should be accurately examined, and such course be taken as was likeliest to make the speediest discovery of the truth. He issued out his writs immediately, and assembled his courts. His princes, dukes, counts, and barons were all present—never was senate so full, nor never was affair of that importance before it. The holy father that beheld all affirms positively that Pluto delivered himself in this manner :—

"Right trusty and well beloved,

"Though our kingdom was assigned us from heaven, and the fatal decree has anciently determined our dominion; though that sentence be irrevocable, and above the cognisance of any human power; yet seeing his prudence is most safe that is dictated by laws, and his judgment most solid that is fortified with others, we are resolved to take your counsels along with us, which way we are to steer in an affair that otherwise may prove in time of great dishonour to our government. The souls of married men, that are continually flocking into our dominions, do unanimously exclaim against their wives as the only persons that send them tumbling hither. To us it seems impossible; yet, forasmuch as a peremptory and determinate sentence upon their bare allegations would not suit with our Satanical mercy, so a careless pretermission on the other side could not be without reflection on our justice. That matters of such importance, therefore, may have their due disquisition, and our administration be defended from obloquy or scandal,—that no inconveniency may follow for want of deliberation, and that some better expedient may be found out than ourselves have happily thought on, we have thought good to call you together, being confident and assured, by the assistance of your counsels, the honour and reputation of our empire will be continued as unquestionable for the future as it has been preserved hitherto by our own proper care and solicitude."

There was not one present but acknowledged it a business of importance, and well worthy an exact consideration. It was the opinion of the whole board that all imaginable means were to be used to find out the truth, but what means these were could not be agreed on. Some were of opinion a single person was to be despatched into this world, and no more; others judged it better to send several, and that the discovery would be more certain from the experience of many than of one; and a third sort, more brisk and severe in their counsels, thought that clutter unnecessary, and that clapping good store of them together upon the rack would be enough, doubtless, to extort a confession. However, it was at last carried by the plurality of voices that a single person only should be sent, and in this resolution the whole company acquiesced. Nevertheless, there being nobody found that would voluntarily undertake the employment, it was concluded the election should be by lot; and at the same time, having made the billets and shuffled them, the lot fell upon Belphegor.

One may say, and say true, that fortune never decided anything so justly, for Belphegor was no ordinary devil; and Pluto having made him formerly Generalissimo of his armies, 'tis to be presumed he was no novice. For all this, he had a month's mind to be quit of his embassy; but the order being unalterable, he was forced to submit, and accept these conditions, that were solemnly decreed: That an hundred thousand ducats should be paid him immediately, to defray the expenses of his journey; that he should assume the shape of a man; that he should take a woman to his wedded wife, and live with her (if possible) ten years; that at the end of the term (pretending to die), he should give her the slip, repair immediately to his old quarters, and make affidavit upon his own experience of all the pleasures and calamities of matrimony. It was declared to him also, that during this metamorphosis he was to be subject to the pains and misfortunes of humanity,—as sickness, imprisonment, and poverty; but that, if by his cunning and dexterity he could disentangle himself, it should be allowed him, and not imputed as any scandal or reproach. Belphegor accepts the conditions, receives his ducats, and having drawn a spruce party of horse out of his guards, and furnished himself with pages and footmen good store, he set out immediately for this world, and arrived at Florence in a very fair equipage. He chose that place above all other for the conveniency of improving his money, and putting it to interest with greater advantage. He called himself Don Roderick of Castile; he took a very noble house in the Fauxburg of All-Saints, and, that his quality might be undiscovered, he gave out that he was a Spaniard; that being young, he took a voyage into Syria; that he had dwelt some time in Aleppo, where he had got most part of his estate; but being weary there, he was come into Italy as a country more agreeable with his humour, with intention (if any fair opportunity was offered) to marry.

Don Roderick seemed to be a very handsome man, about thirty years of age, and in short time after his arrival he made it evident enough that he was rich, and by his liberality that he knew how to make the best use of his wealth; insomuch that several gentlemen of Florence that had more daughters than money took all possible pains to insinuate how welcome he should be into their alliance. Don Roderick, that had choice of mistresses, preferred one that was transcendently handsome before them all. The story says she was called Honesta, and was the daughter of Americ Donati, who had three more also to marry, and three sons between twenty and twenty-five years of age. But though Seigneur Americ was of one of the noblest families of Florence, yet he was looked upon as down the wind, and one that was overlaid with too many children, and the unavoidable charges of his nobility. But Don Roderick took an order for that, defraying the whole expense of his wedding out of his own purse, managing all things with that splendour and magnificence that there was nothing omitted that was desirable upon such an occasion. It was mentioned before, as one of the conditions proposed to Belphegor, that as soon as he was out of the infernal dominions he should be subject to all the passions of mankind; and accordingly, he began immediately to take delight in the honours and gallantry of the world, and, as cunning a devil as he was, to be wheedled with the flatteries and applauses of men. But that which delighted him so much cost him dear. Besides that, he had not been long with Honesta but he fell stark mad in love with her; and finding something or other extraordinary in her that I cannot think of, he was so far enamoured he never thought himself happy before; insomuch as, when she was melancholy or out of humour, he would curse his commission, and take his corporal oath his very life was tedious. On the other side, it was not to be forgot that Honesta, marrying Roderick, and bringing him beauty and nobility instead of a portion, she thought it not fit to leave her pride and untractableness behind her. These two good qualities were so eminently in her, that Roderick, who had been used to Lucifer's, and had more than once experienced it, swore point-blank his wife's insolence was beyond it. For when she once found the fondness and passion her husband had for her, believing she could manage him with a switch, and order him as she pleased, she carried herself like his sovereign, and handled him without pity or respect; and if it happened he denied her anything, she gave him immediately to understand that she was also as eloquent in scolding as others of her quality. By this you may judge what a cooler this was to Don Roderick; nevertheless, the consideration of his father-in-law, his wife's brothers, the kindred he had by that blessed marriage, but above all, the passion and tenderness he had for her, made him endure all patiently. I shall not mention the expense of her clothes, which, though never so rich, he was forced to change every week, according to the ordinary vanity of the ladies in Florence. Besides these, there were other things of no less inconvenience. He was forced (to preserve the peace) to assist his father-in-law in the marriage of his other daughters, which cost him a good round sum. Moreover, that all things might go well, and his correspondence continue with his comfort, he was glad to send one of her brothers into the Levant with woollen stuffs, another into France and Spain with silks, and to furnish the third with wherewithal to set up a goldsmith's shop in Florence. All which afflictions together were sufficient to discompose any devil of a thousand, yet he had other thrown into the bargain. There is not any town in all Italy more extravagant in their expenses in their carnivals and feasts of St. John than Florence; and Honesta upon that occasion must needs have her Roderick outdo all people of his rank, in the sumptuousness of his entertainments, in the magnificence of his balls, and other divertisements that are usual at those times. He suffered all these calamities for the same reasons he endured the rest; and though, perhaps, these difficulties were very hard and unpleasant, he would have thought them supportable could he have been satisfied his patience would have procured any quietness in his family, and that he might have peaceably awaited the hour of his destruction. But Don Roderick found the clear contrary. Besides the expense she occasioned, her insolence was accompanied with a thousand other inconveniences, insomuch as he could keep neither man nor maid servant in his house above three days together. This was severe trouble to him, to find it was impossible for him to keep anybody about him, though never so well experienced or affected to his affairs; nor indeed could anybody blame them for taking their leaves, when the devils themselves that he brought along with him did choose rather to return, and toast the bottoms of their feet against the fire of hell, than live in this world under the dominion of so super-devilish a woman.

Roderick's life being thus miserably uncomfortable, and the stock that he had reserved exhausted by her extravagant expenses, he was reduced to that pass he subsisted only upon the hopes of the advantage he should make by the return of some vessels he had sent into the east and west. Having very good credit in that town, he resolved to keep up his rank, and borrowed money of such as are used in that place to put it out;

but those kind of people being such as are not usually sleepy or negligent in their affairs, they took notice immediately he was not over-punctual to his day. His purse being already empty, and he reduced to the highest extremity, at one dash he receives news of two as disastrous accidents as could possibly befall him. The first was, that one of Honesta's brothers had lost at hazard, all that Roderick had intrusted in his hands; and the other, that his other brother-in-law, returning into Italy, was himself cast away and all his goods. The business was no sooner known in Florence but his creditors had a meeting, where, giving him over for one that was irrecoverably lost, and not daring to discover themselves because the time of payment was not yet come, they concluded he was to be watched very close, lest he should chouse them and show them a light pair of heels.

Don Roderick of Castile, on the other side, considering with himself his affairs were past remedy, resolves to take horse and depart without any more ado, which he performed without much difficulty, living conveniently for that by the Port del Prato. Yet he was no sooner marched off but the alarm was taken by his creditors. They repair immediately to the magistrates, and pursue him not only with post and officers, but, lest a certain number of ducats should debauch that kind of cattle, who are no better in Italy than other places, and prevail with them for an abatement of their speed, they follow him themselves in a full body, with impatience of hearing some tidings of him. Roderick in the meantime was no fool, but considered very well what he had to do. As soon as he was galloped about half a league from the town, he leaves the highway and his horse with it (the country being inclosed and full of ditches on both sides), and was forced to make the rest of his journey on foot, which he did very successfully; for, wandering up and down under the shelter of the vines and reeds that abound much in those parts, he arrived at last at Peretola, at the house of Jean Matteo del Bricca, bailie to Jean del Bene.

By good fortune he meets Matteo carrying fodder to his cattle. He accosts him immediately, and promises him, as he was a gentleman, that if he would deliver him from the catchpoles that were in pursuit of him with design to clap him up and starve him in prison, he had an invention in his pate would make him rich out of hand, and of this he would give such evidence before he departed as should assure him of his truth and fidelity. "And if I do not," says he, with a damn'd imprecation, "I will be content to be delivered up into their clutches that persecute me." Now you must understand that though Matteo was a hind and a peasant, yet the fellow had cunning enough, and knew on which side his bread was buttered. He considered, if he undertook him, and miscarried, he had nothing to lose, and that if he succeeded he should be made for ever.

Without any more ado, therefore, he promises him protection, and clapping him close upon a dunghill that was before the gate, he covered himself over with brush-faggots and reeds, and such other fuel as lay there in readiness for the fire. And, indeed, he was no sooner in his retirement but in came the creditors with full cry. They swaggered and laid about them like lords, but all to no purpose. Matteo could not be persuaded to confess so much as he saw him; insomuch as, marching on still in the pursuit, but with as little success as they came thither, they gave Roderick and their money over for lost, and returned to Florence every jot as wise as they were before. The coast being clear in this manner, and the alarm over, Matteo steals to the place where he had left Roderick, gives him a little fresh air, and conjures him to be as good as his word. Roderick was very honest in that point, and I dare say never any devil, as to matters of gratitude, had more of a gentleman. He gave him thanks for the great obligation he had received; he swore over and over again he would do whatever lay in his power to discharge himself of his promise; and in the heat and height of his compliments, to convince him he meant as he said, he gives him the whole story as you have had it, and at last told him the very way he had pitched upon to make him a prince. "Know then," says he, "that whenever you hear of any lady that is possessed, 'tis no other devil but I that have possessed her, and be sure I will never leave her till you come yourself and force me from my quarters; after which you have wit enough to make your own terms for your payment." They had very few words more; he only gave him the summerset once or twice, and showed him two or three juggling tricks, and vanished.

Awhile after, there was a great noise about the town that Ambrosio Amidei's daughter, that was married to Bonaculo Thebalducci's son, was possessed. Her father and mother did not fail to use all the remedies are usual in so deplorable a case. They brought before her St. Zanobi's head and St. J. Gaulbert's cloak, which was nuts to Belphegor, and made him do nothing but laugh. There was nobody in her but Don Roderick de Castile, who was as ingenious a gentleman devil as one would wish; and that the world might take notice that this was no fantastic imagination, nor fit of the nightmare, nor any such trifle, but that she was really possessed, she spake Latin better than Tully ever writ, disputed in philosophy, and discovered the secrets and sins of several people that were there, who were very much surprised to find the devil concern himself with those kind of affairs.

Amongst the rest was one holy father he did great discourtesy to, in blurting out before the whole company as if he had kept a young lass four years together in his cell in the habit of a young monk; and after all this, let anybody judge whether the possession was not like to be true. Ambrosio, in the meantime, was in great affliction for his daughter. He had tried all the ways that physic or religion could propose, but to no purpose, so as he was brought to the highest point of despair when Matteo came to him, and undertook to cure his daughter if he would give him five hundred florins, which he designed to lay out in land at Peretola. In short, Matteo was an honest fellow, and would have done the miracle gratis, and like a gentleman, but his pockets were hollow, and he had great occasion for money at that time. Seignior Ambrosio accepts the conditions, and Matteo falls to work. He began very civilly, with certain masses and other ceremonies, that he might appear the more formal in the business. At length he stole to the lady's ear, calls Roderick, and tells him he was come thither to him, and did require him to be as good as his word. "Content," says Roderick; "and that you may see I shall deal with you like a person of quality, take notice, that because this expedition is not enough to enrich you and do your business, I will befriend you more than once; for which reason, as soon as I am departed from hence, away I'll march into the daughter of Charles, King of Naples; and don't fear but I'll stick to her till you come to exorcise me, so as there you may make up your markets at a blow, and become considerable for ever. But be sure after that I be troubled with you no more." And as soon as he had said so, he whipped out of the lady, and was gone, to the great joy and astonishment of the whole town.

Belphegor in the meantime was as good as his word. As he promised Matteo, away he goes, and in two or three days' time it was all over Italy that the daughter of Charles, King of Naples, was in the same condition, which was good news for Matteo, who was at this bout to gain the philosopher's stone. The king tried all means possible: the monks went to work with their prayers and their crosses, but to no purpose; the devil would not budge till Matteo came himself, who had formerly obliged him. The king had news of what had happened at Florence, and sends away immediately for Matteo to his court, who came accordingly, and after some few ceremonious formalities, counterfeited for concealment of the mystery, he cures his daughter. However, Roderick, before his departure, as is reported in the chronicle, accosted him in this manner: "You see, Matteo, I have been as good as my word; you see you are become rich in a trice, and may take your ease for the future, so as, if I be not mistaken, I have discharged myself as to you very honestly. Hereafter have a care how you come near me, for as hitherto I have done you knight service, henceforward I will do you as much mischief as I can." Matteo, being returned to Florence very wealthy (for the King of Naples had given him above five thousand ducats), he thought of nothing now but enjoying that peaceably he had got, never imagining Roderick would do him any harm; but his designs were much frustrated by a report out of France that Lewis the Seventh's daughter was possessed in the same way as the daughter of the King of Naples had been. Matteo was not ignorant of the power of Lewis; on the other, he remembered Roderick's last words. The king used all means possible, but without any success. He was told what feats Matteo had done, and despatched a post to him immediately, to desire his company at Paris; but Matteo, pretending indispositions, that rendered him incapable of serving his majesty, the king was forced to write to the magistrates, who sent away Matteo immediately.

Being arrived at Paris, he was in great affliction, because he knew not which way for his life to perform what was expected from him. At last he goes to the king, and tells him that true it was indeed he had formerly wrought some cures in that kind, but that it was not in reason to be expected he could dispossess all people he met with, seeing there were some devils so refractory and cross-grained, neither threats, nor enchantments, nor devotion itself would do any good on. That he said not this out of any repugnancy or unwillingness to do as he was desired, but that in case his endeavours were ineffectual he might have his majesty's pardon. The king was stark mad at the story, and told him in plain terms, if he did not rout the devil out of his daughter, as he had done out of others, he would hang him forthwith, for he saw no reason why miracles were not as feasible at Paris as at Florence and Naples. These words touched Matteo to the quick; he thought there was no pleasure to be taken in being hanged in that manner, and that what the king had said was without any equivocation. However, he recollected himself a little, or at least pretended so, and calling for the princess that was possessed, he makes his approaches, and whispering her in the ear, told Roderick he was his very humble servant, and put him in mind of the good office he had done him, when he delivered him out of the talons of the law; adding, withal, that if he left him in the lurch in the extremity of danger he was then in, the whole world would cry out on his ingratitude. Roderick heard him with no more patience than needs must; he swaggers, swears, storms, and lays about him like a devil in good earnest, gives him a thousand and a thousand ill words, but they could distinguish only these few at the last: "How, now, you rascally traitor, have you the impudence to come near me again? Have you forgot it was I that made you your fortune? But I'll make all the world see, and you too, with a pox to you, that I can take away as well as give; besides which, you shall not fail to be hanged before I get away from Paris."

Poor Matteo, seeing no other remedy for his misfortunes, he fell athinking some other way; and having sent back the lady to her chamber, he made this speech to the king: "Sir, I have told you before that there are certain ill-natured, capricious spirits one knows not which way to deal withal, and of this sort is that which possesses your daughter. If what we shall administer might be sufficient, your majesty should be happy in your desire, and mine also; but if things prove otherwise, and your majesty be not satisfied with my endeavours, I shall submit, and your majesty may deal with me as I deserve. In the meantime, I desire your majesty would give order a theatre be erected in the church-yard of Notre Dame, big enough to receive all the nobility and clergy in the town. Let this theatre, if your majesty think good, be hung with cloth of gold and other rich stuffs, and an altar set up in the middle on Sunday next. I would desire your majesty to be there, with all the princes and nobility in Paris; and after a grand mass is sung, let the princess be brought also. Besides this, it is necessary there should be twenty persons at least, with trumpets, horns, drums, hoboys, and cymbals, ready in some byplace, when I throw up my cap into the air, to advance towards the theatre with all the noise they can make; which music, with some other ingredients that I have, will send the devil packing from the princess." The king gave order all things should be done as Matteo requested, and Sunday being come, and the theatre thronged with a multitude of persons of quality, and the church-yard of Notre Dame full of people, the princess was led in by two bishops, and followed by several lords of the court. Roderick was in a terrible amaze to behold so magnificent a preparation, and pondering with himself, was overheard to pronounce these words: "I would fain know what this rascally peasant means to do. I have seen many places—I have more than once seen the whole pomp of heaven, nor am I ignorant of what is most formidable in hell, yet can I not tell what to make of this; but I'll handle him like a rogue as he is, and if I fail, Pluto requite me." Matteo came up close to him, and desired him very civilly to depart; but Roderick cried out, "Oh, the wondrous cunning that is in you! Do you think by this whimsey to save yourself from my power and the indignation of the king? But think what you will, you scoundrel, I am resolved you shall hang for it, or else let me pass for the most miserable, poor-spirited devil in the world." Matteo persisted in his request, but Belphegor gave him worse language than before. But all that frighted not Matteo; for without losing more time, he threw his hat up in the air, and at an instant the trumpets, horns, and all the rest of the music struck up and advanced towards the theatre. Roderick was startled at the noise, and made it manifest that there are some devils as fearful as men; and not able to imagine the reason, he called out to Matteo, and asked what was the matter? Matteo, being a cunning rogue every inch of him, as if he had been terribly frighted, informs him thus: "Alas! poor Roderick," says he, "'tis your wife Honesta is come to seek you at Paris." He said no more, but it is not to be imagined what disorder these four or five words put the devil into: they took away his wit and judgment, so as, without any consideration whether the news was possible or not, without speaking one word, away he stole from the princess, choosing rather to go back into hell, and give up his accounts there, than to return again into the thraldom of matrimony, that had already cost him so many sorrows and dangers. As soon as he arrived, he demanded audience, and in the presence of Pluto, Æacus, Minos, and Radamanthus, all of them councillors of state, he declared that the souls of men were in the right on it, and that 'twas their wives that sent them to hell.

Matteo, who had been too crafty for the devil, returned to Florence in great triumph. The Chronicle mentions not any great matter the king gave him, but it says, that having gained sufficiently by the two former, he esteemed himself very happy that he had escaped hanging in Paris.

FINIS.

www.ingramcontent.com/pod-product-compliance
Lightning Source LLC
Chambersburg PA
CBHW032311280326
41932CB00009B/773
9783337340902